ASSEMBLY LANGUAGE

AND

COMPUTER ORGANIZATION

FOR THE 86-FAMILY COMPUTERS

ASSEMBLY LANGUAGE

AND

COMPUTER ORGANIZATION
FOR THE 86-FAMILY COMPUTERS

KAREN A. LEMONE

Worcester Polytechnic Institute

HarperCollins*CollegePublishers*

```
Dedication   =   "Michael"   ; for support and love
```

Sponsoring Editor: John Lenchek
Project Coordination, Text and Cover Design: Elm Street Publishing Services, Inc.
Compositor: Carlisle Communications, Ltd.
Printer and Binder: R. R. Donnelley & Sons Company
Cover Printer: Lehigh Press Lithographers

Assembly Language and Computer Organization for the 86-Family Computers
Copyright © 1993 by HarperCollins College Publishers

Library of Congress Cataloging-in-Publication Data
Lemone, Karen A.
   Assembly language and computer organization for the 86-family
computers / Karen Lemone.
     p.   cm.
   Includes bibliographical references and index.
   ISBN 0-06-500747-6
   1. Assembler language (Computer program language)   2. Computer
organization.   3. Intel 80xxx series microprocessors.
QA76.73.A8L46 1992   92–25646
005.265 — dc20   CIP

92 93 94 95 9 8 7 6 5 4 3 2 1

Contents

11   Assembly   292

12   Floating-Point Instructions   314

APPENDICES

Preface

This introduction to assembly language programming for the 86-family is addressed to both practitioners and student audiences. The personal-computer user who is not familiar with academic perspectives is introduced to them in a gentle manner. Students who have little experience in "hands-on" issues are similarly aided to gain this proficiency.

This book presumes only that the reader is familiar with one high-level language, such as Pascal, C, BASIC, FORTRAN, or Ada. It conforms with current ACM and IEEE recommendations concerning introductory computer organization and assembly language courses.

Features of this book include

1. Fundamental concepts of computer organization, assembly language, and the structure of computer systems. The exercises stress concepts and principles and include problems about other machines and representations. Appendix F introduces machine organization concepts in general. I teach this material following Chapter 2. It may be omitted, however, with no loss of continuity.
2. The high-level language-assembler interface. In particular the interface between C and assembler is stressed. Appendix D describes the Quick C environment commands for editing, assembling, linking, and debugging.

3. Extensive use of the debugger interface since this is a tool system programmers use in developing assembly language programs. Appendix E, however, includes simple-to-use I/O macros for those who prefer this form of I/O.

4. Differences between the various members of the 86-family: 8086, 8088, 80186, 80286, 80386, 80486, 8087, 80287, and 80387.

3. Segmentation issues.

4. Floating-point number concepts and instructions.

5. Machine code to make students more comfortable with the assembly language/machine code interface. This material may also be omitted.

6. Exercises stress concepts and principles. Includes exercises on comparative architecture.

7. Section outlines appear at the beginning of each chapter.

Acknowledgments

Although I have made every effort to eliminate errors, inevitably some slip through. I would appreciate hearing about them. You can reach me through the Computer Science Editor, HarperCollins College Publishers, 1900 East Lake Avenue, Glenview, IL 60025.

The following people contributed to this book, and I am grateful to them all: David Ames, Mark Arnold, Raymond Bell, Rich Bouchard, Jr., Gerald Cahill, Paul Cousineau, Nestor Descampo, Patrick Fay, Tricia Gagnon, Mary Hardel, James H. Hu, Gary Gu, Paul Marciello, Allen Martin, Kathy Merck, David Paist, Rob Roy, Tyson Sawyer, Michael Smith, Jan Thomas, Rajeer Tipnis, Bill Todd, Ed Urquhart, David Vasconcelos, Lester Waters, and Ed Woodhull.

The clever cartoons were drawn by George Capalbo.

Karen A. Lemone

0

Computer Systems

The first computers consisted solely of hardware. Programmers would write a program and then operate it themselves. First, the program would be loaded from cards, from paper tape, or from the computer's switches into the computer's memory. Then the appropriate buttons would be pushed to execute the stored program.

DOS

Today, in addition to hardware, computers come equipped with software programs. There is one program in particular that acts as an interface between people and the computer; it is called an operating system. The operating system used for the programs in this book is MS-DOS. This operating system was originally designed for the IBM Personal Computer (PC). However, the programs also will work on IBM PC compatible computers, often referred to as "PC-clones." MS-DOS was first used for computers that used a basic component called the INTEL 8088. This basic component is called a *microprocessor* or *chip*. (Strictly speaking, a microprocessor is a central processing unit (CPU) implemented as an integrated circuit. And an integrated circuit is often referred to as a chip.)

The 86-Family

The 8088 chip is similar to another chip, the 8086. Newer versions of these chips are called (as of this writing) the 80286, 80386, and 80486. Collectively, these chips are referred to as the *86-family,* and computers that contain one of these chips are referred to as the 86-family computers. The notation *80XXX* is also used for 86-family.

When we use the term *DOS,* we mean *MS-DOS* for machines with one of these chips. (DOS may mean something else on other ·computers.) This book describes the architecture of the 86-family computers and the assembly language for these machines.

Assembly language references the internal components of a computer and requires the presence of an *assembler.* An assembler is purchased separately from the computer and the operating system. There are a number of assemblers on the market. The programs in this book were written using the Microsoft MASM assembler environment. Appendix A describes another assembler, the Quick C assembler (also by Microsoft). There are other assemblers available for the 86-family; they may differ slightly from the one described here.

Chapter 12 of this book describes an additional component called a *numeric coprocessor,* which allows floating-point operations to be performed by hardware. Versions of this are called the 80287 and 80387. Versions of the 80486 include floating-point functions, so there is no 80487.

Counting

Counting is done differently in assembly language. Practically all items that are counted are done so from 0 rather than from 1. Thus, the first memory location is called location 0 rather than location 1. We have purposely called this chapter ''Chapter 0'' to emphasize this point.

Manuals

Unlike high-level languages, every detail of the assembly language will not be found in this text. When unsure of how an instruction works, the reader is advised (1) to consult the manual and (2) to ''try it'' on the computer. In addition to hardware and software, as just described, no computer system is complete without manuals.

Chapter 1 introduces us to assembly language programming and to the MASM assembly language.

1

Overview of Assembly Language Programming

1.0   Introduction

Modern *high-level languages,* such as Ada, Pascal, C, and BASIC, enable the programmer to solve problems from the perspective of the problem rather than from the perspective of the computer. These languages contain various and often sophisticated features for structuring data and ever-evolving constructs for manipulating data. *Assembly languages,* on the other hand, are low-level languages that access the computer's components directly to solve problems. In most cases, high-level languages are superior for problem solving. There are, however, several situations in which assembly languages are useful.

Applications where it is necessary to interface with the computer and the computer's parts often require assembly language. The compiler writer needs to know the assembly language used by the computer for which the compiler is being designed. There are also some system operations, such as interrupt routines, that frequently are accessible only on the assembly language level. Even the application programmer may find that certain sequences of code execute faster, take up less space, or manage the machine parts such as memory or the input/output (I/O) devices better when written in assembly language. In addition, learning an assembly language adds breadth and perspective to computer science knowledge.

The assembly language described in this book is called MASM©* and is available (at a price) for 86-family computers. We will often refer to such an assembler as an 86-family assembler, emphasizing that it is an assembler for machines whose basic component is one of the microprocessors described in Chapter 0.

1.1 Machine Language and Assembly Language

1.1.1 Machine Language

Machine language is the computer's native language. There are only two symbols in machine language: 0 and 1. These symbols are called *binary digits*, or *bits*. Each statement in machine language consists of a sequence of bits called a *bit pattern:*

$$1011100000000000000000010$$

An executable computer program consists of a collection of bit patterns. A bit pattern may represent an instruction, a piece of data, or even the location of an instruction or piece of data. In the preceding bit pattern, the leftmost 8 bits indicate that data (the rightmost 16 bits) are to be moved into a register.

Registers are special storage places in which high-speed operations are performed:

$$\underbrace{10111000}_{\text{Move to AX}} \quad \underbrace{00000000\ 00000010}_{2}$$

---

*MASM is a product of Microsoft Corporation.

If the preceding bit string is a machine instruction then it means "Move into the AX register the value 2." The bit patterns are interpreted in groups of 8 bits, or bytes. The first byte is the operation code (opcode). In this case the byte "10111000" means MOVE the following data into the AX register. The following two bytes, or 16 bits, represent the high and low halves of a 16-bit representation of the value 2.

The "heart" of the computer, called the *central processing unit* (CPU), interprets this instruction, which initially is stored in the computer's memory. Registers are part of the CPU. When it executes a program, the CPU distinguishes between a bit pattern representing an instruction and a bit pattern representing data. That is, the CPU understands this machine language. Humans, however, find such sequence of 0's and 1's somewhat incomprehensible and quite difficult to remember. Dealing with bit patterns requires the programmer to remember the numeric code for each instruction and the location in memory of each data item—all in binary. For these reasons we do not write programs in machine language if we can avoid it. Instead, we write in a more understandable notation called assembly language.

1.1.2 Assembly Language

In assembly language, as in high-level languages, a data item may be addressed by a symbolic name such as *A, Min, Result,* or *Factorial*. In addition, a descriptive, mnemonic code is used instead of a bit pattern to represent each instruction. For instance,

```
MOV     AX,2
```

is the 86-family assembly language equivalent for the preceding machine code. It is much easier to understand and to remember that this means "Move a 2 into the AX register" than to remember a sequence of 0's and 1's.

Unfortunately, computers cannot understand assembly language; they understand only the bit patterns of machine language. Thus, before an assembly language program can be executed, it first must be translated into machine language. A program called an assembler performs this translation.

| Assembly Language Program | → | Assembler | → | Machine Language Program |

EXAMPLE 1

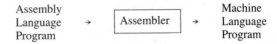

```
MOV AX,2  →  | 86-family Assembler |  →  10111000000000010000000000
```

Notice that in Example 1, the 16 bits representing 2 are written with the low-order bits (00000010) first and the high-order bits (00000000) last. This is because the 8 bits representing the instruction (10111000) are stored first, then the low-order bits of the number and finally, the high-order bits of the number.

1.2 Thinking in Assembly Language

1.2.1 Code Segments

Programming in assembly language is similar to operating a calculator. Each data value must be entered, and, in general, each operation such as addition or multiplication must be performed separately. High-level languages, on the other hand, can perform more than one operation in a single statement. Consider the following assignment statement, which adds 2 and 3 and assigns the sum to the variable named *Result:*

```
Result := 2 + 3
```

Languages such as C, BASIC, and FORTRAN would write this

```
Result = 2 + 3
```

(We use ``:='' in this text to denote the assignment operation.) To accomplish this addition and assignment in 86-family assembly language, we must first enter the value 2 into a register. Register AX will be chosen (somewhat at random—it is the only register we know about at the moment):

```
MOV    AX,2
```

The instruction MOV tells the CPU to copy the number 2 into register AX. Next, add a 3 to the contents of AX:

```
ADD    AX,3
```

Finally, we will move the sum to the location whose symbolic name is *Result*.

```
MOV    Result,AX
```

The entire sequence

```
MOV    AX,2
ADD    AX,3
MOV    Result,AX
```

is one way to calculate 2 + 3 in 86-family assembly language and to store the sum at the location whose name is *Result*. In 86-family assembly language, a *code segment* is the place where such instructions are written.

1.2.2 Instruction Parts

Notice that there are two parts to each of the previous instructions: an *operation* and some *operands*.

Operation	Operands
MOV	AX,2

The operation tells the computer what action to perform, and the operands indicate the object or objects on which to perform this action. We will see two additional (and optional) instruction parts later.

Calculating A + B.   Let's consider the more general case of calculating A + B and storing the sum in *Result*.

```
Result := A + B
```

The 86-family assembly language instructions for this are

Operation	Operands
MOV	AX,A
ADD	AX,B
MOV	Result,AX

Information about *A, B,* and *Result* must be described somewhere. In the 86-family, this place is called a *data segment*.

1.2.3 Data Segments

When a high-level language assignment statement such as

```
Result := A + B
```

is executed, values must have been assigned to the variables A and B. Similarly, in our 86-family assembly language program, A and B must be defined. *A, B,* and *Result* are all symbolic names for memory locations. In assembly language, a memory location must be allocated for each. The *assembler directive* (also called a *pseudo-op*)

```
A   DW   2
```

allots 16 bits of memory (called a *word*) for *A* and puts a 2 into it; i.e., it *de*fines a *w*ord. Similarly,

```
B   DW   3
```

instructs the assembler to put aside 16 bits for *B* and to initialize it to 3. The instruction

```
Result  DW   ?
```

allocates 16 bits for the symbolic name *Result* but assigns no initial value to this location. In particular, this location is not necessarily initialized to be 0. Thus, the entire sequence for our example is

```
A        DW   2
B        DW   3
Result DW    ?
```

1.2.4 Labels

In the preceding data segment, *A, B,* and *Result* are called labels. *Labels* are user-defined names. They can be placed in front of either instructions or assembler directives. *User-defined names* can consist of letters, digits, and the characters "?," ".," "@," "_," and "$." Names may not begin with a digit. If they contain a dot (.), the dot must be first. Names can be any length, but only the first 31 characters are recognized.

All program variables as well as labels must obey these rules for valid user-defined names. In addition, user-defined names cannot be the names of processor parts such as AX. Nor can they be the names of instructions or assembler directives. Notice, however, that more symbols are allowed in names than in typical high-level languages.

Labels are a third instruction part and are optional in the sense that not all instructions have labels.

1.2.5 Comments

It is important to include comments in programs so that you and others can better understand how your program works. In fact, an assembly language program should be commented extensively because assembly language programs are much less readable than most high-level language programs.

Comments begin with a semicolon (;) and continue until the end of the line. Comments are a fourth instruction part and are optional. Alternatively, comments may also begin with the word COMMENT and then can continue past the end of the line. The comment is surrounded (i.e., delimited) by two identical nonblank characters (which cannot be used within the comment).

EXAMPLE 2

```
COMMENT "The following calculates
          Result := 2 + 3"
;
MOV   AX,2           ; get 2
ADD   AX,3           ; add 3
MOV   Result,AX      ; put sum in Result
```

Note that in Example 2, the remark after COMMENT is surrounded by quotation marks ("). The first nonblank character after COMMENT is used as the delimiter of the comment. The comment is ended by repeating this delimiter.

1.3 A Complete Program

To put the code segment and data segment together to form a complete MASM assembly language program requires the addition of some structuring and bookkeeping statements. Figure 1-1 shows a skeletal outline of a typical MASM assembly language program.

In Figure 1-1, we have drawn boxes around the parts of the assembly language program. These parts will be described in the following sections. Words in italics represent parts of the program to be filled in by the programmer. Thus, *Code Segment* might be defined by the programmer to be the three statements from Example 2. All other words—except comments—must be written exactly as shown. We will give brief explanations of their meanings here. In some cases, a detailed explanation will be postponed until later chapters.

1.3.1 The Data Segment

The *data segment* of an 86-family assembly language program is the part of the program where symbols are defined. In the MASM assembly language, it is preceded by

```
.DATA
```

Figure 1-1 Outline of MASM assembly language program

```
;    Comments describing program
;
          Bookkeeping Instructions 1
```

```
;
;    Data Segment Follows
     .DATA
     Data Segment
```

```
;    Code Segment Follows
;
     .CODE
;
          Bookkeeping Instructions 2
;
;    Main Program
;
          Code Segment
;
          Bookkeeping Instructions 3
```

```
     END          Transfer Address
```

This is called an *assembler directive* and may be different in other assemblers. The following example shows the previously defined data segment with the addition of ".DATA":

EXAMPLE 3

```
.DATA
;
A       DW      2
B       DW      3
Result  DW      ?
;
```

Note that comment lines have been added for spacing.

1.3.2 The Code Segment

The code segment of an 86-family assembly language program is the part of the program containing executable instructions. In the MASM assembly language, it is preceded by

```
.CODE
```

The following example shows a code segment for our "Result := A + B" example with the addition of ".CODE":

EXAMPLE 4

```
      .CODE
;
;
      Bookkeeping Instructions 2
;
      MOV    AX,A        ; get A
      ADD    AX,B        ; add B
      MOV    Result,AX   ; put sum in location Result
;
      Bookkeeping Instructions 3
;
      END    Transfer Address
```

1.3.3 Bookkeeping Instructions

There are three sets of bookkeeping instructions shown in Figure 1-1. We will show each set.

The first set, called *Bookkeeping Instructions 1*, consists of the following statements:

```
        DOSSEG       ; use Microsoft SEGment Convention
        .MODEL SMALL
;
;       Stack Segment
;
        .STACK    100H
```

The DOSSEG directive facilitates linking an assembly language module with other assembly language modules or with high-level language modules. We will be doing such linking in a later chapter.

The .MODEL SMALL directive is used where the program has one code segment and one data segment. Although we will not be explicitly using the segment of memory called the *stack,* it is necessary to allocate space (100 base 16 locations) anyway.

The second set of bookkeeping instructions, denoted *Bookkeeping Instructions 2* in Figure 1-1, consists of:

```
Label       MOV        AX,@DATA
            MOV        DS,AX
```

The two instructions initialize the user's data segment. *Label* is a user-defined name. The *transfer address* in the operand of the END statement must be the same name.

The last set of bookkeeping instructions, denoted *Bookkeeping Instructions 3* in Figure 1-1, consists of

```
MOV     AH,4CH
INT     21H
```

These statements allow the program to terminate correctly.

All of these bookkeeping instructions will be discussed in later chapters.

1.4 Pragmatics

Now that we have seen a complete 86-family assembly language program, it is time to consider how to enter and execute such a program. There are five basic steps to entering and running a program using the MASM Editor. These steps are listed here and then described in detail. Steps 0 through 4 are the usual steps for entering or running any program (in C, Pascal, FORTRAN, etc.), except that these programs would be compiled instead of assembled. Step 4 is a useful method for debugging assembly language programs and is the recommended way for viewing the results of the program's execution. (Instructions for simulating traditional print statements for assembly language programs are described in Appendix E, if the reader wishes to use them.) Appendix D shows how to perform these steps using the Quick C assembler.

Step 0: Boot: Load the operating system from a disk.
Step 1: Edit: Create or correct the program.
Step 2: Assemble: Translate the program to machine language. The MASM assembler performs this step. If there are errors, return to Step 1.

Step 3: Link: Assign memory locations to the assembled program.
This is done automatically.

Step 4: Execute: Use the CodeView debugger to execute the program and diagnose any errors. If there are errors, return to Step 1.

This section describes these steps in detail. We will create, assemble, link, execute, and view the results of the 86-family assembly language program shown in Figure 1-1. The commands described are for the DOS operating system with one disk drive and a built-in hard drive.

1.4.1 The Operating System and Editor

Step 0: Load the operating system. This step involves turning the computer on and letting the computer boot from the hard drive without a disk in the floppy drive(s). Some questions may appear on the screen. Answer the questions to get to the DOS "prompt," which is usually:

C> or sometimes C:\>

This means DOS is ready to accept commands. You may now need to change to the directory where the MASM files are stored. This is done with the change directory command, CD, followed by the name of the directory that contains MASM.

Step 1: Create a program using an editor. We will use the Microsoft Editor, *M*, to create the program. Insert a formatted (see DOS command FORMAT) disk into drive A. We will name our program *Sum.ASM*. We precede this by *a:* to indicate that it is to be stored on the disk in drive A. If you want the program to be stored on the C drive omit the *a:*. To create and edit our program type:

C> m a:sum.asm

The Microsoft Editor responds by asking if the user wants to create a new file by this name. Press *Y* to indicate yes. The editor creates the file, and the editor is ready for the program to be typed in. The screen is mostly blank with some information about the file at the bottom. Begin typing in the program as shown in the following example. Use the arrow keys to move within the file. Use the delete and insert keys to edit if a mistake is made. When finished, the screen should appear as follows:

```
;   This program calculates Result := A + B when A = 2, B = 3.
;
; Bookkeeping statements 1
;
    DOSSEG              ; Use Microsoft SEGment conventions
    .MODEL  Small       ; Use small memory model
;
; Stack Segment follows
;
    .STACK  100H
;
; Data Segment follows
;
    .DATA
A        DW   2
B        DW   3
Result   DW   ?
;
; Code Segment follows
;
    .CODE
;
; Bookkeeping statements 2
;
Start:  MOV AX,@Data        ; Define current
        MOV DS,AX           ; Data Segment
;
; Main Program
;
        MOV AX,A            ; Get A
        ADD AX,B            ; Compute A + B
        MOV Result,AX       ; Result := A + B
;
; Bookkeeping statements 3
;
        MOV AH,4C00H        ; To successfully
        INT 21H             ; Return to DOS
;
        END Start           ; End of program.  Start is transfer address
```

Copyright (C) Microsoft Corp 1987, 1988. All rights reserved
c:\masm\bin\sum.asm (macro) Length=(36) Window=(15,1)

Type the function key F8 to save the file and exit from the editor.

1.4.2 The Assembler

The assembler translates the program to machine language.

Step 2: Assemble the program. The Microsoft Macro Assembler is called MASM. To assemble the program type:

```
masm/zi a:sum
```

The ''/zi'' tells the assembler to include symbolic and line number information when assembling; this information will be needed by the debugger in Step 4. The assembler now identifies itself and asks a series of questions. We will respond with *a:Sum* to all of them (*a:* to store everything on the disk in drive A and *Sum* to keep some of the intermediate files from being null). The default names are in brackets.

```
Object filename [SUM.OBJ]:a:sum
Source listing  [NUL.LST]:a:sum
Cross reference [NUL.CRF]:a:sum

Warning Severe
Errors  Errors
0       0
```

The two 0's are the assembler's cryptic way of indicating that there were no errors. If the assembler reports any errors, check your program closely with the one given here, and use *M* to correct any errors.

1.4.3 The Linker

The *linker* assigns memory locations to the program. Linking can also be used to link more than one assembled (or compiled) program into one single program. Once a program has been linked, it is ready to be executed.

Step 3: Link the assembled program. Type *link/co* (''/co'' is used to prepare for debugging). The linker also asks a number of questions, and we will respond with the same types of answers as in Step 2:

```
link/co
Object Modules [.OBJ]:a:sum
Run File [A:SUM.EXE]:a:sum
List File [NUL.MAP]:
Libraries: [.LIB]:
```

Note that only a carriage return was typed for the last two lines.

1.4.4 The Debugger

The debugger allows us to see how the program executes.

Step 4: Execute the program using the debugger. We can execute the program, one instruction at a time, examining registers and memory locations along the way. Alternatively, we could tell the debugger to execute the whole program and then examine registers and memory. The MASM debugger is called CodeView. Type

```
C> cv a:sum.exe
CV>
```

The "CV>" prompt means the debugger is now ready to accept commands. Note: The values shown here are for the author's memory configuration and will vary from system to system.

```
 File  View  Search  Run  Watch  Options  Language  Calls  Help  F8=Trace F5=Go
------------------------------. sum.ASM .-------------------------------------
1: ;  This program calculates Result := A + B when A = 2, B = 3.  AX = 0000
2:    ;                                                           BX = 0000
3:; Bookkeeping statements 1                                      CX = 0000
4:    ;                                                           DX = 0000
5:          DOSSEG          ; Use Microsoft SEGment conventions   SP = 0100
6:          .MODEL  Small   ; Use small memory model              BP = 0000
7:    ;                                                           SI = 0000
8:    ; Stack Segment follows                                     DI = 0000
9:    ;                                                           DS = 6AA7
10:         .STACK  100H                                          ES = 6AA7
11:   ;                                                           SS = 6ABA
12:   ; Data Segment follows                                      CS = 6AB7
13:   ;                                                           IP = 0010
14:         .DATA
15:   A        DW   2                                             NV UP
16:   B        DW   3                                             EI PL
17:   Result   DW   ?                                             NZ NA
18:   ;
PO NC
-----------------------------------------------------------------
```

We will execute this program one statement at a time, using the TRACE command. Each time an instruction is executed, the debugger will update the contents of the registers on the right side of the screen and highlight the next instruction to be executed. Enter a *t* at the prompt and watch the value of register AX (because the program changes AX). Continue with the TRACE command until the message "program terminated normally" appears. Notice the value of AX after each step. We use the DW (*d*isplay *w*ord) command to display the contents of *Result*. Therefore, type

```
DW result
```

The debugger responds with

```
56F6:0000      0005    424E    3030    0090    0000    0000    0010    0011
56F6:0010 0000 0000 0000 5307 4D55 4F2E 4A42 0000
```

The location (56F6:0000) contains our result, which is written as

```
0005
```

In Chapter 2, we will discuss how such numbers are stored in the 86-family. We leave the debugger by using the quit command, Q:

```
CV> Q
```

1.4.5 Prompts

Note that when the operating system is waiting for a command, it displays "C>"; when the CodeView debugger is waiting for a command, it displays a "CV>".

For a faster, though not necessarily better, alternative to viewing results using the debugger, we can add prewritten instructions that perform input and output similar to the I/O instructions found in high-level language. Appendix F contains three instructions *PrintString$, ReadWord$* and *PrintWord$* for displaying results on the screen. The author believes, however, that viewing *Result* using the debugger is a better way to learn how to program in assembly language.

1.5 Summary

This chapter is intended to be motivational. We have seen that we will need to become more familiar with the 86-family architecture (e.g., its registers), with the binary number system, and with the way data are stored. Chapters 2 and 3 discuss these concepts. Chapter 4 then introduces the instruction set for the 86-family assembly language. Appendix G discusses more general computer organization.

An 86-family assembly language program has a separate segment for code (executable instructions) and data. There are two other segments to be discussed: (1) the extra segment and (2) the stack segment, both described in Chapter 2.

An assembly language program is translated into machine code by another program called an assembler. In this chapter, we saw some instructions that were intended for the assembler itself:

```
DOSSEG
.MODEL
.CODE
.DATA
.STACK
DW
;
COMMENT
END
```

They are called assembler directives, or pseudo-ops, and are not themselves translated by the assembler into machine code, although they often (e.g., DW) cause the assembler to produce machine code.

The machine instructions we saw in this chapter were

```
MOV
ADD
INT
```

MOV and ADD are discussed in Chapter 4, INT in Chapter 10.

Exercises

Asterisked exercises indicate programs to run. A single asterisk refers to using the debugger to view results as described in Appendix A. A double asterisk refers to the high-level language I/O instructions described in Appendix E. The reader can choose either or both of these approaches to viewing results. We do recommend that the reader learn to use the debugger in either event.

1. What are the symbols used in machine language, and what are they called?
2. What is the function of the assembler?
3. What are the parts of an assembly language instruction, and what does each do?
4. What is the name of the section within an 86-family assembly language program where data is "declared" and possibly initialized?
5. What is the name of the section within an 86-family assembly language program that contains the executable statements?
6. Using the program in Figure 1-1 as a guide, write a complete assembly language program to calculate

   ```
   B := 2 * A.
   ```

   You need only the instructions from this chapter.

7. Follow Steps 0 through 4 described in this chapter for the program in Exercise 6.
   * (a) Use the debugger as described.
   ** (b) Use the I/O statements from Appendix E.

2

Machine Organization: 86-Family Architecture

2.0 Introduction to 86-Family Architecture

2.0.1 Word Length

Word length is often defined as the number of bits in a register. Computers differ in their word lengths. Many of the first personal computers had a word length of 8 bits. The 86-family and other recently developed microprocessors have a word length of 16 bits. The 80386 and 80486 allow word lengths of either 16 bits or

32 bits. Other computers, for example, the Apple MacIntosh computer, have a word length of 32 bits.

2.0.2 Other Differences in Architecture

Computers differ in ways besides word length. Their differences may include the number and uses of registers, the amount of memory that can be addressed, and the number and functions of peripheral devices (such as disks, line printers, and screen displays), to name a few. In this chapter, we will look at the different sizes for storage elements; the size, number, and uses of registers; and the way the 86-family addresses memory.

2.1 86-Family Storage Elements

2.1.1 Bits

The smallest storage element on any computer is the bit, which, as we saw in Chapter 1, can have a value of 0 or 1 (see Figure 2-1). Clearly, a bit cannot represent much information. In fact, it can contain only one of two values — 0 or 1. Thus we usually represent information in groups of consecutive bits, called, on 86-families, nibbles, bytes, words, doublewords, quadwords, and tenbytes.

2.1.2 Nibbles

The next larger size of information is a *nibble* (sometimes spelled nybble), which is a sequence of 4 bits (see Figure 2-2). The bits in a nibble are numbered from right to left, with the rightmost bit (the least significant bit) numbered 0 and the leftmost bit (the most significant bit) numbered 3.

Figure 2-1 A bit

Figure 2-2 A nibble

2.1.3 Bytes

The next larger size of storage element is a *byte,* which is a sequence of 8 bits (see Figure 2-3). Bytes are one of the most important storage elements—many operations are performed on bytes, and memory is addressable (i.e., accessible) by bytes.

2.1.4 Words

Many of the larger sized storage elements can now be found by multiplying by 2. A *word* equals 2 bytes, or 16 bits. We will view words in two different ways:

1. As a horizontal sequence of 16 bits (see Figure 2-4)
2. As a vertical sequence of 2 bytes (see Figure 2-5)

The first viewpoint is useful when we look at the contents of 16-bit registers. The second viewpoint is more useful when we look at memory locations. In memory,

Figure 2-3 A byte

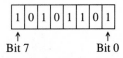

Figure 2-4 A word written horizontally

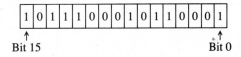

Figure 2-5 The same word written vertically byte by byte

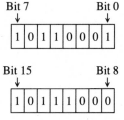

the least significant byte (bits 0 through 7) of a word is stored in lower numbered memory locations, and the most significant byte (bits 8 through 15) is stored in the next higher numbered location. The debugger also displays the least significant byte of a word first.

2.1.5 Doublewords

Two words represent a *doubleword*. For reasons similar to those mentioned earlier, we will show the same doubleword three ways:

1. As a horizontal sequence of 32 bits (see Figure 2-6)
2. As a vertical sequence of 2 words (see Figure 2-7)
3. As a vertical sequence of 4 bytes (see Figure 2-8)

If this doubleword were in memory, bits 0 through 7 would come first, bits 8 through 15 would be in the next higher numbered byte, bits 16 through 23 in the next, and so on.

2.1.6 Quadwords

A *quadword* is 2 doublewords, hence 4 words or 8 bytes (see Figures 2-9 and 2-10).

Figure 2-6 A doubleword written horizontally

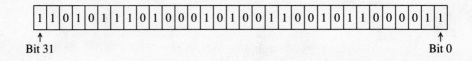

Bit 31   Bit 0

Figure 2-7 The same doubleword written vertically as 2 words

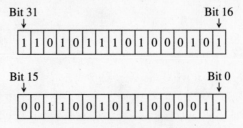

Figure 2-8 The same doubleword written vertically byte by byte

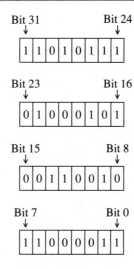

Figure 2-9 A quadword written as 2 doublewords

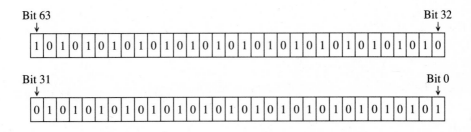

2.1.7 Tenbytes

The largest single unit of storage on the 86-family is a sequence of 10 bytes called a *tenbyte*. It would look like a quadword, but with 2 more bytes.

2.1.8 Data Storage

Bits, nibbles, bytes, words, doublewords, quadwords, and tenbytes are units of storage. They do not indicate what type of data is stored in them. In the next chapter, we shall see that bits may be used to store Booleans (i.e., 1 for True, 0 for False) and that bytes, words, and doublewords are used frequently

Figure 2-10 A quadword written vertically byte by byte

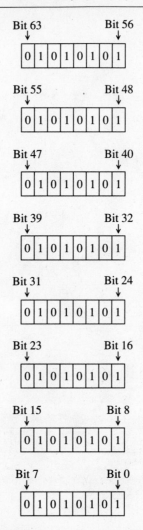

to store integers. Certainly the larger the storage unit, the larger the integer that can be stored there. In addition, we will see that doublewords are large enough to store small decimal point numbers, although larger (''double-precision'') decimal point numbers may require a quadword or tenbyte storage size. We will also see that bytes are large enough to store characters (e.g., letters).

2.2 Registers

The 86-family computers have 14 registers. The bits in each register are numbered from 0 through 15 and from right to left (see Figure 2-11). The 8088 and 80286 have 16-bit registers. The 80386 and 80486 have the same fourteen 16-bit registers, but, in addition, they allow the registers to be extended by 16 bits, effectively producing 32-bit registers.

These registers are divided into five distinct groups:

1. Four segment registers (the 80386/80486 have 6)
2. Four data registers
3. Two pointer and two index registers
4. The instruction pointer
5. The Flags register

We will discuss each of these groups separately.

2.2.1 Segment Registers

The 86-family has separate ''work areas'' for the parts of an assembly language program: an area for data, an area for the code, a special memory area called the stack, and an extra area for storing more data (see Figure 2-12). Each of these areas can be up to 64K (1K in ''computerese'' is defined to be 2**10, approximately 1,000) bytes in length and is called a segment. Thus, the work area for data is called the data segment, the work area for the executable instructions is called the code segment, the stack area is called the stack segment, and the extra data area is called the extra segment. It is possible, even reasonable, to let these four areas overlap; in fact, they can all be the same. The 80386 and 80486 have two more segments for programs that use more than four segments.

The various *segment registers*—denoted DS for data segment register, CS for code segment register, SS for stack segment register, and ES for extra segment register—contain the address of (i.e., point to) the beginning of each segment. We show this in Figure 2-13 for the data segment and the data segment register, DS. A similar picture could be drawn for any of the other segments.

Figure 2-11 A typical 16-bit register

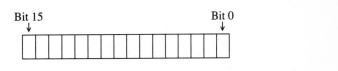

Figure 2-12 Segments

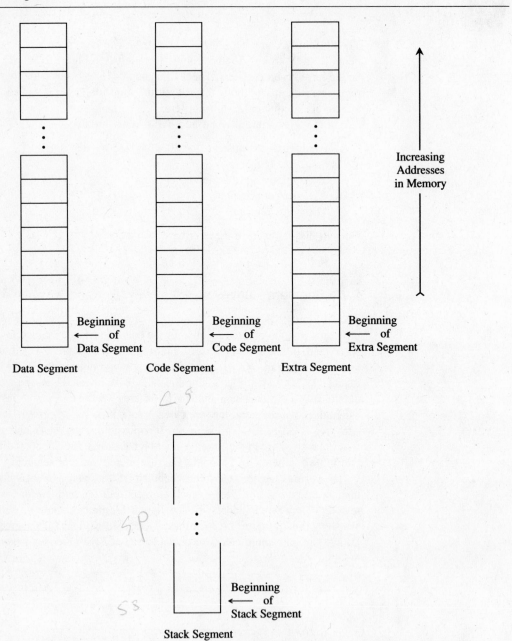

Data Segment   Code Segment   Extra Segment

Stack Segment

Figure 2-13 Segments and segment registers

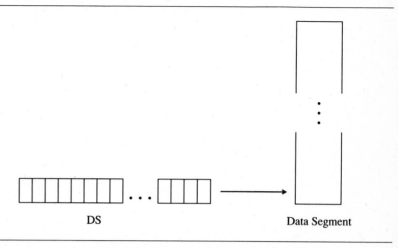

Thus, if the data segment begins in memory location 0, then DS would contain a 0. There are instructions for loading memory location values into segment registers. In Chapter 1, we did this in a somewhat cumbersome way with a series of MOV instructions. In Chapter 4, we will see that many other instructions deal directly with the segment registers.

2.2.2 Data Registers

The four 16-bit data registers are

1. The accumulator, AX
2. The base register, BX
3. The count register, CX
4. The data register, DX

These four registers may also be used in the 80386 and 80486. For larger values, the 32-bit extensions are denoted EAX, EBX, ECX, and EDX.

Each "X" register can be subdivided into a high part and a low part. For example, the low-order 8 bits of AX are denoted AL and the high-order 8 bits are denoted AH (see Figure 2-14). The way we refer to these registers affects the way these registers are modified. For example

```
MOV   AX,2
```

results in zeros in the high-order bits of AX:

AX | 0 | 0 | 0 | 0 | 0 | 0 | 0 | 0 | 0 | 0 | 0 | 0 | 0 | 0 | 1 | 0 |

Figure 2-14 The data registers

AX	AH	AL

BX	BH	BL

CX	CH	CL

DX	DH	DL

whereas

```
MOV  AL,2
```

does not affect the high-order byte:

AX	? ? ? ? ? ? ? ? 0 0 0 0 0 0 1 0

All four registers may be used to store data, but some of these are altered by various instructions. For example, the count register, CX, is altered by the LOOP instruction, and DX is used in multiply and divide instructions. Some instructions produce less machine code when specific registers are used. Thus, when we learn the instruction set, it is important that we note whether an instruction affects a register, and how it affects it.

2.2.3 Pointer and Index Registers

The segment registers point to the beginning of the various memory segments. The *pointer registers* are used to calculate *offsets* (i.e., *displacements*) into these segments. There are two pointer registers:

1. The stack pointer (SP)
2. The base pointer (BP)

The stack pointer. The *stack pointer* is used to hold the current stack location (see Figure 2-15). Here SS contains the address of the beginning of the stack segment and SP contains the offset. In Chapter 8, we will see that stack operations *decrease* SP, i.e., it moves "down" in the diagram in Figure 2-15.

The base pointer. The *base pointer* is also used to point to offsets within segments (e.g., it can point to the stack offset). It is used primarily in conjunc-

Figure 2-15 The stack pointer

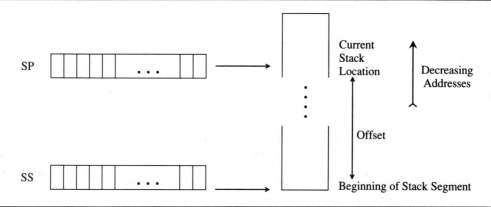

tion with base-indexed addressing mode (described in Chapter 5) for accessing elements between the beginning of the stack and the top of the stack.

There are two *index registers:*

1. Source index (SI)
2. Destination index (DI)

Index registers are used the same way subscripts are used in high-level languages. They enable us to access the elements in an array or table. Often, there is no significance to the words *source* and *destination,* and SI and DI can be used interchangeably. In Chapter 9, however, we will see some instructions that do distinguish between source and destination and use DI and SI explicitly. As usual, EDI and ESI denote the 32-bit extensions for the 80386 and 80486.

2.2.4 The Instruction Pointer

The *instruction pointer,* IP, contains the current offset in the code segment in the same sense that SP (or sometimes BP) contains the current offset in the stack segment. In fact, the IP contains the offset of the address in the code segment of the next instruction to be executed. When the CPU has finished executing one instruction, it consults the contents of the IP to find the offset of the next instruction to execute. The IP is then updated (automatically) to contain the offset of the next instruction to execute within the code segment. In other machines, the register that performs functions similar to the IP is often called the program counter. EIP is the 32-bit extension register for the 80386 and 80486.

Figure 2-16 The Flags register

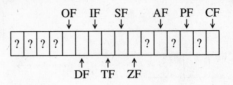

2.2.5 The Flags Register

The *Flags register* contains information about the most recently executed instruction. Although the Flags register is 16 bits long, only bits 0, 2, 4, and 6 through 11 are used (see Figure 2-16). These bits are called *status bits* and contain information during execution about the last executed instruction. A status bit is said to be *set* if it contains a 1 and *cleared* if it contains a 0. Many assembly language instructions affect the status bits in some way. The nine flags are:

1. CF, the *carry flag*: set by arithmetic instructions that involve a carry out of, or a borrow into, the most significant bit of the operand containing the result of the instructions.
2. PF, the *parity flag*: set if the operation results in an even number of 1's in the lower 8 bits. Checking the parity of a data value before and after a hardware operation can often detect transmission errors.
3. AF, the *auxiliary carry flag*: set by arithmetic instructions that involve a carry out of, or a borrow into, bit 3 of the operand containing the result. We will see in Chapter 3 that this can happen when we are dealing with binary-coded decimal (BCD) numbers.
4. ZF, the *zero flag*: set if the result of an operation is 0.
5. SF, the *sign flag*: set if the result of an operation is negative.
6. TF, the *trap flag*: used for executing a program (e.g., by the debugger) one instruction at a time (when set).
7. IF, the *interrupt enable* flag: allows the 86-family to recognize interrupts (when set) or to ignore them (when cleared).
8. DF, the *direction flag*: determines whether to increment or decrement an index register during string instructions. A decrement takes place if DF is set.
9. OF, the *overflow flag*: set by signed operations whose results do not fit into the designated storage unit (e.g., a word).

We will refer to these status bits in Chapter 4 when we discuss instructions that affect them.

The registers are an integral part of the CPU. The CPU retrieves information from memory and determines what operations to perform, and when.

DEBUG's Flag Abbreviations.   The system debugger has special symbols to indicate whether a flag is set or cleared:

OV:	OF is set
NV:	OF is cleared
DN:	DF is set
UP:	DF is cleared
EI:	IF is set
DI:	IF is cleared
NG:	SF is set
PL:	SF is cleared
ZR:	ZF is set
NZ:	ZF is cleared
AC:	AF is set
NA:	AF is cleared
PE:	PF is set
PO:	PF is cleared
CY:	CF is set
NC:	CF is cleared

At the beginning of our DEBUG session back in Chapter 1, the flags are shown as

```
NV UP DI PL NZ NA PO NC
```

indicating that they are all cleared initially. We urge the reader to look back at the debugger output in Chapter 1 to see how the flag register changes as each instruction executes.

The 80386 and 80486 Flags register, Eflags, consists of the Flags register plus a higher order 16 bits.

2.3 Memory

Computer memory consists of an ordered sequence of storage units, each with its own address. Like most computers, the 86-family memory is *byte-addressable,* which means that each byte has its own address. Thus, if A is the address of a word, then A is actually the address of the first byte of the word, $A+1$ is the address of the second byte of the word, and $A+2$ is the address of the next word.

```
.
.
.
   | A
   | A + 1
   | A + 2
.
.
.
```

In Chapter 4, we will learn instructions that have both byte and word versions; i.e., we will be able to execute that instruction on a single byte or on 2 bytes (a word). There are some doubleword versions for 80386 and 80486 machines.

The stack is an exception to this byte-addressable rule: The stack is only word-addressable. There are ways to "get at" the individual bytes in a stack word, but not to address them separately.

Since there are 16 bits in a segment register and a segment register contains the address of the beginning of a segment, it would seem that we can address only 2^{16} different addresses for the beginning of a segment. Not so! Before the address of a segment is computed, the segment register is multiplied by 16, which is equivalent to a shift of 4 bits to the left, i.e., to an append of four 0's to its binary contents. For example, if CS contains 1110000000000000, then CS*16 is 11100000000000000000, which is the actual beginning of the code segment.

Thus a segment register can effectively address (2^{16}) times (2^4) bytes of memory. This figure, 2^{20}, is called a *megabyte,* since it represents approximately a million bytes of memory. Memory may be viewed as in Figure 2-17.

A segment register addresses the *beginning* of a segment. The offset *into* the segment is contained in another register, e.g., IP for the code segment, SP or BP for the stack segment. Thus, the contents of this offset must be added to the contents of the segment register times 16 to compute the *effective address.* Figure 2-18 shows the computer in a state where the next instruction to be executed is in location 11100000000000001101. This is because the CS register contains 1110000000000000. This effectively addresses 11100000000000000000. When the 0000000000001101 offset in IP is added, 11100000000000001101 results.

Figure 2-19 shows the arithmetic for the configuration of Figure 2-18. It should be noted that although there are 2^{20} effective addresses available, the assembly language programmer is restricted to using 4 segments at any one time, each 2^{16} in length. Thus the programmer's work area is 4 times 2^{16}, or 2^{18}, which equals 262,144 bytes.

Figure 2-17 Memory

Memory Address	Example Memory Contents
1 1 1 1 1 1 1 1 1 1 1 1 1 1 1 1 1 1 1 1	0 0 0 0 0 0 0 0
1 1 1 1 1 1 1 1 1 1 1 1 1 1 1 1 1 1 1 0	0 0 0 0 0 0 0 0
0 0 0 0 0 0 0 0 0 0 0 0 0 0 0 0 0 0 1 0	0 1 0 1 0 1 1 0
0 0 0 0 0 0 0 0 0 0 0 0 0 0 0 0 0 0 0 1	0 0 0 0 0 0 0 0
0 0 0 0 0 0 0 0 0 0 0 0 0 0 0 0 0 0 0 0	1 1 0 1 0 0 0 0

Figure 2-18 Referencing the next instruction

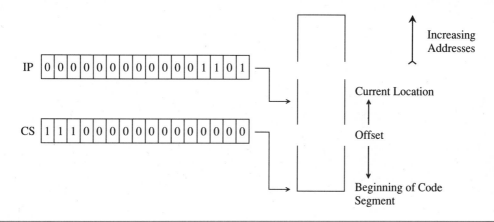

Figure 2-19 Calculating the effective address

```
CS:            1 1 1 0 0 0 0 0 0 0 0 0 0 0 0 0

CS * 16:  1 1 1 0 0 0 0 0 0 0 0 0 0 0 0 0 0 0 0 0     ( Beginning of Code Segment )
     IP:       +  0 0 0 0 0 0 0 0 0 0 0 0 1 1 0 1
CS * 16 + IP:  1 1 1 0 0 0 0 0 0 0 0 0 0 0 0 1 1 0 1     ( Actual Location in Memory )
```

80286 Addressing. The 80286 supports the 8086/8088 method of addressing. The 80286 also has a second method of addressing. Because it has a 24-bit address bus, it can address 2^{24}, or 16 megabytes, of memory. This method of addressing is called protected mode and uses the segment:offset combination to compute the 24-bit address. The offset is used in the same way as in the 8086/8088. The segment register content, however, is used as the index of a table, called a descriptor table. That entry in the table contains the 24-bit address. This amount is then added to the offset.

80386 Addressing. The 80386 also supports the 8086/8088 segment:offset addressing. In addition, the 80386 (operating in ''virtual mode'') can operate as though one machine were really several 8086/8088's.

The third method of addressing on the 80386 is similar to protected mode on the 80286, except that the 80386 has 32 addressing lines and 32-bit registers, thus allowing 2^{32} byte addresses (4 gigabytes) to be stored.

By a similar use of a descriptor table as for the 80286, the 80386 can address up to 2^{46} (64 terabytes) of virtual memory.

2.4 Summary

The architecture of the 86-family described in this chapter is a logical architecture; that is, it is a viewpoint of the physical architecture that is suitable for writing assembly language programs. The experienced programmer might want to acquire more knowledge of the physical architecture, including information about how the various parts of the computer are connected as well as about the actual parts that contain information about these connections. This information can be found in appropriate Intel literature or any of the many "chip" books. In addition, Appendix F discusses computer organization in general.

The 86-family storage elements are divided into multiples and fractions of 16 bits, where 16 is the size of a register. These elements are called nibbles (¼ of 16), bytes (½ of 16), words (16), doublewords (2 times 16), quadwords (4 times 16), and tenbytes (5 times 16).

Many of the 14 registers are general-purpose registers; they may be used to perform general calculations such as arithmetic operations. The instruction pointer, IP, is modified by an executing program. The segment registers point to the beginning of a memory segment, which may be up to 64,000 bytes (approximately) in length.

Memory is accessed using a 20-bit address—accomplished by shifting a segment register left 4 bits and adding an offset from another register. Although this addressing was first developed for the 16-bit members of the 86-family, it may also be used for the 32-bit members and is called real mode. The 80386 and 80486 also permit 32-bit addressing.

Exercises

1. Fill in the chart:

Storage element	Size in bits	Largest contents
Bit	_____	_____
Byte	_____	_____
Word	_____	_____
Doubleword	_____	_____

2. Memory addresses are how many bits long? Explain the relationship between a segment register and the length of an address.
3. What registers are used for general-purpose storing and manipulation of data?
4. What register contains the address of the beginning of the stack segment? What register(s) are usually used to point to the top of the stack?

5. What register contains the offset into the code segment of the next instruction to execute?
6. What register contains status bits? List the status bits and what they stand for.
7. What is the address of the next instruction to be executed if CS contains 0000001100000000 and IP contains 0000000000000001?
8. Show the doubleword

   10010001100111101000101011001010

   as (a) 2 words and as (b) 4 bytes.
9. What does register AX contain after the instructions

   ```
   MOV   AH,1
   MOV   AL,10
   ```
   are executed?

10. What flags would be set by the following instructions after the ADD takes place?

    ```
    MOV   AX,-100
    ADD   AX,-500
    ```

11. Write an instruction (or instructions) that will set the overflow bit, OF. Use the debugger to see the change.
12. Follow Steps 0–4 from Chapter 1 to enter, assemble, link, and debug the following program, using the debugger to examine the contents of the registers and memory location *Result*. Note the differences in content because of the byte-sized storage elements.

```
;   This program calculates Result := A + B when A = 2, B = 3.
;
; Two necessary bookkeeping statements follow
;

        DOSSEG          ; Use Microsoft SEGment conventions
        .MODEL  Small   ; Use small memory model
;
; Stack Segment follows
;
        .STACK  100H
;
; Data Segment follows
;
        .DATA
A       DB   ?
B       DB   ?
Result  DB   ?


; Code Segment follows
;
        .CODE
```

```
        ;
        ; Two more necessary bookkeeping statements follow
        ;
Start:    MOV AX,@Data        ; Define current
          MOV DS,AX           ; Data Segment
        ;
        ; Main Program
        ;



          MOV AL,A            ; Get A
          ADD AL,B            ; Compute A + B
          MOV Result,AL       ; Result := A + B


        ;
          MOV AH,4CH
          INT 21H             ; Back to DOS
        ;
          END Start           ; End of program.  Start is transfer address
```

13. Write, assemble, link, and debug an assembly language program to calculate

    ```
    B := 2*A
    ```

where *A* and *B* are byte-sized values. Pick an appropriate value for *A*. (*Note*: This can be done using an ADD instruction.)

3

Data and Instruction
Representation

3.0 Introduction

Assembly language programs, like high-level language programs, perform manipulations on *data* to produce desired results. Languages differ in the kinds of data they use and in the operations that can be performed on the data.

All data is ultimately represented to the computer in binary. We can, however, choose to look at these bit strings as if they were a character or a sequence of characters, or an integer or a sequence of integers. There are ways to inform the computer that the bit string is to be considered as a particular data type. The

86-family's circuitry and instruction set then enable us to operate on this data in appropriate ways.

In this chapter, we will offer historical perspective to the topic of data storage. For example, when we discuss negative numbers, we will describe ways that other machines represent negative numbers as well as how the 86-family does it. Similarly, there have been other ''codes'' for representing characters besides the one used by the 86-family. In fact, IBM used a different code for representing characters in its computers prior to the PC. It is interesting to view other alternate representations for data.

3.1 Binary, Decimal, and Hexadecimal Numbers

Although the computer operates on binary-coded data, it is often more convenient for us to view this data in hexadecimal (base 16). There are three reasons for this:

1. Binary machine code is usually long and difficult to assimilate. Hexadecimal, like decimal, is much easier to read.
2. There is a direct correspondence between binary and hexadecimal. Thus, we can easily translate from hexadecimal to binary.
3. The 86-family storage elements are multiples or fractions of 16. Thus it is convenient to show contents as multiples and fractions of 16 — hexadecimal. This is clear from the discussion of storage elements in Chapter 2. There, we saw that storage sizes were 4 bits (a nibble), 8 bits (a byte), 16 bits (a word), 32 bits (a doubleword), 64 bits (a quadword), and 80 bits (a tenbyte) — all multiples and fractions of 16.

Thus, although we think in decimal and the computer thinks in binary, hexadecimal is a number system that captures some of the important elements of both. In the remainder of this section we will discuss the binary, decimal, and hexadecimal number systems and the methods for converting from one number system to another. Readers who are already comfortable with these concepts might wish to skip to Section 3.2.

3.1.1 Conversions

Binary to Hexadecimal. To see the one-to-one correspondence between hexadecimal and binary, notice that if we use b to represent a bit and

$$b_n b_{n-1} \ldots b_2 b_1 b_0$$

is a binary number, then it has a value of

$$2^n b_n + \ldots + 2^8 b_8 + 2^7 b_7 + 2^6 b_6 + 2^5 b_5 + 2^4 b_4$$
$$+ 2^3 b_3 + 2^2 b_2 + 2^1 b_1 + 2^0 b_0$$

or

$$\ldots + 256 b_8 + 128 b_7 + 64 b_6 + 32 b_5 + 16 b_4 + 8 b_3 + 4 b_2 + 2 b_1 + b_0$$

which can be written

$$\ldots + 1 b_8) * 16^2 + (8 b_7 + 4 b_6 + 2 b_5 + 1 b_4) * 16^1$$
$$+ (8 b_3 + 4 b_2 + 2 b_1 + 1 b_0) * 16^0$$

Each of the sums in parentheses is a number between 0 (if all the b values are 0) and 15 (if all the b values are 1). These are exactly the *digits* in the hexadecimal number system (see Figure 3-1). Thus, to convert from binary to hexadecimal, we must ''gather up'' groups of 4 binary digits.

Figure 3-1 Number system comparison

Binary	Decimal	Hexadecimal
1	1	1
10	2	2
11	3	3
100	4	4
101	5	5
110	6	6
111	7	7
1000	8	8
1001	9	9
1010	10	A
1011	11	B
1100	12	C
1101	13	D
1110	14	E
1111	15	F
10000	16	10
10001	17	11
.	.	.
.	.	.
.	.	.

EXAMPLE 1

Convert the following binary word to hexadecimal.

$$\underbrace{0010}_{2}\underbrace{1011}_{B}\underbrace{0011}_{3}\underbrace{1000}_{8}$$

That is, $0010101100111000_2 = 2B38_{16}$.

Hexadecimal to Binary. To convert from hexadecimal to binary, we perform the opposite process from that used to convert from binary to hexadecimal. Thus, we must expand each hexadecimal digit to four binary digits.

EXAMPLE 2

Convert $D0_{16}$ to binary.

$$\underbrace{\text{D} \quad 0}_{11010000}$$

That is, $D0_{16} = 11010000_2$.

Binary to Decimal

Method. Write the binary sequence in its place-value summation form and then evaluate it.

EXAMPLE 3

$$
\begin{aligned}
10101010_2 &= 1*2^7 + 0*2^6 + 1*2^5 + 0*2^4 + 1*2^3 + 0*2^2 \\
&\quad + 1*2^1 + 0*2^0 \\
&= 2^7 + 2^5 + 2^3 + 2^1 \\
&= 128 + 32 + 8 + 2 \\
&= 170_{10}
\end{aligned}
$$

Decimal to Binary

Method 1. Use a table of powers of 2 to reduce the decimal sequence to a summation of powers of 2; see Figure 3-2.

EXAMPLE 4

$$
\begin{aligned}
345_{10} &= 2^8 + 89 \qquad (2^9 \text{ is larger than } 345) \\
&= 2^8 + 2^6 + 25 \\
&= 2^8 + 2^6 + 2^4 + 9 \\
&= 2^8 + 2^6 + 2^4 + 2^3 + 1 \\
&= 2^8 + 2^6 + 2^4 + 2^3 + 2^0 \\
&= 1*2^8 + 0*2^7 + 1*2^6 + 0*2^5 + 1*2^4 + 1*2^3 \\
&\quad + 0*2^2 + 0*2^1 + 1*2^0 \\
&= 101011001_2
\end{aligned}
$$

Figure 3-2 Powers of 2

n	2^n
0	1
1	2
2	4
3	8
4	16
5	32
6	64
7	128
8	256
9	512
10	1024
11	2048
12	4096
13	8192
14	16384
15	32768
16	65536
.	.
.	.
.	.

Method 2. Divide the decimal number successively by 2: remainders are the coefficients of 2^0, 2^1, 2^2, ...

EXAMPLE 5

Convert 345_{10} to binary.

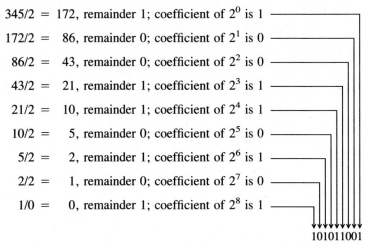

$345/2 = 172$, remainder 1; coefficient of 2^0 is 1

$172/2 = 86$, remainder 0; coefficient of 2^1 is 0

$86/2 = 43$, remainder 0; coefficient of 2^2 is 0

$43/2 = 21$, remainder 1; coefficient of 2^3 is 1

$21/2 = 10$, remainder 1; coefficient of 2^4 is 1

$10/2 = 5$, remainder 0; coefficient of 2^5 is 0

$5/2 = 2$, remainder 1; coefficient of 2^6 is 1

$2/2 = 1$, remainder 0; coefficient of 2^7 is 0

$1/0 = 0$, remainder 1; coefficient of 2^8 is 1

101011001

Thus, $345_{10} = 101011001_2$.

This method works because we want to find the coefficients b_0, b_1, b_2, . . . (which are 0 or 1) of 2^0, 2^1, 2^2, . . . and so on. Thus, in the preceding example,

$$345_{10} = b_{10}2^{10} + b_9 2^9 + b_8 2^8 + \cdots + b_1 2^1 + b_0 2^0$$

Dividing by 2,

$$345/2 = b_{10}2^9 + b_9 2^8 + \cdots + b_1 + (b_0/2)$$

Thus b_0 is the remainder on division by 2 and $(b_{10}2^9 + b_9 2^8 + \cdots + b_1)$ is the quotient.

Decimal to Hexadecimal

Method 1.   Use a table of powers of 16 (see Figure 3-3) to reduce the decimal sequence to a summation of powers of 16 similar to Method 1 for converting from decimal to binary.

EXAMPLE 6

$$
\begin{aligned}
302_{10} &= 1*16^2 + 46 \quad (16^3 \text{ is greater than } 302) \\
&= 1*16^2 + 2*16^1 + 14 \\
&= 1*16^2 + 2*16^1 + E*16^0 \quad (14_{10} = E_{16}) \\
&= 12E_{16}
\end{aligned}
$$

Method 2.   Divide the decimal number successively by 16; remainders are the coefficients of 16^0, 16^1, 16^2, . . .

EXAMPLE 7

302/16 = 18, remainder 14; coefficient of 16^0 is E ─────────────┐

18/16 = 1, remainder 2; coefficient of 161 is 2 ──────────────┐ │

1/16 = 0, remainder 1; coefficient of 162 is 1 ───────────┐ │ │

                          1 2 E

Therefore, $302_{10} = 12E_{16}$.

Figure 3-3 Powers of 16

n	16^n
0	1
1	16
2	256
3	4096
4	65536
5	1048576
6	16777216
7	268435456
8	4294967296
9	68719476736
10	1099511627776
11	17592186044416
.	.
.	.
.	.

This works for the same reason that Method 2 for decimal-to-binary conversion works. That is, division by 16 produces as a remainder the coefficient (h_0) of 16^0, and as a quotient the decimal number minus the quantity (h_0*16^0).

Hexadecimal to Decimal

Method. Write the hexadecimal number in its place-value summation form and then evaluate.

EXAMPLE 8

$$CA14_{16} = C*16^3 + A*16^2 + 1*16^1 + 4*16^0$$
$$= 12*4096 + 10*256 + 16 + 4$$
$$= 51732_{10}$$

Binary Fractions to Decimal Fractions. Binary fractions are easy to understand if we remember what the place-value summation form of a decimal fraction is. For example,

$$.237_{10} = 2*10^{-1} + 3*10^{-2} + 7*10^{-3}$$

Similarly,

$$.1011_2 = 1*2^{-1} + 0*2^{-2} + 1*2^{-3} + 1*2^{-4}$$

EXAMPLE 9

Convert $.1011_2$ to a decimal fraction.

$$
\begin{aligned}
.1011_2 &= 1*2^{-1} + 0*2^{-2} + 1*2^{-3} + 1*2^{-4} \\
&= 1/2 + 1/8 + 1/16 \\
&= 11/16 \\
&= .6875_{10}
\end{aligned}
$$

Decimal Fractions to Binary Fractions

Method.   Multiply the decimal fraction successively by 2; the integer parts of the result are the coefficients of 2^{-1}, 2^{-2}, 2^{-3}, . . . The decimal portions are again multiplied by two. This continues until there is no fractional part or until the desired accuracy is achieved.

EXAMPLE 10

$.6875*2 = 1.3750$; integer part is 1; coefficient of 2^{-1} is 1
$.3750*2 = 0.7500$; integer part is 0; coefficient of 2^{-2} is 0
$.7500*2 = 1.5000$; integer part is 1; coefficient of 2^{-3} is 1
$.5000*2 = 1.0000$; integer part is 1; coefficient of 2^{-4} is 1

Thus, $.6875_{10} = .1011_2$

3.1.2 Arithmetic

Doing arithmetic in the binary and hexadecimal number systems is, perhaps, best shown by examples and best learned by practice. (It sometimes helps to do a few similar decimal examples slowly first.)

EXAMPLE 11   (DECIMAL ARITHMETIC)

$$
\begin{array}{r}
45 \\
+ \ 57 \\
\hline
102
\end{array}
$$

(Remember: $7 + 5$ is 2 with a 1 "carry" in decimal; $5 + 4 +$ the "carried" 1 is 0 with a 1 "carry.")

EXAMPLE 12   (BINARY ARITHMETIC)

$$
\begin{array}{r}
1011 \\
+ \ 1001 \\
\hline
10100
\end{array}
$$

(Remember: $1 + 1$ is 0 with a 1 "carry" in binary.)

EXAMPLE 13   (BINARY ARITHMETIC)

$$\begin{array}{r} 1110 \\ -101 \\ \hline 1001 \end{array}$$

(Remember: To subtract 1 from 0, borrow a 1 from the place to the left; the borrowed 1 becomes 10_2 ($= 2_{10}$) when moved one place to the right.)

EXAMPLE 14   (HEXADECIMAL ARITHMETIC)

$$\begin{array}{r} 1A \\ +5 \\ \hline 1F \end{array}$$

(In decimal A + 5 is 10 + 5 = 15; $15_{10} = F_{16}$.)

EXAMPLE 15   (HEXADECIMAL ARITHMETIC)

$$\begin{array}{r} FF \\ +3 \\ \hline 102 \end{array}$$

(F + 3 is 15 + 3 in decimal; $18_{10} = 12_{16}$, so we write down a 2, carry a 1.)

EXAMPLE 16   (HEXADECIMAL ARITHMETIC)

$$\begin{array}{r} 13 \\ -A \\ \hline 9 \end{array}$$

(Borrow 1 from the 1 part of 13; it becomes a $10_{16} = 16_{10}$ when moved to the right. In decimal, 16 + 3 = 19, 19 − 10 = 9, and $9_{10} = 9_{16}$.)

We encourage the reader to become familiar with the three number systems and adept at converting from one to another, as well as proficient at doing arithmetic in each number system. The exercises contain problems that the reader should try. Answers are given to many of them.

In the remainder of this chapter, we will look at how the 86-family stores various data types. We will frequently view this storage in the various number systems.

3.2 Representing Booleans

Boolean (also called logical) information can be coded using a single bit. True may be coded as 1 and False as 0. When larger storage elements are used to represent Booleans, the entire element is filled with copies of the True or False indicator (see Figure 3-4). In a byte, True is coded as FF (base 16) and False by all 0's. Similarly, True stored in a word is FFFF.

3.3 Representing Positive and Negative Integers

3.3.1 Positive Integers

We can easily see how positive integers are stored. For example, 345 is stored as 101011001. This will not fit into a byte because it has more than 8 bits, but it fits easily into a word (2 consecutive bytes).

EXAMPLE 17

Show 65712_{10} as a binary (a) byte, (b) word, (c) doubleword, (d) quadword.

$$65712_{10} = 10000000010110000_2$$

Thus,

(a) Does not fit in a byte (it's too large).
(b) Does not fit in a word (it's too large).
(c) 00000000000000010000000010110000
(d) 00000000000000000000000000000000
    00000000000000010000000010110000

3.3.2 Signed Integers

Storing negative integers presents a more difficult problem since the negative sign has to be represented (by a 0 or a 1) or some indication has to be made (in binary!) that the number is negative. There have been many interesting and ingenious ways invented to represent negative numbers in binary. We will discuss three of these here:

Figure 3-4 Representation of true in a byte

1. Sign and magnitude
2. One's complement
3. Two's complement

Sign and Magnitude.   This is the simplest method. Knuth used sign and magnitude in his mythical MIX computer. In sign and magnitude representation of signed numbers, the leftmost (most significant) bit represents the sign—0 for positive, 1 for negative.

EXAMPLE 18

31 stored in a byte using sign and magnitude representation is

$$00011111$$
$$31$$
$$(+)$$

-31 becomes

$$10011111$$
$$31$$
$$(-)$$

There are two drawbacks to sign and magnitude representation of signed numbers:

1. There are two representations of 0: $+0 = 00000000$ and $-0 = 10000000$. Thus the CPU has to make two checks every time it tests for 0. Checks for 0 are done frequently, and it is inefficient to make two such checks.
2. $a + (-b)$ is not the same as $a - b$. What this means is that the logic designer must build separate circuits for subtracting; the adding circuit used for $a + b$ is not sufficient for calculating $a - b$.

EXAMPLE 19

The following shows that $52 - 31$ and $52 + (-31)$ are not the same in sign and magnitude representation:

$$
\begin{array}{rl}
52 = & 00110100 \\
-31 = & -00011111 \\
\hline
21 = & 00010101
\end{array}
\qquad
\begin{array}{rl}
52 = & 00110100 \\
+-31 = & +10011111 \\
\hline
21 \neq & 11010011
\end{array}
$$

One's Complement.   This method of storing signed integers was used in computers more in the past than it is currently. Control Data Corporation's 6000 and

Cyber 70 series of computers used this method. In one's complement, the leftmost bit is still 0 if the integer is positive. For example, 00011111 still represents +31. To represent the negative of this, however, we replace all 0's with 1's and all 1's with 0's. Thus 11100000 represents −31. Note that the leftmost bit is again 1.

EXAMPLE 20

Using a word of storage, −31 is stored as

$$1111111111100000$$

since 31 is stored as

$$0000000000011111$$

The second drawback to sign and magnitude has been eliminated; $a - b$ is the same as $a + (-b)$. Thus the circuit designer need only include an adder; it can also be used for subtraction by replacing all subtractions $a - b$ with $a + (-b)$. The following example shows, however, that this adder must do a little more than just "add."

EXAMPLE 21

$52 - 31$ and $52 + (-31)$ are the same in one's complement representation.

```
  52 =   00110100              52 =   00110100
 -31 = - 00011111         + -31 = + 11100000
  21 =   00010101                  100010100
                                   └──────► +1
                            21 =   00010101
```

The "adder" for one's complement arithmetic is more complicated; it must carry around any overflow bit in order to work correctly for subtraction.

The first drawback is still with us, however. In one's complement, there are still two representations of 0 — 00000000 (positive 0) and 11111111 (negative 0) — when viewed as a byte.

Two's Complement. This method of storing signed integers is used in most present-day computers, including the 86-family. The two's complement is formed by (1) forming the one's complement and then (2) adding 1. Note that this is how one's complement was implemented. See Example 21.

EXAMPLE 22

Using two's complement and a byte:

31 is stored as 00011111
-31 is stored as 11100001, since

$$\begin{array}{ll} 11100000 & \text{(one's complement of } +31) \\ \underline{\quad +1} & \\ 11100001. & \end{array}$$

$-(-31)$ is stored as 00011111, since

$$\begin{array}{ll} 00011110 & \text{(one's complement of } -31) \\ \underline{\quad +1} & \\ 00011111 & \end{array}$$

The reader should check that $a - b = a + (-b)$ and that there is only one way to represent 0, i.e., $+0$ and -0 are stored the same.

3.4 Representing Floating-Point Numbers

Storing floating-point numbers presents a problem similar to that of storing signed integers (Section 3.3). For integers, some indication of a positive or negative sign had to be represented; here some method must be devised for showing where the decimal point should go. That is, we must distinguish between the fractional part to the right of the decimal point—called the mantissa—and the integer portion to the left of the decimal point.

Again, different methods have been used in the past and different methods continue to be used by the various manufacturers of computers. There have been so many different ways of coding a floating-point number into binary that the Institute of Electrical and Electronics Engineers (IEEE) has proposed a standard format. The 86-family prior to the 80486 requires an additional chip to use this format and the instructions that accompany it. This chip is called the Intel 8087-family or math coprocessor chip.

There are actually two formats—one that requires 32 bits and one that is used for 64 bits. We will describe the 32-bit format, called the *short real format,* here.

3.4.1 Short Real Format

The first step to understanding how a binary fraction is stored using short real format is to *normalize* it. This is similar to putting a decimal point number into the familiar scientific notation in which we have a *sign*, an *exponent*, and a *mantissa*. To normalize a binary fraction, we write it so that the first 1 is just to the left of the binary point.

EXAMPLE 23

$$0.000111101 \text{ normalized is } 1.11101 * 2^{-4}$$

The next step is to represent the important parts of the normalized fraction in 32 bits. The important parts are those that will allow us to "recover" the original number (and allow the computer to perform operations on it). These parts are the

1. Sign
2. Exponent (whose base is understood to be 2)
3. Mantissa

In the IEEE short real format, the sign is stored in the leftmost bit, the exponent is stored in the next 8- bits, after some alteration (which we will describe), and the mantissa is stored in the rightmost 23 bits, again after a minor adjustment.

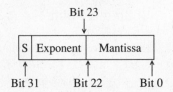

1. To store the sign: 0 for positive, 1 for negative.
2. To store the exponent: Add 127 (1111111_2) to it. The number 127 is called a bias, and the resulting exponent is called a biased exponent. Biased exponents may range from 1 to 254, so that exponents range from -126 to $+128$.
3. To store the mantissa: Remove the leftmost 1 and store the rest of the fraction left-adjusted. This technique of not storing the first 1 before the binary point is a common way to store mantissas. It is called *hidden bit* storage. Computer circuitry "knows" that the 1 is really part of the mantissa.

EXAMPLE 24

Show 0.0390625 (base 10) as it would be stored in short real format.

Step 1: Convert the fraction to binary (see Chapter 2).

$$.0390626_{10} = .0000101_2$$

Step 2: Normalize the binary fraction.

$$.0000101 \text{ normalized is } 1.01*2^{-5}$$

Step 3: Calculate the sign, the exponent, and the mantissa.

Sign: 0, since this is a positive number
Exponent: $-5 + 127 = 122$ (base 10) $= 01111010$ (base 2)
Mantissa: .01 left-adjusted into a field of width 23 is:

$$.01000000000000000000000$$

The entire number is

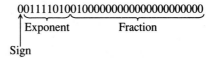

$$00111101001000000000000000000000$$

Sign / Exponent / Fraction

EXAMPLE 25

What number is stored as

$$10111110111101000000000000000000 \text{ ?}$$

We recover the parts:

$$1|01111101|1110100000000000000000000$$

Sign: 1, so the number is negative
Exponent: $01111101_2 = 125_{10}$
$\qquad\qquad 125 - 127 = -2$
Mantissa: affixing 1 to the left of .11101000000000000000000 results in
1.11101000000000000000000, which is 1.11101_2

Multiplying by 2^{-2} gives $.0111101_2$

$$= \frac{1}{4} + \frac{1}{8} + \frac{1}{16} + \frac{1}{32} + \frac{1}{128}$$

$$= -0.4765625_{10}$$

3.5 Binary-Coded Decimals

There is another way of representing numbers in the 86-family. It is a useful format for dealing with decimal point numbers, although the programmer must keep track of where the decimal point is. In a binary-coded decimal, a nibble is used to store each decimal digit. Thus 39 would require 2 nibbles, 1 for the 3 and 1 for the 9.

$$39_{10} = 00111001_2 \text{ (BCD)}$$

A number like this can be created in various ways. One simple way is for the programmer to move 9 into the low-order bytes of a location or register and then to move the 3 into the high-order bytes:

```
MOV   AL,9
MOV   AH,3
```

Since the computer does not know that the binary code represents a BCD number, some care must be taken when operations, especially arithmetic, are performed on something the programmer knows is a BCD number. For example, the BCD number 39 is, in binary, 00111001 and might be interpreted by the 86-family as 57_{10}. There are, however, instructions for converting a BCD number to a more compatible format before performing arithmetic.

It may seem that BCD numbers are more trouble than they are worth since the programmer must do a lot of bookkeeping to store them and operate on them. They are useful, however, in many business applications for keeping track of money "to the penny."

3.6 Representing Characters and Strings

A *character* is a letter, a digit, a "special" character, or even a nonprinting character such as a carriage return (CR). The possible characters include:

Letters:	`A,B,...,Z,a,b,...z`
Digits:	`0,1,...,9`
Special Characters:	`+,-,—,/,$,` etc.
Nonprinting Characters:	`bell (BEL), linefeed (LF), carriage return (CR),` etc.

There are fewer than 128 possible printing and control characters. Since a byte can represent integers from 0 to 257, it should be possible to devise a code whereby all possible characters can be represented in a byte or less.

Many methods have been devised for storing characters. Most present-day computers use a code called ASCII, which stands for American Standard Code for Information Interchange. Figure 3-5 shows the ASCII codes for the various characters. Shown are (1) the character's code number in decimal, (2) its corresponding hexadecimal form (it would take too much space to show the actual binary form), and (3) the character's official name where it is not clear from the

Figure 3-5 ASCII code equivalents

ASCII Value			ASCII Value		
Decimal	Hexadecimal	(Control) Character	Decimal	Hexadecimal	Character
000	00	NUL (null)	048	30	0
001	01	SOH	049	31	1
002	02	STX	050	32	2
003	03	ETX	051	33	3
004	04	EOT	052	34	4
005	05	ENQ	053	35	5
006	06	ACK	054	36	6
007	07	BEL (beep)	055	37	7
008	08	BS	056	38	8
009	09	HT (tab)	057	39	9
010	0A	LF (line feed)	058	3A	:
011	0B	VT (home)	059	3B	;
012	0C	FF (form feed)	060	3C	<
013	0D	CR (carr. ret.)	061	3D	=
014	0E	SO	062	3E	>
015	0F	SI	063	3F	?
016	10	DLE	064	40	@
017	11	DC1	065	41	A
018	12	DC2	066	42	B
019	13	DC3	067	43	C
020	14	DC4	068	44	D
021	15	NAK	069	45	E
022	16	SYN	070	46	F
023	17	ETB	071	47	G
024	18	CAN	072	48	H
025	19	EM	073	49	I
026	1A	SUB	074	4A	J
027	1B	ESC	075	4B	K
028	1C	FS (cursor rt.)	076	4C	L
029	1D	GS (cursor lft.)	077	4D	M
030	1E	RS (cursor up)	078	4E	N
031	1F	US (cursor down)	079	4F	O
032	20	sp	080	50	P
033	21	!	081	51	Q
034	22	"	082	52	R
035	23	#	083	53	S
036	24	$	084	54	T
037	25	%	085	55	U
038	26	&	086	56	V
039	27	'	087	57	W
040	28	(	088	58	X
041	29	)	089	59	Y
042	2A	*	090	5A	Z

(continued)

Figure 3-5 (*Continued*)

| ASCII Value | | | ASCII Value | | |
Decimal	Hexadecimal	Character	Decimal	Hexadecimal	Character
043	2B	+	091	5B	[
044	2C	,	092	5C	\
045	2D	-	093	5D	]
046	2E	.	094	5E	^
047	2F	/	095	5F	_
096	60	\	112	70	p
097	61	a	113	71	q
098	62	b	114	72	r
099	63	c	115	73	s
100	64	d	116	74	t
101	65	e	117	75	u
102	66	f	118	76	v
103	67	g	119	77	w
104	68	h	120	78	x
105	69	i	121	79	y
106	6A	j	122	7A	z
107	6B	k	123	7B	(
108	6C	l	124	7C	|
109	6D	m	125	7D	)
110	6E	n	126	7E	-
111	6F	o	127	7F	DEL
128-255	80-FF	nonstandard			

key or combination of keys needed to type the character. (A combination of keys is needed for some of the control codes. The author's printer associates graphics characters with some of the ASCII codes; for example, π is (227_{10}). We will be concerned here, however, with the codes for the more common characters, such as letters of the alphabet.

EXAMPLE 26

The character Q is stored as

$$51_{16} = 01010001_2$$

The character format for an integer is not the same as its arithmetic form. Thus a character "3" is represented by the ASCII code 33_{16}, whereas the value 3 that we would perform arithmetic upon would be denoted (in hex) by 3. In Section 3.8, we will learn some directives for informing the assembler what *type* the data is. Note that the ASCII code (in hexadecimal) for the digit i is $30 + i$. For example, the ASCII code for the digit 8 is 38. Also, note that the ASCII code for corresponding uppercase and lowercase letters differs by 20 (hexadecimal).

EXAMPLE 27

The character *a* is stored in ASCII as

$$61_{16} = 01100001_2$$

while the character *A* is stored as

$$41_{16} = 01000001_2.$$

A sequence of characters is called a *string*.

EXAMPLE 28

The string *IBM PC* is stored in ASCII as:

| 49 | 42 | 4D | 20 | 50 | 43 |

Note that the space (20) is stored; it is a character.

3.7 Representing Addresses

In Chapter 2, we saw that addresses are stored in a segment register (base of segment) plus another register (offset). The beginning of a segment is called a segment *paragraph* address and begins at a multiple of 16. Certain register combinations are assumed by the 86-family to contain address offsets for particular segments. Thus SP is assumed to contain the offset into the stack segment, IP the offset into the code segment, and BX the offset into the data segment. In Chapter 5, we will see that it is possible to override these built-in assumptions.

3.8 Data Storage Directives

Assembler directives are instructions to the assembler. Although they may generate machine code, the directives themselves are not translated into machine language. In appearance they look very much like assembly language instructions that are translated into machine code.

This section will discuss those directives that reserve, reference, and initialize memory locations of various sizes. Data storage directives exist for all the previously described data types.

3.8.1 Allocating Memory

The following are used to allot and initialize memory locations.

```
DB    DW    DD    DQ    DT
```

where DB means *define byte*, DW means *define word*, DD means *define doubleword*, DQ means *define quadword*, and DT means *define tenbyte*.

EXAMPLE 29

```
A    DD    2
```

instructs the assembler to reserve a doubleword and to generate code that stores the integer 2 into 4 consecutive bytes whose (first) address is *A*.

EXAMPLE 30

```
Input   DW   20, 23, 102, -76, 0
```

allots 16-bit words containing 20, 23, 102, -76, and 0. The address of the first word has the symbolic name *Input*. Machine code is generated which will store 23 at *Input* + *2* (bytes) since a word is 2 bytes.

EXAMPLE 31

```
Answer   DW   ?
```

allocates 2 bytes for the location whose symbolic name is *Answer*, but does not initialize this location to any value.

EXAMPLE 32

```
String1   DB   "hello"
```

allots 5 bytes and stores (the ASCII code for) the characters *h, e, l, l,* and *o*. The strings and characters defined using DB may be enclosed within either single quotes (') , double quotes ("), or any character not included in the string. This is useful when we want to include one of (') or (") in the string.

DD is used to allocate space for either 32-bit integers or short real format floating-point numbers.

EXAMPLE 33

```
Pi   DD   3.14
```

DUP.   It is possible to duplicate the value of the expression by preceding the expression with a repeat factor followed by the DUP operator. This is useful for initializing lists and tables (arrays).

EXAMPLE 34

```
Array   DB   100 DUP(0)
```

initializes to zero 100 bytes starting at the location whose name is *Array*.

3.9 Data Assignment Directives

Data storage directives assign names to memory locations and optionally initialize these locations. The following two directives assign *values* to symbols rather than to memory locations.

```
EQU        =
```

where EQU is read "equate" and = is read "equals." Both assign a value to a symbolic name, but they differ in that = allows the value to be changed. Both assign this value during assembly, not during execution.

EXAMPLE 35

```
A = 2
```

EXAMPLE 36

```
A   EQU   2
```

In the first example above, *A* can be assigned another value. In the second example, it cannot.

EXAMPLE 37

```
A = 2
 . . .
A = A + 1
```

For the data *storage* directives, the labels associated with the directive (if any) denote names of memory locations. During execution, when this symbol is referenced, that memory location is consulted. For the data *assignment* directives, the labels associated with the directive do *not* denote memory locations. During assembly, when this symbol is referenced, the symbol table (a table of symbols and values) is consulted to find the value that has been assigned to the symbol by EQU or =.

The expression used with = and EQU can assume (1) values that are integer arithmetic expressions that have 16-bit values or less, (2) previously defined symbols, or (3) assembler symbols (such as register names or instructions). For other values that = and EQU may assume, see the pseudo ops section of the Microsoft Macro Assembler Reference Manual.

EXAMPLE 38

```
Copy   Equ   Mov
       . . .
       Copy  AX,2
```

replaces the MOV instruction name with the perhaps more accurate name *Copy*. The kind of renaming shown in the previous example is particularly useful when the programmer is familiar with the mnemonics of another assembly language.

3.10 Operators and Expressions

The assembler can perform many calculations as it translates the assembly language to machine code. We discuss these here but emphasize that these calculations, like the assignment statements in Section 3.9, are performed during *assembly,* not during *execution.* MASM assembly language allows traditional arithmetic expressions using various arithmetic operators. It is also possible to perform operations on the underlying bit strings using what we shall call *bit string operators.* In addition, there are two sets of operators called *value-returning operators* and *attribute operators.* For operands, these operators have, in many cases, expressions whose values are addresses.

3.10.1 Arithmetic Expressions

An *arithmetic expression* may be (1) a constant, (2) a variable, or (3) an expression combined with an arithmetic operator.

Constants.   The MASM assembler interprets all constants to be in decimal unless one of the following symbols is attached to the end of the constant.

B	(binary)
H	(hexadecimal)
O or Q	(octal)
D	(decimal)

Use of D for decimal is optional.

EXAMPLE 39

```
HexVal  DB  1AH
```

.RADIX.   The assembler presumes values are in decimal. If we wish to use other number systems, we must attach a code indicating the base. For example, 2AH is 2A in hexadecimal. If we are using another base besides 10 for most of our values, then we can omit the codes following the constant by putting

```
.RADIX  Expression
```

before any such constants, where *Expression* evaluates to an integer from 2 to 16. Thus

```
.RADIX  16
MOV     AH,1A
```

allows us to omit the ''H'' from our hexadecimal number.

In defining hexadecimal constants, the first character must be a digit from 0 to 9. Thus A_{16} must be coded as 0AH (because AH would be interpreted as a user-defined name).

Arithmetic Operators.   An arithmetic operator is one of the following operators:

```
*   /   MOD
  +  −
```

The first set of operators has precedence over the second set. Thus 2 + 3 * 4 evaluates to 14 rather than to 20 (as it would if evaluation were strictly from left to right). +, −, *, and / are the usual operators for addition, subtraction, multiplication, and division. MOD returns a remainder when the first operand is divided by the second.

EXAMPLE 40

```
Loc  EQU  5 MOD 2
```

assigns 1 to the name *Loc*.

3.10.2 Bit String Expressions

In high-level languages, expressions such as *NOT Flag* where *Flag* is a Boolean (called logical in some languages), results in a True if *Flag* is false and a False if *Flag* is true. In assembly language, operators such as NOT produce a more general result. In fact, NOT applied to an operand will change all the 1 bits to 0 and all the 0 bits to 1. We thus distinguish between bit string operators such as NOT and the relational operators described next, which *always* return values of True and False.

Bit String Operators.   The bit string operators are

```
SHL        SHR
      NOT
      AND
   OR    XOR
```

They are shown in order of decreasing precedence.

SHL and SHR interpret the left operand in binary and shift the bits by the number of bits indicated in the second operand.

EXAMPLE 41

```
Myst    =    00000101B SHL 2
```

will assign a 20 to the name *Myst* since 5 = ...0101 and ...0101 shifted left 2 bits is ...10100, which equals 20.

We will see a use for these operands when we use *masks* in Chapter 9.

AND, OR, and NOT are called bit string operators. AND compares the bits of each of its operands and returns a 1 in each bit position for which both operands contain a 1. Otherwise, that position is set to 0. Appendix F contains further information about Boolean operators.

EXAMPLE 42

```
A   DB   00101011B AND 11001100B
```

causes the assembler to assign a value 00001000 to the symbol A.

OR compares each bit position in the two operands and produces a 1 if *either* of them is a 1.

EXAMPLE 43

```
A   DB   00101011B OR 11001100B
```

XOR compares each bit position and returns a 1 if one and only one of the respective bits is a 1. Thus, A will be given the value 11101111.

EXAMPLE 44

```
A   DB   00101011B XOR 11001100B
```

causes the assembler to initialize location A to 11100111.

3.10.3 Boolean Expressions

In Section 3.2, we saw that the assembler recognizes 1 (or multiple copies of it) as True and 0 (or multiple copies of it) as False. Operators for Boolean expressions are called *relational operators*.

Relational Operators. Relational operators return values that are (the computer's representation of) True and False. The relational operators are

    EQ NE LT LE GT GE

and denote *eq*ual, *n*ot *e*qual, *l*ess *t*han, *l*ess than or *e*qual, *g*reater *t*han, and *g*reater than or *e*qual. They operate on two operands and return a value of True (FF_{16} for a byte quantity) or False (00_{16} for a byte).

EXAMPLE 45

```
ByteSize    EQU  8
NibbleSize  EQU  4
Chunk  = ...
       ...
              MOV  AX, Chunk GT ByteSize
              MOV  BX, ((Chunk  EQ  ByteSize) AND 2)
```

moves a True (FFFF) to AX if *Chunk* has a value larger than 8, moves a 2 to BX if *Chunk* equals 8, and moves a False (all 0's) to BX if *Chunk* is some other value.

3.10.4 Other Expressions

In some sense, expressions are defined by the operators that compute them. The following set of operators return values that are either addresses or information about addresses.

Value Returning Operators

    SEG OFFSET SIZE TYPE LENGTH

SEG and OFFSET return values that are addresses. SEG returns the operand's segment address—essentially the value of the segment register for the segment in which the operand is defined. OFFSET returns the operand's offset in whatever segment it occurs.

EXAMPLE 46

```
MOV   AX,SEG A
MOV   BX, OFFSET A
```

moves *A*'s address into a combination of the AX and BX registers.

The preceding example presumes that we do not know what segment defines *A*. This is rarely the case. If we need *A*'s complete address—not just its offset—and we know that *A* is in our data segment entitled *Data*, then the following example is equivalent to the preceding one.

EXAMPLE 47

```
MOV   AX, Data
MOV   BX, OFFSET A
```

TYPE, LENGTH, and SIZE return values that describe the amount of memory allotted to their operands.

TYPE returns a number indicating what type of data the operand is, 1 for byte and 2 for word. It also may be applied to a label and returns -1 if the label is NEAR (in the same segment) and -2 if the label is FAR (in another segment).

EXAMPLE 48

```
Array   DB   5 DUP(0)
         . . .
Chunk  = TYPE Array
```

assigns a value of 1 to symbol *Chunk* since *Array* has been declared as having a byte type.

LENGTH returns the number of units (bytes, words, etc.) allotted to an operand using the DUP operator.

EXAMPLE 49

```
Array   DB        5 DUP (0)
         . . .
ArrayLength   =  LENGTH   Array
```

assigns a value of 5 to *ArrayLength*.

SIZE returns the number of actual byte memory locations allotted to its operand.

EXAMPLE 50

```
ByteArray    DB   5 DUP (0)
WordArray    DW   5 DUP (0)
                 . . .
ByteArrayChunk   = SIZE ByteArray
WordArrayChunk   = SIZE WordArray
```

assigns a value of 5 to *ByteArrayChunk* and a value of 10 to *WordArrayChunk.*

Attribute Operators.   Attribute operators also return values and are generally used to create operands similar to existing ones, but with a different property. The attribute operators are

```
PTR   SegmentOperators
      PTR   THIS
      HIGH  LOW
            SHORT
```

once again shown in order of decreasing precedence. As before, the italics indicate that more is needed to describe segment operators. In this chapter, we will discuss only PTR, THIS, HIGH, and LOW, postponing discussion of SHORT and the segment operators to Chapters 4 and 5, where their use may be seen more easily.

PTR interprets, i.e., overrides, its second operand to be the value (which must be BYTE, WORD, NEAR, or FAR) of its first operand.

EXAMPLE 51

```
WordArray   DW   12, 32, 507, -44, 0
ByteArray   =    BYTE  PTR  WordArray
```

asigns another name, *ByteArray,* which can be used to access the bytes of array *WordArray.* Thus *ByteArray + 1* refers to the high-order byte of the first word in *WordArray.*

THIS can be used to name and assign a type (BYTE or WORD) to the next available memory location. (We will see another use for THIS in Chapter 4.)

EXAMPLE 52

```
ByteArray   EQU   THIS BYTE
WordArray   DW    12, 32, 507, -44, 0
```

accomplishes the same result as the preceding example.

LABEL.   Still another way to refer to a label with either a different size or with a different NEAR or FAR attribute is with LABEL. Thus

```
ByteArray   LABEL   BYTE
WordArray   DW      12, 32, 507, -44, 0
```

creates a new label, *ByteArray,* which allows us to refer to the bytes in *Word-Array.*

HIGH and LOW return the high- and low-order bytes of a word operand.

EXAMPLE 53

```
HexStuff  =   1234H
          . . .
          MOV   AL, LOW HexStuff
```

moves the hexadecimal value 34 into the lower half of AX.

3.11 The Location Counter

In this chapter, we have been primarily concerned with the operations that can be performed during assembly rather than those that occur during execution.

Assembly is the process of translating an assembly language program into machine code. The assembler assumes that the machine code is to be stored in consecutive locations, beginning at offset 0.

For example,

```
List  DB  5,4,3,10,2
```

produces the following machine code:

Location	Machine code		Assembly language
0000 0005	05 04 03 0A 02	List	DB 5,4,3,10,2

During assembly, the assembler maintains a *location counter* (LC), which contains the location *relative to 0* of the current byte of machine code being generated. Thus when the fourth number in *List* is being translated into machine code, the location counter has a value of 3. After the machine code for the numbers in *List* has been generated, the machine code to be listed on the next line will start with a location counter value of 0005.

The dollar sign ($) is a special symbol used to denote the current value of the location counter. The assembly language programmer may use this value in a program.

EXAMPLE 54

```
List    DB      5,4,3,10,2
Here = $-List
```

assigns the location counter value (5) to the name *Here*.

Even.   We can force the location counter to the next higher even number by inserting the EVEN directive. Some operations execute faster if they are on an even boundary.

3.12   Machine Code Representation of Instructions—Part 1

Figure 3-6 is from the assembler *listing* of the program from Chapter 1 that calculates $A + B$ when $A = 2$ and $B = 3$. It shows the location counter value (LC), machine code, and source program.

EXAMPLE 54 (FROM FIGURE 3-6)

LC	Machine code	Assembly language
000A 000D	A1 0000 R	MOV AX,A ; Get A

Since the machine code (A1 0000) occupies 3 bytes—remember, each hexadecimal digit occupies half a byte—the location counter's value is incremented by 3. 000A + 3 = 000D in hexadecimal.

We will reexamine the machine code in this listing in Chapter 5 after describing the instruction set and addressing modes.

3.13   Summary

In this chapter, we have examined the various ways data is represented in the 86-family. The following data types are described:

Booleans
  Positive and negative integers
  Floating-point numbers
  Binary-coded decimals
  Characters and strings
  Addresses

Accompanying many of these types are assembler directives (also called pseudo-ops) for declaring and initializing them to the assembler. Most of them are declared implicitly by reserving an amount of memory of the right size; e.g., characters and strings are declared using the DB directive.

In addition, the assembler can recognize certain types of expressions. Expressions can be defined by the operators associated with them. The following operators are described. They are listed in decreasing order of precedence. Where the description of the operator is postponed, we include a reference in parentheses to the chapter where it is described. As usual, italics indicate that the syntax is still to be described.

```
LENGTH    IZE   WIDTH (Chapter 9)    MASK (Chapter 9)
   SegmentOverride  PTR   OFFSET   SEG   TYPE   THIS
                    HIGH   LOW
                MOD   SHL   SHR
                        +      -
              EQ   NE   LT   LE   GT   GE
                       NOT
                       AND
                  OR         XOR
                    SHORT (Chapter 9)
```

Figure 3-6 Assembler listing from Chapter 1

LC	Machine Code	Assembly Language

```
                ;  This program calculates Result := A + B when
                ;  A = 2, B = 3.
                ;
                ; Two necessary bookkeeping statements follow
                ;
                DOSSEG            ; Use Microsoft SEGment conventions
                .MODEL  Small     ; Use small memory model
                ;
                ; Stack Segment follows
                ;
                .STACK  100H
                ;
                ; Data Segment follows
                ;
                .DATA
0000  0000                        A      DW  ?
0002  0000                        B      DW  ?
0004  0000                        Result DW  ?


                ;
                ; Code Segment follows
                ;
                .CODE
                ;
                ; Two more necessary bookkeeping statements follow
                ;
0000  B8 ---- R        Start:  MOV AX,@Data     ; Define current
0003  8E D8            MOV DS,AX        ; Data Segment
                ;
                ; Main Program
                ;
0005  A1 0000 R        MOV AX,A              ; Get A
0008  03 06 0002 R     ADD AX,B              ; Compute A + B
000C  A3 0004 R        MOV Result,AX         ; Result := A + B
000F  B4 4C            MOV AH,4CH
0011  CD 21            INT 21H               ; Back to DOS
                ;
                        END Start             ; End of program.
                                              ; Start is transfer address
```

The assembler keeps track of the machine code it has generated by adjusting its location counter. The machine code example in this chapter will be reexamined in Chapter 5, after we have learned the instruction set (Chapter 4) and the many methods that the 86-family uses to reference addresses (Chapter 5).

Exercises

1. Why is hexadecimal a convenient number system for representing 86-family machine code?
2. Convert the following binary numbers to hexadecimal:
   a. 0110111100111101
   b. 1011010011110101
   c. 11001010
   d. 11001
3. Convert the following hexadecimal numbers to binary:
   a. 8C4E
   b. F5
   c. 56
   d. 0FFFF
4. Using a byte, show the
   a. sign and magnitude
   b. one's complement
   c. two's complement
   representation of 0.
5. Convert 127_{10} to binary.
6. Show how the 86-family would store -53_{10}.
7. What number is represented in the 86-family by 11111110?
8. Fill in the following hexadecimal multiplication table:

*	1	2	3	4	5	6	7	8	9	A
1										
2										
3										
4										
5										
6										
7										
8										
9										
A										

9. What short-format floating-point number is stored as follows?

10111111000000000000000000000000

10. How is 0.0 stored using the short format?
11. Show the hexadecimal ASCII code for *ascii*.
12. Is *b* less than *B*?
13. Write a data storage directive that will initialize memory location *K* to the byte integer 12.
14. Write a data storage directive to reserve six consecutive words in memory, starting at location *List*.
15. Write a data assignment statement that will allow the six words allocated in Exercise 14 to be accessed bytewise.
16. Given the instruction

```
Input:      DW   5, 10, 15, 20, 25
```

and that the location counter value for *Input* is 2000, what is the location counter value for the number 20?
17. Given the following instructions

```
Input       DB    "abcdefghijklmn"
Endinput = $
```

what is *Endinput*'s value if the location counter value at *Input* is 0?
18. What is the "." called in the binary fraction 1011.0011?
19. What range of numbers can be stored:
    a. in a byte?
    b. in a word using (1) sign-and-magnitude; (2) one's complement; (3) two's complement?

4

86-Family Instruction Set

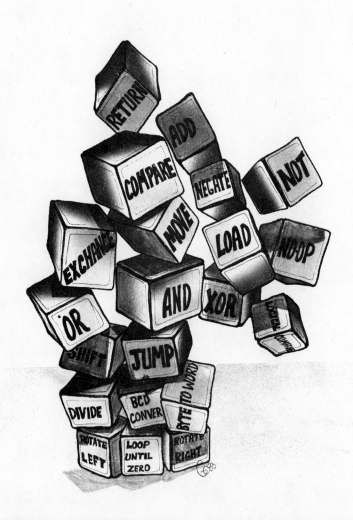

4.0 Introduction

The first assembly languages "permitted" programmers to code in a more convenient number system than binary—usually in octal (base 8). The assembler did little more than translate from this number system to binary. The programmer was still responsible for assigning memory locations to both data and executable instructions.

Modern assemblers allow programmers to write instructions using easy-to-remember mnemonic codes. In addition, modern assemblers allow data to be referenced by symbolic names. No longer does the assembly language programmer have to assign specific memory locations to data and instructions (although most assemblers will allow it).

The MASM assembler allows data and instructions to be written using such mnemonic instructions and operands. In addition, it contains many other constructs that facilitate programming and direct contact with machine parts.

4.0.1 Instructional Types

The 86-family reflects computer science experience acquired over the past few decades. Thus there are instructions for incrementing (adding 1 to) and decrementing (subtracting 1 from) an operand, instructions for manipulating strings (both character and bit strings), instructions for looping, and instructions for performing arithmetic operations and for transferring control. Not all instructions are described in this chapter. I/O instructions are described in Chapter 10. Stack and subroutine call instructions are described in Chapter 8. Bit and character string manipulation instructions are described in Chapter 9. We divide the instructions in this chapter into the following categories:

Data movement
Arithmetic
Control
Miscellaneous

We will concentrate on the 8- and 16-bit data subset of operatives, which work on all members of the 86-family; 32-bit operations require use of the EAX-EDX registers.

4.0.2 Notation

We will use the following notation to describe assembly language statements in this chapter:

Purpose. A brief description of the intent of the statement.
Syntax. An explicit specification of how the statement is to be constructed.
Machine Code. The op(eration) code, usually in table form, listing the machine code in hexadecimal for the various forms of the instruction. Most opcodes depend on both the instruction type and its operands. In this chapter, we omit machine code for 32-bit operations, but it may be found in Appendix B.
Semantics. An English language description of the meaning of the statement.
Pragmatics. Commentary pointing out the (possibly nonobvious) implications of the other parts of the description.
Examples. Sample well-formed statements.

These categories may be omitted or varied for instructions when the resulting description is clear.

To describe the operands of the various instructions (where there are any), we will use the following abbreviations

Reg: A register.

Mem: A memory location.

Reg8: The high or low end of the data registers, i.e., one of AL, AH, BL, BH, CL, CH, DL, DH.

Reg16: A 16-bit general register, i.e., one of AX, BX, CX, DX, SP, BP, SI, or DI. Specific exceptions will be noted.

Reg32: A 32-bit general register, i.e., one of EAX, EBX, ECX, EDX, ESP, EBP, ESI, EDI.

Mem8: A byte memory location.

Mem16: A word memory location.

Mem32: A doubleword memory location.

Imm: An immediate value, i.e., data that represents itself; e.g., an integer or symbol that has been defined using EQU or = . Byte, word, and doubleword-size immediate data are denoted Imm8, Imm16, and Imm32 respectively.

SR: One of the segment registers DS, CS, ES, or SS. Again, specific exceptions will be noted.

4.1 Data Movement Instructions

Data movement instructions move information from one part of the computer to another. In this chapter, we will see movement from register to memory, from memory to register, and from register to register. The 86-family does not allow memory-to-memory movement of data. We will see data movement from other computer parts, e.g., the system stack and the I/O devices, in other chapters. Not all instructions allow all types of movement, so it is important to read each instruction description carefully.

4.1.1 Move

Purpose.   To copy data to and from memory and registers.

Syntax

    MOV   *Destination,Source*

where

Destination may be Mem8, Mem16, Mem32, Reg8, Reg16, Reg32, or SR, *except* CS is not allowed.

Source may be Mem8, Mem16, Mem32, Reg8, Reg16, Reg32, SR, or Imm.

Machine Code

Instruction		Opcode	Instruction		Opcode
MOV	AL,Mem8	A0	MOV	CL,Imm8	B1
MOV	AX,Mem16	A1	MOV	DL,Imm8	B2
MOV	Mem8,AL	A2	MOV	BL,Imm8	B3
MOV	Mem16,AX	A3	MOV	AH,Imm8	B4
MOV	Reg8,Reg8	8A	MOV	CH,Imm8	B5
MOV	Reg16,Reg16	8B	MOV	DH,Imm8	B6
MOV	Reg16,DS	8C	MOV	BX,Imm8	B7
MOV	Mem16,DS	8C	MOV	AX,Imm16	B8
MOV	SR,Reg16	8E	MOV	CX,Imm16	B9
MOV	SR,Mem16	8E	MOV	DX,Imm16	BA
MOV	Mem8,Reg8	88	MOV	BX,Imm16	BB
MOV	Mem16,Reg16	89	MOV	SP,Imm16	BC
MOV	Mem8,Imm8	C6	MOV	BP,Imm16	BD
MOV	Mem16,Imm16	C7	MOV	SI,Imm16	BE
MOV	AL,Imm8	B0	MOV	DI,Imm16	BF

Semantics.   MOV copies the contents of the source operand into the destination operand; it does not destroy the source operand contents.

Pragmatics

In the preceding machine code, Reg8 and Reg16 do not include AL, AX, or the three allowable segment registers since operands that include these have their own opcode.

Source and *Destination* cannot both be memory locations.

When *Source* is Imm, *Destination* cannot be a segment register.

Since more than one operand has the same machine code (e.g., 8C and 8E occur twice), the computer will need more information to perform. This information is in another byte called the addressing mode byte, which we will discuss in the next chapter.

MOV instructions affect the Flags register in unpredictable ways (usually there is no effect).

EXAMPLE 1

```
MOV  SI,DI
```

Here, the contents of register DI are copied to register SI.

4.1.2 Exchange

Purpose. To swap the contents of two registers or a register and a memory location.

Syntax

        XCHG   *Operand1,Operand2*

where

    neither operand is a segment register.

Machine Code

Instruction		Opcode	Instruction		Opcode
XCHG	Reg8,Reg8	86	XCHG	AX,BX	93
XCHG	Reg8,Mem8	86	XCHG	BX,AX	93
XCHG	Mem8,Reg8	86	XCHG	SP,AX	94
XCHG	Reg16,Reg16	87	XCHG	AX,SP	94
XCHG	Reg16,Reg16	87	XCHG	BP,AX	95
XCHG	Mem16,Reg16	87	XCHG	AX,BP	95
XCHG	AX,CX	91	XCHG	SI,AX	96
XCHG	CX,AX	91	XCHG	AX,SI	96
XCHG	DX,AX	92	XCHG	DI,AX	97
XCHG	AX,DX	92	XCHG	AX,DI	97

Semantics. XCHG exchanges *Operand1* with *Operand2*. It does not affect the Flags register.

Pragmatics

    Note that the machine code is different if both operands are registers and one is the AX register.
    Data can be exchanged only between storage elements of the same size.

EXAMPLE 2

```
    A       DW      . . .
            .
            .
            .
            XCHG        A,AX
            XCHG        CX,AX
            XCHG        BL,AL
```

4.1.3 Translate

Purpose. To access an element in a list of elements.

Syntax

```
XLAT        ListName
```

where

the *ListName* is a byte address.

Machine Code

Instruction		Opcode
XLAT	Mem8	D7

Semantics. XLAT consults the AL register, where an index or offset should be stored. It then moves this element of the list name to the AL register. The address of the list name must also have been stored (in the BX register) before XLAT is executed. XLAT does not affect the Flags register.

Pragmatics

The index in AL is destroyed.
Because of the byte limitation, this is limited to a 256-byte list.
An index of *N* will fetch the *N + 1*st element; i.e., if AL contains 3, then the 4th element in the list is fetched.

EXAMPLE 3

```
Array       DB      5,4,3,2,1,0
            .
            .
            .
            MOV     AL,3
            MOV     BX,offset Array
            XLAT    Array
```

moves the fourth element (remember, we count from 0) of *Array,* the 2, into AL. .

4.1.4 Load Effective Address

Purpose. To move an address of a memory location to a register.

Syntax

```
LEA    Reg16,Mem16
```

Machine Code

Instruction		Opcode
LEA	Reg16,Mem16	8D

Semantics. LEA moves an address, not the contents of that address. It accomplishes the same result as MOV OFFSET (see Chapter 3). LEA does not affect the Flags register.

Pragmatics. LEA is more general than MOV OFFSET, allowing the source to be subscripted. Subscripts are discussed in Chapter 5.

EXAMPLE 4

```
Array      DB     5,4,3,2,1,0
             .
             .
             .
           MOV  AL,3
           LEA  BX,Array
           XLAT Array
```

performs the same action as the previous example.

4.1.5 Load Data Segment Register

Purpose. To move a segment and offset address to DS and another register.

Syntax

```
LDS    Reg16, Mem32
```

where

Reg16 is any nonsegment register.
Mem32 is a doubleword memory location.

Machine Code

Instruction		Opcode
LDS	Reg16,Mem32	C5

Semantics. LDS moves the higher order word (most significant 16 bits) of the *Mem32* doubleword to DS, and the lower order word (least significant 16 bits) of the *Mem32* doubleword to the specified register. LDS does not affect the Flags register.

Pragmatics. The programmer must have put an address into the doubleword memory operand prior to executing this instruction.

4.1.6 Load Extra Segment Register

Purpose. Same as for LDS, except the register involved is the extra segment register.

Syntax

```
LES     Reg16,Mem32
```

where

Reg16 is not a segment register.

Machine Code

Instruction		Opcode
LES	Reg16,Mem32	C4

Semantics. Same as for the LDS, with ES substituted for DS.

We will see other data movement instructions in later chapters (Flags instructions in Chapter 9).

4.2 Arithmetic Instructions

This section describes instructions for incrementing, decrementing, negating, and performing addition, subtraction, multiplication, and division. Also included here are instructions that aid in converting data to the format necessary to perform these operations.

Arithmetic instructions set the status bits in the Flags register in the ways described in Section 2.2.5.

4.2.1 Increment

Purpose.   To increase an operand by 1.

Syntax

    INC   *Operand*

where

Operand may be Mem8, Mem16, Mem32, Reg8, Reg16, or Reg32.

Machine Code

Instruction		Opcode
INC	AX	40
INC	CX	41
INC	DX	42
INC	BX	43
INC	SP	44
INC	BP	45

Instruction		Opcode
INC	SI	46
INC	DI	47
INC	Reg8	FE
INC	Mem8	FE
INC	Mem16	FF

Semantics.   See Purpose.

EXAMPLE 5

```
A        DB      1
AA       DW      2
         .
         .
         .
         INC     A
         INC     AA
         INC     AX
         INC     AL
```

4.2.2 Decrement

Purpose.   To decrease a register or memory location by 1.

Syntax

```
DEC        Operand
```

where

    Operand may be Mem8, Mem16, Mem32, Reg8, Reg16, or Reg32.

Machine Code

Instruction		Opcode
DEC	AX	48
DEC	CX	49
DEC	DX	4A
DEC	BX	4B
DEC	SP	4C
DEC	BP	4D

Instruction		Opcode
DEC	SI	4E
DEC	DI	4F
DEC	Reg8	FE
DEC	Mem8	FE
DEC	Mem16	FF

Semantics.   See Purpose.

EXAMPLE 6

```
A       DW      2
        .
        .
        .
        DEC     AX
        DEC     A
        DEC     BL
```

4.2.3 Negate

Purpose.   To change the sign of a byte or word register or memory location.

Syntax

```
NEG     Operand
```

where

    Operand may be Reg8, Reg16, Reg32, Mem8, Mem16, or Mem32.

Machine Code

Instruction		Opcode
NEG	Reg8	F6
NEG	Mem8	F6
NEG	Reg16	F7
NEG	Mem16	F7

Semantics. NEG negates its operand by changing it to its two's complement.

Pragmatics

To form the two's complement, the 86-family subtracts the operand's value from 1 and then adds 1.

The addressing mode byte contains further information about the operand.

EXAMPLE 7

```
NEG     AL
NEG     AX
```

4.2.4 Add

Purpose. To add the contents of two operands.

Syntax

```
ADD     Destination, Source
```

where

either *Destination* or *Source* is an 8-bit, 16-bit, or 32-bit register (or both are). Both cannot be memory operands.

Source may also be Imm8, Imm16, or Imm32.

Machine Code

Instruction		Opcode
ADD	Reg8,Mem8	02
ADD	Reg16,Mem16	03
ADD	Mem8,Reg8	00
ADD	Reg8,Reg8	02

Instruction		Opcode
ADD	Mem16,Reg16	01
ADD	Reg16,Mem16	03
ADD	AL,Imm8	04
ADD	AX,Imm16	05
ADD	Reg8,Imm8	80
ADD	Reg16,Imm16	81
ADD	Reg16,Imm8	83
ADD	Mem16,Imm8	83

Semantics. The operands are added and the result is stored in the first (*Destination*) operand.

Pragmatics. Addition can result in incorrect sums if the sign bit is set. For example, if 01010101 (decimal 85) is added to itself, the result is 10101010, which is −86 (for byte-sized storage locations). In section 4.2.5 we will see a way to adjust this.

EXAMPLE 8

```
A       DW      2
        .
        .
        .
ADD     AX,BX
ADD     A,AX
ADD     AL,3
ADD     AX,456
ADD     A,48
```

4.2.5 Add with Carry

Purpose. Same as ADD, but used when the sum may involve a carry out of the most significant bit.

Syntax

```
ADC     Destination, Source
```

where

Destination and *Source* can assume the same values as for ADD.

Machine Code

Instruction		Opcode		Instruction		Opcode
ADC	Mem8,Reg8	10	ADC	Reg8,Imm8	80
ADC	Mem16, Reg16	11	ADC	Mem8,Imm8	80
ADC	Reg8,Mem8	12	ADC	Reg16,Imm16	81
ADC	Reg16,Mem16	13	ADC	Mem16,Imm16	81
ADC	AL,Imm8	14	ADC	Reg16,Imm8	83
ADC	AX,Imm16	15	ADC	Mem16,Imm8	83
ADC	Reg8,Reg8	12	ADC	Reg16,Reg16	13

Semantics.   ADC adds the two operands, adds one to the sum if CF is set (i.e., if there is a carry), and returns the result to the first (destination) operand.

Pragmatics

If there is no carry, ADC and ADD execute identically.

ADC is used (usually in conjunction with ADD) to add two numbers that are larger than 16 bits: ADD adds the lower 16 bits, producing 17 bits; if the 17th bit is 1, then the CF flag is set, and ADC adds it in when adding the next higher 16 bits.

EXAMPLE 9

```
A         DW      . . .
RestA     DW      . . .
          .
          .
          .
          ADD     AX,A        ; add lower 16 bits
          ADC     BX,RestA    ; add higher 16 bits
                              ; including carry from
                              ; lower, if any
```

adds a 32-bit number from *A* and *RestA* to AX and BX, respectively. The result is in the combination BX and AX.

4.2.6 Subtract

Purpose.   To subtract two operands and store the difference in the first.

Syntax

```
SUB      Destination, Source
```

where

Destination and Source are byte or word register or memory operands. Both cannot be memory operands.

Machine Code

Instruction		Opcode
SUB	Mem8,Reg8	28
SUB	Mem16,Reg16	29
SUB	Reg8,Mem8	2A
SUB	Reg8,Reg8	2A
SUB	Reg16,Mem16	2B
SUB	Reg16,Reg16	2B
SUB	AL,Imm8	2C
SUB	AX,Imm16	2D
SUB	Reg8,Imm8	80
SUB	Reg16,Imm16	81
SUB	Reg16,Imm8	83
SUB	Mem16,Imm8	83

Semantics. The source operand is subtracted from the destination operand and the result is stored in the destination.

Pragmatics. As with addition, subtraction can result in incorrect results when the sign bit changes inappropriately.

EXAMPLE 10

```
A       DW      2
        .
        .
        .
        SUB     AL,BL
        SUB     BX,A
```

4.2.7 Subtract with Borrow

Purpose. To perform subtraction when the difference may involve a borrow into the most significant bit.

Syntax

```
SBB     Destination, Source
```

where

the operands are the same as for SUB.

Machine Code

	Instruction	Opcode
SBB	Mem8,Reg8	18
SBB	Mem16,Reg16	19
SBB	Reg8,Mem8	1A
SBB	Reg8,Reg8	1A
SBB	Reg16,Mem16	1B
SBB	Reg16,Reg16	1B
SBB	AL,Imm8	1C
SBB	AX,Imm16	1D
SBB	Reg8,Imm8	80
SBB	Reg16,Imm16	81
SBB	Mem16,Imm8	83
SBB	Reg16,Imm8	83

Semantics. If the carry flag, CF, is set, SBB subtracts 1 from the difference.

EXAMPLE 11

```
A          DW      . . .
RestA      DW      . . .
           .
           .
           .
           SUB     AX,A
           SBB     BX,RestA
```

performs a 32-bit subtraction.

4.2.8 Multiply Unsigned Integers

Purpose. To multiply an unsigned byte, word, or doubleword integer by another unsigned byte, word, or doubleword integer.

Syntax

```
MUL     Operand
```

where

Operand is a byte or word memory location or register.

Machine Code

Instruction		Opcode
MUL	Mem8	F6
MUL	Reg8	F6
MUL	Mem16	F7
MUL	Reg16	F7

Semantics.   MUL multiplies the byte, word, or doubleword operand by the contents of AL, AX, or EAX, respectively. For word multiplications, the result is returned in the pair DX and AX; for byte multiplications, the product is returned in AH and AL; for doubleword multiplication, the product goes into the EDX and EAX registers.

Pragmatics.   It is not possible to multiply by an immediate value. To perform such a multiplication, first move the immediate value to a register or memory location.

EXAMPLE 12

```
A       DW       . . .
B       DW       . . .
        .
        .
        .
        MOV     AX,A
        MUL     B
```

multiplies *A* by *B*, storing the high-order word of the product in DX and the low-order word in AX.

4.2.9 Multiply Signed Integers

Purpose.   Same as MUL, but used for signed integers.

Syntax

(1)   IMUL   *Operand*

where

   Operand is the same as for MUL.

Or, for 80386 and above,

(2)   `IMUL`   *Destination, Source*

where

> *destination* is Reg16 or Reg32 and *source* is Reg16, Reg32, Mem16, Mem32, or Imm8.

There is also a three-operand version for the 80386 and above (see Appendix B).

Machine Code

Instruction		Opcode
IMUL	Reg8	F6
IMUL	Mem8	F6
IMUL	Reg16	F7
IMUL	Mem16	F7

4.2.10 Divide Unsigned Integers

Purpose.   To divide an unsigned byte, word, or doubleword by a byte or word.

Syntax

    `DIV`   *Divisor*

where

> *Divisor* is a Mem8, Mem16, Reg8, or Reg16.

Machine Code

Instruction		Opcode
DIV	Reg8	F6
DIV	Mem8	F6
DIV	Reg16	F7
DIV	Mem16	F7

Semantics.   DIV expects the dividend (the number to be divided) to be in AX (for a word) or in DX and AX (for a doubleword). The quotient is returned to AX (or just AL for a word dividend), and the remainder is returned to DX (or AH for a word dividend).

Pragmatics

Like MUL, DIV cannot divide by an immediate value. To perform such division, the programmer must put the immediate value in a register or memory location.

If the divisor is 0, the 86-family aborts the program and issues a ''divide overflow'' message.

EXAMPLE 13

```
A       DW      2
B       DD      . . .
        .
        .
        .
        MOV             AX,Word Ptr B
        MOV             DX,Word Ptr B+2
        DIV             A
```

divides *B* by 2. The quotient will be in AX, the remainder in DX.

4.2.11 Divide Signed Integers

Purpose.   Same as DIV, but for signed integers.

Syntax

```
    IDIV        Divisor
```
where

Division is Reg8, Reg16, Reg32, Mem8, Mem16, or Mem32.

Machine Code

Instruction		Opcode
IDIV	Mem8	F6
IDIV	Reg8	F6
IDIV	Mem16	F7
IDIV	Reg16	F7

4.2.12 Writing a Small Program

We will use MOV and some of the arithmetic instructions to write a small program.

Problem.   Write an assembly language program to find the average of two word integers, *X* and *Y.* (Use *X* = 2 and *Y* = 3 for data.)

Discussion.   Since there are two integers, we must calculate

$$\text{Average} := (X + Y)/2$$

When we run the program, the integer part of the quotient will be in AX and the remainder in DX. The program is shown in Figure 4-1.

Figure 4-1 Finding the average of *X* and *Y*

```
; This program computes the average of two word integers.
;
; Two necessary bookkeeping statements follow
;
        DOSSEG              ; use Microsoft SEGment conventions
        .MODEL  SMALL       ; use small memory conventions
;
        .STACK  100H
;
; Data segment follows
;
        .DATA
;
X       DW   2
Y       DW   3
;
; Code segment follows
;
        .CODE
;
; Necessary bookkeeping statements follow
;
Start:  MOV AX,@DATA
        MOV DS,AX
;
; Main program
;
        MOV AX,X            ; get x
        ADD AX,Y            ; SUM := x + y
        MOV BL,2            ; for div by 2
        DIV BL              ; AVG := SUM  / 2
;
        MOV AX,4C00H
        INT 21H             ; back to DOS
        END Start
```

4.2.13 Implementing a MOD Function

Many high-level languages, including Pascal, C, Ada, BASIC, and FORTRAN, include a "mod" function, which is used to calculate remainders on integer division. Thus *A MOD B* computes the remainder when the integer A is divided by the integer B. There is an assembler directive to compute MOD but no executable 86-family instruction. We can simulate one, however, using DIV and examining the remainder. The following program illustrates this idea.

Problem. Write an assembly language program to test whether or not a positive integer, *N,* is even.

Discussion. We know that even integers have no remainder when divided by 2. Thus we wish to code the following algorithm.

```
IF N MOD 2 = 0
    THEN DX := 0
    ELSE DX := 1
```

There is not much to code since, for word division by 2, DX will automatically be 0 or 1! The program is shown in Figure 4-2.

4.3 Conversion Instructions

The previous instructions performed binary arithmetic on byte, word, and doubleword binary numbers. ADD, SUBtract, and MULtiply expect to operate on numbers of the same size, e.g., both bytes, both words, or both doublewords. If one of the operands is not the same size as the other, or not the correct size for the instruction, it can be converted by using CBW (Convert Byte to Word), CWD (Convert Word to Doubleword), CDQ (Convert Double to Quad) on 80386 and above, or CWDE (Convert Word to Extended Double) on 80386 and above.

In addition, when performing arithmetic on binary-coded decimal (BCD) integers, the result may not be a BCD integer. There are instructions for converting binary-coded decimal integers back to correct BCD when the arithmetic is performed.

4.3.1 Convert Byte to Word

Purpose. To convert a byte to a word.

Figure 4-2 Testing if N is even

```
; This program tests whether an integer N is even.
;
        DOSSEG              ; use Microsoft SEGment conventions
        .MODEL   SMALL
;
        .STACK   100H
;
; Data segment follows
;
        .DATA
;
N       DW   9
;
; Code segment follows
;
        .CODE
;
; Necessary bookkeeping statements follow
;
Start:  MOV AX,@DATA
        MOV DS,AX
;
; Main program
;
        MOV DX,0            ; Extend N to 32 bits
        MOV AX,N            ; get N
        MOV CX,2            ; get divisor (2)
        XOR DX,DX           ; clear DX
        DIV CX              ; DX := N mod 2
;
        MOV AX,4C00H
        INT 21H             ; back to DOS
        END Start
```

Syntax

    CBW

Machine Code

Instruction	Opcode
CBW	98

Semantics.   CBW extends the byte in AL to a word in AX by replacing AH with all 0's if the byte is positive, and all 1's if the byte is negative.

Pragmatics.   It may not appear at first that this "works," especially when the byte is negative. The following example illustrates that CBW does make it possible to do word arithmetic by converting a byte this way.

EXAMPLE 14

```
A     DB      -30
B     DW      256
      .
      .
      .
      MOV     AL,A      (puts 11100010 into AL)
      CBW               (converts AX to 1111111111100010)
      ADD     AX,B      (adds        0000000100000000)
                        (result is   0000000011100010)
```

4.3.2 Convert Word to Doubleword

Purpose.   To convert a word to a doubleword.

Syntax

```
CWD
```

Machine Code

Instruction	Opcode
CWD	99

Semantics.   CWD "sign-extends" the word in the AX register to DX and AX in the same way CBW converts a byte to a word.

EXAMPLE 15

```
A     DW      . . .
      .
      .
      .
      MOV     AX,A
      CWD
      IDIV    BX
```

divides *A* by the word in BX.

4.4 Control and Iteration Instructions

The instructions in the preceding sections were shown as if they are always executed one after another. Although this is often the case, it is also sometimes necessary to execute instructions out of sequential order. For example, if we want to repeat a sequence of instructions 10 times, we will need to transfer back to these instructions repeatedly.

The 86-family has instructions for transferring unconditionally (JMP), instructions for comparing two operands (CMP and TEST), and various instructions for transferring based on the result of this comparison (e.g., JE—jump if the two operands are equal).

When a transfer is to be made, it is often to a user-defined label. If the label is within the same code segment, it should be followed by a colon (:).

4.4.1 Jump

Purpose. To transfer unconditionally to an instruction either within or outside of the current code segment.

Syntax

```
JMP     Operand
```

where

Operand is a user-defined label or a register or memory address (16 or 32 bits).

Machine Code

	Instruction	Opcode
JMP	label within same segment	E9
JMP	label within − 128 or + 127 bytes	EB
JMP	label outside segment	EA
JMP	Reg16	FF
JMP	Mem16	FF

Semantics. If the operand is a label, JMP transfers control to the instruction with that label; if the operand is a register or memory reference, JMP presumes that the contents of the register or memory reference contain the address to which to transfer.

Pragmatics

Note that if the operand is a register or memory reference, the programmer must have stored an address there prior to the JMP instruction's execution. JMP is roughly equivalent to the GOTO instruction found in most high-level languages.

EXAMPLE 16

```
        JMP     There
     .
     .
     .
There:
```

EXAMPLE 17

```
LEA     There,AX
JMP     AX
```

4.4.2 Compare

Purpose. To compare one operand with another.

Syntax

```
CMP     Operand1,Operand2
```

where

Operand1 is a byte or word register or memory location.
Operand2 is a byte or word register, memory location, or immediate data

One of the operands must be a register.

Machine Code

Instruction		Opcode
CMP	Reg8,Reg8	3A
CMP	Mem8,Reg8	38
CMP	Mem16,Reg16	39
CMP	Reg8,Mem8	3A
CMP	Reg16,Mem16	3B
CMP	AL,Imm8	3C

	Instruction	Opcode
CMP	AX,Imm16	3D
CMP	Reg8,Imm8	80
CMP	Mem8,Imm8	80
CMP	Reg16,Imm16	81
CMP	Mem16,Imm16	81
CMP	Reg16,Imm8	83
CMP	Mem16,Imm8	83

Semantics.   Without changing the values of either operand, CMP calculates the difference between the right operand and the left operand and sets the flags appropriately. Thus, ZF is set if the two operands are equal; CF is set if the left unsigned operand is greater than the right unsigned operand; SF is set if the difference is negative, i.e., if the left operand is less than the right for signed numbers.

Pragmatics

In reality, the programmer cares little about the flag settings; the conditional jump instructions below consult them for decision making.

We will defer an example until the conditional jump instructions are introduced (Example 18).

4.4.3 Logical Compare

Purpose.   To compare two operands as bit strings rather than as numbers.

Syntax

TEST   *Operand1,Operand2*

where

Operand1 and *Operand2* are as in CMP.

Machine Code

	Instruction	Opcode
TEST	Reg8,Mem8	84
TEST	Reg16,Mem16	85
TEST	AL,Imm8	A8
TEST	AX,Imm16	A9
TEST	Reg8,Imm8	F6

Instruction		Opcode
TEST	Mem8,Imm8	F6
TEST	Reg16,Imm16	F7
TEST	Mem16,Imm16,	F7

Semantics.   TEST does a logical AND of the two operands (without changing their value) and sets the flags appropriately.

Pragmatics.   Similar to CMP, TEST generally immediately precedes one of the following conditional jump instructions.

4.4.4 Conditional Jump

The conditional jump instructions cause a transfer of control based on the values in the Flags register. From the programmer's point of view, the transfer usually takes place as a result of comparing (via CMP or TEST) two operands. Thus, there is a jump if two operands are equal (JE), if the left operand is greater than the right (JG), and so on. In all cases, the programmer should think of the comparison as the left operand being compared with the right.

There is more than one mnemonic for each opcode, reflecting the fact that there is more than one way to state a relation. For example, "greater than" is logically the same as "not less than or equal to." Thus JG can also be written JNLE. It increases the readability of the program to use the instruction mnemonic that best reflects the meaning of the operation.

The syntax for any of the conditional jumps is

```
ConditionalJump        ShortLabel
```

where *ConditionalJump* is one of the following instructions, and *ShortLabel* is a label within -128 and $+127$ bytes.

The following table shows the opcode, mnemonic, and meaning for the various conditional jump instructions:

Opcode	Mnemonic	Meaning
6B	JNP	Jump if Not Parity
6B	JPO	Jump if Parity Odd
70	JO	Jump on Overflow
71	JNO	Jump on No Overflow
72	JB	Jump if Below (unsigned)
72	JNAE	Jump if Not Above or Equal (unsigned)
72	JC	Jump if Carry
72	JP	Jump if Parity
72	JPE	Jump if Parity Even
73	JAE	Jump if Above or Equal (unsigned)

Opcode	Mnemonic	Meaning
73	JNB	Jump if Not Below
73	JNC	Jump if No Carry
74	JE	Jump if Equal
74	JZ	Jump if Zero
75	JNE	Jump if Not Equal
75	JNZ	Jump if Not Zero
76	JBE	Jump if Below or Equal (unsigned)
76	JNA	Jump if Not Above (unsigned)
77	JA	Jump if Above (unsigned)
77	JNBE	Jump if Not Below or Equal (unsigned)
78	JS	Jump if Sign
79	JNS	Jump if Not Sign
7C	JL	Jump if Less Than
7C	JNGE	Jump if Not Greater Than or Equal
7D	JNL	Jump if Not Less Than
7D	JGE	Jump if Greater Than or Equal
7E	JLE	Jump if Less Than or Equal
7E	JNG	Jump if Not Greater
7F	JNLE	Jump if Not Less Than or Equal
7F	JG	Jump if Greater Than
E3	JCXZ	Jump if CX is Zero

Note that there are conditional jumps based directly on testing an individual flag as well as a combination of flags. There is even a jump based on the contents of the CX register. We will see another instruction in section 4.4.6 that not only jumps based on the contents of CX, but also alters the CX contents at the same time.

Some of the conditional jumps are appropriate only for signed integers, while others are appropriate only for unsigned. Thus, JA is used for a jump when the first value is larger than the second, but they are unsigned; JG is used in the same situation when the values are signed.

Since the conditional jumps transfer based on the contents of the Flags register, CMP or TEST instructions are not always strictly needed. The following examples execute in the same way. If speed of execution is not critical, the first is somewhat more readable than the second and is perhaps "better" code. (There are assembly language programmers, however, who might disagree.)

EXAMPLE 18

```
SUB   AX,BX
CMP   AX,0    ; If AX = 0
JE    There   ;   Then Goto There
.
.
.
There:
```

EXAMPLE 19

```
SUB     AX,BX
JZ      There    ; If AX = 0 Then Goto There
.
.
.
There:
```

4.4.5 A Program

We will use some of the instructions from the last section as well as previous sections to calculate the absolute value of a word integer, X.

Problem. Write an assembly language program to convert a word integer, X, to its absolute value.

Discussion. The problem requires us to calculate

$$X: = |X|$$

The program is shown in Figure 4-3.

4.4.6 Iteration

We can use the CMP instruction and a conditional jump instruction to repeat a sequence of instructions. Figure 4-4 shows this type of iteration for a program that calculates 5 factorial (5∗4∗3∗2∗1).

Most high-level languages have instructions that facilitate repeating a group of instructions. These constructs, called loops, come in various flavors: DO loops (FORTRAN and C), FOR loops (BASIC, Pascal), WHILE loops (Pascal, some FORTRANs, C, and Ada), and REPEAT loops (Pascal). The 86-family has a loop construct similar to a FOR loop or a DO loop that counts down rather than up.

The vanilla-flavored loop structure (called, imaginatively, LOOP) repeats a sequence of instructions while the CX register is nonzero, decrementing CX on each iteration.

Two other loop instructions, LOOPN (also called LOOPE) and LOOPNZ (also called LOOPNE), are similar to LOOP except, in addition to checking CX, they check the flag bit ZF before they iterate; this gives the programmer a "way out" of the loop even if CX is not 0. In all cases, it is the programmer's responsibility to initialize CX and to be aware of when ZF might be set or cleared.

Loop Until Count Complete.

Purpose.   To repeat a sequence of instructions.

Figure 4-3 Calculating the absolute value of *X*.

```
;  This program calculates the absolute value of a word integer.
;
; Two necessary bookkeeping statements follow
;
    DOSSEG              ; Use Microsoft SEGment conventions
    .MODEL  SMALL       ; Use small memory model
;
; Stack Segment follows
;
    .STACK  100H
;
; Data Segment follows
;
    .DATA
;
X    DW   -4
;
; Code Segment follows
;
    .CODE
;
; Two more necessary bookkeeping statements follow
;
Start:  MOV AX,@DATA      ; Define current
        MOV DS,AX         ; Data Segment
;
; Main Program
;
        CMP X,0           ; if X >= 0
        JGE Pos           ;    then go to POS
        NEG X             ;    else X := -X
;
Pos:    MOV AH,4CH
        INT 21H           ; Back to DOS
;
        END Start         ; End of program.  Start is transfer address
```

Syntax

```
    LOOP      ShortLabel
```

where

the *ShortLabel* is within −128 to +127 bytes.

Machine Code

Instruction		Opcode
LOOP	*ShortLabel*	E2

Figure 4-4 Calculating 5 factorial

```
;   Looping
;
; Two necessary bookkeeping statements follow
;
    DOSSEG              ; Use Microsoft SEGment conventions
    .MODEL  SMALL       ; Use small memory model
;
; Stack Segment follows
;
    .STACK  100H
;
; Data Segment follows
;
    .DATA
;
Fact    DW  ?
;
; Code Segment follows
;
    .CODE
;
; Two more necessary bookkeeping statements follow
;
Start:  MOV AX,@Data        ; Define current
        MOV DS,AX           ; Data Segment
;
; Main Program
;
COMMENT /
        Fact := 1
        LOOP FOR I := 1 to 5
                Fact := Fact * i
        END LOOP
        /
        MOV Fact,1          ; FACT := 1
        MOV AX,Fact         ; prepare for mult
        MOV CX,1            ; I := 1
Loop:   MUL CX              ; FACT := FACT * I
        INC CX              ; I := I + 1
        CMP CX,5            ; if I <= 5
        JLE Loop            ;    go to LOOP
        MOV Fact,AX         ; store in FACT
;
        MOV AH,4CH
        INT 21H             ; Back to DOS
;
        END Start           ; End of program.  Start is transfer address
```

Semantics. LOOP decrements the CX register, and if it is not zero, the instruction pointer, IP, is changed to *ShortLabel* so that the next instruction executed is at *ShortLabel*.

Pragmatics. The programmer must initialize CX.

EXAMPLE 20

```
              MOV      CX,10
StartLoop     . . .
              LOOP     StartLoop
```

executes the instructions represented by the dots 10 times. Note that CX is initialized before the loop is entered.

Loop if Zero—Loop if Equal.

Purpose. To repeat a sequence of instructions for a count and while some condition is true.

Syntax

```
    LOOPE    ShortLabel
```

or

```
    LOOPZ    ShortLabel
```

where

ShortLabel   is as in LOOP.

Machine Code

Instruction		Opcode
LOOPE	*ShortLabel*	E1
LOOPZ	*ShortLabel*	E1

Semantics. LOOPZ (LOOPE) loops while $CX \neq 0$ and $ZF = 1$.

Pragmatics

As in LOOP, the programmer must initialize CX.
The programmer must be aware of what conditions will clear ZF (because the loop will stop iterating then).

EXAMPLE 21

```
            MOV     CX,10
StartLoop:  . . .
            CMP     AX,0
            LOOPE   StartLoop
```

iterates up to 10 times while AX = 0.

Loop if Not Zero—Loop if Not Equal.

Purpose. To iterate for a count and while a condition is not true.

Syntax

```
    LOOPNZ    ShortLabel
```

or

```
    LOOPNE    ShortLabel
```

Machine Code

Instruction		Opcode
LOOPNZ	*ShortLabel*	E0
LOOPNE	*ShortLabel*	E0

Semantics. LOOPNZ (LOOPNE) continues to loop while CX is zero and while ZF is cleared.

Pragmatics. As in the previous loop instructions, the programmer must initialize CX and be aware of when ZF is cleared.

EXAMPLE 22

```
            MOV     CX,10
StartLoop:  . . .
            CMP     AX,0
            LOOPNE  StartLoop
```

iterates up to 10 times while AX is nonzero.

Figure 4-5 shows the factorial program of Figure 4-4, but using the LOOP instruction. The label "LOOP" is also replaced with "Loopl" for clarity. (It is perfectly legal to have an instruction label called "LOOP".)

Figure 4-5 Factorial of Figure 4-4, now using LOOP

```
;   This program computes 5 factorial using LOOP.
;
; Two necessary bookkeeping statements follow
;
    DOSSEG              ; Use Microsoft SEGment conventions
    .MODEL  SMALL       ; Use small memory model
;
; Stack Segment follows
;
    .STACK  100H
;
; Data Segment follows
;
    .DATA
Fact    DW  ?
;
; Code Segment follows
;
    .CODE
;
; Two more necessary bookkeeping statements follow
;
Start:  MOV AX,@DATA        ; Define current
        MOV DS,AX           ; Data Segment
;
; Main Program
;
COMMENT /
        Fact := 1
        Loop FOR I := 5 DOWN TO 1
            Fact := Fact * I
        END Loop
        /
        MOV     Fact,1      ; FACT := 1
        MOV     AX,Fact     ; prepare for mult
        MOV     CX,5        ; I := 5
Loop1:  MUL     CX          ; FACT := FACT * I
        LOOP    Loop1
        MOV     Fact,AX     ; store in FACT
;
        MOV AH,4CH
        INT 21H             ; Back to DOS
;
        END Start           ; End of program.  Start is transfer address
```

4.5 Summary

This chapter has introduced many of the 86-family instructions, most with examples of their use as well as complete programs for the various groups. We have seen instructions for moving data, performing arithmetic operations, converting from one data type to another, comparing and branching, and looping.

In Chapter 6, we will look at standard constructs (e.g., IF statements and WHILE loops) and problems (e.g., searching and sorting). The exercises in this chapter are intended to familiarize the reader with the instruction set. More practical examples are postponed to Chapter 6.

Not all instructions are described in this chapter. Chapters 8 through 12 contain more 86-family instructions while Chapters 7 through 11 contain more assembler directives for controlling 86-family programs.

Exercises

1. What do the following instructions do?

```
a. MOV    CH,2      (Show CX)
b. ADD    CH,2      (Show CX)
c. MUL    CH,2      (Show CX)
d. DIV    CH,2      (Show CX)
e. MOV    AH,"h"
   MOV    AL,"i"    (Show AX)
f. NEG    AX        (Where AX contains 4100H)
g. Elem       DB    5
              .
              .

              .
              CMP   Elem,0
              JL    Here
   There:     MOV   ax,2
              JMP   Around
              .

              .
   Here:      MOV ax,1    (Show AX)
   Around:    . . .
```

2. Write an instruction or instructions to
   a. Put a 6 into the lower part of the AX register.
   b. Transfer the word at memory location called *Datum* to BX.
   c. Exchange the contents of register BX with register AX.
   d. Exchange the contents of byte location *DataByte* with byte location NutherByte.
   e. Access the fifth element of a byte array *Table*.
   f. Access the first byte of the fifth element of the word array *WTable*.
   g. Divide the doubleword *Dividend* by the word *Divisor*. Put the result into word location *Quotient*.
   h. Same as part g, except *Dividend* is a word; *Divisor* is a byte.
   i. Multiply a 32-bit unsigned operand by an unsigned 32-bit operand.
   j. Same as part m, but for signed 32-bit integers.

    k. Calculate A^B, where A is a word and B is a byte.

    l. Calculate the sum of the first 10 integers.

    m. Calculate the sum of the first 100 integers.

    n. Multiply AX by 2.

3. For each problem in Exercise, 1, list the opcodes (to the extent possible, given the information in this chapter).

4. Write a sequence of instructions to add two 48-bit numbers.

5. Extend the program of Figure 4-1 to find the average of two doublewords.

6. Extend the program of Figure 4-1 to find the average of three doublewords.

7. Extend the program of Figure 4-5 to compute 10 factorial.

86-Family Addressing Modes

5.0 Introduction

86-family instructions specify addresses of data in various ways. Sometimes the operand is itself the address:

EXAMPLE 1

```
MOV   Store,AX
```

In Example 1, the CPU goes to AX and copies the contents into the memory location whose name is *Store*.

Sometimes the operand contains the address of the data, rather than the actual data:

EXAMPLE 2

```
MOV    Store,[BX]
```

In Example 2, the brackets mean that BX contains the address of the data, rather than the data itself. The CPU goes to that address, which is called the effective address (EA) and copies those contents into the memory location whose name is *Store*. This is an example of indirect addressing, and it allows a program to calculate an address during execution.

The various ways of specifying an address, i.e., of calculating an EA, are called addressing modes. In this chapter, we will consider five categories of addressing modes:

1. Direct mode
2. Immediate mode
3. Indirect mode
4. Displacement mode
5. Indexed mode

5.0.1 Addressing Mode Byte

An addressing mode byte contains information about the actual address of the operand or operands. All PC instructions are of the form

OptionalLabel   *Operation*   *Operands*   *OptionalComment*

The field for *Operands* can be null (no operands), as in the operation RET:

```
RET
```

or there can be one operand, as in the operation NEG:

```
NEG    AX
```

or there can be two operands or more, as in MOV:

```
MOV    AX,BX
```

If the operand is null, there is no addressing mode byte in the machine code. If there are two operands, one of them must be a register in direct mode (no brackets) or immediate data (e.g., 3). Instructions with one operand have addressing mode bytes when the operand is not a register in direct mode or when the addressing mode byte contains further information describing the instructions. When there is an addressing mode byte, it follows the instruction byte.

EXAMPLE 3

```
8B   C3        MOV   AX,BX
F7   D8        NEG   AX
CB             RET
```

In Example 3, 8B is the machine code for the instruction MOV when both operands are 16-bit registers (see Chapter 4). The following byte, C3, represents the addressing mode information. The machine code for NEG is F7, but since this does not specify the instruction uniquely (NOT, for example, has the same machine code), another byte that completes the instruction as well as describing the operand AX is needed. RET has no operands and thus no addressing mode byte. When we describe each addressing mode, we also will describe the machine code for the addressing mode byte.

Each addressing mode has its own encoding in the addressing mode byte. There are three distinct fields in this byte:

1. The mode field, which is 2 bits long
2. The register field, which is 3 bits long
3. The register/memory field (denoted r/m), which is 3 bits long

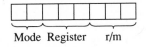

Mode   Register   r/m

Mode Field. This can have one of four values—00, 01, 10, or 11—and encodes mode information. For example, if there are two operands and they are both in direct mode, then the mode field is 11. Each of the following addressing modes has a specific value for the mode field.

Register Field. This is used to encode two types of information. If one of the operands is a register in direct mode, then this field is its encoding, using the following codes:

AX or AL : 000
CX or CL : 001
DX or DL : 010
BX or BL : 011
SP or AH : 100
BP or CH : 101
SI or DH : 110
DI or BH : 111

When both operands are registers in direct mode, the register field encodes the destination (i.e., first) operand.

If there is no operand in direct mode (e.g., when an immediate value is ADDed to a memory location), the register field is used to complete the description of the operation. In Chapter 4, we saw instructions that had the same machine code as other instructions, NEG and NOT, for example. In these cases, the 3 bits are not needed to describe a register and are thus free to complete the instruction description.

Table 5-1 shows the codes for those instructions whose machine code does not specify them uniquely and for those instructions that do not really need a register field (denoted Reg in Table 5-1). The mode and r/m field encode the information for the operand when there is just one; when there are two operands, these fields describe the operand that is not the immediate data.

r/m Field. This field completes the addressing mode field partially described in the first 2 bits of the addressing mode byte.

Table 5-1 Instruction codes

Instruction	Operand(s)	Mode Reg r/m
MOV	Register/Memory,Imm	Mode 000 r/m
PUSH	Register/Memory	Mode 110 r/m
ADD	Register/Memory,Imm	Mode 000 r/m
ADC	Register/Memory,Imm	Mode 010 r/m
INC	Register/Memory	Mode 000 r/m
SUB	Register/Memory,Imm	Mode 101 r/m
SBB	Register/Memory,Imm	Mode 011 r/m
DEC	Register/Memory,Imm	Mode 001 r/m
NEG	Register/Memory	Mode 011 r/m
CMP	Register/Memory,Imm	Mode 111 r/m
MUL	Any	Mode 100 r/m
IMUL	Any	Mode 101 r/m
DIV	Any	Mode 110 r/m
IDIV	Any	Mode 111 r/m
NOT	Any	Mode 010 r/m
SHL/SAL	Any	Mode 100 r/m
SHR	Any	Mode 101 r/m
SAR	Any	Mode 111 r/m
ROL	Any	Mode 000 r/m
RCL	Any	Mode 010 r/m
RCR	Any	Mode 011 r/m
AND	Register/Memory,Imm	Mode 100 r/m
TEST	Register/Memory,Imm	Mode 000 r/m
OR	Register/Memory,Imm	Mode 001 r/m
XOR	Register/Memory,Imm	Mode 110 r/m
JMP	Indirect within segment	Mode 010 r/m

When the memory being described is a memory location name (e.g., *Store*), this field contains 110, and the mode field contains 00.

When both operands are registers, then this field encodes the source (i.e., second) operand. We will describe the other values for this field when we discuss each addressing mode. The chapter summary will bring all these rules together in one place.

The reader need not be concerned about memorizing machine code. It is something to be ''looked up.''

5.1 Direct Mode

We use direct mode when the register or memory location contains the actual contents to be operated upon. This is one of the simplest of the addressing modes and is also called direct addressing. All of the examples in this text so far have used direct mode; that is, all the registers and memory locations have contained the actual contents on which to operate.

EXAMPLE 4

```
MOV    BX,AX
MOV    Store,CX
```

In Example 4, all the operands—AX, BX, CX, and *Store*—are in direct mode.

5.1.1 Addressing Mode Byte for Direct Mode

When both operands are registers in direct mode, the mode field is 11; if only one operand is in direct mode, then the mode field is 00. The following shows the machine code for the previous example to the left of the instruction.

EXAMPLE 5

```
8B D8              MOV    BX,AX
89 0E 0005 R       MOV    Store,CX
```

We can examine each of the machine code fields in Example 5:

```
MOV    BX,AX
```

8B: Opcode for MOV when both operands are 16-bit registers (see MOV opcodes in Chapter 4).

D8: Addressing mode byte. In binary, D8 is

$$11011000 \quad \text{or} \quad 11 \quad 011 \quad 000$$

The mode field is 11, indicating that both operands are registers in direct mode. The register field is 011, indicating that the destination operand is BX. The r/m field is 000, indicating that the source operand is AX.

```
MOV   Store,CX
```

89: Opcode for MOV when the source is a 16-bit register (CX) and the destination is a memory location name (*Store*) (see MOV opcodes in Chapter 4).

0E: Addressing mode byte. In binary, this is

$$00001110 \quad \text{or} \quad 00 \quad 001 \quad 110$$

The mode field is 00, and the r/m field is 110, indicating that the nonregister operand (here *Store*) is a memory location name. The register field is 001, the code for CX.

0005 R: This indicates that *Store* is declared (starting) in the 6th byte of the data segment. Perhaps the data segment looks like

```
.DATA
A       DW    2
B       DW    3
C       DB    4
Store  DW    ?
           .
           .
           .
```

The "R" indicates that 0005 may be relocated (by the linker) somewhere other than location 0005 in memory. We will discuss relocation in Chapter 11.

5.2 Immediate Mode

Immediate mode indicates that one of the operands, most likely, the source operand, contains immediate data.

EXAMPLE 6

```
    MOV    AL,3
```

AL is in direct mode; the 3 is in immediate mode.

5.2.1 Addressing Mode Byte for Immediate Mode

When one of two operands contains immediate data, the addressing mode byte is free to refer to the nonimmediate data operand. Thus the mode field and the r/m field describe the other operand, if necessary; if the opcode contains enough information to describe the instruction and the nonimmediate operand, then there is no addressing mode byte.

Since there is no register for immediate data, the 3 bits in the register field are used to finish describing the operation.

EXAMPLE 7

```
    04 05    ADD    AL,5
```

Examining the machine code for Example 7:

04: Opcode for adding byte immediate data to AL (see ADD opcodes in Chapter 4).

05: The immediate data.

Note that there is no addressing mode byte here—it is not needed.

EXAMPLE 8

```
    83 06 0000 R 30    ADD    Store,48
```

Examining the machine code for Example 8:

83: Opcode for ADD, ADC, SUB, or SBB, with a byte-sized immediate source and a word-sized destination. Thus the machine code does not specify the operation ADD uniquely.

06: Addressing mode byte. In binary, this is

$$00000110 \quad \text{or} \quad 00 \quad 000 \quad 110$$

The mode field is 00, and the r/m field is 110, indicating that the destination is a memory location name. The register field contains 000, indicating that this is an ADD instruction. In the chapter summary, we will list the register field bits for the various instructions that use this field to complete the instruction opcode.

0000: The address where *Store* is declared.

30: Hexadecimal for 48, the immediate data.

5.3 Indirect Mode

We use indirect mode when the register contains the *address* of the data, rather than the actual data we are trying to access. Only BX, BP, SI, or DI can be used in indirect mode; to indicate that they are in indirect mode, they are surrounded by brackets.

EXAMPLE 9

```
List    DW      15,4,10,6,4
        .
        .
        .
        LEA     BX,List
Loop:   MOV     AX,[BX]
        .
        .
        .
        ADD     BX,2
        CMP     BX,10
        JLE     Loop
```

In Example 9, after

```
MOV     AX,[BX]
```

is executed (the first time), AX will contain 15 since BX is in indirect mode and the previous instruction (LEA) put the address of the 15 into register BX. Subsequent executions of this statement, due to the JLE instruction, will copy the remaining elements of the list into AX.

5.3.1 Addressing Mode Byte for Indirect Mode

The mode field and r/m field of the addressing mode byte always describe the operand that is in indirect mode. (If there are two operands, then the other one must be in direct mode and is encoded in the register field.) The mode field for indirect mode contains 00; the r/m field contains the encoding for the register that is in indirect mode.

The encodings for the r/m field in indirect mode are

```
100:  [SI]
101:  [DI]
110:  [BP]
111:  [BX]
```

EXAMPLE 10

```
          List    DW    15,4,10,6,4
                  .
                  .
                  .
                  LEA   BX,List
8B 07  Loop:      MOV   AX,[BX]
                  .
                  .
                  .
                  ADD   BX,2
                  CMP   BX,10 + OFFSET List
                  JL    Loop
```

Looking at the machine code for the instruction labeled *Loop* in Example 10:

8B: Opcode for MOV when both operands are registers.
07: Addressing mode byte. In binary, this is

$$00000111 \quad \text{or} \quad 00 \quad 000 \quad 111$$

The (first) 00 encodes the indirect mode operand. The register field bits—000—encode the AX operand, and the 111 in the r/m field encodes BX in indirect mode as the source.

5.4 Displacement Mode

We use displacement mode to access data that occurs at a byte or word displacement from the address in our register. The integer displacement must be immediate data and may precede the "[ ]", follow it with a " + " or " − ", or be inside the "[ ]" preceded by a " + ". Thus 4[BX], [BX] + 4, and [BX + 4] all indicate a displacement of 4 bytes from the *base* address stored in BX.

EXAMPLE 11

```
List    DB    15,4,6,10,4
                 .
                 .
                 .
        LEA   BX,List
        CMP   AL,4[BX]
```

In Example 11, the instruction

```
CMP   AL,4[BX]
```

compares the contents of AL with the byte at *List + 4*, which is the 5th byte of the list, the 4. (The first element, the 15, is at location *List;* the second element, the 4, is at location *List + 1* byte; and so on.)

5.4.1 Addressing Mode Byte for Displacement Mode

The addressing mode byte for displacement mode is similar to that for indirect mode, because indirect mode is actually displacement mode with a zero displacement. There is an extra byte or word following the addressing mode byte, indicating the actual byte or word displacement. Thus the r/m field contains the same encodings as those shown in Section 5.3. The mode field is 01 for a byte displacement, and 10 for a word displacement.

EXAMPLE 12

```
              List    DB    15,4,6,10,4
                             .
                             .
                             .
                      LEA   BX,List
  3A 47 04            CMP   AL,4[BX]
                             .
                             .
                             .
```

Examining the machine code for CMP AL,4[BX] in Example 12:

3A: Opcode for CMP with AL destination, memory reference source (see Chapter 4).

47: Addressing mode byte. In binary, this is

$$01000111 \quad \text{or} \quad 01 \quad 000 \quad 111$$

The mode field is 01, indicating a byte displacement. (If *List* were declared using DW, then this field would be 10.) The next 3 bits, the register field, contain 000, the encoding for AL. The r/m field is 111, the encoding for [BX] + displacement.

04: The displacement.

5.5 Index Mode

The addressing modes described in the previous sections enable the programmer to access displacements (offsets) from a base address (beginning) of a table or array of data. The programmer must know which element to access in the array or table when the program is coded since the displacements are immediate data.

Index mode is used to access particular elements in the table at execution time. In Examples 11 and 12, we specified the fifth element of the array by

```
4[BX]
```

The displacement (4 here) must be immediate data. Thus, using displacement mode, we cannot specify the *I*th element of *List*. Index mode does allow us to do this.

To access the *I*th element of an array such as *List,* we can store *I* in either the SI or the DI register. Thus, if SI contains 4 and BX contains the base address of *List,* then

```
[SI][BX]
```

addresses the fifth element of *List*. Thus, at execution time SI contains the offset (also called a subscript or index) of the *I*th element in *List*.

SI and DI are the only registers that may be used in index mode. As in indirect and displacement modes, they are surrounded by brackets. Thus [SI][BX] indicates that register BX contains the (beginning) address of a table or list, and we wish to access the element whose index (subscript) is in register SI. This also can be written [BX][SI] or [BX] + [SI] or [BX + SI] or [SI] + [BX] or [SI + BX].

Index mode can be used by itself; thus *List*[*SI*] references the byte table *List* and accesses the element whose index is in SI. Once again, *List*[*SI*] references the contents of element *SI* + *1* in the array since *List* (which may be thought of as *List* + *0*) references element 1 in *List*.

The combination of a base and index can be used to access elements in a two-dimensional array or table; the indirect or displacement mode base can address a particular row or column, and the index mode register can access the actual element in the row or column. For the following table,

12	56	78	5	44
54	89	65	92	6
37	66	15	77	19

if the elements are stored row by row, we can access the second element in the first row by storing the base address of the first element in BX (or BP) and a 1 in SI (or DI). Then

    [BX][SI]

refers to this element, the 56. Once again, a "1" rather than a "2" is stored in SI since the element whose address is in BP (the 12 here) is considered to be the 0th element, and the 56 is then the first element after this 0th element.

To access the second element in the second row, we add the number of elements in a row to BX; in our example, this is 5.

    ADD   BX,5

Then,

    [BX][SI]

references the element in the second row, second column, the 89. Alternatively, rather than add 5 to BX, we can simply use a displacement

    5[BX][SI]

EXAMPLE 13

    List   DW   15,4,6,10,4
            .
            .
            .
            LEA   BX,List
            MOV   SI,4
            MOV   AX,[BX][SI]

After the MOV AX,[BX][SI] instruction is executed, AX contains $List_2$, which is 6. Remember that the first element is $List_0$.

5.5.1 Addressing Mode Byte for Index Mode

The mode field bits are the same as for the previous modes:

00: No displacement
01: Byte displacement
10: Word displacement

The r/m field encodings are

000: [BX] [SI]
001: [BX] [DI]
010: [BP] [SI]
011: [BP] [DI]

In all cases, a displacement may be added to the registers in index mode. Thus [BX][SI] + 2 has the same r/m field as [BX][SI].

EXAMPLE 14

```
List      DW    15,4,6,10,4
                .
                .
                .
          LEA   BX,List
          MOV   SI,2
8B 00     MOV   AX,[BX][SI]
```

Examining the machine code for MOV AX,[BX][SI] in Example 14:

8B: Opcode for MOV when both operands are 16-bit registers.
00: Addressing mode byte. In binary, this is

00000000   or   00   000   000

The 00 mode field here indicates that there is no displacement. The next three bits, 000 — the register field, are the encoding for AX. And the last three 000's are the r/m field and encode index mode for [BX] + [SI] — even though we chose to write it [BX][SI].

In Example 14, we accessed the list elements with

[BX][SI]

where BX contained the address of *List*. We also could have accessed the same element with

List[SI]

In fact, this is more readable code and saves register references. It is also a slower way to access the list.

5.6 **Machine Code Representation of Instructions—Part 2**

5.6.1 Program to Compute $A + B$

The assembler listing for the assembled version of the program from Chapter 1 that calculates $A + B$, when $A = 2$ and $B = 3$, is shown in Figure 5-1.

The first column of Figure 5-1 is the location counter (LC) (see Chapter 3). Following this is the machine code translation for the instruction.

Figure 5-1 Assembler listing of program to compute $A + B$

```
;   This program calculates Result := A + B when A = 2, B = 3.
;
; Two necessary bookkeeping statements follow
;
                      DOSSEG          ; Use Microsoft SEGment conventions
                      .MODEL  Small   ; Use small memory model
;; Stack Segment follows
;
                      .STACK  100H
;
; Data Segment follows
;
                      .DATA
0000  0002            A       DW   2
0002  0003            B       DW   3
0004  0000            Result  DW   ?
;
; Code Segment follows
;
                      .CODE
;
; Two more necessary bookkeeping statements follow
;
0000  B8 ---- R       Start:  MOV AX,@Data    ; Define current
0003  8E D8           MOV DS,AX               ; Data Segment
;
; Main Program
;
0005  A1 0000 R       MOV AX,A        ; Get A
0008  03 06 0002 R    ADD AX,B        ; Compute A + B
000C  A3 0004 R       MOV Result,AX   ; Result := A + B
;
000F  B4 4C           MOV AH,4CH
0011  CD 21           INT 21H         ; Back to DOS
;
                      END Start       ; End of program.
                                      ; Start is transfer address
```

Consider the machine code for MOV AX,A (at LC = 000A):

```
A1  0000  R
```

A1: Opcode for MOV when the source is a memory location name and the destination is AX.

There is no addressing mode byte here; A1 completely describes everything (source and destination type) except the location of memory location *A*.

0000 R: 0000 is the LC value for *A,* with an indication that it may be relocated when the program is linked.

Consider next the machine code for ADD AX,B (at LC = 000D):

03: Opcode for ADD when the source is a word memory location name and the destination is a 16-bit register.

06: Addressing mode byte. In binary, this is

00000110   or   00   000   110

The mode field is 00, and the r/m field is 110. This combination indicates that the effective address (EA) is a memory location name (*B* here). The register field is 000, the encoding for AX.

0002 R: The LC value for *B*.

5.6.2 Program to Compute 5 Factorial

Figure 5-2 shows the assembler listing for the program shown in Figure 4-4 of Chapter 4.

Much of the machine code in Figure 5-2 is similar to that in Figure 5-1. The instruction at the LC value of 001C—JLE Loop—contains a machine code byte somewhat different from what we have seen so far. The machine code is 7E F8.

7E: Opcode for JLE.

F8: The displacement from IP to which to jump during execution. Since IP contains the location of the next instruction, IP contains the (relocated) value of 001E when the transfer is to be made to *Loop*. The displacement F8H in binary is

11111000

This is a negative number (the leftmost bit is 1). Using the techniques of Chapter 2, we decode this to −8. Thus the transfer is to the instruction 8 bytes *back* because of the negative sign. This brings us to an LC value of 16H, which is the instruction labeled *Loop* (as it should be).

Figure 5-2 Assembly listing for calculating 5 factorial

```
;   Looping
;
; Two necessary bookkeeping statements follow
;
                    DOSSEG          ; Use Microsoft SEGment conventions
                    .MODEL  Small   ; Use small memory model
;
; Stack Segment follows
;
                    .STACK  100H
;
; Data Segment follows
;
                    .DATA
;
 0000   0000                  Fact    DW  ?
;
; Code Segment follows
;
                    .CODE
;
; Two more necessary bookkeeping statements follow
;
 0000   B8 ---- R    Start:  MOV AX,@Data      ; Define current
 0003   8E D8                MOV DS,AX         ; Data Segment
;
; Main Program
;
comment /
    fact := 1
    loop for i := 1 to 5
    fact := fact * i
    end loop
        /
 0005   C7 06 0000 R 0001 MOV Fact,1       ; Fact := 1
 000B   A1 0000 R         MOV AX,Fact      ; prepare for mult
 000E   B9 0001           MOV,CX,1         ; I := 1
 0011   F7 E1      Loop:  MUL CX           ; Fact := Fact * I
 0013   41                INC CX           ; I := I + 1
 0014   83 F9 05          CMP CX,5         ; IF I <= 5
 0017   7E F8             JLE Loop         ;   GOTO  Loop
 0019   A3 0000 R         MOV Fact,AX      ; store in Fact
;
 001C   B4 4C             MOV AH,4CH
 001E   CD 21             INT 21H          ; Back to DOS
;
                          END Start        ; End of program.
                                           ; Start is transfer address
```

5.7   32-Bit Addressing

When the .386 directive is used, all the previous addressing modes may be used with the 80386 and 80486 computers. In addition the 32-bit registers may be used whenever their 16-bit counterparts are used.

Also there are fewer restrictions on these 32-bit counterparts. We list these extensions:

1. Any 32-bit general-purpose register may be used in indirect mode (only BX, BP, DI, and SI may be used in 16-bit addressing).

EXAMPLE 15

```
MOV    EBX,[EAX]
```

2. In index mode, one of the 32-bit registers (excluding ESP) can be multiplied by 2, 4, or 8 for accessing word, doubleword, or quadword arrays.

EXAMPLE 16

```
LEA    EDX,Mem32
MOV    AX,[EDX*2]   ; Move a word from Mem32 to AX
```

3. If EBP is used, the default segment register is SS; the other registers assume the DS register is to be used.

EXAMPLE 17

```
MOV    EAX,[EBP*2]    ; Move a word at SS:[EBP]
                      ; to AX
MOV    AX,[EDX*2]     ; Move a word at DS:[EDX]
                      ; to AX
```

It is legal to mix 16-bit addressing with 32-bit addressing.

EXAMPLE 18

```
MOV    EAX,[BX]     ; Move a 32-bit word at
                    ; DS:[BX] to EAX
MOV    AX,[EBX]     ; Move a 16-bit word at
                    ; DS:[EBX] to AX
```

5.8 Summary

This chapter describes the various ways that registers may be used to access data, as well as the machine code translation for these addressing modes.

It is important to be able to read machine code when debugging assembly language programs, especially when disassembling and analyzing someone else's code. (Disassembling is the process of translating machine code back to the instruction mnemonics. The debugger has a command to do this.)

We urge the reader to examine the machine code for the rest of the programs in Figure 5-1 and Figure 5-2, as well as for other programs. See, for example, Chapter 4. Chapter 1 describes how to get these assembler listings. If the original file is named *Sum.ASM,* then the listing after assembly will be in the file *Sum.LST.*

We summarize both the addressing modes and the machine code for them in Figure 5.3.

Instructions with no operands have no addressing mode byte.

Single operand instructions have an addressing mode byte when the operand is not fully described within the opcode.

Double operand instructions have addressing mode bytes when the opcode does not describe the operands fully.

If one of two operands is a memory location name or a nondirect addressing mode, then the other operand is in direct mode. In this case, the nondirect mode operand is described in the mode and r/m fields. The direct mode operand is described in the register field, using the encoding described in Section 5.0.

When the mode field = 00 and the r/m field = 110, the addressing mode byte denotes an operand that is a memory location name.

When the mode field is 11, there are two operands, both of which are registers in direct mode.

In Chapter 4, all opcodes were given in hexadecimal. It is possible (but not really necessary) to break these down into binary. When this is done, it is easy to see that the binary code ends in 0 for instructions with byte operands and in 1 for word operands.

Other analyses can be made on the opcode.

Exercises

1. What is an addressing mode?
2. When does an instruction contain an addressing mode byte? What are its parts?
3. If there are two operands, how do we know which operand is coded in the various parts of the addressing mode byte, if there is one?

Figure 5-3 Addressing modes and machine codes

Addressing mode	Syntax	Machine code
Direct (data is in register) or Direct (1 operand is a memory reference)	Reg Mem	Mode Field: 11 Register Field: Destination register code. r/m Field: Source register code. Mode Field: 00 r/m Field: 110

Indirect
(address of data is in register)
	[Reg]	Mode Field: 00 (indicates no displacement).
		Register Field: 1) code for direct mode operand.
		     or 2) rest of the opcode when other
		     operand is Immediate.
		r/m Field: 100 - [SI]
		              100 - [DI]
		              110 - [BP]
		              111 - [BX]

Displacement (address of data is at a displacement from address in register)	Disp[Reg] or [Reg] + Disp or [Reg + Disp]	Mode Field: 01 for byte Displacement. 10 for word displacement. Register Field: See Indirect. r/m Field: See Indirect.

Index
(for arrays of data)
	[Reg] or [Reg1][Reg]
	or [Reg][Reg1]
	or [Reg1] + [Reg]
	or [Reg1 + Reg] etc.
		Mode Field: See Displacement.
		Register Field: See Indirect.
		
		r/m Field: 000 - [BX] + [SI]
		              001 - [BX] + [DI]
		              010 - [BP] + [SI]
		              011 - [BP] + [DI]
		              See Indirect for [SI] or [DI]
		              alone.

4. What will be the contents of both AX and BX after the following instruction is executed?

```
MOV   [BX],AX
```

5. Show AX, BX, and locations 2012–2015 in memory after the following instruction is executed.

```
MOV   AX,2[BX]
```

The initial values are:

AX contains 0000
BX contains 2012
Location 2012 contains 45

Location 2013 contains 67
Location 2014 contains 01
Location 2015 contains 23

6. Write an instruction to move the contents of DX to the location whose address is contained in BX.

7. Write all the equivalent representations of

   `[BX][DI].`

8. What instruction is represented by each of the following machine code bytes:
   a. `8E D8`
   b. `03 07`
   c. `01 07`
   d. `03 05`
   e. `24 0A`
   f. `3A 77 01`
   g. `FF 0E 0000 R`
   h. `FF 8C 0000 R`
   i. `FF 06 0000 R`
   j. `FF 84 0000 R`
   k. `EB FE`
   l. `75 FA`
   m. `89 38`
   n. `D3 D0`
   o. `D1 16 0000 R`
   p. `D3 16 0000 R`
   q. `1C 04`

9. Translate the following instructions into machine code:
   a. `ADD    [DI],AX`
   b. `ADD    AX,[DI]`
   c. `CMP    AX,DX`
   d. `CMP    A,AX    (where A is at LC = 0000)`
   e. `DEC    AX`
   f. `DEC    BL`
   g. `DEC    A       (where A is at LC = 0001)`
   h. `DIV    A        (where A is at LC = 0001)`

10. Write a complete program to add 1 to every element of the list whose elements initially are 5, 4, 3, 15, 2, 0.

6

Implementing Control Structures and Algorithms in Assembly Language

6.0 Introduction

High-level language programs consist of statements. These statements perform useful work through the use of *control structures* that enable the programmer to control the way the program executes. It can be shown that any calculation that can be performed on a computer can be performed using just three control structures: (1) sequencing, (2) selection, and (3) repetition.

Sequencing is simple. It means that two statements that follow each other are to be executed one after the other. The most common statement used in any of these three control structures is the *assignment* statement.

In Chapter 1 we saw that the single assignment statement

```
Result := A + B
```

requires more than one assembly language instruction:

```
MOV    AX,A          ; get A
ADD    AX,B          ; add B
MOV    Result,AX     ; store in Result
```

Assignment statements are the most frequently used statements in high-level languages such as Pascal, BASIC, FORTRAN, C, and Ada.

In addition to assigning values to variables, we may wish to specify that a choice is to be made among a number of alternative statements. Such constructs are called selection statements. The GOTO statement, the IF statement, the IF-THEN-ELSE statement, and the CASE or SWITCH statement are common selection statements found in many high-level languages.

Most useful computer programs require that a statement or a sequence of statements be repeated. Repetition (also called iteration) is performed in high-level languages with loops. Recusion is another way to repeat. Pascal contains WHILE loops, REPEAT loops, and FOR loops. FORTRAN contains DO loops (similar to the FOR loop in Pascal and BASIC). Recent versions of FORTRAN and BASIC may also contain the WHILE loop construct. C and Ada contain FOR loops and WHILE loops.

In addition, there are certain techniques that a programmer must be familiar with in any language. These include the ability to count, to compare two values, and to perform various operations on lists of data. Typical list operations are to find the smallest, largest, and average element in a list; to search a list to find an element; or to count its number of occurrences. Sorting a list is an important list operation.

In this chapter, we illustrate many of these techniques. Further examples are described in the chapter exercises.

The examples in this chapter are shown in seven forms:

1. Pseudocode (in many cases this is the same as the Pascal)
2. BASIC
3. FORTRAN
4. Pascal
5. C
6. Ada
7. Assembly Language

In many cases, our examples do not use all of the features of these languages. For example, most 86-family BASIC compilers allow variables of any length, whereas some other versions of BASIC limit variables to one or two letters. In our BASIC examples, therefore, we have limited our variables to one letter.

We do not attempt to teach these other languages. We have chosen Pascal, BASIC, FORTRAN, C, and Ada as "intermediaries" between the pseudocode and the assembly language because many people are familiar with at least one of them. Only the pseudocode version will be shown in the rest of the book. We hope the reader will become comfortable with representing algorithms (programs) in pseudocode as well as in assembly language.

6.1 Assignment Statements

In high-level languages, assignment statements are of the form

```
LeftHandSide := RightHandSide
```

where *LeftHandSide* is a variable name, such as *Result,* and *RightHandSide* is a variable or a number of variables connected by operators, for example, $A + B$. BASIC, FORTRAN and C all use "=" for assignment rather than ":=".

To implement this as closely as possible in assembly language, a MOV instruction is needed for at least one of the variables on the right-hand side to move it into a register; an arithmetic or logical instruction is needed for each operation to be performed; and a final MOV is needed to store the result of the calculation into the variable whose name is on the left-hand side. The size of the result also must be considered since some operations on one size of data, say words, produce other-sized results, say doublewords. The multiply instruction, MUL, produces a result larger than its operands.

EXAMPLE 1

Pseudocode

```
R = (A + B) * C
```

Pascal

```
Result := (A + B) * C;
```

FORTRAN

```
Result = (A + B) * C
```

C

```
result = (a + b) * c;
```

Ada

```
Result := (A + B) * C;
```

Assembly Language

```
MOV    AX,A            ; Get A
ADD    AX,B            ; Add B
IMUL   C               ; Multiply by C
MOV    Result,AX       ; Store 32-bit
MOV    Result+2,DX     ; product
```

The following example shows a similar operation:

EXAMPLE 2

Pseudocode

```
B := A²
```

BASIC

```
B = A^2
```

Pascal

```
B := A * A;
```

FORTRAN

```
B = A**2
```

C

```
b = a * a;
```

Ada

```
B :=A**2;
```

Assembly Language

```
MOV    AX,A            ; Get A
IMUL   A               ; Compute A**2
```

```
MOV    B,AX          ; Store 32-bit
MOV    B+2,DX        ; product
```

6.2 Selection Statements

High-level languages use constructs such as IF, IF-THEN, and IF-THEN-ELSE statements to control statement execution, i.e., to select the statements to be executed next. These selection statements do not translate to assembly languages very well (although we will see in Chapter 10 that the MASM assembler has its own IF construct for controlling what statements get *assembled*). The following example illustrates the difficulty with translating these high-level constructs to assembly language:

EXAMPLE 3

Pseudocode

```
IF New > Max
   THEN Max := New
END IF
```

BASIC

```
10   IF N > M THEN M = N
20
```

Pascal

```
IF New > Max THEN
   Max := New;
```

FORTRAN

```
IF (New .gt. Max) THEN
     Max = New
ENDIF
```

C

```
if (new > max)
   max = new;
```

Ada

```
IF New > Max THEN
    Max := New;
END IF;
```

Assembly Language

```
MOV   AX,New
CMP   AX,Max        ; If New > Max
JLE   There

MOV   Max,Ax        ;    Then Max := New
There:
```

Note that in Example 3 we essentially changed the logic of the problem to

```
IF New ≤ Max
   THEN
   ELSE Max := New
```

Another way to express this is

```
IF NOT(New ≤ Max)
   THEN Max := New
```

Two alternatives, as in IF-THEN-ELSE, are equally clumsy to implement:

EXAMPLE 4

Pseudocode

```
IF A < B
   THEN Min := A
   ELSE Min := B
END IF
```

BASIC

```
10 LET M = B
20 IF A < B THEN M = A
30
```

Pascal

```
IF A < B
   THEN Min := A
   ELSE Min := B;
```

FORTRAN

```
IF (A .lt. B) THEN
    Min = A
ELSE
    Min = B
ENDIF
```

C

```
if (a < b)
    min = a;
else
    min = b;
```

Ada

```
IF A < B THEN
    Min := A;
ELSE
    Min := B;
ENDIF
```

Assembly Language

```
            MOV    AX,A    ; get A
            CMP    AX,B    ; if A < B
            JGE    Label1
            MOV    Min,AX  ;    then Min := A
            JMP    Label2
Label1:     MOV    AX,B
            MOV    Min,AX  ;    else Min := B
Label2:
```

Once again, Example 4 does not seem to be a comfortable translation of the IF-THEN-ELSE structure. There are other ways to code this, e.g., comparing the operands in reverse order,

```
IF B < A
```

which is equally cumbersome compared to the original pseudocode. It is easy to make mistakes when coding such constructs into assembly language.

6.3 Loops

Loops are coded in a more straightforward manner than the selection constructs of the previous section. As we saw in Chapter 4, there is even a built-in LOOP statement, which, with its variants LOOPE and LOOPNE, simulates the loop constructs found in high-level languages. Example 5 shows a typical use of LOOP.

EXAMPLE 5

Pseudocode

```
Sum := 0
LOOP FOR I := 1 TO N
     Sum := Sum + I
END LOOP
```

BASIC

```
10 LET S = 0
20 FOR I = 1 to N
30    LET S = S + I
40 NEXT I
```

Pascal

```
Sum := 0;
FOR I := 1 to N DO
   Sum := Sum + I;
```

FORTRAN

```
Sum = 0
DO 25 I = 1,N
    Sum = Sum + I
25 CONTINUE
```

C

```
sum = 0;
for(i=0;i<=n;++i)
    sum += i;
```

Ada

```
Sum := 0;
FOR I IN 1..N
    Sum := Sum + I;
END LOOP;
```

Assembly Language

```
;    AX contains Sum
;    CX contains I, the count - initialized to
;       upper limit, N
;
              MOV       AX,0        ; Sum := 0
              MOV       CX,N        ; I := N
                                    ; LOOP
Loop1:        ADD       AX,CX       ; Sum := Sum + I
              LOOP      Loop1       ; I := I-1
                                    ; END LOOP
              MOV       Sum,AX
;
```

Notice that in Example 5 we changed the logic from a loop that counts "up" to a loop that counts "down" since that is the way that the LOOP instruction operates.

In Example 6, it is not really convenient to use the LOOP instruction. Here, we create a loop using conditional and unconditional transfer instructions, similar to the GOTO loop, which is anathema to modern structured programming. (A GOTO loop is a loop that is created by using a GOTO statement to iterate a sequence of instructions.)

EXAMPLE 6

Pseudocode

```
Sum := 0
I := 0
LOOP WHILE Sum <= 100
    I := I + 1
    Sum := Sum + I
END LOOP
```

BASIC

```
10 S = 0
20 I = 0
```

```
30  IF NOT (S <= 100) THEN 70
40     I = I + 1
50     S = S + I
60     GOTO 30
70
```

Pascal

```
Sum := 0;
I := 0;
WHILE Sum <= 100 DO
   BEGIN
      I := I + 1;
      Sum := Sum + I;
   END;
```

FORTRAN

```
        Sum = 0
        I = 0
200     IF (.NOT. (Sum .LE. 100)) GO TO 400
           I = I + 1
           Sum = Sum + I
           GO TO 200
400
```

C

```
sum = 0;
i = 0;
while (sum <= 100) {
   ++i;
   sum += i;
  }
```

Ada

```
Sum := 0;
I := 0;
WHILE Sum <= 100 LOOP
   I := I + 1;
```

```
        Sum := Sum + I;
    ENDLOOP;
```

Assembly Language

```
            ; AX contains Sum
            ; CX contains count (I) - initialized to 1
            ;
                MOV     AX,0        ; Sum := 0
                MOV     CX,1        ; I := 1
    Loop2:      CMP     AX,100      ; LOOP WHILE Sum <= 100
                JG      After
                INC     CX          ;    I := I + 1
                ADD     AX,CX       ;    Sum := Sum + I
                JMP     Loop2       ; END LOOP
    After:      MOV     Sum,AX
    ;
```

The WHILE loop construct *WHILE Condition DO* is difficult to simulate in assembly language. We have simulated it by writing:

```
    Label1    IF NOT Condition   Goto Label2
              ...
              Goto Label1
    Label2
```

Both the BASIC and Fortran versions were written using this logic, although many 86-family versions of these languages *do* allow the WHILE construct.

6.4 Arrays

In Chapter 5 we discussed how to use indirect mode and index mode to access array elements. In this section we will illustrate some standard practical problems using arrays.

6.4.1 Finding the Largest Element in a List

Consider the problem of finding the largest integer in an array *List,* consisting of positive integers and whose last element is a 0. The technique used here initializes a variable, *Max,* to be 0. Each element of the list is examined, beginning with the first. As each element in the list is examined, *Max* is changed to contain the value of any element larger than *Max*'s current value. In this way *Max* either contains 0, implying that the list is empty, or the largest of the positive elements in the list. It is quite easy to make this problem more general, i.e., to find the largest element in a list of positive, negative, and zero elements. All that must be changed is (a) the way *Max* is initialized and (b) the method by which we know the entire list has been examined. We leave this to the reader (see Exercise 4 at the end of the chapter).

EXAMPLE 7

Pseudocode

```
I := 1
Max := 0
LOOP WHILE List(I) <> 0
   IF List(I) > Max
      THEN Max := List(I)

      END IF
I := I + 1
END LOOP
```

BASIC

```
10  I = 1
20  M = 0
30  WHILE L(I) <> 0
40     IF L(I) > M THEN M = L(I)
50     I = I + 1
60  WEND
70
```

Pascal

```
I := 1;
Max := 0;
WHILE List[I] <> 0 DO
   BEGIN
     IF List[I] > Max
         THEN Max := List[I];
     I := I + 1;
   END;
```

FORTRAN

```
I = 1
Max = 0
WHILE (List(I) .NE. 0)
```

```
IF (List(I) .gt. Max) Max = List(I)
I = I + 1
ENDWHILE
```

C

```
i = 1;
max = 0;
while (list[i] != 0) {
    if (list[i] > max)
        max = list[i];
    ++i;
}
```

Ada

```
I := 0;
Max := 0;
WHILE List(I) /= 0 LOOP
    IF List(I) > Max THEN
        Max := List(I);
    END IF;
    I := I + 1;
ENDLOOP;
```

Assembly Language

```
; List consists of an array of 16-bit positive integers
; terminating with a 0
; AX contains Max

; BX points to current List element
;
;
        MOV     AX,0                    ; Max := 0
        LEA     BX,List
                                        ; LOOP
Loop1:  CMP     WORD PTR [BX],0 ;           WHILE List(I) <> 0
        JE      Fini
        CMP     [BX],AX         ;               IF List(I) > Max
        JLE     Next
        MOV     AX,[BX]         ;                   THEN Max := List(I)
Next:   ADD     BX,2            ;           get next List element
        JMP     Loop1           ; END LOOP
Fini:   MOV     Max,AX
;
```

The complete program is shown in Figure 6-1, using the list 5, 4, 13, 2, 11, 0.

Figure 6-1 Finding the largest element in a list

```
;  This program finds the largest element in a list.
;
; Two necessary bookkeeping statements follow
;
    DOSSEG              ; Use Microsoft SEGment conventions
    .MODEL  SMALL    ; Use small memory model
;
; Stack Segment follows
;
    .STACK  100H
;
; Data Segment follows
;
    .DATA
;
List    DW  5,4,13,2,11,0
Max     DW  ?
;
; Code Segment follows
;
    .CODE
;
; Two more necessary bookkeeping statements follow
;
Start:  MOV AX,@Data     ; Define current
        MOV DS,AX        ; Data Segment
;
; Main Program
;
; AX contains MAX
; BX points to current LIST element
;
        MOV AX,0                 ; MAX := 0
        LEA BX,List
                                 ; loop
Loop11: CMP WORD PTR [BX],0  ;    while LIST(I) <> 0)
        JE  Fini2
        CMP [BX],AX          ;        if LIST(I) > MAX
        JLE Next
        MOV AX,[BX]          ;            then MAX := LIST(I)
Next:   ADD BX,2             ;    get next LIST element
        JMP Loop11           ; end loop
Fini2:  MOV Max,AX
;
        MOV AH,4CH
        INT 21H                  ; Back to DOS
;
        END Start                ; End of program.  Start is transfer address
```

6.4.2 Searching

Searching a list for a desired element (often called a *key*) is a common programming procedure. Many applications involve a searching operation: the registry of motor vehicles searches for the owner of a particular license plate; the insurance company searches for the holder of a particular policy number; the department store searches for the account number of a customer to find the current balance.

Searching procedures are complicated by many factors, in particular the type of element for which the search is made and the method used to perform the search. It is generally more difficult to search for character-type data (e.g., names of persons or things) than to search a list of numbers. If the list is ordered in some way or is very long, it is not efficient merely to start looking at the beginning of the list (although for short lists it is reasonable).

The search algorithm we illustrate here is the simplest (and slowest) of all. We assume we have an unordered list of integers and search for an element called *Key,* counting the number of occurrences of *Key.* We begin our search with the first element and look at every element until we reach the last. Since the list is unordered, we must look at the entire list to be sure we have found all occurrences of *Key.* This is called a sequential linear search.

EXAMPLE 8

Pseudocode

```
Count := 0
LOOP FOR I := 1 TO N
    IF List(I) = Key
        THEN Count := Count + 1
    END IF
END LOOP
```

BASIC

```
10  C = 0
20  FOR I = 1 TO N
30      IF L(I) = K THEN C = C + 1
60  NEXT I
```

Pascal

```
Count := 0;
FOR I := 1 To N
```

```
        IF List[I] = Key
           THEN Count := Count + 1;
```

FORTRAN

```
        Count = 0
        DO 25 I = 1,N
           IF (List(I) .eq. Key) Count := Count + 1
     25 CONTINUE
```

C

```
        count = 0;
        for (i=1;i<=n;++i);
           if (list[i] == key)
              ++count;
```

Ada

```
        Count := 0;
        FOR I IN 1..N LOOP
           IF List(I) = Key THEN
              Count := Count + 1;
           END IF;
        END LOOP;
```

Assembly Language

```
; DX contains Key
; CX contains Count
; DI contains current List offset
; BX points to beginning of List
; N contains length of List in bytes
;
;
                MOV     DX,Key
                MOV     CX,0           ; Count := 0
                MOV     DI,0           ; I := 0
                LEA     BX,List        ; get List address
Loop1:          CMP     DI,N           ; LOOP FOR I := 1 TO N
                JE      Fini
                CMP     [BX][DI],DX    ;       If List(I) = Key
                JNE     After2
                INC     CX             ;          THEN increment Count
```

```
After2:           ADD     DI,2         ;       (2 for word)
                  JMP     Loop1        ; END LOOP
Fini:             MOV     Count,CX
```

A complete program for performing a search of the same list as in Figure 6-1, counting the occurrences of 2, is shown in Figure 6-2.

6.4.3 Sorting

Like searching, sorting a list is one of the more common applications performed by computers (or, more accurately, by computer programs). The registry probably keeps its license-plate file ordered; the department store may keep its account list ordered; and the insurance company's policy-number file quite likely is ordered. Keeping an already sorted list in order as additions and changes are made is a different process from that of taking an unordered list and putting it in order in the first place.

If the list is very long, sorting can be a slow process. Many efficient sorts have been ''invented,'' and we refer the interested reader to any good data structure book.

The sort algorithm we show here is relatively slow as sorting algorithms go, but it is perfectly appropriate for sorting small lists or when speed is not as critical as is getting a program written fast. It is called a *selection* or *exchange* sort, and it is very simple to program in a high-level language and not too difficult in assembly language.

We shall use the selection sort to put a list into ascending order. The technique is: (a) search the entire list to find the smallest element—this is similar to the algorithm shown in Example 7 that searches for the largest element; (b) when this smallest element has been found, swap it with the first element—do not be bothered that the element that was originally first is not in its proper position; (c) search the list, starting with the second element, swapping the (second) smallest element with the second element; (d) continue this process, starting with the third element, the fourth, and so on.

The procedure is shown below for the list 5, 4, 3, 1, 2.

Before	Pass 1:	5	4	3	1	2
Before	Pass 2:	1	4	3	5	2
Before	Pass 3:	1	2	3	5	4
Before	Pass 4:	1	2	3	5	4
After	Pass 4:	1	2	3	4	5

In Example 9 we use this algorithm to sort a list of n elements, using a selection sort. Note that the assembly language program is written for the list $List_0$, $List_1$, . . . As usual, *List* or $List_0$ denotes the first element in the list.

Figure 6-2 Searching a list; counting occurrences of a key

```
;   This program searches a list, counting occurences of a key.
;
; Two necessary bookkeeping statements follow
;
    DOSSEG              ; Use Microsoft SEGment conventions
    .MODEL  SMALL       ; Use small memory model
;
; Stack Segment follows
;
    .STACK  100H
;
; Data Segment follows
;
    .DATA
;
List    DW  5,4,13,2,11,0
N = $ - List
Key     DW  2
Count   DW  ?
;
; Code Segment follows
;
    .CODE
;
; Two more necessary bookkeeping statements follow
;
Start:  MOV AX,@DATA     ; Define current
        MOV DS,AX        ; Data Segment
;
; Main program
;
; DX contains KEY
; CX contains COUNT
; DI contains current LIST offset
; BX points to beginning of LIST
; N contains length of LIST in bytes
;
        MOV     DX,Key
        MOV     CX,0         ; COUNT := 0
        MOV     DI,0         ; I := 0
        LEA     BX,List      ; get LIST address
Loop3:  CMP     DI,N         ; loop for I := 1 to N
        JE      Fini
        CMP     [BX][DI],DX  ; if LIST[I] = KEY
        JNE     After
        INC     CX           ; then increment COUNT
After:  ADD     DI,2
        JMP     Loop3        ; end loop
Fini:   MOV     Count,CX
;
        MOV AH,4CH
        INT 21H              ; Back to DOS
;
        END Start           ; End of program.  Start is transfer address
```

EXAMPLE 9

Pseudocode

```
LOOP FOR I := I TO N-1
    Min := List(I)
    Place := I
    LOOP FOR J := I+1 TO N
        IF List(J) < Min THEN
            Place := J
            Min := List(J)
        END IF
    END LOOP
    Temp := List(I)
    List(I) := List(Place)
    List(Place) := Temp
END LOOP
```

BASIC

```
10  FOR I = 1 TO N-1
20      M = L(I)
30      P = I
40      FOR J = I+1 TO N
50          IF (L(J) < M) THEN P = J : M = L(J)
60      NEXT J
70      T = L(I)
80      L(I) = L(P)
90      L(P) = T
100 NEXT I
```

Pascal

```
FOR I := 1 TO N-1 DO
    BEGIN
        Min := List[I];
        Place := I;
        FOR J := I+1 TO N DO
            IF List[J] < Min THEN
                BEGIN
                    Place := J;
                    Min := List[J];
                END;
        Temp := List[I];
        List[I] := List[Place];
        List[Place] := Temp;
    END;
```

FORTRAN

```
          DO 25 I = 1, N-1
              Min = List(I)
              Place = I
              DO 24 J = I+1, N
                  IF (List(J) .ge. Min) GO TO 24
                  Place = J
                  Min = List(J)
24            CONTINUE
              Temp = List(I)
              List(I) = List(Place)
              List(Place) = Temp
25
```

C

```
for (i=1;i<n-1;++i) {
   min = list[i];
   place = i;
   for (j+=i;j<=n;++j)
      if (list[j] < min) {
         place = i;
         min = list[j];
      }
   temp := list[i];
   list[i] := list[j];
   list[j] := temp;
}
```

Ada

```
FOR I IN 1..N-1 LOOP
   Min := List(I);
   Place := I;
   FOR J IN I+1..N LOOP
      IF List(J) < Min THEN
         Place := J;
         Min := List(J);
      END IF;
   END LOOP;
   Temp := List(I);
   List(I) := List(Place);
   List(Place) := Temp;
END LOOP;
```

Assembly Language

```
; AX : (1) contains PLACE
;    : (2) used as TEMP during swap
; BX points to LIST beginning
; CX contains COUNT - initialized to the number
;                      of elements - 1
; DX : (1) contains MIN
;    : (2) used as a TEMP during swap
; DI contains current base (I)
; SI contains current position (J)
; N contains number of BYTES in word array LIST
;
;
         LEA BX,List
         MOV CX,N/2-1          ; COUNT = #elements - 1
         MOV Count,CX          ; save count
         MOV DI,0              ; loop for I := 0 to #elements - 2
Loop1:   MOV DX,[BX][DI]       ; MIN := LIST[0]
         MOV AX,DI             ; PLACE := I
         MOV SI,DI
         ADD SI,2              ; loop for J := I + 1 (word)
Loop2:   CMP [BX][SI],DX       ; if LIST[J] < MIN
         JGE After
         MOV AX,SI             ;    PLACE := J
         MOV DX,[BX][SI]       ;    MIN := LIST[J]
After:   ADD SI,2              ;   (for WORD elements)
         LOOP Loop2            ; end loop
         MOV SI,AX             ; SI <--- PLACE
;
         MOV AX,[BX][DI]       ; swap
         MOV DX,[BX][SI]       ; LIST[I]
         MOV [BX][DI],DX       ; with
         MOV [BX][SI],AX       ; LIST[PLACE]
;
         DEC Count             ; decrement count
         MOV CX,Count
         ADD DI,2
         CMP DI,N-2
         JL  Loop1             ; end loop
```

The complete program is shown in Figure 6-3 for the list 5, 4, 13, 2, 11, 0.

6.5 Summary

In this chapter we have shown how many of the common programming constructs from high-level languages may be implemented in assembly language. Constructs such as assignment statements translate easily into assembly language, although it takes more statements to implement them.

Figure 6-3 Sorting a list

```
;  Sort.
;
; Two necessary bookkeeping statements follow
;.
    DOSSEG            ; Use Microsoft SEGment conventions
    .MODEL  SMALL     ; Use small memory model
;
; Stack Segment follows
;
    .STACK  100H
;
; Data Segment follows
;
    .DATA
List    DW  5,4,13,2,11,0
N = $-List
Count   DW  ?
MIN     DW  ?
;
; Code Segment follows
;
    .CODE
;
; Two more necessary bookkeeping statements follow
;
Start:  MOV AX,@DATA     ; Define current
        MOV DS,AX        ; Data Segment
;
; Main Program
;
; AX : (1) contains PLACE
;    : (2) used as TEMP during swap
; BX points to LIST beginning
; CX contains COUNT - initialized to the number
;                     of elements - 1
; DX : (1) contains MIN
;    : (2) used as a TEMP during swap
; DI contains current base (I)
; SI contains current position (J)
; N contains number of BYTES in word array LIST
;
;
        LEA BX,List
        MOV CX,N/2-1        ; COUNT = #elements - 1
        MOV Count,CX        ; save count
        MOV DI,0            ; loop for I := 0 to #elements - 2
Loop1:  MOV DX,[BX][DI]     ; MIN := LIST[0]
        MOV AX,DI           ; PLACE := I
        MOV SI,DI
        ADD SI,2            ; loop for J := I + 1 (word)
```

Figure 6-3 (*Continued*)

```
Loop2:    CMP [BX][SI],DX       ; if LIST[J] < MIN
          JGE After
          MOV AX,SI             ;     PLACE := J
          MOV DX,[BX][SI]       ;     MIN := LIST[J]
After:    ADD SI,2              ;   (for WORD elements)
          LOOP Loop2            ; end loop
          MOV SI,AX             ; SI <--- PLACE
          MOV [BX][DI],DX       ; with
          MOV [BX][SI],AX       ; LIST[PLACE]
;
          DEC Count             ; decrement count
          MOV CX,Count
          ADD DI,2
          CMP DI,N-2
          JL  Loop1             ; end loop
;
          MOV AH,4CH
          INT 21H               ; Back to DOS
;
          END Start             ; End of program.   Start is transfer address
```

The implementation of most assignment statements involving variables will begin and end with a MOV: the first MOV for one of the variables on the right; the last MOV or pair of MOV's for the variable on the left. In between these two MOV's will be (at least) one instruction for every operation performed in the assignment statement.

Some control statements, such as GOTO's, implement quite naturally into assembly language (via JMP). Others, such as IF-THEN and IF-THEN-ELSE statements, do not translate in a straightforward way. The programmer often must think in convoluted ways to code these statements into assembly language. Thus

```
IF Condition
THEN Statements
ELSE Other Statements
```

is often coded using reverse logic:

```
IF  NOT  Condition
THEN
        Other Statements
        (go around ELSE)
ELSE
        Statements
```

If there is no ELSE clause, then *Other Statements* will be null. Traditionally, loops have been coded using JMP-type instructions. Many modern architectures, including the 86-family, have included loop logic; hence the assembly language has at least one loop instruction. The 86-family assembly language has an instruction LOOP and two variants, LOOPE and LOOPNE, which essentially allow implementation of FOR loops (DO loops in FORTRAN). Implementation of WHILE loops is not as straightforward and suffers from some of the same problems as the IF-THEN-ELSE statement. Thus

```
WHILE Condition DO
      Statements
```

often must be interpreted as

```
IF NOT Condition
   THEN go around ELSE
   ELSE
       Statements
       Go back to IF
```

This is the logic used in the implementation of the WHILE loop in Example 7.

With practice, these assembly language interpretations of high-level constructs will become easy to code. Programming is not a spectator sport. Competence requires practice!

Exercises

1. Find at least two ways other than those shown in the text to code:
   a. `IF new > max`
      `THEN max := new`
   b. `IF new > max`
      `THEN max := a`
      `ELSE max := b`

2. The Pascal statement

```
        CASE control of
1:          a := 10;
2,3,4:      a := 100;
OTHERWISE a := 0
END;
```

   evaluates the variable *Control*. If the value is 1, then "*A := 10*" is executed; if *Control* = 2 or 3 or 4, then the statement "*A := 100*" is executed. If it is none of these, the statement "*A := 0*" is executed. Code this into assembly language.

3. Recode the program of Example 6 using a LOOPNE instruction instead of JMP. (Hint: The sum of the first N integers is greater than N, so a loop from 1 to N may be used.)

4. Extend Example 7 to find the maximum of an arbitrary length list of positive, negative, and zero integers.

5. The following algorithm represents another way of sorting, called a *BubbleSort*. Add your own data segment, code this into assembly language, and execute it.

```
loop for i := 1 to n-1
  loop for j := 1 to n-1
    if list_j > list_{j+1} then
       temp := list_j
       list_j := list_{j+1}
       list_{j+1} := temp
    end if
  end loop
end loop
```

6. Although the *BubbleSort* of Exercise 5 is "quick to program," it executes very slowly. In Chapter 8 (Exercise 10), we will discuss another, more rapid way of sorting, called *QuickSort*, which—although harder to program—executes much more rapidly, on the average. (Its worst case, however, is as slow as the *BubbleSort*.) For now, make the following (minor) improvements to *BubbleSort*.

   a. Initialize a Boolean variable called *Change* to False, and change its value to True only if a change takes place during an iteration of the outer loop:

```
change := true
i := 1
loop while change and i <= n-1
  change := false
  loop for j := 1 to n-1
    if list_j > list_{j+1} then
       temp := list_j
       list_j := list_{j+1}
       list_{j+1} := temp
       change := true
    end if
  end loop
end loop
```

   b. If the end of the list is already in order, the inner loop continues to check anyway. Change the Boolean in (a) to an integer that records *where* the last interchange took place so that the inner loop can stop when it gets that far.

7. Write an assembly language program to search through a list and store the address of the first occurrence of a key in a location called *Loc*. Use your own list and key to test the program.

8. Same as Exercise 6, but assume the list is in (ascending) order. Thus there is no need to search the entire list; the program can stop when (a) the key is found or (b) when an element larger than the key is encountered.

9. Same as Exercise 7, but initiate the search in the middle of the list. If the element in the middle is not the key, then check to see if the key is smaller or larger than this middle element. If the key is smaller, go to the middle of the first half of the list. If it is larger, go to the middle of the second half of the list. Again, check this new

middle element to see if it is the key. Continue checking and halving until either the key is found or all elements have been checked (this is somewhat tricky). This is called a *binary search,* and the algorithm for it can be found in most data structure texts.

10. Keeping a list in order is different from putting it in order to begin with. Declare a list of 100 words whose first 10 elements are 2, 5, 8, 14, 33, 45, 46, 66, 72, 99. Add the element 50 to this list by finding its proper position.

11. Similar to Exercise 9, but delete the 46.

12. Sorting names is trickier than sorting numbers. Using the names of 10 friends, write a program to sort them into alphabetical order. Assume the names are in the following form:

Last First Middle-Initial

with one space between the last and first names, and one space between the first name and middle initial. (Hint: Space is less than any alphabetic character in ASCII.) Assume each name is contained in a doubleword (cut off names that are longer).

7

Introduction to Macros

7.0 Introduction

The 86-family instruction set is extensive. We can code into assembly language any algorithm that we can code in a high-level language. There are times, however, when a sequence of the same instructions is coded so frequently that we may wish there were a single instruction to perform that sequence. For example, suppose we are writing a program that needs the absolute value of various arguments throughout the program. We may find ourselves wishing we could say:

```
        ABS     AX      ; AX := |AX|
```
or
```
        ABS     Result  ; Result := |Result|
```
But since there is no such instruction, we code:
```
        CMP     AX,0
        JGE     Pos
        NEG     AX
Pos:
```
or
```
        CMP     Result,0
        JGE     Pos1
        NEG     Result
Pos1:
```

Each time we want to take the absolute value, we code the same sequence of instructions, being careful to use unique labels.

There is, however, a feature in most assembly languages that allows the programmer to "invent," or create, such instructions. This feature is called a *macro*.

7.1 Defining and Using Macros

Macros are used in assembly languages to replace sequences of code with one instruction. This is done so the programmer does not have to code the same operations over and over. It increases the readability of a program by replacing a relatively mysterious sequence of code with a mnemonic name.

7.1.1 Defining a Macro

The format for a MASM macro definition is:

```
MacroName MACRO    ParameterList
          Body of Macro
     ENDM     MacroName
```

where *MacroName* is any user-defined name, *ParameterList* is a list of formal parameters that are also user-defined names, and *Body of Macro* is the assembly language instructions that *MacroName* is to represent. *ParameterList* may be empty; if nonempty, and if there is more than one parameter, they may be separated by spaces, tabs, or commas.

EXAMPLE 1

```
Abs        MACRO     X
           LOCAL     Pos
           CMP       X,0
           JGE       Pos
           NEG       X
Pos:       NOP
           ENDM      Abs
```

In Example 1, *MacroName* is *Abs*. There is one element in *ParameterList: X*. The LOCAL assembler directive (described in Section 7.1.2) immediately follows the macro definition. It lists labels to be used within the macro.

7.1.2 Using a Macro

The format to call (i.e., use) a macro is

```
MacroName         ArgumentList
```

where *MacroName* is the same name as in the macro definition, and *ArgumentList* contains the names to be substituted for the formal parameters in the macro. The values of the arguments are not substituted; rather, the argument names themselves are substituted. A macro call is executed during assembly. The assembler replaces each macro call with its definition. This is called *macro expansion*.

EXAMPLE 2

```
ABS        AX         ; AX := |AX|
...
ABS        Result     ' Result := |Result|
```

will be expanded to

```
           ABS        AX
+          CMP        AX,0
+          JGE        ??0000
+          NEG        AX
```

```
+??0000:NOP

            ABS     Result
+           CMP     Result,0
+           JGE     ??0001
+           NEG     Result
+ ??0001:NOP
```

```
LOCAL
```

In Example 2, the label *Pos,* from Example 1, was replaced by local labels each time the macro was invoked to prevent the label from being multiply defined. This is the purpose of the Local assembler directive shown in Example 1. Local, if it is used, must immediately follow the MACRO statement—not even comments can intervene.

Figure 7-1a shows a complete program containing the *Abs* macro. Although macros may be defined anytime before they are used, it is usual to place all macro definitions at the beginning of a program.

Figure 7-1b shows this same program after it has been assembled.

Why Use a Macro? As can be seen from Figure 7-1, macros do not save storage space; every time the macro is used, it is replaced by the statements in its definition. Macros do, however, save "programmer space"; that is, they allow the programmer to write fewer lines of code. In addition, as stated earlier, macros can make assembly language programs more readable by replacing mysterious sequences of code with a mnemonic name, e.g., *Abs*. We also can keep frequently used macros in a file called a library and tell the assembler to include them.

Include. To include macros that reside in an external file, use the following statement:

```
INCLUDE FileName
```

where *FileName* is the name of a file containing only macro definitions. It is best to put the INCLUDE statement at the beginning of the program.

EXAMPLE 3

```
INCLUDE Arith.MLB
```

where *Arith.MLB* is the name of a file containing the desired macros. Such a file must be created with the desired macros prior to assembly of a program that INCLUDEs it.

Figure 7-1a The *Abs* macro

```
       .SALL
       ;
       ; X := abs(X)
       ;
Abs         MACRO    X
            LOCAL    Pos
            CMP      X,0
            JGE      Pos
            NEG      X
Pos:        NOP
            ENDM     Abs
       ;
       ; Two necessary bookkeeping statements follow
       ;
           DOSSEG              ; Use Microsoft SEGment conventions
           .MODEL   SMALL      ; Use small memory model
       ;
       ; Stack Segment follows
       ;
           .STACK   100H
       ;
       ; Code Segment follows
       ;
            .CODE
       ;
       ; Two more necessary bookkeeping statements follow
       ;
Start:     MOV AX,@DATA        ; Define current
           MOV DS,AX           ; Data Segment
       ;
       ; Main Program
       ;
           MOV AX,4
           Abs AX
           MOV BX,-4
           Abs BX
       ;
           MOV AH,4CH
           INT 21H             ; Back to DOS
       ;
           END Start           ; End of program.  Start is transfer address
```

Figure 7-1b The *Abs* macro after assembly

```
;
; X := |x|
;
                        Abs     MACRO   X
                                LOCAL   Pos
                                CMP     X,0
                                JGE     Pos
                                NEG     X
                        Pos:    NOP
                                ENDM    Abs
;
; Two necessary bookkeeping statements follow
;
                                DOSSEG       ; Use Microsoft SEGment conventions
                                .MODEL  Small    ; Use small memory model
;
; Stack Segment follows
;
                                .STACK  100H
;
; Code Segment follows
;
                                .CODE
;
; Two more necessary bookkeeping statements follow
;
 0000  B8 ---- R      Start:    MOV AX,@Data    ; Define current
 0003  8E D8                    MOV DS,AX       ; Data Segment
;
; Main Program
;
 0005  B8 0004                  MOV  AX,4
                                Abs  AX
 0008  3D 0000    1             CMP  AX,0
 000B  7D 02      1             JGE  ??0000
 000D  F7 D8      1             NEG  AX
 000F  90         1   ??0000:   NOP
 0010  BB FFFC                  MOV  BX,-4
                                Abs  BX
 0013  83 FB 00   1             CMP  BX,0
 0016  7D 02      1             JGE  ??0001
 0018  F7 DB      1             NEG  BX
 001A  90         1   ??0001:   NOP
;
 001B  B4 4C                    MOV AH,4CH
 001D  CD 21                    INT 21H         ; Back to DOS
;
                                END Start       ; End of program.
                                                ; Start is transfer address
```

7.1.3 Using a Macro to Calculate $A * B + C$

We can write a macro that calculates $A * B + C$ and then call it from our main program:

```
Calc      MACRO     A,B,C,Result
          MOV       AX,A
          MOV       CX,B

          IMUL      CX

          ADD       AX,C
          MOV       Result,AX
          MOV       Result+2,DX
          ENDM      Calc
```

(Strictly speaking, we should add the instruction ''ADC DX,0'' following the ''ADD AX,C.'')

Figure 7-2a shows this program before assembly, and Figure 7-2b shows this same program after assembly.

It is important to note that the macro in Figure 7-2 changed registers AX, CX, and DX. If the listing does not show the full macro expansion, the programmer may not notice and may use these registers inappropriately.

7.1.4 Sorting

In the sorting program of Chapter 6, we swap $List_{place}$ with $List_i$. The program becomes easier to read with a swap macro.

```
Swap      MACRO     X,Y
          MOV       AX,X
          MOV       DX,Y
          MOV       X,DX
          MOV       Y,AX
          ENDM      Swap
```

Notice that it is necessary to have four assembly language instructions to swap, rather than the traditional three needed by high-level languages. This is because one of the operands of a MOV must be a register. (Of course we could have used XCHG.)

Figures 7-3a and 7-3b show the complete program before and after assembly.

Figure 7-2a Macro to calculate $A * B + C$

```
;  This program uses a macro to calculate A * B + C.
;
Calc    MACRO   A,B,C,Result
        MOV     AX,A
        MOV     CX,B
        MUL     CX
        ADD     AX,C
        MOV     Result,AX
        MOV     Result+2,DX
        ENDM    Calc
;
; Two necessary bookkeeping statements follow
;
    DOSSEG              ; Use Microsoft SEGment conventions
    .MODEL  SMALL       ; Use small memory model
;
; Stack Segment follows
;
    .STACK  100H
;
; Data Segment follows
;
    .DATA
;
Product1    DW  ?
Product2    DW  ?
            DW  ?
;
; Code Segment follows
;
    .CODE
;
; Two more necessary bookkeeping statements follow
;
Start:  MOV AX,@DATA    ; Define current
        MOV DS,AX       ; Data Segment
;
; Main Program
;
        Calc    2,3,4,Product1
        Calc    2000,3000,4000,Product2
;
        MOV AH,4CH
        INT 21H         ; Back to DOS
;
        END Start       ; End of program.  Start is transfer address
```

Figure 7-2b Macro to calculate $A * B + C$ after assembly

```
Microsoft (R) Macro Assembler Version 5.10              12/5/90 22:00:36
                                                        Page    1-1


;   This program uses a macro to calculate A * B+ C.
;
                    Calc    MACRO    A,B,C,Result
                            MOV      AX,A
                            MOV      CX,B
                            MUL      CX
                            ADD      AX,C
                            MOV      Result,AX
                            MOV      Result+2,Dx
                            ENDM     Calc
;
; Two necessary bookkeeping statements follow
;
                            DOSSEG            ; Use Microsoft SEGment conventions
                            .MODEL   Small    ; Use small memory model
;
; Stack Segment follows
;
                            .STACK   100H
;
; Data Segment follows
;
                            .DATA
;
 0000   0000    Product1    DW  ?
 0002   0000    Product2    DW  ?
 0004   0000                DW  ?
 ;
 ; Code Segment follows
 ;
                            .CODE
 ;
 ; Two more necessary bookkeeping statements follow
 ;
 0000   B8 ---- R  Start:   MOV AX,@Data      ; Define current
 0003   8E D8              MOV DS,AX          ; Data Segment
 ;
 ; Main Program
 ;
                            Calc    2,3,4,product1
 0005   B8 000    1         MOV     AX,2
 0008   B9 0003   1         MOV     CX,3
 000B   F7 E1     1         MUL     CX
 000D   05 0004   1         ADD     AX,4
 0010   A3 0000 R 1         MOV     Product1,AX
 0013   89 16 0002 R 1      MOV     Product1+2,DX
                            Calc    2000,3000,4000,product2
 0017   B8 07D0   1         MOV     AX,2000
 001A   B9 0BB8   1         MOV     CX,3000
```

Figure 7-2b (*Continued*)

```
001D  F7 E1         1    MUL     CX
001F  05 0FA0       1    ADD     AX,4000
0022  A3 0002 R     1    MOV     Product2,AX
0025  89 16 0004 R 1     MOV     Product2+2,DX
;
0029  B4 4C              MOV AH,4CH
002B  CD 21              INT 21H          ; Back to DOS
;
                         END Start        ; End of program.
                                          ; Start is transfer address
```

Figure 7-3a *Swap* macro

```
         ;  This program uses a swap macro for a sort.
         ;
         Swap    MACRO    X,Y
                 MOV      AX,X
                 MOV      DX,Y
                 MOV      X,DX
                 MOV      Y,AX
                 ENDM     Swap
         ;
         ; Two necessary bookkeeping statements follow
         ;
             DOSSEG              ; Use Microsoft SEGment conventions
             .MODEL  SMALL       ; Use small memory model
         ;
         ; Stack Segment follows
         ;
             .STACK   100H
         ;
         ; Data Segment follows
         ;
             .DATA
         ;
         List    DW   5,4,13,2,11,0
         N = $-List
         Count   DW   ?
         Min     DW   ?
         ;
         ; Code Segment follows
         ;
             .CODE
         ;
         ; Two more necessary bookkeeping statements follow
         ;
         Start:  MOV  AX,@DATA   ; Define current
                 MOV  DS,AX      ; Data Segment
         ;
         ; Main Program
```

Figure 7-3a (*Continued*)

```
;
; AX : (1) contains PLACE
;     : (2) used as TEMP during swap
; BX points to LIST beginning
; CX contains COUNT - initialized to the number
;                     of elements - 1
; DX : (1) contains MIN
;     : (2) used as a TEMP during swap
; DI contains current base (I)
; SI contains current position (J)
; N contains number of BYTES in word array LIST
;
;
          LEA BX,List
          MOV CX,N/2-1          ; COUNT = #elements - 1
          MOV Count,CX          ; save count
          MOV DI,0              ; loop for I := 0 to #elements - 2
Loop1:    MOV DX,[BX][DI]       ; MIN := LIST[0]
          MOV AX,DI             ; PLACE := I
          MOV SI,DI
          ADD SI,2              ; loop for J := I + 1 (word)
Loop2:    CMP [BX][SI],DX       ; if LIST[J] < MIN
          JGE After
          MOV AX,SI             ;    PLACE := J
          MOV DX,[BX][SI]       ;    MIN := LIST[J]
After:    ADD SI,2              ;    (for WORD elements)
          LOOP Loop2            ; end loop
          MOV SI,AX             ; SI <--- PLACE
;
          Swap    [BX][DI],[BX][SI]   ; swap LIST[I]
                                      ; with LIST[PLACE]
;
          DEC Count            ; decrement count
          MOV CX,Count
          ADD DI,2
          CMP DI,N-2
          JL  Loop1            ; end loop
;
          MOV AH,4CH
          INT 21H            ; Back to DOS
;
          END Start          ; End of program.  Start is transfer address
```

Figure 7-3b *Swap* macro after assembly

```
Microsoft (R) Macro Assembler Version 5.00              9/17/92 17:00:57
                                                        Page     1-1


                              SWAP      MACRO     X,Y
                                        MOV       AX,X
                                        MOV       DX,Y
                                        MOV       X,DX
                                        MOV       Y,AX
                                        ENDM      SWAP


                              DOSSEG
                              .MODEL SMALL
        0100                  .STACK 100H

        0000                  .DATA
        0000  0005 0004 000D 0002  LIST DW        5,4,13,2,11,0
              000B 0000
        = 000C                N=$-LIST
        000C  ????            COUNT     DW        ?
        000E  ????            MIN       DW        ?

        0000                  .CODE
        0000  B8 ---- R       START:    MOV       AX,@DATA
        0003  8E D8                     MOV       DS,AX
        0005  8D 1E 0000 R              LEA       BX,LIST
        0009  B9 0005                   MOV       CX,N/2-1
        000C  89 0E 000C R              MOV       COUNT,CX
        0010  BF 0000                   MOV       DI,0
        0013  8B 11           LOOP1:    MOV       DX,[BX][DI]
        0015  8B C7                     MOV       AX,DI
        0017  8B F7                     MOV       SI,DI
        0019  83 C6 02                  ADD       SI,2
        001C  39 10           LOOP2:    CMP       [BX][SI],DX
        001E  7D 04                     JGE       AFTER
        0020  8B C6                     MOV       AX,SI
        0022  8B 10                     MOV       DX,[BX][SI]
        0024  83 C6 02        AFTER:    ADD       SI,2
        0027  E2 F3                     LOOP      LOOP2
        0029  8B F0                     MOV       SI,AX
                                        SWAP      [BX][DI],[BX][SI]
        002B  8B 01         1           MOV       AX,[BX][DI]
        002D  8B 10         1           MOV       DX,[BX][SI]
        002F  89 11         1           MOV       [BX][DI],DX
        0031  89 00         1           MOV       [BX][SI],AX
        0033  8B 01                     MOV       AX,[BX][DI]
        0035  8B 10                     MOV       DX,[BX][SI]
        0037  89 11                     MOV       [BX][DI],DX
        0039  89 00                     MOV       [BX][SI],AX
        003B  FF 0E 000C R              DEC       COUNT
        003F  8B 0E 000C R              MOV       CX,COUNT
        0043  83 C7 02                  ADD       DI,2
        0046  83 FF 0A                  CMP       DI,N-2
        0049  7C C8                     JL        LOOP1
        004B  B4 4C                     MOV       AH,4CH
        004D  CD 21                     INT       21H
        004F                            END       START
```

7.1.5 Searching

We will implement the entire search-and-count operation from Figure 6-2 as a macro called *SrchCnt*. To illustrate that macros do not have to be at the beginning, we have put the macro just before it is used, but this is not necessarily good practice. Figures 7-4a and 7-4b show the listings before and after assembly.

Figure 7-4a *SrchCnt* macro

```
;   This program uses a macro to search a list.
;
;  Two necessary bookkeeping statements follow
;
     DOSSEG             ; Use Microsoft SEGment conventions
     .MODEL   SMALL     ; Use small memory model
;
;  Stack Segment follows
;
     .STACK   100H
;
;  Data Segment follows
;
     .DATA
;
Array    DW  5,4,13,2,11,13
Answer   DW  ?
;
;  Code Segment follows
;
     .CODE
;
;  Two more necessary bookkeeping statements follow
;
Start:   MOV AX,@DATA       ; Define current
         MOV DS,AX          ; Data Segment
;
;  Define macro
;
SrchCnt MACRO     List,N,Key,Count
        LOCAL     Loop3,After,Fini
;
;  DX contains KEY
;  CX contains COUNT
;  DI contains current LIST offset
;  BX points to beginning of LIST
;  N contains length of LIST in bytes
;
         MOV      DX,Key
         MOV      CX,0       ; COUNT := 0
         MOV      DI,0       ; I := 0
         LEA      BX,List    ; get LIST address
```

Figure 7-4a (*Continued*)

```
        Loop3:  Cmp     DI,N            ; loop for I := 1 to N
                JE      Fini
                CMP     [BX][DI],DX     ; if LIST[I] = KEY
                JNE     After
                INC     CX              ; then increment COUNT
        After:  ADD     DI,2
                JMP     Loop3           ; end loop
        Fini:   MOV     Count,CX
                ENDM    SrchCnt
        ;
        ; Main program
        ;
                SrchCnt Array,12,13,Answer  ; put the number of
                                            ; 13's contained in
                                            ; ARRAY's 6 elements
                                            ; into ANSWER
        ;
                MOV AH,4CH
                INT 21H                 ; Back to DOS
        ;
                END Start               ; End of program.  Start is transfer address
```

Figure 7-4b *SrchCnt* macro after assembly

```
;   This program uses a macro to search a list.
;
; Two necessary bookkeeping statements follow
;
                        DOSSEG          ; Use Microsoft SEGment conventions
                        .MODEL  Small   ; Use small memory model
;
; Stack Segment follows
;
                        .STACK  100H
; Data Segment follows
;
                        .DATA
;
 0000   0005 0004 000D 0002 Array   DW  5,4,13,2,11,13
        000B 000D
 000C   0000                Answer  DW  ?
;
; Code Segment follows
;
                        .CODE
;
; Two more necessary bookkeeping statements follow
;
```

Figure 7-4b (*Continued*)

```
0000  B8 ---- R    Start:  MOV   AX,@Data      ; Define current
0003  8E D8                MOV   DS,AX         ; Data Segment
;
; Define macro
;
                   SrchCnt MACRO  List,N,Key,Count
                           LOCAL  Loop3,After,fini
;
; DX contains KEY
; CX contains Count
; DI contains current List offset
; BX points to beginning of List
; N contains length of List in bytes
;
                           MOV   DX,Key
                           MOV   CX,0          ; Count := 0
                           MOV   DI,0          ; I := 0
                           LEA   BX,List       ; get List address
                   Loop3:  CMP   DI,N          ; loop for I := 1 to N
                           JE    Fini
                           CMP   [BX][DI],DX   ; if List[I] = Key
                           JNE   After
                           INC   CX            ; then increment Count
                   After:  ADD   DI,2
                           JMP   Loop3         ; end loop
                   Fini:   MOV   Count,CX
                           ENDM  SrchCnt
;
; Main program
;
                           SrchCnt Array,12,13,Answer  ; put the number of
0005  BA 000D  1           MOV   DX,13
0008  B9 0000  1           MOV   CX,0          ; Count := 0
000B  BF 0000  1           MOV   DI,0          ; I := 0
000E  8D 1E 0000 R 1       LEA   BX,Array      ; get List address
0012  83 FF 0C  1  ??0000: CMP   DI,12         ; loop for I := 1 to N
0015  74 0A     1          JE    ??0002
0017  39 11     1          CMP   [BX][DI],DX   ; if List[I] = Key

0019  75 01     1          JNE   ??0001
001B  41        1          INC   CX            ; then increment Count
001C  83 C7 02  1  ??0001: ADD   DI,2
001F  EB F1     1          JMP   ??0000        ; end loop
0021  89 0E 000C R 1 ??0002: MOV     Answer,CX
                                                ; 13's contained in
                                                ; Array's 6 elements
                                                ; into Answer
;
0025  B4 4C                MOV AH,4CH
0027  CD 21                INT 21H             ; Back to DOS
;
                           END Start          ; End of program.
                                              ; Start is transfer address
```

Figure 7-4 shows a macro that might be better as a procedure (see Chapter 8) because (1) it is used only once, and (2) the code is fairly long. Macros are more useful as short sequences of code invoked many times.

7.1.6 Data Initialization

Macros are often used to allocate or initialize data. The following initializes *Count* words to zero, starting at location *Place*.

```
Alloc    MACRO    Count,Place
Place    DW       Count DUP (0)
         ENDM     Alloc
```

One use of this macro might be to allocate space for and initialize an array $Array_0$, $Array_1$, . . . $Array_{99}$:

```
Alloc          100,Array
```

Note that the macro *Alloc* can be called only once since its label *Place* does not occur in a LOCAL directive. The following directive might be used after this macro is called to ensure that it is not used again inadvertently.

PURGE.   The PURGE directive deletes the definition of a macro. Its form is

```
PURGE    MacroNames
```

where *MacroNames* is a list of (defined) macro names. It is possible to redefine a macro, although this is rarely good programming practice—it is usually considered ''wizardry'' since it requires a wizard to follow a program through that redefines its macros. It is not necessary to purge a macro before redefining it.

7.2   Macro Listing Directives

In the previous example, the assembly listing shows a source line only if it generates machine code. To include in the listing the complete macro text for all expansions, we must use the pseudo-op

```
.LALL
```

To suppress all text and object code of macro expansions in the listing, we use

```
.SALL
```

To include (again, after using .SALL or .LALL) the source line for all lines that generate object code, we use

```
.XALL
```

.XALL is the default, i.e., if neither .SALL nor .LALL is used, the assembler assumes .XALL is intended.

Figures 7-5a and 7-5b show the same program from Figure 7-1a, but with the addition of .LALL (Figure 7-5a) and .SALL (Figure 7-5b).

Figure 7-5a *Abs* macro with .LALL

```
                              .LALL
                              ;
                              ; x := abs(x)
                              ;
                              abs      macro   x
                                       local   pos
                                       cmp     x,0
                                       jge     pos
                                       neg     x
                              pos:     nop
                                       endm    abs
                              ;
                              ; Two necessary bookkeeping statements follow
                              ;
                                  DOSSEG            ; Use Microsoft SEGment con
                              ventions
                                  .MODEL  Small    ; Use small memory model
                              assume cs:@code,ds:@data,ss:@data
                              ;
                              ; Stack Segment follows
                              ;
                                  .STACK  100H
0000                          STACK segment 'STACK'
0100                          @CurSeg ends
                              ;
                              ; Code Segment follows
                              ;
                                  .CODE
0000                          _TEXT segment 'CODE'
                              ;
                              ; Two more necessary bookkeeping statements fol
                              low
                              ;
0000  B8 ---- R               Start:  MOV AX,@Data     ; Define current
0003  8E D8                           MOV DS,AX         ; Data Segment
                              ;
                              ; Main Program
                              ;
0005  B8 0004                         mov ax,4
                                      abs ax
0008  3D 0000         1                cmp     ax,0
000B  7D 02           1                jge     ??0000
000D  F7 D8           1                neg     ax
000F  90              1       ??0000:  nop
0010  BB FFFC                         mov bx,-4
                                      abs bx
0013  83 FB 00        1                cmp     bx,0
0016  7D 02           1                jge     ??0001
0018  F7 DB           1                neg     bx
001A  90              1       ??0001:  nop
                              ;
001B  B4 4C                           MOV AH,4CH
001D  CD 21                           INT 21H            ; Back to DOS
                              ;
                                      END Start          ; End of program.  Star
                              t is transfer address
001F                          @CurSeg ends
```

7.3   **Special Macro Operators**

MASM contains four special operators for making macro use more flexible. These operators are:

$$\& \quad ! \quad \% \quad ;;$$

7.3.1 Ampersand—&

The ampersand operator (&) is used within a macro definition. During assembly, when the macro is expanded, it acts as a concatenation operator. (Microsoft calls it the *substitution* operator.)

EXAMPLE 4

```
Alloc       MACRO     Number,Place
Place&Number    DW    Number DUP (0)
            ENDM      Alloc

;
            .DATA
;

            Alloc     100,Array
```

will expand to

```
        .
        .
        .
;

            .DATA
            Alloc     100,Array
+Array100   DW        100 DUP (0)
```

The concatenation operator is also needed to insert into a quoted string:

EXAMPLE 5

```
Alloc       MACRO     Number,Place,InitVal
Place       DW        Number DUP ("&InitVal")
            ENDM      Alloc
            . . .
            .DATA
            Alloc     100,Array,0
```

Figure 7-5b *Abs* macro with .SALL

```
                            .SALL
                            ;
                            ; x := abs(x)
                            ;
                            abs       macro   x
                                      local   pos
                                      cmp     x,0
                                      jge     pos
                                      neg     x
                            pos:      nop
                                      endm    abs
                            ;
                            ; Two necessary bookkeeping statements follow
                            ;
                                DOSSEG              ; Use Microsoft SEGment con
                            ventions
                                  .MODEL  Small   ; Use small memory model
                            ;
                            ; Stack Segment follows
                            ;
                                  .STACK  100H
                            ;
                            ; Code Segment follows
                            ;
                                  .CODE
                            ;
                            ; Two more necessary bookkeeping statements fol
                            low
                            ;
0000  B8 ---- R             Start:  MOV AX,@Data    ; Define current
0003  8E D8                         MOV DS,AX       ; Data Segment
                            ;
                            ; Main Program
                            ;
0005  B8 0004                       mov ax,4
                                    abs ax
0010  BB FFFC                       mov bx,-4
                                    abs bx
                            ;
001B  B4 4C                         MOV AH,4CH
001D  CD 21                         INT 21H         ; Back to DOS
                            ;
                                    END Start       ; End of program.  Star
                            t is transfer address
```

will expand to

```
                      .
                      .
                      .
                      .DATA
                      Alloc     100,Array,0
       + Array        DW        100 DUP ("0")
```

effectively initializing *Array* to the character 0 (30H) as opposed to the number 0 (0H).

7.3.2 Exclamation Point—!

Since macro expansion is essentially a string substitution, we need a way to tell the assembler that symbols normally having special meaning are to be interpreted literally. Suppose, for example, that we wish to create a character array of 100 semicolons:

The sequence from Example 5 will not work:

```
Alloc    MACRO    Number,Place,InitVal
Place    DW       Number DUP ("&InitVal")
         ENDM     Alloc
         ...
         .DATA
         ALLOC    100, Array,;
```

because the assembler will think the ";" is the beginning of a comment. The literal operator (!) prevents this.

EXAMPLE 6

```
Alloc    MACRO    Number,Place,InitVal
Place    DW       Number DUP ("&InitVal")
         ENDM     Alloc
         .
         .
         .
         .DATA
         Alloc    100,Array,!;
```

will expand to

```
         .DATA
Alloc    100,Array,!;
+Array   DW       100 DUP (";")
```

7.3.3 Percent—%

The percent operator (%) performs an operation opposite from "!". When assembler-defined symbols are used as arguments in macro calls, their values will not be used since a macro call causes a string substitution rather than an evaluation of arguments. In some cases, we may actually want the value. The operator "%" allows us to do this:

EXAMPLE 7

```
Alloc     MACRO     Number,Place
Place     DW        Number DUP (0)
          ENDM      Alloc
          ...
          .DATA
n = 100
          Alloc     %n,Array
```

will expand to

```
          .DATA
Alloc     %n,Array
+Array    DW 100 DUP (0)
```

7.3.4 Double Semicolon—;;

The double semicolon operator (;;) is used for comments that are to appear only in the source listing. They will not appear in the listing after assembly, even if the .LALL directive is used.

7.4 Summary

This chapter is an introduction to macros. There are other directives that are frequently used in conjunction with macros to control the code generated during assembly. We will discuss these directives in Chapter 11.

Macros save ''programmer space'' and time. They do not save storage space since each macro call is replaced by its definition during assembly. It is often useful to think of this macro expansion as a string substitution similar to that performed by various editing operations. The analogy is helpful and quite accurate.

Since macros may change the contents of registers, it is easy to make errors when using macros. You can help prevent this by including comments at the beginning of the macro that document which registers are to be changed, and fully listing the macro each time it is used. An even better technique is to save and restore the registers within the macro so that the programmer can use them safely.

We encourage the reader to create, maintain, and use macro libraries. They will save time when a new program uses an operation or procedure already used in another program.

═════ **Exercises**

1. What are the advantages of using macros in an assembly language program?
2. What two assembler directives define a macro?
3. What happens at assembly time to a macro call?
4. Change the *Abs* macro to return the absolute value of an argument without changing the value of the original argument.
5. Write a macro that swaps byte 1 with byte 2 in a word. Use it to swap the contents of AL and AH. Put something in them so you can see if your macro works.
6. In Section 4.2, we wrote a program that implemented a MOD operator. Write a macro called *Mod* that, given two arguments, returns the remainder when the first is divided by the second.
7. Show register contents and appropriate memory locations (if any) after executing

    `Calc 2000,3000,4000,BX`

    where *Calc* is the macro of Figure 7-2a or 7-2b.
8. a. Write a macro called *ECount* that searches a string (of up to 30 characters) and counts the number of occurrences of the letter *e*. (Hint: Remember that each ASCII character is stored in a byte.)
    b. Use this macro to store the number of *e*'s into AX. Use

    `String      DB    "There are a lot of e's here"`
    as data.
9. a. Write a macro called *ItoA* that converts a hexadecimal integer to its ASCII representation.
    b. Write a macro called *AtoI* that converts a string of digits in ASCII to a hexadecimal number.
10. Write a macro called *Dly1ms* that will generate a delay of one millisecond.
11. Write a macro called *LongDelay* that will generate a delay of one or more seconds.
12. Create a file of macros that do some common functions such as compute absolute value, clear a group of registers, exponentiation, and factorial. Write a program that incorporates (via INCLUDE) these macros and uses them.
13. The BASIC instruction

    `ON X GO TO LABEL1,LABEL2,LABEL3, ...`

    transfers processing to one of the listed labels, depending upon the value of *X*. For example, if *X* = 3, then processing goes to *LABEL3*. Implement a macro called *OnGoto* that has formal parameters *X* and address labels to which to transfer, depending upon the value of *X*.
14. Use the ampersand operator (&) to define a macro *Errors*, which expands as

    `Error# DB Message`

    where # and *Message* are arguments. For example, the macro might be called by

    `Error 3,<Too many characters>`

15. Write a macro called *Heading* that will insert your name and the date as comments into a program listing. For example,

```
;
; Programmer: Robert W. Roy
; Date: January 1, 1992
```

16. Expand the following macro:

```
Outer   MACRO   A,B
   Inner   MACRO   C,A

        MOV     AL,A
        MUL     C
        MOV     C,AX
     ENDM    Inner
     Inner   A,B
     MOV     AX,B
ENDM   Outer
     ...
     Outer Delta,Alpha
```

Stacks and Procedures

8.0 Introduction

A procedure in assembly language resembles a procedure (sometimes called a subroutine) in a high-level language: it consists of a sequence of instructions that may be "called" from various points outside the procedure. That is, there is a single sequence of code, but it may be executed repeatedly.

Procedures in assembly language require more explicit control by the programmer than required in high-level languages. When an executing program transfers control to a procedure, it must save information in order to return. In particular, it must save the value of the instruction pointer (IP) so that execution can proceed from where it left off. A part of memory called the *stack* temporarily stores this information. We will discuss stacks first.

8.1 Stacks

A stack is a pile or list of items that can be accessed one at a time and from only one end, usually called the *top*. Items are removed from the top and added to the top. Thus, another name for a stack is a last-in-first-out (LIFO) list. A dishwell in a cafeteria operates as a stack, with plates being added to and removed from the top of the pile.

A portion of each user's address space is allocated as a stack, which may be visualized as a consecutive sequence of 16-bit words, only one of which may be accessed at a time. Values are stored and removed from the word at the top of the stack. The stack segment register (SS) contains the address of the bottom of the stack, and SP (or sometimes BP) contains the offset (from SS) of the top word in the stack.

As words are added to the stack, the addresses *decrease*. Thus, if the top of the stack is at location 204 (of the stack segment), then the next available location is 202 since each element in the stack is a word (2 bytes). We write "SP →" to indicate that SP contains the address of (i.e., points to) the top of the stack. Similarly, "SS →" indicates that SS contains the address of the bottom of the stack. Remember that each stack entry contains a 16-bit word. In Figure 8-1, if *Top* is really location 204 of the stack segment, then *Top + 1* is location 206.

8.1.1 Adding and Removing Elements from the Top of the Stack

There are two basic operations on a stack:

1. PUSH: Decreases the stack pointer (SP) by 1 word (2 bytes); then stores a word on the stack. The format for a PUSH instruction is

   PUSH   *Operand*

   where

   > *Operand* is a register or memory address. The register can be any register except the flags register. In particular, it can be a segment register.

   > The word at *Operand* is copied onto the top of the stack.

2. POP: Removes the top word from the stack, then adds 1 word (2 bytes) to the stack pointer (SP). The format is as follows:

   POP   *Operand*

   where

   > *Operand* is a memory location or any register except CS or the Flags register.

Figure 8-1 Illustration of a stack

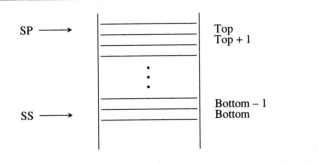

The word on the top of the stack is copied into *Operand*.

In addition, there are instructions for pushing and popping the Flags register:

    PUSHF

and

    POPF

In both cases, the stack word bits correspond to the corresponding bits in the flag register. Thus, POPF moves bit 11 to the OV position in the Flags register (see Chapter 2 for a description of the bits in the Flags register).

We divide the machine code for the various stack instructions into the categories PUSH, POP, PUSHF-POPF:

PUSH	
Instruction	Opcode
PUSH AX	50
PUSH CX	51
PUSH DX	52
PUSH BX	53
PUSH SP	54
PUSH BP	55
PUSH SI	56
PUSH DI	57
PUSH ES	06
PUSH CS	0E
PUSH SS	16
PUSH DS	17
PUSH Mem16	77*

* The register field of the addressing mode byte for Push Mem16 contains 110. (See Chapter 5.)

POP	
Instruction	Opcode
POP AX	58
POP CX	59
POP DX	5A
POP BX	5B
POP SP	5C
POP BP	5D
POP SI	5E
POP DI	5F
POP ES	07
POP SS	17
POP DS	1F
POP Mem16	8F*

* The register field for this instruction is 000.

PUSHF/POPF	
Instruction	Opcode
PUSHF	9C
POPF	9D

8.1.2 Reversing a List

In addition to being a convenient temporary storage area, the stack's last-in-first-out character allows information to be accessed in reverse order. The program in Figure 8-2 reverses the following list

```
Input DB "abcdefghijklmn"
```

and stores it in reverse order at the location whose name is *Output*.

8.2 Procedures

Procedures are used in assembly language for the same two reasons they are used in higher-level languages:

1. They save storage space by allowing a branch to a sequence of frequently used code.
2. They help to segment a program, making it easier to code, debug, and maintain.

Figure 8-2 Program to reverse a list

```
;   This program reverses a list.
;
; Two necessary bookkeeping statements follow
;
    DOSSEG              ; Use Microsoft SEGment conventions
    .MODEL   SMALL      ; Use small memory model
;
; Stack Segment follows
;
    .STACK   100H


;
; Data Segment follows
;
    .DATA
Input    DB   "abcdefghijklmn"
Count=$ - Input
Output   DB   Count    DUP(?)
;
; Code Segment follows
;
    .CODE
;
; Two more necessary bookkeeping statements follow
;
Start:  MOV AX,@DATA     ; Define current
        MOV DS,AX        ; Data Segment
;
; Main Program
;
        LEA     BX,Input
        MOV     SI,0
Loop1:  MOV     AX,0                         ; loop for I := 1 to Count
        MOV     AL,Byte ptr [BX][SI]
        PUSH    AX                           ;       push Input(i) onto stack
        INC     SI
        CMP     SI,Count
        JL      Loop1                        ; end loop
;
        LEA     BX,Output
        MOV     SI,0
Loop2:  POP     AX                           ; loop for I := 1 to Count
        MOV     Byte Ptr[BX][SI],AL
        INC     SI                           ;       pop stack into output(i)
        CMP     SI,Count
        JL      Loop2                        ; end loop
;
        MOV AH,4CH
        INT 21H          ; Back to DOS
;
        END Start        ; End of program.  Start is transfer address
```

Procedure calls involve two essential actions:

1. *Linkage:* Since the procedure may be called from different places in the program, the procedure must be able to access the correct address to which to return.
2. *Argument transmission:* The procedure must be able to access the values for its parameters (arguments).

8.2.1 Linkage

Although it is possible to JMP to a procedure and JMP back, the programmer would be responsible for all the linkage and argument transmission. There are two instructions that handle much of this overhead, one for transferring control to a procedure:

```
CALL
```

and one for transferring control back:

```
RET
```

CALL. CALL has one operand, which may be a label or an indirect reference to a register or memory location, where indirect means that the register or memory location contains the address of the procedure.

If the procedure is in the same segment, it is said to be NEAR and can be explicitly stated or omitted. For example,

```
CALL      Sort
```

and

```
CALL      NEAR      Sort
```

both execute identically and imply that procedure *Sort* is in the same segment.

To declare a procedure such as *Sort,* the NEAR directive may be attached or omitted:

```
Sort      PROC
...
```

and

```
Sort      PROC      NEAR
```

are identical.

If the procedure to be called is in another segment from the calling procedure, then again it is optional whether to include FAR as an attribute to the call:

```
CALL      FAR      Sort
```

and

```
    CALL    Sort
```

execute identically.

The procedure itself must have a FAR attribute to be called from another segment:

```
    Sort    PROC    FAR
```

When the CALL is executed, one of two events occurs, depending on whether the procedure is NEAR or FAR:

1. If the procedure is NEAR, then the contents of the IP are pushed onto the stack.
2. If the procedure is FAR, then the contents of CS are first pushed onto the stack, and then the contents of the IP are pushed onto the stack.

In both cases, IP is now replaced by the address of the procedure. If the procedure is NEAR, it resides within the current code segment. If it is FAR, the 86-family assumes that it is declared in another segment.

If the operand of CALL is a register or memory location, then it is assumed that the operand contains an address—the address of the procedure. Again, NEAR calls may be both explicit and implicit. Thus

```
    CALL    BX
```

or

```
    CALL    WORD PTR [BX]
```

perform the same action and require that BX contain the address within the current code segment of the procedure to be called.

To call a FAR procedure with a register or memory operand, the DWORD attribute must be used, e.g.,

```
    CALL    DWORD  PTR [BX]
```

Once again, NEAR procedures are assumed to be in the current code segment, and FAR procedures are assumed to be in another segment, perhaps the current data segment.

If BP is used to call the procedure, the address of the procedure is presumed to be on the stack; that is, the programmer should have PUSHed such an address onto the stack before the CALL using BP is executed.

Override Operator. The calling program presumes that the called program is either in the current code segment (for NEAR procedures) or declared in another segment (for FAR procedures). If no segment is specified, the 86-family presumes that the procedure is in the current data segment. If the procedure is in neither of these places, its segment address may be explicitly stated:

```
CALL    WORD    PTR    ES:[BX]
```

Here, the procedure is located in the extra segment (ES), and BX contains its address relative to ES.

The machine code for various versions of CALL are shown below:

Instruction	Opcode
CALL (NEAR) Mem16	DB
CALL (FAR) Mem16	9A
CALL (NEAR) Indirect	FF*
CALL (FAR) Indirect	FF**

*The register field is 011.
**The register field is 010.

RET.   RET undoes the actions performed by CALL:

1. If the procedure CALLed was NEAR, then the top word on the stack is popped into IP.
2. If the procedure CALLed was FAR, then the top word on the stack is popped into IP, and the next word is popped into CS.

RET can contain an operand that adds a specified immediate value to the stack after IP and (perhaps) CS have been restored. This is useful if other values have been pushed onto the stack by the procedure; it essentially restores the stack to its condition prior to the procedure call. If N values were PUSHed onto the stack, then an operand of $2*N$ in RET will restore the stack to its previous value.

Thus

```
RET    6
```

first pops the 1- or 2-word return address into IP and perhaps CS, and then adds 6 to the stack before returning to the calling procedure. If three 16-bit, i.e., word, arguments were passed to the procedure via the stack, then this will in essence pop them from the stack.

The machine code for RET depends, as does CALL, on whether the call was NEAR or FAR and on whether there is a value to be popped. There are three forms allowed: (1) RET and commencing with MASM Version 5.0, (2) RETN (Return NEAR), and (3) RETF (Return FAR).

Instruction	Opcode
RET (NEAR) or RETN	C3
RET (NEAR) or RETN *Imm*	C2
RET (FAR) or RETF	CB
RET (FAR) or RETF *Imm*	CA

8.2.2 Argument Transmission

There are three common ways for transmitting arguments to procedures:

1. Placing them in a register
2. Putting them on the stack
3. Putting their address into a register or onto the stack

We show the first two of these three methods for transmitting arguments in Figures 8-3a and 8-3b. The procedure *Calc* called in these two examples is exceedingly simple; it merely calculates the sum of two operands. More complicated (i.e., more useful) examples are shown in the remainder of this book and assigned in the exercises at the end of the chapter.

Figure 8-3b uses AX and BP in its calculations. We save their initial values by PUSHing them onto the stack when first entering the procedure, and restoring them via POPs when exiting from the procedure.

The procedures in Figure 8-3 explicitly describe with comments how the procedure expects its arguments to be transmitted. This is good programming technique and allows the programmer to write the correct sequence of code to call the procedure. It is also useful when using the same procedure in different programs; the programmer can either adapt to the procedure's argument transmission expectations or easily modify the procedure to expect different argument transmission. We will be modifying procedure *Calc* in Sections 8.2.3 and 8.3 to be able to CALL it from a separately assembled or compiled program.

8.2.3 Independent Assembly

We can assemble procedures and main programs separately if we obey some extra rules. Such separate assembly is called *independent assembly,* and we will need two new assembler directives to accomplish it. Let us assume that we are going to assemble procedure *Calc* and a program that calls it separately. Figure 8-4 shows procedure *Calc* before we have fixed it so it can be assembled independently.

Figure 8-3a Procedure to calculate a sum

```
;   This program uses a procedure to calculate a sum.
;
; Two necessary bookkeeping statements follow
;
    DOSSEG              ; Use Microsoft SEGment conventions
    .MODEL  SMALL       ; Use small memory model
;
; Stack Segment follows
;
    .STACK  100H
;
; Data Segment follows
;
    .DATA
;
A       DW  2
B       DW  3
Result  DW  ?
;
; Code Segment follows
;
    .CODE
;
; Two more necessary bookkeeping statements follow
;
Start:  MOV AX,@DATA     ; Define current
        MOV DS,AX        ; Data Segment
;
; Main Program
;
        MOV     AX,A     ; put A into AX
        MOV     BX,B     ; put B into BX
        CALL    Calc
        MOV     Result,Ax ; Store sum in RESULT
;
        MOV AH,4CH
        INT 21H          ; Back to DOS
;
Calc    PROC
;
; This procedure adds the contents of AX and BX
; returning the sum in AX.
;
        ADD AX,BX        ; Sum := AX + BX
        RET
Calc    ENDP
;
        END Start        ; End of program.  Start is transfer address
```

Figure 8-3b Procedure and stack to calculate a sum

```
;   This program uses a procedure and the stack to find Result := A + B.
;
; Two necessary bookkeeping statements follow
;
    DOSSEG              ; Use Microsoft SEGment conventions
    .MODEL  SMALL       ; Use small memory model
;
; Stack Segment follows
;
    .STACK  100H
;
; Data Segment follows
;
    .DATA
;
A       DW  2
B       DW  3
Result  DW  ?
;
; Code Segment follows
;
    .CODE
;
; Two more necessary bookkeeping statements follow
;
Start:  MOV AX,@DATA    ; Define current
        MOV DS,AX       ; Data Segment
;
; Main Program
;
        LEA     AX,Result
        PUSH    AX
        PUSH    B
        PUSH    A
        CALL    Calc
;
        MOV AH,4CH
        INT 21H             ; Back to DOS
;
Calc    PROC
;
; This procedure computes Result := A + B
; It presumes that the values of A and B and the
; address of Result are on the stack with Result's
; address pushed first; then B, then A.
;
        PUSH    AX          ; save AX
        PUSH    BP          ; save BP
        MOV     BP,SP       ; get args
        MOV     AX,6[BP]    ; get A
        ADD     AX,8[BP]    ; add B
        MOV     BP,10[BP]   ; get address of result
        MOV     [BP],AX     ; store in result
        POP     BP          ; restore BP
        POP     AX          ; restore AX
        RET     6           ; pop args off stack
;
Calc    ENDP
;
        END Start           ; End of program.  Start is transfer address
```

Figure 8-4 The procedure *Calc*

```
; This procedure computes Result := A + B
; It presumes that the values of A and B and the
; address of Result are on the stack with Result's
; address pushed first; then B, then A.
;
        DOSSEG
        .MODEL  Small
        .CODE
Calc    PROC    Near
        PUSH    AX              ; save AX
        PUSH    BP              ; save BP
        MOV     BP,SP           ; get args
        MOV     AX,6[BP]        ; get A
        ADD     AX,8[BP]        ; add B
        MOV     AX,10[BP]       ; get address of Result
        MOV     [BP],AX         ; store in Result
        POP     BP              ; restore BP
        POP     AX              ; restore AX
        RET     6               ; pop args off stack
;
Calc    ENDP
        END
```

PUBLIC and EXTRN. *Calc* must be altered in order to be known to the linker. First, a statement must be added containing the PUBLIC assembler directive, which allows this procedure to be known (i.e., made PUBLIC) to other procedures. PUBLIC allows other procedures or programs *entry* into procedure *Calc*. It is of the form

        PUBLIC   *Name, Name,. . . ,Name*

where *Name* can be any variable name or label except those names defined by = or EQU. If there is more than one procedure or label to be made public, they are separated by commas.

Figure 8-5 shows procedure *Calc* made PUBLIC.

   Since our main program is going to call procedure *Calc*, we must tell the assembler not to worry when it sees a reference to this name. Otherwise the assembler will tell us that *Calc* is an undefined symbol. This is done with an EXTRN statement, which is of the form:

        EXTRN   *Name:Type, Name:Type, ... Name:Type*

where *Name* is a procedure name or label and *Type* is NEAR or FAR; or *Name* is a data name and *Type* is BYTE, WORD, DWORD, or the name defined by EQU.

Figure 8-5 *Calc* made PUBLIC

```
        DOSSEG
        .MODEL  SMALL
        PUBLIC  Calc   ; Allows Calc to be called from an external program
        .CODE

;
Calc    PROC
;
; This procedure computes Result := A + B
; It presumes that the values of A and B and the
; address of Result are on the stack with Result's
; address pushed first; then B, then A.
;
        PUSH    AX          ; save AX
        PUSH    BP          ; save BP
        MOV     BP,SP       ; get args
        MOV     AX,6[BP]    ; get A
        ADD     AX,8[BP]    ; add B
        MOV     BP,10[BP]   ; get address of result
        MOV     [BP],AX     ; store in result
        POP     BP          ; restore BP
        POP     AX          ; restore AX
        RET     6           ; pop args off stack
;
Calc    ENDP
;
        END
```

Figure 8-6 shows the changes to our main program that calls procedure *Calc*.

Assembling our assembly language main program and our assembly language procedure produces two object (.OBJ) modules. These object modules may be linked together, and then the resulting module—called the *execution* or *load* module—may be executed. Figure 8-7 shows these steps.

Figure 8-8 shows the actual commands to perform this sequence. We have stored our main assembly language program in the file FIG8-6.ASM and our procedure *Calc* in the file FIG8-5.ASM. We link FIG8-5.OBJ to FIG8-6.OBJ. The resulting file is called FIG8-6.EXE. We execute it using the debugger.

Stack Use.   When procedure *Calc* is called, it pushes the following onto the stack: *Result*'s address, then *B*'s value, then *A*'s value, and finally the contents of IP. CS is not pushed onto the stack since *Calc* is a NEAR procedure. The first actions performed by *Calc* are to PUSH the current values of AX and BP since the procedure is going to use these registers and we want to save their values.

Figure 8-6 Changes to main program that calls *Calc*

```
;
; Two necessary bookkeeping statements follow
;
    DOSSEG            ; Use Microsoft SEGment conventions
    .MODEL  SMALL     ; Use small memory model
;
; Stack Segment follows
;
    .STACK  100H
;
; Data Segment follows
;
    .DATA
;
A       DW   2
B       DW   3
Result  DW   ?
;
; Code Segment follows
;
    .CODE
    EXTRN    Calc:NEAR
;
; Two more necessary bookkeeping statements follow
;
Start:  MOV AX,@DATA      ; Define current
        MOV DS,AX         ; Data Segment
;
; Main Program
;
        LEA     AX,Result
        PUSH    AX
        PUSH    B
        PUSH    A
        CALL    Calc
;
        MOV AH,4CH
        INT 21H           ; Back to DOS
;
        END Start         ; End of program.  Start is transfer address
```

When we are done, we will POP them from the stack. After procedure *Calc* has executed the instructions

```
PUSH    AX
PUSH    BP
MOV     BP,SP
```

Figure 8-7 Execution of object modules

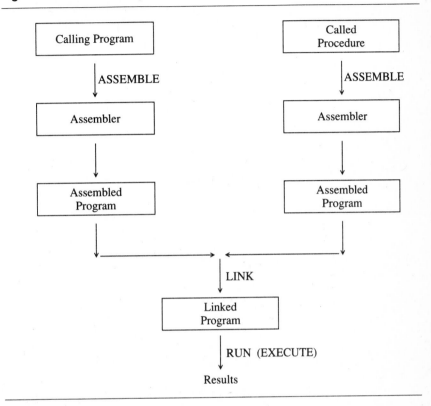

the stack is as follows:

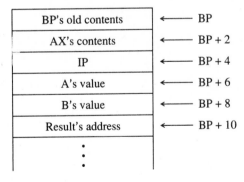

Thus, when we want to access *A*'s value we use 6[BP], and so on. When we execute

```
RET    6
```

Figure 8-8 Actual commands to perform sequence in Figure 8-7

```
C> masm/zi fig8-5
Microsoft (R) Macro Assembler Version 5.10
Copyright (C) Microsoft Corp. 1981, 1988. All rights reserved.
Object filename [FIG8-5.OBJ]:
Source Listing [NUL.LST]:
Cross reference [NUL.CRF]:
0 Warning Errors
0 Severe Errors

C> masm/zi fig8-6
Microsoft (R) Macro Assembler Version 5.10
Copyright (C) Microsoft Corp. 1981, 1988. All rights reserved.
Object filename [FIG8-6.OBJ]:
Source Listing [NUL.LST]:
Cross reference [NUL.CRF]:
0 Warning Errors
0 Severe Errors

C>link/co fig8-6+fig8-5
Microsoft (R) Overlay Linker Version 3.64
Copyright (C) Microsoft Corp. 1983 - 1988. All rights reserved.
Run File [FIG8-6.EXE]:
List File [NUL.MAP]:
Libraries [.LIB]

CV>
```

the RET instruction automatically POPs the stored IP value back into IP. The 6 operand will move SP past the three arguments, in effect, "popping" them from the stack.

8.3 Calling Assembly Language Procedures from High-Level Languages

In Chapter 1, we saw some reasons for using assembly language rather than machine language. Some of these reasons are:

1. Operations are mnemonic and easy-to-remember words such as MOV, rather than numeric opcodes such as $B8_{16}$ (or 10111000_2).
2. Addresses are symbolic names such as *Loop, Begin,* and *Result,* rather than absolutes such as $000D_{16}$ or 0000000000001101_2.

A similar, and probably longer, list could be made stating reasons for using high-level languages instead of low-level languages like assembly language. The reader realizes by now that assembly language is somewhat cumbersome. Constructs such as assignment statements, loops, and conditionals usually require more code than do their counterparts in a high-level language. Yet some actions can be performed only in assembly language (e.g., certain screen actions), and others can be performed faster, take up less space, or better manage machine parts such as memory or the I/O devices.

It is not always necessary to write the entire program in assembly language. It is possible to CALL procedures written in one language from procedures or programs written in another.

Consider procedure *Calc* from our previous examples. We will call *Calc* from BASIC, Pascal, FORTRAN, and C. In all the examples, except for C, *Calc* is called as a procedure. It could equally well be called as a function since it returns one value (see Exercise 13).

In the previous section, we saw that this procedure can be assembled separately and then linked to another assembled program. It can also be linked to a compiled program.

BASIC, however, passes *addresses* of its arguments rather than their *values*. Thus we must add code to access the values at these addresses. It is necessary to alter procedure *Calc* again.

Figure 8-9 shows this new version of procedure *Calc*.

Figure 8-9 New version of *Calc*

```
        DOSSEG
        .MODEL  SMALL
        .CODE
        PUBLIC  Calc
;
Calc    PROC FAR
;
; This procedure computes Result := A + B
; It presumes that the values of A and B and the
; address of Result are on the stack with Result's
; address pushed first; then B, then A.
;
        PUSH    AX          ; save AX
        PUSH    SI          ; save SI
        PUSH    BP          ; save BP
        MOV     BP,SP       ; get args
        MOV     SI,14[BP]   ; get A's address
        MOV     AX,[SI]     ; get A
        MOV     SI,12[BP]   ; get B's address
        ADD     AX,[SI]     ; add B
        MOV     BX,10[BP]   ; get address of Result
        MOV     [BX],AX     ; store in Result
        POP     BP          ; restore BP
        POP     SI          ; restore SI
        POP     AX          ; restore AX
        RET     6           ; pop args off stack
;
Calc    ENDP
        END
```

BASIC's CALL statement will push the arguments onto the stack before the call is made. Thus these arguments (three here) must be popped when the procedure returns to the main BASIC program.

There are many ways to execute an assembly language program from BASIC, none of them simple. One way is to assemble our procedure *Calc* and let BASIC "poke" the machine code into a safe location. To do this we need to know what the machine code is for our procedure. We can get it from the .LST file, the listing after assembly. Figure 8-10 shows the .LST file for Figure 8-9.

In Figure 8-10, we see that the 1st byte of machine code is "50" and the last 3 bytes are "CA," "06," and "00." [Remember that 0006 is stored with the

Figure 8-10 .LST file for Figure 8-9

```
Microsoft (R) Macro Assembler Version 5.10              7/10/92 20:05:07
                                                        Page    1-1


                                DOSSEG
                                .MODEL  SMALL
                                .CODE
                                PUBLIC  Calc
                                ;
 0000               Calc        PROC FAR
 ;
 ; This procedure computes Result := A + B
 ; It presumes that the values of A and B and the
 ; address of Result are on the stack with Result's
 ; address pushed first; then B, then A.
 ;
 0000  50                       PUSH    AX          ; save AX
 0001  56                       PUSH    SI          ; save SI
 0002  55                       PUSH    BP          ; save BP
 0003  8B EC                    MOV     BP,SP       ; get args
 0005  8B 76 0E                 MOV     SI,14[BP]   ; get A's address
 0008  8B 04                    MOV     AX,[SI]     ; get A
 000A  8B 76 0C                 MOV     SI,12[BP]   ; get B's address
 000D  03 04                    ADD     AX,[SI]     ; add B
 000F  8B 5E 0A                 MOV     BX,10[BP]   ; get address of Result
 0012  89 07                    MOV     [BX],AX     ; store in Result
 0014  5D                       POP     BP          ; restore BP
 0015  5E                       POP     SI          ; restore SI
 0016  58                       POP     AX          ; restore AX
 0017  CA 0006                  RET     6           ; pop args off stack
 ;
 001A              Calc         ENDP
                                END
```

Figure 8-11 BASIC program for *Calc*

```
Ok
list
10 DEFINT A-Z
20 DEF SEG=&H1700
30 FOR I = 0 TO 26
40 READ J
50 POKE I,J
60 NEXT
70 CALC = 0
80 PRINT "input A and B"
90 INPUT A,B
100 CALL CALC(A,B,RESULT)
110 PRINT RESULT
120 END
130 DATA &H50,&H56,&H55,&H8B,&HEC,&H8B,&H76,&H0E,&H8B,&H04
140 DATA &H8B,&H76,&H0C,&H03,&H04,&H8B,&H5E,&H0A,7H89
150 DATA &H07,&H5D,&H5E,&H58,&HCA,&H06,&H00
Ok
run
input A and B
? 2,3
 5
 Ok
```

least significant byte (06) before the most significant byte (00).] We put all the machine code into BASIC data statements and poke it into memory, starting at location 17000H (92K). This is a safe place in the author's system. Figure 8-11 shows this BASIC program, the commands for running it, and the actual results.

Figures 8-12 and 8-13 show *Calc* computed as a function (the value is returned in AX), and called from MS-Quick BASIC.

Pascal has facilities for passing arguments both by value and by address. In Figure 8–14, *A* and *B* are value parameters. Procedure *Calc* must be changed accordingly. Figure 8-15 shows a procedure *Calc* that can be called from the main program of Figure 8-14.

Figure 8-16 is similar to Figure 8-7, but now the calling program is compiled rather than assembled.

Figure 8-17 shows the steps described in Figure 8-16 for the Pascal program of Figure 8-14 and the procedure of Figure 8-15. The Pascal program is in a file called CalcPas.

Figures 8-18 and 8-19 show *Calc* and its call from C.

Figure 8-12 *Calc* computed as a function

```
; This procedure computes Result = A + B.
; It presumes the ADDRESSES of A and B are on the stack.
; BASIC type PUSH order: A, then B.
; Result is returned in AX.
; BASIC uses the MEDIUM memory model
; The procedure is responsible for removing A and B from the stack.
;
; Stack diagram:
;
;            -------------
;           |             |
;           |   A OFFSET   | <- [BP+8]
;           |-------------
;           |   B OFFSET   | <- [BP+6]
;           |-------------
;           |   RET SEG    | <- [BP+4]
;           |
;           |  RET OFFSET  | <- [BP+2]
;           |-------------
;           |  saved BP    | <- [BP]
;            -------------
;                              <- next space on top of stack
;
; Written by Tyson D. Sawyer

        DOSSEG
        .MODEL MEDIUM

        PUBLIC CalcBas

        .CODE

CalcBas:

        PUSH BP                  ; save BP register
        MOV BP, SP               ; point BP to stack frame
        PUSH BX                  ; preserve BX

        MOV BX, [BP+8]           ; get A's address
        MOV AX, [BX]             ; get A
        MOV BX, [BP+6]           ; get B's address
        ADD AX, [BX]             ; add B

        POP BX                   ; restore BX
        POP BP                   ; restore BP
        RETF 4                   ; far return to caller

        END
```

Figure 8-13 *Calc* called from MS-Quick BASIC

```
'*****************************************
'*                                       *
'*                                       *
'* This program demonstrates calling     *
'* the assembly language program,        *
'* 'CalcBas.ASM' from MS-Quick BASIC.    *
'*                                       *
'* NOTE:                                 *
'*                                       *
'*     The '%' character indicates that  *
'*     the related variable or function  *
'*     is of 16 bit INTEGER type.        *
'*                                       *
'* Written by Tyson D. Sawyer            *
'*                                       *
'*****************************************


DECLARE FUNCTION CALCBAS% ALIAS "CALCBAS"

DO

     INPUT "ENTER A:", A%
     INPUT "ENTER B:", B%

     RESULT% = CALCBAS(A%, B%)

     PRINT "THE RESULT IS "; RESULT%
     PRINT

LOOP WHILE (A% <> 0 AND B% <> 0)
```

Figure 8-14 Pascal program to call *Calc*

```
(* Original program by Tyson D. Sawyer         *)
(* Modified program by Paul Cousineau          *)
(*                                             *)
(* This procedure calls the CalcPas Procedure  *)
(* Written in assembly language                *)


{$F+}                    (* Forces far calls   *)
{$L CalcPas}             (* link with CalcPas  *)

Function CalcPas(A,B: integer): integer; external;

var
   A, B, Result        : integer;
   Code                : integer;
   InputString         : string;

begin
    repeat
         Write ('Enter A:');
         Readln(InputString);
         val (InputString, A, Code);
         if InputString <> '' then
             begin
                   Write('Enter B:');
                   Readln (InputString);
                   val (InputString, B, Code);

                   Result := CalcPas (A, B);
                   Writeln('Result =',Result);
                   Writeln('');
             end;
    until InputString =''
end.
```

Figure 8-15 Function *Calc* called from main program of Figure 8-14

```
;               Title CalcPas.asm
;
; This procedure computes Result = A + B.
; It presumes the VALUES of A and B are on the stack.
; PASCAL type PUSH order: A, then B.
; Result is returned in AX.
; CalcPas is responsible for removing A and B from the stack.
; PASCAL uses the LARGE memory model, thus requiring a FAR return.
;
; NOTE:
;       Turbo Pascal REQUIRES that the code segment of external
;       object files be labeled 'CODE' or 'CSEG'.  MASM names the
;       code segment _TEXT or modual_TEXT if the .MODEL and .CODE
;       directives are used.  Therefore these directives can not
;       be used and explicit segment notation must be used.
;
; Stack diagram:
;
;
;           ------------
;                A        <- [BP+8]
;           ------------
;                B        <- [BP+6]
;           ------------
;             RET SEG     <- [BP+4]
;
;            RET OFFSET   <- [BP+2]
;           ------------
;            saved BP     <- [BP]
;           --------------
;                          <- next space on top of stack
;
; Written by Tyson D. Sawyer


        DOSSEG

        PUBLIC PASCAL CalcPas

CODE    SEGMENT WORD PUBLIC 'CODE'
        ASSUME CS:CODE

Calc_Pas:

        PUSH BP                 ; save BP register
        MOV BP, SP              ; point BP to stack frame

        MOV AX, [BP+8]          ; get A
        ADD AX, [BP+6]          ; add B

        POP BP                  ; restore BP
        RETF 4                  ; far return to caller

CODE    ENDS

        END
```

Figure 8-16 Assembled calling program

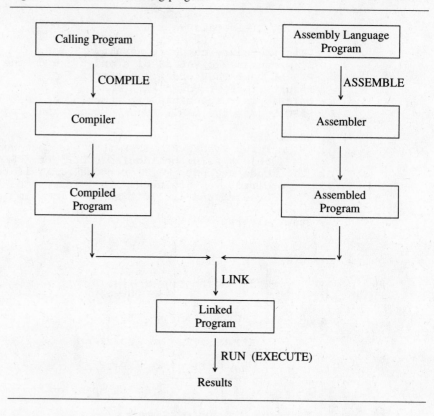

Figure 8-17 Actual commands to perform sequence in Figure 8-16

```
C:\>masm CALCPAS.ASM
Microsoft (R) Macro Assembler Version 5.00
Copyright (C) Microsoft Corp 1981-1985, 1987.  All rights reserved.

Object filename [calcpas.OBJ]:
Source listing  [NUL.LST]:
Cross-reference [NUL.CRF]:

  51614 + 391042 Bytes symbol space free

     0 Warning Errors
     0 Severe  Errors

C:\>tpc CALC.PAS
Turbo Pascal Version 5.5  Copyright (c) 1983,89 Borland International
CALC.PAS(34)
34 lines, 0.3 seconds, 2528 bytes code, 910 bytes data.
C:\>
```

Figure 8-18 C version of *Calc*

```
;         Title CalcC.asm
;
; C appends a '_' character to the beginning of external labels
; This procedure computes Result = A + B.
; It presumes the VALUES of A and B are on the stack.
; C type PUSH order: B, then A.
; Result is returned in AX.
; The calling program is responsible for removing A and B from the stack.
; C defaults to the SMALL memory model, thus using a NEAR return.
;
; Stack diagram:
;
;           |             |
;           |-------------|
;           |      A      |  <- [BP+6]
;           |-------------|
;           |      B      |  <- [BP+4]
;           |-------------|
;           | RET OFFSET  |  <- [BP+2]
;           |-------------|
;           |  saved BP   |  <- [BP]
;           ---------------
;                            <- next space on top of stack
;
; Written by Tyson D. Sawyer


        DOSSEG
        .MODEL SMALL

        PUBLIC _CalcC

        .CODE

_CalcC:
        PUSH BP                 ; save BP register
        MOV BP, SP              ; point BP to stack frame

        MOV AX, [BP+4]          ; get A
        ADD AX, [BP+6]          ; add B

        POP BP                  ; restore BP
        RET                     ; return to caller

        END
```

Figure 8-19 *Calc* and its call from C

```
/*******************************************/
/*                                         */
/*                                         */
/* This program calls the CalcC procedure  */
/* written in assembly language.           */
/*                                         */
/* Written by Tyson D. Sawyer              */
/*                                         */
/*******************************************/


#include <stdio.h>
#include <stdlib.h>

main()
        {
        int A;
        int B;
        int Result;
        char InputString[30];
        int CalcC (int A, int B);

        do
            {
            printf ("Enter A: ");
            gets (InputString);
            A = atoi (InputString);

            if (*InputString != '\0')
                {
                printf ("Enter B: ");
                gets (InputString);
                B = atoi (InputString);

                Result = CalcC (A, B);

                printf ("Result = %i\n\n", Result);
                }
            }
        while (*InputString != '\0');
        }
```

8.4 Summary

This chapter describes procedures and the stack instructions and operations related to their linkage and argument transmission. Linkage is performed more or less automatically by CALL and RET. Argument transmission is the responsibility of the programmer when the calling program is itself an assembly language program. Passing arguments via registers or on the stack are two common ways to pass these arguments.

When an assembly language program is called from another language, the calling program pushes the arguments onto the stack before making the call. The assembly language programmer must know where these arguments are. Since these calls are generally made to FAR procedures, this means that the 2 top words on the stack contain the return address. The arguments thus lie ''underneath'' these 2 words. Generally, the arguments are accessed by setting BP equal to the stack pointer and using displacement mode addressing mode on BP. It is the assembly language programmer's responsibility to POP these arguments off the stack, using RET. Also, it is considered good programming technique to PUSH (i.e., save) any registers used in the procedure and to POP (i.e., restore) them before RETurning. This should not be done, of course, for procedures that return values in registers.

Since different languages support different parameter types, the assembly language programmer must know in what form the argument is pushed when the call is made. BASIC and FORTRAN pass addresses; Pascal can pass both addresses and values.

Assembly language programs rarely exist in themselves. Usually, they are called from high-level languages. For this reason, many of the examples in the remainder of this book will be shown in procedure form with comments explaining how the procedure expects to access its arguments.

Exercises

1. What is another name for a stack?
2. Why is the stack pointer decreased in a PUSH instruction?
3. Can addresses be stored on the stack?
4. Where are the contents of the IP saved in a NEAR call? In a FAR call?
5. What two actions do procedure calls invoke?
6. Show the contents of the stack after the MOV BP,SP instruction is executed in the version of procedure *Calc* called from the BASIC program of Figure 8-11.
7. Same as Exercise 6, but for the Pascal program of Figure 8-14.
8. Implement the SEARCH program from Chapter 6 as a procedure.
    a. Call it as a NEAR procedure from an assembly language program.
    b. Call it as a FAR procedure from an assembly language program.
    c. Call it as a procedure from your favorite high-level language.

9. Same as Exercise 8, but for the *Sort* program in Chapter 6.
10. The following method is used by many system SORT routines. On the average, it sorts faster than the *Selection Sort* or *BubbleSort* of Chapter 6, and is called *Quick-Sort:*
    a. Pick any element of the array at random; call it *X*.
    b. Initialize variables *Up* and *Down* to the index of the first element and last element in the array, respectively.
    c. Move up the array, incrementing *Up* until an element larger than *X* is found.
    d. Move down the array, decrementing *Down* until an element less than or equal to *X* is found.
    e. Exchange the elements at *Up* and *Down*.
    f. Continue moving *Up* up and *Down* down, exchanging when necessary, until *Up* and *Down* pass. At this point, (any instance of) *X* is in its correct place in the array, and all elements to the left are less than *X,* and all elements to the right are greater than *X*.
    g. Apply parts a through f for the array whose elements are less than *X*.
    h. Apply parts a through f for the array whose elements are greater than *X*.
    In high-level languages, this often would be written recursively (see Chapter 9 for a definition of recursion). In assembly language, however, where efficiency is important, a nonrecursive solution that keeps track of partitioning requests (parts g and h) via a stack is more appropriate.
    Write a program to implement *QuickSort*.
11. Write a program that calls *Selection Sort, BubbleSort,* and *QuickSort,* counting the number of comparisons each makes (alternatively, count the number of elements exchanged). Run the program on various lists of numbers. Is *QuickSort* ever "slower" (more comparisons or exchanges) than the other two? Is there any ordering of the array such that *BubbleSort* is better? What ordering of the array makes each do the least amount of work? The most? What are your conclusions about the efficiency of the three methods?
12. Write a procedure called *Squeez* that eliminates all the blanks in a short line of text. Use the following string as data:

    ```
    a  bc d ef g
    ```

Data Structures in Assembly Language

9.0   Introduction

In Chapters 5 and 6, we described arrays. Arrays are a way of structuring data — they are *data structures*. All the elements of an array are of the same type; for example, we can have byte arrays, word arrays, even tenbyte arrays if we wish. In Chapter 12, we will see arrays whose elements are all floating-point numbers. Arrays of characters are called *strings* and occur so often that there are special instructions for performing operations on them.

Sometimes, however, our data consist of elements that are not of the same type. For example, a calendar date in the 20th century may be described with three parts:

1. Month: an integer from 1 to 12
2. Day: an integer from 1 to 31
3. Year: an integer from 1900 to 1999

Although these are all integers, the first two may be stored in a byte, whereas the last requires a word of storage. Thus in assembly language these parts are different types. We will call such data types *structures*. If all the parts consist of bit strings, then they are called *records*. These terms differ somewhat from their use in high-level languages, such as Pascal and C.

9.1 Bit Strings

In previous chapters, we have operated on data whose smallest size is a byte. A byte is the smallest piece of information that we can move from or to memory and registers. Once the data are in a register, however, there are operations that can be performed on the individual bits.

The instructions for operating on bit strings are similar syntactically to the bit string operators described in Chapter 3. There, however, the operators produced results during *assembly*. The instructions described in this section are evaluated during *execution*.

Logical, or Boolean, instructions traditionally return values that are True or False. We would like to emphasize that these instructions return True or False only when the bit string operand is initially True (all 1's) or False (all 0's). If the operands are not True or False, they produce a more general result.

We will divide these instructions into 5 groups:

1. Boolean instructions: AND, OR, XOR, NOT
2. Rotate instructions: ROL, ROR, RCL, RCR
3. Shift instructions: SAL, SAR, SHL, SHR, SHLD, SHRD
4. Flags register instructions: CLC, CLD, CLI, CMC, STC, STD, STI
5. Scan and test instructions: BSF, BSR, BT, BTC, BTR, BTS

9.1.1 Boolean Instructions

AND

Purpose. To "and" two byte, word, or doubleword operands.

Syntax

> AND   *Operand1, Operand2*

where

> *Operand1* is a byte, word, or doubleword register or memory location.
> *Operand2* is a byte, word, or doubleword register, memory location, or immediate value.
> One of the operands must be in direct mode.

Machine Code

	Instruction	Opcode
AND	Mem8,Reg8	20
AND	Mem16,Reg16	21
AND	Reg8,Mem8	22
AND	Reg16,Mem16	23
AND	AL,Imm8	24
AND	AX,Imm16	25
AND	Reg8,Imm8	80
AND	Mem8,Imm8	80
AND	Reg16,Imm16	81
AND	Mem16,Imm16	81

Semantics.   AND compares each bit of its operands, respectively, and returns 1 in that place of the first operand only if both bits are 1. The overflow and carry flags are cleared, while the sign, zero, and parity flags may be set or cleared in the usual ways.

EXAMPLE 1

> AND   AX,BX

If AX contains 1111010000000011B and BX contains 1110000011110010B before execution, then AX contains 1110000000000010B after execution. BX is unaltered.

OR

Purpose.   To "or" byte, word, or doubleword operands.

Syntax

> OR *Operand1,Operand2*

where

> the operands follow the same rules as for AND.

Machine Code

	Instruction	Opcode
OR	Mem8,Reg8	08
OR	Mem16,Reg16	09
OR	Reg8,Mem8	0A
OR	Reg16,Mem16	0B
OR	AL,Imm8	0C
OR	AX,Imm16	0D
OR	Reg8,Imm8	80
OR	Reg16,Imm16	81

Semantics. OR compares each bit, respectively, of its operands and returns 1 to that place in the first operand if either (or both) bit(s) is (are) 1. The status bits are set and cleared in the usual way.

EXAMPLE 2

```
OR      AX,BX
```

If AX contains 1111010000000011B and BX contains 1110000011110010B before execution, then AX contains1111010011110011B after execution. BX is unaltered.

Exclusive OR

Purpose. To "exclusive or" two byte or word operands.

Machine Code

	Instruction	Opcode
XOR	Mem8,Reg8	30
XOR	Mem16,Reg16	31
XOR	Reg8,Mem8	32
XOR	Reg16,Mem16	33
XOR	AL,Imm8	34
XOR	AX,Imm16	35
XOR	Reg8,Imm8	80
XOR	Mem8,Imm8	80
XOR	Reg16,Imm16	81
XOR	Mem16,Imm16	81

Semantics. XOR compares its operands bit-wise and returns a 1 to the corresponding position in the first operand if one, and *only* one, of the bits is 1. The status bits are set and cleared in the usual ways.

EXAMPLE 3

```
XOR     AX,BX
```

If AX contains 1111010000000011B and BX contains 1110000011110010B before execution, then AX contains 0001010011110001B after execution. BX is unaltered.

NOT

Purpose. NOT complements its operand, i.e., converts all 1's to 0's and all 0's to 1's.

Syntax

```
NOT     Operand
```

where

Operand is a byte, word, or doubleword memory location or register.

Machine Code

	Instruction	Opcode
NOT	Mem8	F6
NOT	Reg8	F6
NOT	Mem16	F7
NOT	Reg16	F7

Semantics. NOT subtracts its operand from 0FFH (remember H denotes hexadecimal) for bytes and from 0FFFFH for words. The flags register is unaffected.

EXAMPLE 4

```
NOT     AX
```

If AX contains 1110000011110010B before this instruction is executed, it contains 0001111100001101B after it is executed.

These instructions are often used to create "masks," a powerful use of bit strings.

Masks. The set and cleared bits in a byte, word, or larger element often have significance. When bit strings are used in this way, they are called masks. For example, a mask can be used to convert a digit to its ASCII representation.

```
Digit = 05  ; Digit to be changed
ASCIIMask  = 030H
     . . .
     MOV      AX,Digit
     OR       AX, ASCIIMask
```

Here, the masked bits are 11 in the byte (*ASCIIMask*) 00110000. This effectively leaves all the original bits in the digit set while converting to the character representation. The example shows a 5 (0101) being changed to its ASCII value of 53 (35H).

A mask can be used to perform the reverse process of converting an ASCII representation of a number to its numerical value:

```
ASCIIDigit = 35H    ; ASCII representation of 5
NumericalMask = OFH
     . . .
     MOV      AX,ASCIIDigit
     AND      AX,NumericalMask
```

We can write a simple routine for converting an uppercase letter to lowercase by noticing that the only difference is that bit 5 is set for the ASCII representation of lowercase letters and is cleared for uppercase:

```
Letter = "Q"
Mask5 = 20H
     MOVB AL,Letter
     OR   AL,Mask5 ; changes contents to lowercase
```

We will see numerous examples of masks in the remainder of this book. To summarize, using a mask to modify bits in a register performs the following actions:

Operation	Action of mask bit on register
AND	1: retain previous value; 0: clear bit to 0
OR	1: set bit to 1; 0: retain previous value
XOR	1: toggle (i.e., change) bit; 0: retain previous value

9.1.2 Rotate Instructions

These instructions perform a circular rotation on their first operand by the number of bits specified in the second operand. For example, if the shift is a simple rotate left (ROL) of, say, AL by 1 bit, and AL contains

10101111

before the instruction is executed, it will contain

01011111

after it is executed. Note that the leftmost 1 has rotated around to the rightmost bit because all the rest of the bits are shifted left one:

$$10101111 = 01011111$$

Rotate instructions are often used to access the bits in a byte or word. For example, converting hexadecimal numbers to their ASCII codes is done 4 bits at a time. In such conversions, the first 4 bits are converted. Then all the bits to be converted are shifted left (4 bits), and the next 4 bits are converted. Other applications for rotate instructions include those where groups of bits are operated on at one time. Rotating allows these bits to be accessed as a group from one end of the byte or word.

As we will see, the opcodes for the various rotate instructions are identical; the addressing mode byte contains distinguishing information.

Rotate Left

Purpose.   To rotate left circularly the byte or word first operand by the number of bits specified in the second operand.

Syntax

```
ROL     Operand, Count
```

where

Operand is a byte, word, or doubleword memory location or register.
Count is an immediate value (1 for 86-family members before the 80286; 0–15 for the 80286; 0–31 for 80386 and 80486) or is contained in CL.

Machine Code

	Instruction	Opcode
ROL	Reg8,1	D0
ROL	Mem8,1	D0
ROL	Mem16,1	D1
ROL	Reg16,1	D1
ROL	Mem8,CL	D2
ROL	Reg8,CL	D2
ROL	Reg16,CL	D3
ROL	Mem16,CL	D3

Semantics.   ROL rotates each bit to the left, putting the leftmost bit into the rightmost bit. The rotation continues until the rotation has been accomplished the number of times indicated by the number in CL (unless *Count,* the second operand, is 1). The high-order bits are also rotated into the carry flag (CF). The overflow flag (OF) is set or cleared for single bit variants of this instruction.

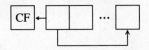

EXAMPLE 5

```
ROL   AX,1
MOV   CL,3
ROL   BX,CL
```

If AX contains 0050H and BX contains 5000H before these instructions are executed, they contain 00A0H and 8002H, respectively, after these instructions are executed.

Rotate Right

Purpose.   To rotate a register or memory operand circularly right by a specified number of bits.

Syntax

```
ROR   Operand,Count
```

where

Operand and *Count* are as in ROL.

Machine Code

	Instruction	Opcode
ROR	Mem8,1	D0
ROR	Reg8,1	D0
ROR	Mem16,1	D1
ROR	Reg16,1	D1
ROR	Mem8,CL	D2
ROR	Reg8,CL	D2
ROR	Reg16,CL	D3
ROR	Mem16,CL	D3

Semantics. Same as for ROL, except rotation is right circularly.

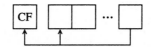

Rotate Left Through Carry

Purpose. To rotate left circularly a byte, word, or doubleword operand through the carry flag (CF).

Syntax

```
RCL    Operand,Count
```

where

Operand and *Count* are as in ROL.

Machine Code

	Instruction	Opcode
RCL	Reg8,1	D0
RCL	Mem8,1	D0
RCL	Mem16,1	D1
RCL	Reg16,1	D1
RCL	Mem8,CL	D2
RCL	Reg8,CL	D2
RCL	Reg16,CL	D3
RCL	Mem16,CL	D3

Semantics. RCL moves each bit left; the current carry flag, CF, is moved into the rightmost bit; the new leftmost bit is moved into the CF. The overflow flag is the same as for ROL.

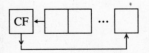

Pragmatics. Think of CF as a 17th bit to the left of the 16-bit register or memory location, or as a 9th bit to the left of an 8-bit register or memory operand.

EXAMPLE 6

```
RCL     AX,1
MOV     CL,3
RCL     BX,CL
```

If AX contains 0050H, BX contains 5000H, and CF contains 1 before these instructions are executed, then AX contains 00A1H, BX contains 8001H, and CF contains 0 after they are executed.

Rotate Right Through Carry

Purpose. To rotate a byte or word circularly right through the carry bit.

Syntax

```
RCR     Operand, Count
```

where

Operand and *Count* are as in ROR.

Machine Code

	Instruction	Opcode
RCR	Mem8,1	D0
RCR	Reg8,1	D0
RCR	Mem16,1	D1
RCR	Reg16,1	D1
RCR	Mem8,CL	D2
RCR	Reg8,CL	D2
RCR	Mem16,CL	D3
RCR	Reg16,CL	D3

Semantics. Each bit is rotated right; the carry bit is put into the leftmost bit; the rightmost bit is put into CF. This continues for count rotations.

9.1.3 Shift Instructions

The shift instructions shift bits left and right, but not circularly. Shifts in any assembly language traditionally have been used to perform fast multiply and divide instructions. For example, shifting left *Count* bits multiplies by 2^{COUNT}. Similarly, shifting right *Count* bits divides by 2^{COUNT}.

SAL and SAR are used to shift signed numbers (when we wish to preserve the sign), and SHL and SHR are used for unsigned numbers. Again, the opcodes for these four instructions are identical; the distinguishing bits were discussed when we looked at addressing modes in Chapter 5.

Shift Arithmetic Left

Purpose. To shift the bits in a byte or word left.

Syntax

```
    SAL     Operand, Count
```

where

Operand and *Count* are as in ROL.

Machine Code. Same as for rotate instructions.

Semantics. SAL shifts *Operand* left by *Count,* bringing *Count* zeros into the right-hand end. The last left-most bit shifted off is copied into CF. The sign, zero, and parity flags may also be set or cleared in the usual way.

EXAMPLE 7

```
    MOV   CL,3
    SAL   AX,CL   ; Multiply by +8
```

Shift Logical Left. Shift logical left, SHL, is identical in every way to SAL.

Shift Arithmetic Right

Purpose. To shift a signed byte or word right bit by bit.

Syntax

```
SAR     Operand, Count
```

where

Operand and *Count* are the same as for the other rotate and shift instructions.

Machine Code. Same as for rotate instructions.

Semantics. SAR shifts bits right, replicating the sign bit in the leftmost bit, rather than bringing in 0's on the rightmost end as do SHL and SAL. The last bit shifted off is copied into the carry flag.

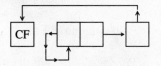

EXAMPLE 8

```
MOV     CL,3
MOV     AX,-16
SAR     AX,CL ; Divide by 8
```

After this is executed, AX contains -2 (shifting right 3 divides by 2^3 or 8).

Shift Logical Right

Purpose. To shift the bits in an unsigned byte or integer right.

Syntax

```
SHR     Operand,Count
```

where

Operand and *Count* are as before.

Machine Code. Same as for other shift and rotate instructions.

Semantics. SHR shifts each bit in *Operand* right *Count* bits, bringing 0's in on the left.

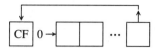

EXAMPLE 9

```
MOV   CL,3
MOV   AX,16
SHR   AX,CL ; Divide by 8
```

9.1.4 Flags Instructions

Many instructions affect or consult the flags bits automatically; the programmer scarcely needs to be aware of them. The conditional jump instructions are an example. Still others use the flags explicitly, and the programmer does need to be aware of their value. For example, RCL and RCR rotate including the carry flag, CF, as part of the rotation.

Load AH from Flags

Purpose. To move some of the bits in the flags register to the AH register.

Syntax

```
LAHF
```

Machine Code

Instruction	Opcode
LAHF	9F

Semantics. The following shows which flags bit goes to which bit (0–7) of AH.

$$
\begin{aligned}
\text{Bit } 7 &\leftarrow \text{SF} \\
\text{Bit } 6 &\leftarrow \text{ZF} \\
\text{Bit } 4 &\leftarrow \text{AF} \\
\text{Bit } 2 &\leftarrow \text{PF} \\
\text{Bit } 0 &\leftarrow \text{CF}
\end{aligned}
$$

The Flags register itself is unchanged.

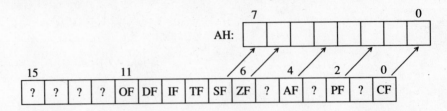

Pragmatics. The programmer should make no assumptions about bits 1, 3, and 5 after LAHF is executed. They may or may not be 0.

Store AH in Flags

Purpose. To move the contents of AH to the flags register.

Syntax

    SAHF

Machine Code

Instruction	Opcode
SAHF	97

Semantics. The following shows which bits of AH are moved to which flags bit.

Bit 7 → SF
Bit 6 → ZF
Bit 4 → AF
Bit 2 → PF
Bit 0 → CF

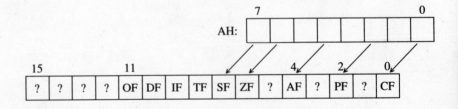

Pragmatics

The other bits in the flags register are not affected.
There are also instructions for setting and clearing various flags.

Clear Carry Flag

Purpose.   To clear the carry flag (CF) to 0.

Syntax

```
CLC
```

Machine Code

Instruction	Opcode
CLC	F8

Set Carry Flag

Purpose.   To set the carry flag (CF) to 1.

Syntax

```
STC
```

Machine Code

Instruction	Opcode
STC	F9

Complement Carry Flag

Purpose.   To change the carry flag (CF) from 0 to 1 or from 1 to 0.

Syntax

```
CMC
```

Machine Code

Instruction	Opcode
CMC	F5

Semantics. If CF is 0, it becomes 1; if CF is 1, it becomes 0.

Clear Direction Flag

Purpose. To clear the direction flag (DF) to 0.

Syntax

```
CLD
```

Machine Code

Instruction	Opcode
CLD	FC

Set Direction Flag

Purpose. To set the direction flag (DF) to 1.

Syntax

```
STD
```

Machine Code

Instruction	Opcode
STD	FD

Clear Interrupt Flag

Purpose. To clear the interrupt flag (IF) to 0.

Syntax

```
CLI
```

Machine Code

Instruction	Opcode
CLI	FA

Set Interrupt Flag

Purpose.   To set the interrupt flag (IF) to 1.

Syntax

    STI

Machine Code

Instruction	Opcode
STI	FB

We will see uses for these various flags instructions in later chapters.

9.1.5 Scan and Test Instructions

The instructions described in the preceding sections have counterparts in other machines and architectures. The 86-family members, beginning with the 80386, also have a set of instructions that can find, set, and clear bits in strings that are not a multiple of the usual byte-sized data.

These instructions are similar in flavor to the character string instructions in Section 9.2.

Bit Scan Instructions.   There are two Bit Scan instructions: one for scanning forward (from bit 0) and one for scanning backward (from the most significant bit toward 0):

```
    BSF     Destination,Source   ; Bit Scan forward
    BSR     Destination,Source   ; Bit Scan backwards
```

In both cases, the source is scanned, and if a set bit is found, the ZF flag (zero flag) is set, and the destination operand is given the value of the offset where the bit is found.

EXAMPLE 10

```
    MOV     AL,01001010B
    BSF     BX,AL            ; BX contains 1
    BSR     CX,AL            ; CX contains 6
```

In Example 10, BX contains 1 after the BSF instruction executes because there is a bit at index 1 (2nd position from the right) when we count from 0. Similarly,

CX contains 6 since the bit string contains a 0 at an offset of 6, and it is the first bit encountered when we scan in reverse (from bit 7).

Machine Code

	Instruction	Opcode
BSF	Reg16,Reg16	OF BC
BSF	Reg32,Reg32	OF BC DB
BSF	Reg16,Mem16	OF BC
BSF	Reg32,Mem32	OF BC 1E
BSR	Reg16,Reg16	OF BD DB
BSR	Reg32,Reg32	OF BD DB
BSR	Reg16,Mem16	OF BD 1E
BSR	Reg32,Mem32	OF BD 1E

Bit Test.   The Bit Test instructions allow a particular bit to be tested. The bit to be tested is stored in the *Destination* operand, and the offset to be tested is the *Source* operand. The *Source* operand may be an immediate or a register (presumedly containing the offset).

The Bit Test instructions are used in conjunction with jump on carry (JC) and jump on not carry (JNC) because the Bit Test instructions copy the bit to be tested to the carry flag in the flags register.

There are 4 forms:

```
BT      Destination,Source    ; Copy bit to CF
BTC     Destination,Source    ; Copy bit to CF, and
                              ; complement it in
                              ; Destination
BTR     Destination,Source    ; Copy bit to CF, and
                              ; leave it cleared in
                              ; Destination
BTS     Destination,Source    ; Copy bit to CF, and
                              ; leave it set in
                              ; Destination
```

EXAMPLE 11

```
        MOV     AL,01000100B
        BT      AL,4
        JC      Here
There   ...     ; Control passes to this point
Here    ...
```

In Example 11, bit 4 is not set, so that when the JC instruction is executed, the jump does not take place (since CF is not set).

9.1.6 An Application: Hamming Codes

In any computer system, errors may occur during data transmission to and from peripheral devices. In addition, memory and storage devices may themselves corrupt data through hardware imperfections. Various mechanisms to detect erroneous data have been developed. We will discuss one, Hamming Codes, here.

When an ASCII-encoded byte is transmitted, we need only 7 bits for the code itself. Often extra bits, called *parity* bits, are added when the byte is transmitted, indicating the number of 1's in the original byte. (Parity bits can be added to other-sized units besides bytes.) *Even parity* sets these bits so that the total bits transmitted (including the parity bits) are even. *Odd parity* sets these bits so that the total bits sent are odd. When the data are received, their parity is checked; if it is not even in an even parity system, we say that a parity error has occurred. Occasionally, stored or transmitted data is *corrupted;* that is, what is received is not what is sent. Adding one or several more bits to each piece of data to help detect a change in the data has been shown to be effective in detecting many errors resulting from faulty transmission and hardware.

Some encoding schemes add only one parity bit/byte. Hamming codes, developed by R. W. Hamming in 1950, add several bits for both detection and correction. The data size is not restricted to just bytes. The original data plus the parity bits will be called a *Codeword* here.

Hamming's method numbers the bits in a Codeword from right to left starting at 1 (not 0!). Bits whose number is a power of 2 (1, 2, 4, 8, 16, and so on) are used as parity bits. The remaining bits in the Codeword are used for data. This involves moving the bits in the original data to various positions in the Codeword. For example, a 7-bit data word would be moved as follows:

$$|7|6|5|4|3|2|1|$$
$$|11|10|9|8|7|6|5|4|3|2|1|$$

The extra parity bits are calculated as follows:

1. Each data bit affects the parity for at least 2 of the parity bits.
2. Data bit number L is expanded into powers of 2, using its number in its new position in the Codeword. For example, bit number 10 is $8 + 2$. (This is bit number 6 in the original data.)
3. The parity bits affected are the bits represented by the power of 2 expansion. Thus, data bit number 10 affects Codeword bits 8 and 2.

4. Codeword bits are affected by any data number that has that power of 2 in its expansion. Thus, for an 11-bit Codeword encoding a 7-bit Dataword, parity bit 1 is affected by data bits 3, 5, 7, 9, and 11, since

$$3 = 2 + 1$$
$$5 = 4 + 1$$
$$7 = 4 + 2 + 1$$
$$9 = 8 + 1$$
$$11 = 8 + 2 + 1$$

Parity bit 2 is affected by data bits 3, 6, 7, 10, and 11. Parity bit 4 is affected by data bits 5, 6, and 7. Parity bit 8 is affected by data bits 9, 10, and 11.

5. Even or odd parity may be used; for even parity, the parity bit is set so that the total number of bits set in the data bits plus the parity bit is even.

For example, if our data is 62 (hexadecimal) = 1100010_2, then these bits will occupy positions 3, 5, 6, 7, 9, 10, and 11:

The parity bits will occupy the other positions. The parity bits for even parity are the following.

Parity bit 1 (affected by bits 3, 5, 7, 9, 11): 0, since bit 3 = 0, bit 5 = 1, bit 7 = 0, bit 9 = 0, bit 11 = 1, which is an even number of 1's; with a parity bit of 0, the total number of 1's is even.
Parity bit 2 (affected by bits 3, 6, 7, 10, 11): 0
Parity bit 4 (affected by bits 5, 6, 7): 1
Parity bit 8 (affected by bits 9, 10, 11): 0

The Codeword is 11000011000, where bits 1, 2, 4, and 8 are parity bits, and bits 3, 5, 7, 8, 10, and 11 contain the original data.

Problem: Write a procedure called *Hamming* that will calculate the Hamming code for arbitrary 16-bit data words.

Discussion: We will need a 5th parity bit so the Hamming code word will be 21 bits long. The method used is described above. The procedure is shown in Figure 9-1 for 32-bit registers (for the 80386 and 80486). Exercise 10 explores how to implement this using 16-bit registers and instructions.

Figure 9-1 *Hamming* procedure

```
;-----------------------------------------------------------------
; Hamming takes a 16-bit dataword and changes it into a 21-bit Hamming
; code. Parity bits are 1,2,4,8,16. They are affected by certain dataword
; bits.                                                    Dec 9,1991
;                                                          D. Vasconcelos
;-----------------------------------------------------------------

PUBLIC  Hamming
EXTRN   DataW:DWORD, CodeW:DWORD

DOSSEG
.MODEL SMALL
.386
        .DATA
        .CODE
Hamming: MOV    AX,@DATA
         MOV    DS,AX


;-----------------------------------------------------------------
; This section copies each dataword bit into proper positions in codeword.
;-----------------------------------------------------------------

        MOV    ECX,2             ; start at bit two in codeword
        MOV    EAX,3             ; next parity bit in codeword
        MOV    EBX,0             ; start at bit zero in dataword

CLoop:  CMP    EAX,ECX           ; is the current bit a parity bit?
        JNE    CCopy             ; if not, branch to bit copy
        INC    ECX               ; else, move to next bit in codeword
        SHL    EAX,1             ; next parity bit is (2*current)+1
        INC    EAX

CCopy:     BT     DataW,EBX ; is the current dataword bit set
           JNC    CNEXT      ; if no, try next bit
           BTS    CodeW,ECX  ; else, set appropriate bit in codeword

        CNext:  INC    ECX        ; next bit of codeword
                INC    EBX        ; next bit of dataword
                CMP    EBX,16     ; more bits in dataword?
                JL     CLOOP


;-----------------------------------------------------------------
; This section computes each parity bit of the codeword.
; NOTE: Since each codeword bit affects only parity bits that are set
;       in the binary representation of the number [ bit 3 (..0011 in
;       binary) has only parity bits 1 & 2 set], anytime a bit in the
;       dataword is set, the correct parity bits can be affected by XORing
;       the binary representation of the bit# with the parity bits.
;       note that: (0 xor 0)=(0 + 0)= 0      (0 xor 1)=(0 + 1)= 1
;                  (1 xor 0)=(1 + 0)= 1      (1 xor 1)=(1 + 1)= 0    (mod 2)
;-----------------------------------------------------------------

           MOV    EBX,1          ; start with bit 1 of codeword
           XOR    ECX,ecx        ; internally bit 0
           XOR    EDX,edx        ; clear parity bit storage
```

Figure 9-1 (*Continued*)

```
PLoop:          BT      CodeW,ECX               ; test bit
                JNC     PNEXT                   ; if clear, no parity bits affected
                XOR     EDX,EBX                 ; else add 1 (mod 2) to appropriate
                                                ; parity bits
PNext:          INC     EBX             ; next codeword bit
                INC     ECX
                CMP     ECX,21
                JL      PLOOP           ; repeat if more bits


;-----------------------------------------------------------------------
;    The last section stores parity bits in proper locations in codeword
;-----------------------------------------------------------------------

                XOR     ECX,ECX                 ; pointer for bits in edx
                XOR     EAX,EAX                 ; pointer to codeword

SPLoop:         BT      EDX,ECX            ; is parity bit set?
                JNC     SPNext             ; if not, try next bit
                BTS     CodeW,EAX          ; else, set appropriate codeword bit

SPNext:         SHL     eax,1              ; next parity bit = (2*current)+1
                INC     EAX
                INC     ECX                ; next bit in edx
                CMP     ECX,16
                JLE     SPLoop             ; repeat if more bits

                RET                        ; program terminates
                END     Hamming
```

9.2 Character Strings

When the computer revolution began, it was believed that the primary use of computers would be for number-crunching—high-speed calculations on very precise numbers. Although computers are used for this purpose, it is no longer their main function. In our increasingly complex world, computers and their peripheral devices, such as tapes and disks, have become manipulators and repositories of an increasingly vast and varying amount of data and information.

At the machine level, these data are essentially a sequence of bytes or words, grouped together and often called *blocks* or *strings* of data. In high-level languages, the term "string" is usually used when we are referring to sequences of characters (generally, bytes), and the more general term "block" is used for any group of data, not necessarily of byte size. In 86-family assembly language, strings can be either sequences of bytes or words. Thus, there is no real difference between the terms "string" and "block."

Common manipulations performed are: moving a block of information from one location to another; comparing one string with another; searching a string or a particular character or group of characters; and accessing or changing some part of a string. In the following sections we discuss the instructions that perform these manipulations.

Strings may be up to 65,536 (64K) bytes in length; this is the size of one segment. The string manipulation instructions do not care what is stored in these bytes; but they do make assumptions about where the strings are located or are to be located, and they use various machine parts, such as ES, SI, DI, and DF (the direction flag). Other registers, such as AX and CX, are used to store information needed by these instructions.

9.2.1 Moving Character Strings

To copy a character string from one location to another, its (source) location first must be loaded into SI, and the location to which it is to be copied (destination) must be loaded into DI. The location to which the string is to be moved must be declared in the extra segment; that is, the offset in DI is used in conjunction with ES. The location from which the string is to be copied need not be declared in the extra segment. If no override operator is used, it is assumed that the source string is declared in the data segment; that is, SI is used in conjunction with DS.

There are three forms for the move-character-string instruction:

1. MOVSB
2. MOVSW
3. MOVS *Destination, Source*

MOVSB (move byte string) is used when the string to be moved is a byte string, i.e., it is declared using DB. MOVSW (move word string) is used for word strings.

MOVS is translated into one of the other two during assembly; *Destination* and *Source* are irrelevant since the source and destination address are in SI and DI, unless the default source (the data segment) is to be overridden. The assembler will report an error if they are inconsistent, however. Thus

        MOVS   *NewName,OldName*

moves characters from *OldName* to *NewName*. Here, *OldName* is declared in the data segment and its offset must be in SI. *NewName* is declared in the extra segment and its offset is in DI. The instruction

        MOVS   *NewName,ES:OldName*

is the same as just given, except *OldName* is also declared in the extra segment.

Machine Code

Instruction		Opcode
MOVSB		A4
MOVS	(bytes)	A4
MOVSW		A5
MOVS	(words)	A5
MOVSD		66 A5
MOVS	(doublewords)	66 A5

Semantics.   The string can be moved from either end — we can start with the characters at the beginning of the string or with the characters that terminate the string. If the direction flag (DF) is 0, then the string is moved from left to right; that is, SI and DI are incremented after each move. If the DF is set, then the string is moved from the other end; that is, SI and DI are decreased after each move. Note that this does not reverse the string. Moving from one end or the other is often convenient or even necessary to prevent overlapping. For example, if we are moving the source string one place to the right to form a destination string, we will want to start with the last character rather than the first.

A common name for strings in any language is *Name*. This cannot be used in MASM, since NAME is itself an assembler directive (see Chapter 11).

When used by themselves, these instructions move only the first byte or word of the string. The prefix operator REP must precede the move-character-string instruction to move the entire string.

REP.   REP precedes a character-string instruction and repeats that instruction until the CX register is zero. CX must, therefore, be loaded with a count prior to the instruction containing REP. CX is decremented automatically each time the instruction is executed. The machine code for REP is

Prefix	Opcode
REP	F2

EXAMPLE 12

```
        LEA     SI,Name1
        LEA     DI,NewName
        MOV     CX,5
        CLD                         ; Move from beginning
    ;
REP MOVS        NewName,Name1       ; Repeat until 5
                                    ; characters are copied.
```

If these instructions are to copy the first 5 character (bytes) in *Name1* to *New-Name*, then the data segment must contain a declaration such as

```
Name1    DB   "Johnson"
```

and the extra segment must have a declaration such as

```
NewName DB   10 DUP (?)
```

9.2.2 Comparing Character Strings

To compare one character string with another, SI is loaded with the address of the first operand, and DI is loaded with the address of the second operand, which must be a string declared in the extra segment. As with the move-string instructions, there are three forms:

1. CMPSB
2. CMPSW
3. CMPS   *Operand1,Operand2*

Like MOVS, CMPS is translated by the assembler into one of the other two, depending on the size of the operands.

Machine Code

Instruction		Opcode
CMPSB		A6
CMPS	(bytes)	A6
CMPSW		A7
CMPS	(words)	A7
CMPSD		66 A7
CMPS	(doublewords)	66 A7

Semantics. The compare-string instructions compare in reverse order from the comparison performed by CMP. CMP compares the *first* operand with the *second;* CMPSB (compare byte string), CMPSW (compare word string), CMPSD and CMPS (compare string) compare the *second* operand with the *first*.

Like the move-string instructions, CX is used to contain a count of the number of characters to compare. Most often, we want to compare characters until we find a place where the two strings differ (or until we have compared the desired number of characters). A variation of REP allows us to do this.

REPE (REPZ). REPE, which can also be coded REPZ, repeats the string instruction only as long as ZF is set and CX is nonzero. If the instruction is a CMPSB or CMPSW, the comparison will continue as long as the strings are the same. As soon as a comparison clears the ZF bit—finds a position where they differ—then the instruction repetition ceases. Otherwise, repetition ceases when CX is 0. The machine code for REPE is

Prefix	Opcode
REPE	F2

REPE can be used with the string compare to find where two strings differ. We know where the strings differ since CX is decremented for each comparison before the ZF bit is checked. For example, if CX was originally 5 and the strings differ in the third position, then CX will now be 2; thus, the original CX value minus the current CX value is the place where the strings differ.

Once again, if DF is 0, the comparison proceeds from left to right; if DF is set, the comparison is from right to left.

EXAMPLE 13

```
            LEA     SI,Name1
            LEA     DI,NewName
            MOV     CX,5
            CLD
  REPE      CMPS    Name1,NewName
            JL      First
            MOV     AX,0
            JMP     After
  First:    MOV     AX,1
  After:
```

If the first 5 characters of *NewName* precede the first 5 characters of *Name1* in ASCII, then AX is set to 1; otherwise AX is cleared. *Name1* and *NewName* are declared as in Example 12, but both should have been given values prior to the CMPS. If this example were to follow Example 12 in execution, then AX would be zero after this is executed, since *Name1* equals "Johnson," *NewName* equals "Johns," and we are comparing only 5 characters.

9.2.3 Searching Character Strings

To search (often called *scan*) a string, we again load DI with the address of the string to be scanned. This string must be declared in the extra segment; the character to be scanned for is in AL for byte strings and AX for word strings. There are the usual three forms, with the last translated into one of the other two during assembly:

1. SCASB
2. SCASW
3. SCAS   *Operand*

Machine Code

Instruction		Opcode
SCASB		AE
SCAS	(bytes)	AE
SCASW		AF
SCAS	(words)	AF
SCASD		66 AF
SCAS	(doublewords)	66 AF

Semantics.   Like moving and comparing characters, scanning can be performed from left to right (DF = 0) or from right to left (DF = 1). Since the instruction scans to find an occurrence of the contents of AX or AL, the scan usually repeats while the string contents and AX (AL) are *un*equal. A form of REP will do this.

REPNE (REPNZ).   This prefix will repeat the string operation while ZF is 1 and CX is nonzero, that is, as long as ZF is not cleared. This means that if AX or AL and the scanned character are unequal, then the instruction is repeated. It thus scans a string until it finds a match. The machine code for this form of the repetition prefix is:

Prefix	Opcode
REPNE	F3

EXAMPLE 14

```
        MOV     AL, "o"        ; Scan for o
        LEA     DI,NewName     ; Scan first
        MOV     CX,5           ; 5 characters
        CLD                    ; of
    REPNE SCASB                ; NewName for o
        JE      . . .
```

The following example counts the words in a text.

EXAMPLE 15 COUNTING WORDS

```
;
; Written by Tyson D. Sawyer
;
; This procedure counts the number of words in a string.
;
; This procedure is written to be called from C.
; The following standard C conventions are used:
;
; 1. The string is an ASCIZ string:
;       An ASCIZ string has no length parameter
;       and is terminated with a zero.
;
; 2. A pointer to the string is passed on the stack.
;
; 3. The word count is returned in the AX register
;
; 4. The calling C procedure will restore the stack.
;
; 5. Count is an external label and therefore must
;       begin with an underscore.
;
; For this procedure a word is defined as any
;   sequence of non-space characters terminated by
;   spaces or the end of the string.


            DOSSEG
            .MODEL SMALL

            PUBLIC _Count

            .CODE

_Count   PROC NEAR

            PUSH BP                      ; save BP register
            MOV BP, SP                   ; point BP to stack frame

            PUSH CX                      ; save CX register
            PUSH SI                      ; save SI register

            MOV SI, [BP+4]               ; get pointer to string
            MOV AX, 0                    ; clear count register
Loop1:
                                         ; Look for beginning of word
            MOV CL, [SI]                 ; get character from string
            CMP CL, 0                    ; is it the end of the string?
            JZ Exit                      ; done if end of string
            CMP CL, ' '                  ; is it a space?
            JNE Label1                   ; find end of word if not
            INC SI                       ; point to next character
            JMP Loop1                    ; get next character
```

```
Label1: INC AX                        ; increment word counter

Loop2:                                ; Look for end of word
        MOV CL, [SI]                  ; get character
        CMP CL, 0                     ; is it the end of the string?
        JZ Exit                       ; done if end of string
        CMP CL, ' '                   ; is it a space?
        JE Loop1                      ; Look for start of next word
        INC SI                        ; point to next character
        JMP LOOP2                     ; get next character

Exit:   POP SI                        ; restore SI
        POP CX                        ; restore CX

        POP BP                        ; restore BP
        RET                           ; return to caller

_Count  ENDP

        END
```

9.2.4 Accessing and Changing String Characters

To access or change a string element after a string has been scanned or two
strings have been compared, we move the address of the element in the string to
be accessed to SI or the address of the element in the string to be changed to DI.
This element is then loaded to or stored from AL or AX. There are the usual four
instructions for accessing and another three for changing.

Accessing:

1. LODSB
2. LODSW
3. LODSD
4. LODS   *Operand*

Changing:

1. STOSB
2. STOSW
3. STOSD
4. STOS   *Operand*

LODS (load string) and STOS (store string) are translated into their byte and
word counterparts during assembly.

Machine Code

Instruction		Opcode
LODSB		AC
LODS	(bytes)	AC
LODSW		AD
LODS	(words)	AD
LODSD		66 AD
LODSD	(doublewords)	66 AD
STOSB		AA
STOS	(bytes)	AA
STOSW		AB
STOS	(words)	AB
STOSD		66 AB
STOS	(doublewords)	66 AB

Semantics.   If DF is 0, SI (for load) or DI (for store) is incremented after the instruction is executed; if DF is set, they are decremented. It is unlikely that this instruction will be preceded by a REPetition factor since some action is probably needed between string accesses to accomplish anything useful. It is more likely that the load-string and store-string instructions will be enclosed together with other instructions within a traditional loop if an access or change is to be repeated.

EXAMPLE 16

```
      MOV     AL, "o"
      LEA     DI,NewName
      MOV     CX,10
      CLD
REPNE SCASB
      DEC     DI
      MOV     AL,"a"
      STOS    NewName
```

This will replace the first "o" in *NewName* with "a." DI is decremented since it contains an offset; that is, DI is 0 when we are scanning the first character, and so on. If this example were executed after Examples 1 and 2, *NewName* would be changed from "Johns" to "Jahns."

In the next section we discuss a typical application for which string instructions are appropriate.

9.2.5 Identifying Identifiers

Compilers and assemblers, as well as other translators, must be able to decide what sequences of characters form legal identifiers and what sequences do not.

Problem.   Write a program that returns a value of 1 in AX if a character string represents a legal identifier and a value of 0 if it does not.

Discussion.   An identifier may be defined as follows:
$s_1\ s_2\ s_3 \ldots s_n$ is an identifier if:

1. $n = 1$ and s_1 is a letter, or
2. s_n is a letter or digit and $s_1\ s_2\ s_3 \ldots s_{n-1}$ is an identifier.

Note that this definition is *recursive;* that is, the definition of identifier uses the word ''identifier'' (see 2). The definition makes sense because it will terminate (see 1). The following is an equivalent definition:
$s_1\ s_2\ s_3 \ldots s_n$ is an identifier if:

1. It begins with a letter, and
2. This letter is followed by a (possibly null) sequence of letters or digits.

Many programming languages define identifiers similarly. There is no limit on the length in the above definitions.

Figure 9-2 shows a procedure called *Ident* for solving this problem.

This program implements the first definition of identifier. *Valid* is initialized to 0, indicating that we are assuming (until we check) that the string is not a valid identifier. It looks first at the last character. If it is a letter or a digit, the procedure looks at the next-to-last character, and so on. When the procedure encounters a nonletter or nondigit, it exits. When it encounters the first character, it checks to see if it is a letter. If it is, *Valid* is changed to 1.

9.3 Numeric Strings

In Section 3.5, we saw another way to represent numbers that consist of a large number of digits either before or after the decimal point. Business languages such as COBOL and RPG have these data types built in. Compilers can be written for these languages more easily if there is a direct (assembly instruction) implementation of such numeric string data types. Even so, these instructions tend to be much slower that the floating-point instructions for the 87-family.

Figure 9-2 *Ident* procedure

```
; Procedure IDENT:
; This procedure checks to see if a string is a valid identifier.
; Input arguments have been pushed on the stack in the following
; order:
;
;    1. Address of a byte string called String
;    2. Count - the number of characters in String
;    3. The address of a word called Valid
;
; The procedure returns 1 in Valid if String is a legal
; identifier and a 0 if it is not.
;
;
Ident   PROC
        PUSH    BP
        PUSH    AX
        PUSH    BX
        PUSH    CX
        PUSH    SI
        MOV     BP,SP
        MOV     BX,12[BP]         ; assume not
        MOV     WORD PTR [BX],0   ; an identifier
        MOV     CX,14[BP]         ; get string length
        MOV     SI,16[BP]         ; get string address
        ADD     SI,CX             ; address of end of string
        DEC     SI                ; offset
        STD                       ; access right of string
Loop1:  DEC     CX                ; offset into string
        LODSB                     ; get last character
        CMP     CX,0
        JL      Exit              ; string is null
        JG      Long
;
; single character - should be a letter
;
        Cmp     AL,"A"            ; Is character
        JL      Exit              ; between
        CMP     AL,"Z"            ; A and Z?
        JG      Exit              ; no
        MOV     BX,12[BP]
        MOV     WORD PTR [BX],1   ; yes
        JMP     Exit
;
; more than one character - should be a letter or digit
;
Long:   CMP     AL,"A"            ; Is character
        JL      DigitChk          ; between
        CMP     AL,"Z"            ; A and Z?
        JG      Exit
        JMP     Loop1             ; yes
;
DigitChk:   CMP AL,"0"            ; Is character
            JL  Exit              ; between
            CMP AL,"9"            ; 0 and 9?
            JG  Exit              ; no
            JMP Loop1             ; yes
```

Figure 9-2 (*Continued*)

```
;
Exit      NOP
          POP    SI
          POP    CX
   POP    BX
   POP    AX
   POP    BP
   RET    6
Ident     ENDP
          END
```

9.3.1 BCD Conversions

To review, if 39 is stored in a byte by storing the 3 in the left nibble and the 9 in the right nibble, then this is called a *packed* binary-coded decimal. If there is only one digit stored in the byte, it is called an *unpacked* binary-coded decimal. In either case, note that the BCD has no more than 1001 (9H) in either nibble.

When the 86-family performs arithmetic, it does not know

1. That the number is in BCD
2. Whether it is packed or unpacked
3. That no nibble can contain a value larger than 9H to be a proper BCD number

Thus, when the 86-family adds 39 + 22, it interprets (wrongly) everything to be in binary and produces the sum 01111001:

$$
\begin{array}{rcl}
39 \ (\text{BCD}) & = & 00111001 \\
22 \ (\text{BCD}) & = & \underline{00100010} \\
& & 01011011 \quad = \quad 5B \ (\text{Not BCD})
\end{array}
$$

The answer not only is incorrect; it is not even a valid BCD since B is not a BCD digit.

If we look at what went wrong, we can easily derive a formula for "fixing up" the result of a BCD arithmetic.

1. The right nibble went "wrong" when the sum exceeded 9. This can be fixed by adding 6 to the right nibble, allowing the 1 carry to be added to the left nibble. To see why 6 is the magic number, add 6 to the various hexadecimal digits. The resulting digit is always the same in value, but is a valid BCD. For example, an addition of the BCD integers 9 and 2 would produce B_{16} (1011 in binary). Adding 6 to B_{16} gives 11_{16}, which is the BCD number for (decimal) 11.
2. If the left nibble exceeds 9, 6 is added to it (60H for the whole byte); the programmer now needs another byte for the 1 carry.

In our case the answer is fixed up by using (1):

$$
\begin{array}{lll}
01011011 & = & \text{5B (Not BCD)} \\
\underline{0110} & & \\
01100001 & = & \text{61 (BCD)}
\end{array}
$$

Note that this not only is a valid BCD, but it is also the right answer and is again stored in BCD packed decimal format.

The instructions that accomplish the above adjustments are DAA and DAS for addition and subtraction results, respectively.

There are separate adjustment instructions if the BCD is unpacked (i.e., one digit to a byte). Here, the left nibble of each byte involved in the arithmetic operation is necessarily 0, before the arithmetic operation is performed. For example, if we add 9 + 1 as BCD numbers:

$$
\begin{array}{lll}
00001001 & = & \text{9 (BCD)} \\
\underline{00000001} & = & \underline{\text{1 (BCD)}} \\
00001010 & = & \text{A (Not BCD)}
\end{array}
$$

Once again, adding 6 does the trick:

$$
\begin{array}{lll}
00001010 & = & \text{A (Not BCD)} \\
\underline{00000110} & = & \underline{6} \\
00010000 & = & \text{10 (BCD)}
\end{array}
$$

There are separate conversion instructions for adjusting unpacked binary BCD arithmetic: AAA, AAS, AAM, and AAD for addition, subtraction, multiplication, and division, respectively.

Before describing each of these instructions, we should emphasize once again that integers do not really exist in BCD format—the programmer creates and keeps track of them. The 86-family has conversion instructions for their use, but the programmer must be aware of when to use them.

ASCII Adjust for Addition

Purpose.   To convert the sum of two unpacked BCD integers to a valid BCD integer.

Syntax

```
AAA
```

Machine Code

Instruction	Opcode
AAA	37

Semantics. AAA adds 6 to the lower nibble of AL and adds 1 to AH if it exceeds 9 or if the auxiliary carry flag has been set.

Pragmatics. Since AAA and all the BCD conversion instructions require that the number to be converted be in AL, operating on a sequence of BCD numbers would require moving the numbers in and out of the AL register. Such operations most likely would be coded within a loop.

EXAMPLE 17

```
A    DB    2
     ...
     MOV   AL,A
     ADD   AL,9
     AAA                    ; Convert to BCD
```

When this sequence is executed, AX contains 0101H, which is BCD for the decimal integer 11.

ASCII Adjust for Subtraction

Purpose. To convert the difference of two unpacked BCD integers to BCD.

Syntax

```
AAS
```

Machine Code

Instruction	Opcode
AAS	3F

ASCII Adjust for Multiplication

Purpose. To convert the product of two unpacked BCD numbers to BCD.

Syntax

```
AAM
```

Machine Code

Instruction	Opcode
AAM	D4 0A

Semantics. AH is replaced by AL divided by 10; AL is replaced by AL mod 10.

Pragmatics. The reader should do a few examples to see how AAM works (and to believe it works correctly).

ASCII Adjust for Division

Purpose. To convert an unpacked BCD integer *before* division is performed so that the result is a valid and correct BCD integer.

Syntax

```
AAD
```

Machine Code

Instruction	Opcode
AAD	D5 0A

Semantics. AH is multiplied by 10 and added to AL. AH is then cleared.

Pragmatics.

Note that AAD is used before the division takes place.
Again, the reader should do a few examples to see how this instruction works.

Decimal Adjust for Addition

Purpose. To adjust the sum of two packed BCD numbers to valid, correct BCD.

Syntax

```
DAA
```

Machine Code

Instruction	Opcode
DAA	27

Semantics. If the right nibble of AL is greater than 9, or if AF is set, 6 is added to it. If AL is greater than 9FH, 60H is added to it.

Pragmatics. See the beginning of this section for a discussion of how DAA works.

Decimal Adjust for Subtraction

Purpose. To adjust the difference of two BCD integers to be valid, correct BCD integers.

Syntax

```
DAS
```

Machine Code

Instruction	Opcode
DAS	17

9.4 Structures

Structures are used when the data we are using consist of parts that—unlike array and strings—vary in type and, hence, in the amount of storage we need to allot to them. These parts are called *fields*. Structures in 86-family assembler correspond to records in Pascal and Ada and to strucs in C. The STRUC assembler directive allows us to describe such data. Its syntax is as follows:

```
StructureName  STRUC
Field1Name     Define   Expression
Field2Name     Define   Expression

StructureName ENDS
```

where *StructureName, Field1Name,* and so forth, are legal variable names, and *Define* is one of DB, DW, DD, DQ, or DT. The *Expression* defines a default value for that field. If the expression is a single value or a string, it may be overridden later. Thus

```
MyStruc     STRUC
MyField1    DB      3
MyField2    DB      3,5
MyField3    DW      10 DUP (0)
MyField4    DB      'Stuff'
MyStruc     ENDS
```

defines a structure called *MyStruc* with 4 fields, called *MyField1, MyField2, MyField3,* and *MyField4,* all with initial values. Only *MyField1* and *MyField4* can be overridden.

Structures are like macros in that no memory is allocated for them until they are "invoked." To invoke a structure, which can be thought of as creating an "instance" of that structure, we write

```
Name      StructureName     <Value1, Value2, ...>
```

where *Name* is the name of our data structure of type *StructureName. Value1, Value2,* . . . indicate values for the respective fields. These values can be null. Thus,

```
Foo      MyStruc  <,,,'things'>
```

overrides *MyField4* and initiates it to *things.* The rest of the fields are now allocated and assigned their default values.

Structures differ from macros in that they may now be used under their instantiation *Name.* The syntax for such a reference is

```
Name.FieldName
```

which refers to the appropriate field of structure *Name.* Thus,

```
MOV      AL,Foo.MyField1
```

will put a 3 into register AL.

Problem.   Write a procedure called *Update* that will take a date in the 20th century and change it to the date of the following day. Assume that the date consists of three fields:

1. Month: a byte integer
2. Day: a byte integer
3. Year: a word integer

and use a structure called *Date* with an instantiation name of *Date20.*

Solution.   Since months vary in the number of days, we will calculate this value via a macro, *DaysInMonth,* that will calculate, from the values of *Month* and *Year,* a value of *LastDay.* Then if our value in *Day* equals *LastDay,* we know we must add 1 to the *Month* parameter. Our algorithm is:

```
IF Day = LastDay
    THEN Day := 1
        IF Month = 12
            THEN Month := 1
                Add 1 to Year
```

```
                    ELSE Add 1 to Month
              ENDIF
          ELSE Add 1 to Day
      ENDIF
```

Our *DaysInMonth* macro will return 31 for the value of *LastDay* for months 1, 3, 5, 7, 8, 10, and 12; 30 for the months numbered 4, 6, 9, and 11; and 27 or 38 when *Month* equals 2. (See Exercise 7 at the end of this chapter.) The complete program is shown in Figure 9-3.

Figure 9-3 *Update* procedure

```
;   This program updates values for MONTH, DAY, and YEAR to the
;   following day.
;
; Two necessary bookkeeping statements follow
;
    DOSSEG              ; Use Microsoft SEGment conventions
    .MODEL  SMALL       ; Use small memory model
;
; Stack Segment follows
;
    .STACK  100H
;
; Macro DAYSINMONTH computes the number of days in a month for
; integer valued months. 1 = Jan, 2 = Feb, etc.
; Rule: "30 days hath September, April, June, and November.  All the
; rest have 31 except February which has 28 and in leap year 29."
;
DaysInMonth MACRO       Mon,Year,LastDay
            LOCAL       Feb,Sept,Leap,Done
            CMP         Mon,2           ; Feb?
            JE          Feb             ; yes
            CMP         Mon,4           ; no
            JE          Sept
            CMP         Mon,6
            JE          Sept
            CMP         Mon,9
            JE          Sept
            CMP         Mon,11
            JE          Sept
            MOV         LastDay,31      ; not Feb, Sept, Apr,
            JMP         Done            ;   June, or Nov.
Feb:        MOV         AX,Year         ; Get year
            MOV         CX,4            ; If divisible
            DIV         CX              ;   by 4 then
            CMP         AH,0            ;   it's a leap
            JE          Leap            ;   year.
            MOV         LastDay,28      ; not a leap year
            JMP         Done
Leap:       MOV         LastDay,29
            JMP         Done
```

Figure 9-3 (*Continued*)

```
Sept:        Mov     LastDay,30      ; 30 days hath Sept,
Done:        NOP                     ;   Apr, Jun, & Nov.
             ENDM    DaysInMonth
;
;
;  Following is a DATE STRUCture with three fields,
;    MONTH, DAY, and YEAR.
;
Date         STRUC

Month        DB  ?
Day          DB  ?
Year         DW  ?

Date         ENDS
;
; Data Segment follows
;
     .DATA
;
Date20  Date    <12,31,1957>    ; Initialize DATE Structure
;
; Code Segment follows
;
    .CODE
;
; Two more necessary bookkeeping statements follow
;
Start: MOV AX,@DATA      ; Define current
       MOV DS,AX         ; Data Segment
;
; Main Program
;
             DaysInMonth Date20.Month,Date20.Year,AL
                                 ; AL<-- lastday
             CMP     AL,Date20.Day    ; if day = lastday
             JNE     DayPlus1         ;   then
             MOV     Date20.Day,1     ;     day := 1
             CMP     Date20.Month,12 ;    if month = 12
             JNE     MonthPlus1       ;     then
             MOV     Date20.Month,1 ;      month := 1
             INC     Date20.Year      ;      add 1 to year
             JMP     Finish           ;     else add 1 to
MonthPlus1: INC     Date20.Month      ;            month
             JMP     Finish           ;     endif
DayPlus1:   INC     Date20.Day        ;   else add 1 to day
                                      ; endif
Finish:     NOP
;
       MOV AH,4CH
       INT 21H           ; Back to DOS
;
             END Start            ; End of program.  Start is transfer address
```

9.5   Records

The structures of Section 9.4 are analogous to records in high-level languages. Records in the 86-family are similar, but they differ in that their fields are bit strings.

Assembly language allows us to access and operate on bits using bit string and Boolean instructions. Converting between ASCII, binary, and hexadecimal requires such access, as do applications that access the system parts, such as I/O ports (see Chapter 10).

We can describe sets of such bit strings using a RECORD assembler directive. RECORDs are similar to STRUCtures, except that the fields are bit strings. The syntax is as follows:

```
RecordName    RECORD    Field1, Field2, Field3, ...
```

where

    RecordName is a legal name
    each *Field* is of the form
           FieldName: *FieldWidth*
    or
           FieldName: *FieldWidth* = *Expression*
    FieldName is a legal name
    FieldWidth is an integer from 1 to 16
    Expression is a default value.

Thus

```
MyRec    RECORD    MyF1 : 6, MyF2 : 8 = '0', MyF3 : 1 = 0
```

describes a record with three bit fields: the first called *MyF1*, which is 6 bits wide; the second called *MyF2*, which is 8 bits wide and initialized to the *character* zero; and the third called *MyF3*, which is 1 bit wide and initialized to 0. (The character zero is 30H, or 00110000 in binary.)

As with STRUCtures, the RECORD is not really allocated until it is instantiated with a statement of the form:

```
Name    RecordName         <Value1, Value2 ...>
```

where *Name* is a legal name, *RecordName* is the name in a RECORD declaration, and *Value1, Value2, . . .* are values for the respective fields.

```
BAR    MyRec    <001100B,,1>
```

creates the following record:

$$\underbrace{0001100001100001}_{\text{MyF1 \quad MyF2}}$$

MyF1   MyF2

MyF3

Since 15 bits are initialized, 2 bytes are used with the most significant (leftmost) bit unused and assigned a 0. In hexadecimal, this would appear as

1861

We can access the entire record under its instantiation name. Thus,

```
MOV     AX,BAR
```

will copy 1861 (hex) into register AX.

Three operators are useful in conjunction with records, WIDTH, SHIFT COUNT, and MASK.

WIDTH.   WIDTH returns the width of a record field. For our example,

```
MOV     CL,WIDTH MyF1
```

puts a 6 into CL, whereas

```
MOV     AX,WIDTH Bar
```

would put 15 into AX, since that is the total width of record *Bar*.

SHIFT COUNT.   This is a strange operator in that it is not explicitly stated, but when reference is made to a field, it is automatically calculated. SHIFT COUNT is the number of bits to the right of the field being referenced. In our example,

```
MOV     CL,MyF1
```

moves the value 9 into register CL since there are 9 bits to the right of MyF1 in record *Bar*.

MASK.   MASK is used to isolate fields in a record. It returns a 1 for each bit of the field in its operand. Thus

```
MASK    MyF1
```

puts 1's into all the bits of *Bar* that represent the fields of *MyF1*,

0111111000000000

When this is ANDed with the entire record, we can get the current value of the field. Thus,

```
MOV     AX,Bar
AND     MASK MyF1
```

isolates the value of *MyF1*, but it is not right adjusted in AX. We can combine these instructions with the SHIFT COUNT:

```
MOV     AX,Bar           ; Get Bar
MOV     CL,MyF1          ; Get shift count
AND     AX,MASK MyF1     ; Isolate MyF1
SHR     AX,CL            ; Right-adjust MyF1
```

Exercise 9 applies many of these ideas to solve the problem in Section 9.4 at the bit level.

9.6 Sets

Sets may be implemented in assembly language by using bit-string, operations and records. Record fields of length one are used to indicate the set elements. Thus

```
Letters   RECORD  A:1, B:1, C:1, D:1, E:1, F:1, ...
```

might represent a set of letters on an 80386 or above (since more than 16 bits are needed). Then to represent vowels, we might use:

```
Vowels  Letter  <1,0,0,0,1,0,0,0,1,0,0,0,0,0,1,0,0,0,0,0,1,0,0,0,0,0>
```

The exercises explore the implementation of standard set operations.

9.7 Summary

Older computer architectures did not have built-in string manipulation instructions. With the modern use of computers for information processing, such instructions have become useful and convenient. Coding the program in Figure 9-2 without string instructions would result in a program that is longer, slower, and more difficult to read. The string instructions permit rapid moving, comparing, scanning, and character accessing and changing of blocks of data.

Each of the string instructions in this chapter exists in four forms: one for byte strings, one for word strings, one for doubleword, and one that is translated into one of the other three. Since this last form allows the string(s) to be used as an operand(s), it is more readable than the other two. On the other hand, the other two allow the same instruction to be used on different string(s) merely by changing the contents of DI and SI.

The string instructions require that one of the strings be declared in the extra segment. If the programmer finds this inconvenient, the extra segment register (ES) can be made to point to one of the other segments. For example,

```
MOV     ES,DS
```

allows the operands that must be declared in the extra segment to be declared in the data segment since ES now contains the same address as DS. Another technique is to give ES the same segment name as CS in an ASSUME statement:

```
ASSUME CS:Code, DS:Data, ES:Code
```

The string instructions make active use of registers. The programmer should be careful not to modify these registers inadvertently, or even to use them without first checking that they are available for use, that is, that no string instruction is apt to use them for its own purposes.

Strings and arrays are useful when the data are all of one type. Structures and records are useful when the data are of varying types and sizes—structures when we are using multiples of bytes and records when we are using multiples of bits. STRUCtures, as described in this chapter, correspond closely to the record types in Pascal and COBOL and to the STRUCT type in the programming language C. Although C and Ada have facilities for accessing bits, there is no direct analogue in common high-level languages to the RECORD assembler directive described here.

Exercises

1. Rewrite macro *ECount* (Exercise 7, Chapter 7) using string instructions.
2. Write a procedure that will count the number of nonblank characters in a string argument.
3. a. Write an assembly language program that calls procedure *Ident* of Figure 9-2.
   b. Write a program in your favorite high-level language to call procedure *Ident*. Make any necessary adjustments in the assembly language program.
4. Extend the procedure of Figure 9-2 to include noncapital letters in a valid identifier.
5. Write a procedure to examine a piece of text and produce a list in alphabetical order of all the distinct words that appear in the text. Use

```
Text DB "The quick sly fox jumped over the lazy brown dog."
```

   as data.
6. Write a procedure that will count the number of words in a text. You may assume that a word is any sequence of nonblank characters surrounded on either side by at least one blank character. Use the text from Exercise 5 to test your program.
7. The program in Figure 9-3 considers 1900 as a leap year. This is untrue. Make the necessary adjustments to the program to reflect this fact.
8. Define a STRUCture that represents a student record with fields for the student's name, current year (an integer from 1 to 4), and a two-letter code representing the student's major. Write a procedure to create a record containing the following information:
   Name: Jill Lemone
   Year: 1
   Major: MBA

9. The program in Figure 9-3 uses an entire byte for the *Day* and *Month* fields, when *Day* needs only 5 bits (the largest number is 31) and month needs at most 4 bits since there are only 12 months. Similarly, *Year* does not need 16 bits. Rewrite this program using RECORDs instead of STRUCtures.

10. Redo the program in Figure 9-1 for an 86-family machine that has only 16-bit registers.

11. Using records as described in Section 9.6, implement

   a. element of, as a macro,

```
MACRO    ElementOf      X,Y
```

   that returns 1 in AL if X is in Y and 0 in AL if X is not an element of Y.

   b. union as a macro,

```
MACRO    Union   X, Y, Z
```

   that returns the union of sets X and Y as set Z.

   c. intersection, as a macro.

```
MACRO    Intersection    X,Y,Z
```

   that returns the intersection of sets X and Y as set Z.

   d. subset, as a macro,

```
MACRO    Subset X,Y
```

   that returns a 1 in AL if X is a subset of Y and a 0 in AL otherwise.

10

I/O and Interrupts

10.0 Introduction

We have given little attention to input and output so far in this book. With the exception of Section 8.3, where high-level language programs read input values and printed output values, all values have been defined inside 86-family assembly language programs—either in the data segment or as immediate values in the code segment. Calculated values have not been printed out; instead we have been using the debugger to examine altered registers and memory locations. The debugger, by the way, can also be used to input data (see MASM 5.1 CodeView and Utilities).

Although this technique of using the debugger is sufficient for many applications, there are commands for input and output; these commands are, respectively, IN and OUT. They perform a different type of input and output from that performed by either the debugger or high-level language READ and WRITE (or PRINT) statements.

IN and OUT operate directly on *ports,* which are addresses (different from main memory addresses), of the computer system's I/O devices.

Interrupts are instructions that cause a new sequence of actions to take place. Thus, in some sense, interrupts are like procedure calls; they differ in that interrupts may be invoked not only by a program but also by the computer itself. In addition, for interrupts, more information is pushed onto the stack, and arguments are not explicitly passed as they are with procedures.

There are two interrupt instructions—INT and INTO—for invoking interrupts, and one instruction—IRET—for returning from an interrupt.

10.1 Input/Output (I/O)

The 86-family I/O instructions IN and OUT perform a more detailed set of input and output operations than we have seen so far. Not only can we INput and OUTput characters, but we can INput and OUTput information about a device. Thus IN can be used to inquire whether disk drive A's motor is turned on. Similarly, OUT can OUTput information that will actually turn disk drive A's motor on.

IN and OUT deal directly with the I/O hardware devices through intermediaries called ports.

10.1.1 Ports

Ports are to computer peripheral devices as traditional ports are to transportation vehicles. Thus we have (air)ports for planes and (sea)ports for boats. Associated with each of these transportation "devices" (vehicles) may be more than one port, and different functions may take place in them. Thus there are ports for cargo and ports for passengers, ports for entry and ports for exit, and ports where vehicles may be safely stored. We can consider these ports gateways.

I/O ports are also gateways, but to hardware devices such as keyboards, disk drives, and other external devices. These ports are numbered, and the ports you access depend on the configuration of your computer. Thus, if you do not have a floppy disk drive, ports 3F0 to 3F7 (hexadecimal) may not interest you since they are the port numbers for the floppy disk drive controller.

These port numbers may be thought of as addresses—addresses of registers that are part of a device; each device may have more than one register associated with it. There are 2^{16} I/O addresses (64K), and these addresses are not part of the addresses in memory that we have been discussing in previous chapters. There is no confusion when a number is used since if it is used with an I/O instruction, the 86-family computers know that this is an I/O address, not a memory address.

Ports can contain data (e.g., an ASCII character), status bits (e.g., information that a device is or is not ready to be used), or control bits (e.g., information that will cause a device to be readied).

The I/O instructions IN and OUT deal directly with ports.

IN.   IN transfers a byte, word, or doubleword of information from an input port to the AL, AX, or EAX register. Its syntax is:

        IN   Reg,*Port*

where *Port* is either (a) an immediate value from 0 to 255 or (b) register DX, which contains a number from 0 to 65,535. Thus, DX must be used for addresses (ports) greater than 255.

The machine code is

Instruction	Opcode
IN AL,Imm8	E4 12
IN AX,Imm8	E5 12
IN AL,DX	E6
IN AX,DX	ED
IN EAX,Imm8	66 E5 12
IN EAX,DX	66 ED

EXAMPLE 1

        MOV   DX,3F4H
        IN   AL,DX

Port 3F4 functions as a status port for the floppy disk controller; after these instructions are executed, AL will contain a 1 in bit 0 if floppy disk drive A is busy and a 0 if it is not. Similarly, bits 1 through 3 are set if disk drives B through D are busy. We will list some of the port addresses for standard devices later.

OUT.   OUT transfers a byte or word from AL, AX, or EAX to an output port. As with IN, the port may be an immediate value from 0 to 255 or DX (in which a port number has been stored). The syntax is

        OUT   *Port*,Reg

The machine code is

Instruction		Opcode
OUT	Imm8,AL	E6 12
OUT	Imm8,AX	E7 12
OUT	DX,AL	EE
OUT	DX,AX	EF
OUT	DX,EAX	66 EF

EXAMPLE 2

```
MOV     AL,20
MOV     DX,3F2H
OUT     DX,AL
```

turns on floppy disk drive A's motor. The 20 essentially sets bits 2 and 4 since 20 (decimal) = 0010100 (binary); bit 4 enables (turns on) drive A's motor, and bit 2 indicates that no data are to be written.

We encourage the reader to execute Examples 1 and 2 with the debugger to see the contents of the registers involved.

The addresses (or port numbers) for the various peripheral devices, as well as port numbers that are unused (some of which you can use for your own devices), are shown in Figure 10-1. We will describe only a few of them here. Physically, many of the devices and the port addresses listed in Figure 10-1 reside, with the 86-family chip, on the computer's *system board*. Some, however, are extensions or expansions of the computer.

8237 DMA Controller Chip. The 8237 direct memory access controller chip coordinates the reads and writes to main memory (from the disk, say) so that the 86-family can perform other activity at the same time. This is done by providing the DMA with a start address and a count of how many bytes to be read or written, and using the IN and OUT commands on the various port addresses of the DMA.

8259 Interrupt Controller Chip. This chip handles interrupts for the 86-family by assigning an interrupt level for the various devices, such as keyboard and printer, that can interrupt the 86-family's processing. For example, the keyboard is assigned an interrupt level of 1, and the printer is assigned a level of 7. Lower numbers have higher priorities so that if the 8259 detects two or more interrupts at the same time, the one with the lower level is dealt with first; a higher level interrupt is not allowed to interrupt a lower level one. We will discuss in Section 10.2 how the 8259 coordinates the processing of interrupts.

Figure 10-1 86-family port addresses

Address (in Hexadecimal)	Device
000-00F	8237 DMA controller chip
020-021	8259 interrupt controller chip
040-043	8253 timer
060-063	8255 programmable peripheral Interface
080-083	DMA page registers
0Ax	Nonmaskable interrupt (NMI) Register
0Cx	Reserved
0Ex	Reserved
100-1FF	Not usable
200-20F	Game control
210-217	Expansion unit
220-24F	Reserved
278-27F	Reserved
2F0-2F7	Reserved
2F8-2FF	Asynchronous communications
300-31F	Prototype card
320-32F	Fixed disk
378-37F	Printer
380-38C	SDLC communications
380-389	Binary synchronous Communications (secondary)
3A0-3A9	Binary synchronous Communications (primary)
3B0-3BF	IBM monochrome display/printer
3C0-3CF	Reserved
3D0-3DF	Color/graphics
3E0-3F7	Reserved
3F0-3F7	Diskette
3F8-3FF	Asynchronous communications (Primary)

8253 Timer. The 8253, as the name implies, can be used as a timer or clock. Its ports can be accessed directly, but we will let some system routines (interrupt handlers) do this for us in Section 10.2.

8255 Programmable Peripheral Interface. The three ports at addresses 60H, 61H, and 62H are also called PA, PB, and PC, respectively, and are set to be either input or output ports. (When the machine is turned on, PA and PC are set up to be input ports and PB to be an output port.) Address 61H functions as a command register. It interfaces with various devices, including the keyboard and speaker.

NMI Register. The nonmaskable interrupt (NMI) is used to report memory parity errors (a parity error is detected if the number of 1's in a piece of data changes). When the computer is turned on, the NMI is masked off, that is, disabled. It can be enabled by putting 80H into port A0; it can be disabled by storing a 0.

Game Control.   The game control adapter allows up to four paddles or two joysticks to be attached. The various ports from 200 to 20F are programmed to provide the correct interface.

Expansion Unit.   We can add more memory and various other upgrades to our computer. Ports 210 and 217 can be programmed or read where appropriate.

Asynchronous Communications.   When the computer is equipped with an 8250 asynchronous communications element, we can use our computer as a terminal to log into and communicate with other computers. Ports 3F8 to 3FF are used to set the baud rate and perform the various other tasks that such communications entail. If a second 8250 is added, then ports 2F8 to 2FF are used.

Printer.   To ready a character for the printer, its ASCII value is placed in port 378H. Port 37AH controls the actual transmission. On systems with a monochrome display, these same functions are performed by ports 3BC and 3BE.

SDLC Communications.   The synchronous data link control (SDLC) communications adapter contains a number of chips that enable parallel communication. (Parallel communication sends bits simultaneously over separate lines.) The Intel 8255A programmable peripheral interface is used in conjunction with an 8253 programmable interval timer and an 8273 SDLC protocol controller. These devices use ports 380 to 38C. Do not confuse the 8255A and the 8253 port addresses in the SDLC with the port addresses for these devices when used separately (see previous discussion).

Diskette.   Ports associated with the floppy disk(s) are at addresses 3F0 to 3F7. Examples 1 and 2 show two of these ports. In Section 10.6, we will use prewritten system routines to access these ports.

10.1.2 Device Drivers

Device drivers are software procedures that control the actions of various hardware devices. Example 3 is a (very simple) device driver that manipulates a device that is a standard option with the 86-family (the floppy disk drive). Other devices also can be attached to the computer and device drivers written to control them. Routines that examine or change values in the I/O ports directly are often called *programmed I/O*. Typically, the status of a port is *polled* (examined) until that port indicates that the device is ready to receive or transmit data. In Sections 10.4 and 10.5 we will perform another form of I/O called *interrupt I/O*. Programmed I/O is generally simpler to implement; it may execute more slowly, however, since a loop may be needed to poll the status of the device.

EXAMPLE 3

```
TestLoop:    MOV    DX,StatPort    ; Read Status Port
             IN     AL,DX
             AND    AL,StatBit     ; Mask for Status Bits
             JZ     TestLoop       ; If StatBit not on, try again
                    .
                    .
                    .
```

Here some status port address (called *StatPort*) is read and a particular bit or bits defined as *StatBit* are checked. If they are 0, the port is polled again.

In Example 3, the device is polled until a bit or bits are set. For some applications, we may want to poll a device until the bits are cleared. Example 3 may not be appropriate for devices that may never alter their status bits for some reason since the loop would then execute forever. In this case a "delay" routine may be written, which delays an amount of time after which the device is no longer polled. (See Exercise 9 in Chapter 7.)

Ports involve manipulating peripheral device characteristics. We have presented an introduction to this topic, but a more in-depth study is beyond the scope of this book.

10.2 Interrupts

We have all been interrupted in various ways—by a friend who wishes to have a word with us, by the telephone, by a fire alarm. These interruptions have different levels of urgency, and we respond to them accordingly. If we are reading a book, we might finish the sentence we are on before acknowledging our friend; we might even ask the friend to wait while we resume and finish the page. Unless we are ignoring all calls, we cannot ask the telephone to wait; we must put down our book and answer it, perhaps finishing our sentence first. But it is unlikely that we would wait in responding to the fire alarm. It is a high-priority interruption. In addition, the fire alarm is an interruption that itself may not be interrupted: we probably are not going to answer a ringing telephone until we have dealt with the fire alarm. On the other hand, when our friend interrupts, we might allow the telephone to interrupt us, that is, to interrupt the interruption, and the fire alarm to interrupt even that interruption.

To carry the analogy a little further, we can distinguish between internal interruptions, such as hunger and pain, and external interruptions, such as the telephone and fire alarm.

Computer system interrupts share these same properties. They cause a suspension of current activity that may be resumed; they have varying priorities; some interrupts are interruptible and some are not; and some interrupts are internal and some are external.

The 86-family has two interrupt instructions, INT and INTO, both of which are described later. In addition, the computer itself may cause an interrupt to occur; that is called a hardware interrupt. For example, if a program attempts to divide by a number that will produce too large a result, a hardware interrupt may occur.

Whether an interrupt is invoked by hardware or software, the same sequence of actions occurs: current activity ceases; the flags register, CS, and IP are pushed onto the stack; the trap flag (TF) and the enable interrupt flag (IF) are cleared to prevent most other interrupts from occurring, for the time being; and control is passed to a prewritten interrupt handler.

This sequence of actions is similar to transferring to a procedure; the differences are: (a) more information is (automatically) pushed onto the stack than for a procedure CALL, (b) we cannot specify parameters, and (c) we may not have purposely initiated the transfer.

Associated with each interrupt is its *type*. It is an interrupt's type that indirectly defines the address where its interrupt handler routine is stored. An interrupt handler routine is a sequence of code that performs some action due to the interrupt.

> The address of the interrupt handler routine for an interrupt of type N is stored starting at address 4N.
> This address uses 4 bytes.

Thus, if an interrupt of type 0 occurs, the address of its interrupt handler routine is stored at locations 0–3; if it is an interrupt of type 1, the address of its interrupt handler routine is stored at locations 4–7; and so on.

Notice that the interrupt handler routine is not stored at these locations, but the *address* of such an interrupt handler routine is stored at these locations. A sequence of such addresses is called an *interrupt vector*. This is useful if a new interrupt handler routine is written that takes more or less space than its predecessor. The address of the routine remains the same. On the other hand, we can write a new interrupt handler routine, store it somewhere, and then just change the address stored at 4N to our new address.

Figure 10-2 Interrupt vector and handler

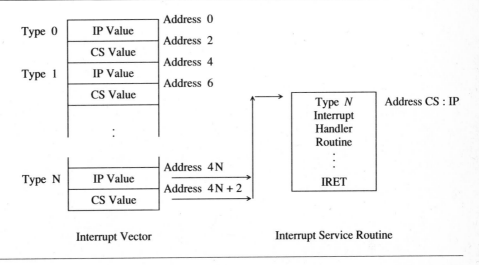

The reason for the multiple of 4 is that it takes 2 words (4 bytes) to specify the address of the interrupt handler routine. The 1st word contains the IP offset of the interrupt handler, and the 2nd word contains the CS base address of the interrupt handler. Thus, for our type 0 interrupt, byte addresses 0 and 1 contain an IP value, and byte addresses 2 and 3 contain a CS value. When this interrupt occurs, these values are loaded into the IP and CS registers, respectively, thus effecting an indirect transfer to this address. The 8259 interrupt controller (see Section 10.1) coordinates these actions, holding onto lower priority interrupts while the 86-family processes a previous or simultaneous interrupt.

The last instruction of the routine will, in many cases, cause transfer back to the routine where the interrupt occurs. This instruction cannot be RET since different information is pushed onto the stack from that pushed by a CALL instruction. There is a special instruction to perform the return, IRET; thus all interrupt handler routines that transfer back will have IRET as their last instruction. Figure 10-2 shows the interrupt vector and an interrupt handler for an interrupt of type *N*.

10.2.1 INT

INT performs a transfer to a (far) interrupt routine indicated by its type. The syntax is

```
INT    Type
```

where *Type* is an immediate value, *n,* and indicates that the address of the routine to which to transfer is itself stored at 4*n.

Machine Code. There are two different opcodes for INT, one for type 3 interrupts and one for all the rest. (Clearly, there is something special about type 3 interrupts!)

Instruction	Opcode
INT 3	CC
INT Imm8	CD

Following the opcode for non-type 3 interrupts is the machine code for the immediate data. There is no such byte for the type 3 interrupt; the ''3'' is not translated — the fact that it is type 3 is recorded in the opcode itself.

10.2.2 INTO

INTO causes a type 4 interrupt to occur if the overflow flag (OF) is set. Its syntax is

```
INTO
```

and its machine code is

```
CE
```

Two flag instructions, CLI (clear IF) and STI (set IF), are used frequently with the interrupt instructions (INT and INTO) to enable and disable interrupts.

In the next section, we will discuss built-in interrupts.

10.3 Predefined Interrupts

The following predefined interrupts can be initiated by an interrupt instruction or, where appropriate, by hardware. We do not describe all predefined interrupts.

In the author's system, the first 32 of these interrupts are used by the I/O service routine, BIOS (basic input/output service). Examining these routines reveals that many of these predefined interrupt routines use IN and OUT to access various device ports—especially the port associated with the hardware that implements interrupts, the Intel 8259 chip. This chip has port numbers (I/O addresses) 20H and 21H.

These interrupt routines are prewritten; the programmer may use them, but should be aware what the service routine actually does when executed.

Type 0 (Divide by Zero).   Type 0 is a divide by 0 interrupt and can be invoked either by the instruction

```
INT 0
```

or by the hardware if a division results in a quotient too large for AL or AX. The interrupt handler routine aborts the executing program and displays a DIVIDE OVERFLOW error; thus it does not execute an IRET when it concludes but returns control to the operating system.

Type 1 (Single Step).   This interrupt is used to execute programs one instruction at a time. The debugger uses INT 1 to transfer to a routine that services a single step interrupt, such as occurs when the T(race) command is requested.

Type 2 (NMI—Nonmaskable Interrupt).   Other interrupts can be ignored by clearing the interrupt enable flag (IF). For a type 2 interrupt, clearing IF does not prevent this interrupt from occurring; that is, it is nonmaskable. It occurs (and should be used) only for catastrophic events, such as power failure or memory errors. In the author's system, this interrupt is used by BIOS to perform a parity check.

Type 3 (Breakpoint).   This interrupt also is useful in debugging. Because it generates only 1 byte of machine code (see "Machine Code" in previous section), it can be easily "slipped into" the code. The debugger inserts a type 3 interrupt at the place where a breakpoint is requested (see Debugger GO command).

Type 4 (Overflow).   This interrupt takes place when an INTO instruction is executed and the overflow flag (OF) is set.

Type 5 (Print Screen).   This interrupt is used to print the current contents of the screen onto the printer. It is activated when the Print Screen key is activated. The cursor position is saved and restored prior to executing the IRET instruction. This interrupt routine itself invokes other interrupts, so that interrupts must be enabled by an STI as one of the first actions taken by the interrupt handler for a type 5 interrupt.

Types 6–IF (Hex). These interrupts are used by BIOS for a variety of tasks; they communicate with the system timer (type 8), keyboard (type 9), disks, printer, and so on.

Types 20 (Hex)–3F (Hex). The operating system, DOS, uses these interrupts. Once again, the programmer is free to use them but (should) not define what the routines do. Since these interrupts, like the previous ones, are documented in hexadecimal in the manuals, we will list them that way. Thus type 20 in hexadecimal is type 32 in decimal. Because these interrupts are implemented by the operating system, further information may be found in the DOS manual. Three of the predefined interrupts are described next.

TYPE 20 (Hex) (program terminate). This is used to terminate (normally) from a program. The interrupt handler routine associated with this interrupt restores system values as they were before the program executed. All .EXE files (the ones we have been executing) contain 100 hexadecimal locations of "prefix" information deposited there by the linker. Offset 0 of this prefix actually contains an INT 20 instruction.

TYPE 21 (Hex) (function calls). DOS provides built-in functions for program termination, displaying output, and interfacing with various peripheral devices. These routines are accessed by putting the appropriate function call integer into AH and then executing INT 21. In this book, we return to DOS by invoking an INT 21H with 4C (hex) in AH. Function number 01 gets a character from the keyboard; function 02 outputs a character to the screen, and function 09 outputs a string to the screen. Other function numbers and the actions performed are listed in the DOS manual.

TYPE 27 (Hex) (terminate and stay resident). INT 20 and INT 21 cause a normal termination, and the operating system DOS considers the space in which the program has resided to be free space. It is possible to terminate a program but enable it or some part of it to stay in memory. Before executing the INT 27 instruction, the programmer should store in DX the location following the last location to remain and in CS the address of the program segment prefix (see Section 10.6.4). This procedure allows the programmer to write new interrupt handlers that remain effectively part of DOS when loaded. They remain until the computer is turned off or rebooted.

10.4 Using Predefined Interrupts

We can use either the BIOS or the DOS predefined interrupts to perform system operations. Procedure TIMER uses the DOS interrupt INT 21H to get the time of day. It can be used to find the time it takes a procedure to execute. Figure 10-3 shows the interrupt being invoked. Figure 10-4 shows this interrupt being invoked to calculate the time to perform procedure *Calc*.

When the program in Figure 10-4 is executed, CX and DX contain the time of day. An example CodeView session of the program follows. The CX value, 0000, represents 00 (hex) hours and 00 (hex) minutes. DX contains 0005 (hex). The 00 value in AH represents 00 (hex) seconds. The 4C (hex) in AH is 0.76 seconds in decimal. The number still must be divided by 64k to get the time it took to execute *Calc* (on an 80486)!

```
 File   View   Search   Run   Watch   Options   Language   Calls   Help | F8=Trace F5=Go
                                  ┤ TIMECALC.ASM ├                              AX = 4C00
 0) A   :   0x0002                                                             BX = FFFF
 1) B   :   0x0003                                                             CX = 0000
 2) Result  :   0x0005                                                         DX = 0005
 36:        T_01:       CALL Calc              ; Result = A + B                 SP = 0100
 37:                    LOOP T_01                                              BP = 0000
 38:                                                                           SI = 0000
 39:                    MOV AH, 2CH            ; read time of day              DI = 0000
 40:                    INT 21H                ; DOS function call             DS = 4748
 41:                                                                           ES = 4733
 42:                    ADD SP, 4              ; remove A and B from stack      SS = 4749
 43:                    POP Result             ; get Result                    CS = 4743
 44:                                                                           IP = 0042
 45:                    MOV AX, 4C00H
 46:                    INT 21H                ; Exit to DOS w/ error level     NV UP
 47:                                                                           EI PL
 48:                    END Timer                                              NZ NA
 49:                                                                           PO NC

Microsoft (R) CodeView (R)  Version 2.2
(C) Copyright Microsoft Corp. 1986-1988.  All rights reserved.
>
```

Figures 10-3 and 10-4 use DOS interrupts, which are clearly documented in the DOS Manual. The BIOS interrupts are described in the Technical Reference Manual and require a little digging to discover all the necessary information. We will describe the process with a few examples. The exercises will explore further useful applications.

Figure 10-3 Invoke INT 21H interrupt

```
;  This example accesses the system time clock via an INT 21H.
;
; Two necessary bookkeeping statements follow
;
    DOSSEG           ; Use Microsoft SEGment conventions
    .MODEL  SMALL    ; Use small memory model
;
; Stack Segment follows
;
    .STACK  100H
;
; Code Segment follows
;
    .CODE
;
; Two more necessary bookkeeping statements follow
;
Start:  MOV AX,@Data     ; Define current
        MOV DS,AX        ; Data Segment
;
; Main Program
;
        STI
        MOV CX,0
        MOV DX,0
        MOV AH,2CH   ; Get time of day
        INT 21H      ; DOS function call
        NOP
;
        MOV AH,4CH
        INT 21H          ; Back to DOS
;
        END Start        ; End of program.  Start is transfer address
```

Accessing the Display Screen. The BIOS interrupts contain procedures for accessing the ports of the various devices. In particular, it is possible to access the ports for the video display. The Technical Reference Manual contains a description of these interrupts just prior to the BIOS listings. We show this table in Figure 10-5.

Figure 10-5 lists 10H as the video display interrupt and states that it can be found at BIOS Entry VIDEO_IO. After some search, this routine is found, and the comments preceding the code—combined with a little experimenting—allow us to set the registers correctly. We show the routine as a procedure; it might just as well be a macro (in a macro library).

Figure 10-4 Program to calculate execution time

```
;   This program calculates a procedure's execution time.
;   Written by Tyson Sawyer
;
; Two necessary bookkeeping statements follow
;
    DOSSEG              ; Use Microsoft SEGment conventions
    .MODEL  SMALL       ; Use small memory model
;
; Stack Segment follows
;
    .STACK  100H
;
    EXTRN   Calc:PROC
; Data Segment follows
;
    .DATA
A       DW  2
B       DW  3
Result  DW  ?


;
; Code Segment follows
;
    .CODE
;
; Two more necessary bookkeeping statements follow
;
Start:  MOV AX,@Data     ; Define current
        MOV DS,AX        ; Data Segment
;
; Main Program
;
        STI
        LEA     AX,Result
        PUSH    AX          ; Set up stack
        PUSH    B           ;   for call
        PUSH    A           ;   to calc
        MOV     BX,0FFFFH    ; Do 64K iteratiions
        MOV     CX,0
        MOV     DX,0
        MOV     AH,2DH       ; Set time of day (to 0)
        INT     21H          ; DOS function call
        MOV     CX,BX        ; Move # of iterations to CX
CLoop:  CALL    Calc
        LOOP    CLoop
        MOV     AH,2CH       ; Read time of day
        INT     21H
        NOP                  ; CALC's run time is in CX-DX
                             ; Divide CX-DX value by 64K
;
        MOV AH,4CH
        INT 21H              ; Back to DOS
;
        END Start            ; End of program.  Start is transfer address
```

```
 File   View  Search   Run   Watch   Options   Language   Calls   Help | F8=Trace F5=Go
                               ╠═══╡ con_io.ASM ╞═══
0)   0002 L A  :  4947:0002 ABCDEFGHIJ                             AX = 0000
                                                                   BX = 0007
 73:     Begin:    MOV AX, @DATA                                   CX = 0000
 74:               MOV DS, AX              ; initialize DS register DX = 0000
 75:                                                               SP = 00FE
 76:               CALL GetKey             ; get a keyboard char from DO BP = 4947
 77:                                                               SI = 0000
 78:               CALL ClearScreen        ; clear the screen      DI = 0000
 79:                                                               DS = 4947
 80:               MOV AH, 20                                      ES = 492F
 81:               MOV AL, 10                                      SS = 4948
 82:               GotoXY AH, AL           ; position cursor at 20, 10  CS = 493F
 83:                                                               IP = 004E
 84:               ReadLine InBuffer, Number
 85:                                       ; Read Number Char's to InBuf  NV UP
 86:                                                               EI PL
 87:               MOV AX, 4C00H           ; AH=4CH = Return to Dos; AL=  NZ NA
 88:               INT 21H                 ; return to DOS         PE NC
 89:
 90:
 91:     ClearScreen:
 92:
 93:               PUSH AX                 ; save AX
 94:               PUSH BX                 ; save BX
 95:               PUSH CX                 ; save CX
 96:               PUSH DX                 ; save DX
 97:
 98:               MOV AH, 6               ; scroll function
 99:               MOV AL, 0               ; clear window
100:               MOV BH, 7               ; White foreground, black bac
101:               MOV CX, 0               ; CH=0, CL=0; upper left corn
102:               MOV DH, 24              ; lower edge at 24
103:               MOV DL, 79              ; right edge at 79
104:               INT 10H                 ; BIOS Video Driver
105:
106:               POP DX                  ; restore DX
107:               POP CX                  ; restore CX
108:               POP BX                  ; restore BX
109:               POP AX                  ; restore AX
110:               RET                     ; return to caller
111:
112:
113:     GetKey:
═══════════════════════════════════════════════════════════════════ ═╡
Microsoft (R) CodeView (R)  Version 2.2
(C) Copyright Microsoft Corp. 1986-1988.  All rights reserved.
>WA 0002 L A
>
```

Similarly, we can write a routine to set the cursor to a row and column. We write this as a macro (it could equally well be a procedure).

```
;
; Written by Tyson D. Sawyer

GotoXY  MACRO X, Y                 ; define GotoXY X, Y macro

        PUSH AX                    ; save AX
        PUSH BX                    ; save BX
        PUSH DX                    ; save DX

        MOV AH, 2                  ; function set cursor position
        MOV DH, X                  ; column X
        MOV DL, Y                  ; row Y
        MOV BH, 0                  ; assume video page 0
                                   ;  Use INT 10H, func. 0FH to
                                   ;  get actual page if necessary.
        INT 10H                    ; BIOS video functions

        POP DX                     ; restore DX
        POP BX                     ; restore BX
        POP AX                     ; restore AX

        ENDM                       ; END Macro
```

Accessing the Keyboard. Consulting Figure 10-5 again, we discover that BIOS interrupt 16H contains routines for accessing the ports associated with the keyboard, and that they can be found at location KEYBOARD_IO in the BIOS listing. We read the comments preceding this routine to discover how to initialize the registers and write the following macro:

```
ReadLine MACRO InBuffer, Number ; define macro
         LOCAL Read             ; Read is only defined within macro

         PUSH AX                ; save AX
         PUSH BX                ; save BX
         PUSH CX                ; save CX
         PUSH SI                ; save SI

         MOV CX, Number         ; move Number to count register
         LEA SI, InBuffer       ; move address of InBuffer to SI
         MOV BH, 0              ; assume video page 0
                                ;  Use INT 10H, func. 0FH to
                                ;  get actual page if necessary.
         MOV BL, 7              ; foreground color if in graphics mode
Read:    MOV AH, 0             ; BIOS - Read Char From Keyboard
         INT 16H                ; BIOS - keyboard driver functions
         MOV [SI], AL           ; store returned character
         INC SI                 ; point to next buffer position
         MOV AH, 0EH            ; BIOS - Write Char
         INT 10H                ; BIOS - Echo Character to Screen
         LOOP Read              ; DEC CX, JNZ Read

         POP SI                 ; restore SI
         POP CX                 ; restore CX
         POP AX                 ; restore AX

         ENDM                   ; END Macro
```

Figure 10-5 86-family software interrupt library

Address (Hex)	Interrupt Number	Name	BIOS Entry
0-3	0	Divide by Zero	D_EOI
4-7	1	Single Step	D_EOI
8-B	2	Nonmaskable	NMI_INT
C-F	3	Breakpoint	D_EOI
10-13	4	Overflow	D_EOI
14-17	5	Print Screen	PRINT_SCREEN
18-1B	6	Reserved	D_EOI
1D-1F	7	Reserved	D_EOI
20-23	8	Time of Day	TIMER_INT
24-27	9	Keyboard	KB_INT
28-2B	A	Reserved	D_EOI
2C-2F	B	Communications	D_EOI
30-33	C	Communications	D_EOI
34-37	D	Disk	D_EOI
38-3B	E	Diskette	DISK_INT
3C-3F	F	Printer	D_EOI
40-43	10	Video	VIDEO_IO
44-47	11	Equipment Check	EQUIPMENT
48-4B	12	Memory	MEMORY_SIZE_DETERMINE
4C-4F	13	Diskette/Disk	DISKETTE_IO
50-53	14	Communications	RS232_IO
54-57	15	Cassette	CASSETTE_IO
58-5B	16	Keyboard	KEYBOARD_IO
5C-5F	17	Printer	PRINTER_IO
60-63	18	Resident BASIC	F600:0000
64-67	19	Bootstrap	BOOT_STRAP
68-6B	1A	Time of Day	TIME_OF_DAY
6C-6F	1B	Keyboard Break	DUMMY_RETURN
70-73	1C	Timer Tick	DUMMY_RETURN
74-77	1D	Video Initialization	VIDEO_PARMS
78-7B	1E	Diskette Parameters	DISK_BASE
7C-7F	1F	Video Graphic Chars	0

We can also access the keyboard using DOS interrupts. The DOS Manual lists this as a function request (INT 21H) with AH initialized to 1. We show this for reading a single character.

```
GetKey:

        PUSH BP                 ; save BP
        MOV BP, SP              ; point BP to current stack frame
        ADD SP, 2              ; reserve space on stack for RetChar
                                ; SP must be changed a word at a time.
                                ; It has no one's bit.
        PUSH AX                 ; save AH (can't push just AH, see above)

        MOV AH, 1              ; DOS Read Character
        INT 21H                ; Read Char into AL
        MOV [bp-2], AL         ; save char so it isn't lost in POP

        POP AX                 ; restore AH
        MOV AL, [BP-2]         ; recover character

        MOV SP, BP             ; restore SP
        POP BP                 ; restore BP

        RET                    ; return to caller

        END Begin
```

10.5 User-Defined Interrupts

To write our own interrupt routines, we must access memory directly since the operand for INT must be an immediate value. INT automatically transfers to the address which is stored in this immediate value multiplied by 4.

The first 256 locations in memory are allocated for interrupt routine addresses called interrupt vectors (see Figure 10-2). Since BIOS uses the first 32 and DOS uses the next 32, and BASIC uses the last 65, the available interrupt vectors are from 40H to 7FH. We recommend that the reader consult the manual for his or her system since some of these may be reserved.

To create an interrupt routine, select an address that is evenly divisible by 4, say, 180H. Store a CS:IP value here. That is, locations 180 and 181 are to contain an IP value; 182 and 183 are to contain a CS value. This CS:IP value is to be the location of the interrupt routine. At this CS:IP value, store your interrupt routine; do not forget to terminate with an IRET. You can invoke your interrupt with an

```
INT    60H
```

since INT will automatically multiply 60H by 4 (which is 180H), performing an indirect transfer to your routine whose *address* is stored in 180H–183H.

Figure 10-6 shows this sequence; the interrupt handler executes an IRET after computing DX = AX + BX.

Figure 10-6 User-defined interrupt

```
; This program demonstrates the use of a user defined interrupt.
; CalcInt.asm is called through INT 60H
; CalcInt.asm is linked with UserInt.asm and its start address is PUBLIC
;
; Written by Tyson D. Sawyer


        DOSSEG
        .MODEL SMALL
        .STACK 100H

        EXTRN CalcInt:PROC



        .DATA

OldOff  dw ?                            ; storage for old INT 60H OFFSET
OldSeg  dw ?                            ; storage for old INT 60H SEGMENT


        .CODE

Begin:  MOV AX, @DATA
        MOV DS, AX                      ; initialize DS register
        MOV AX, 00
        MOV ES, AX                      ; Interrupt vectors in SEG 0000H

                                        ; INT 60H vector at 60H * 4 = 180H

        MOV AX, ES:180H                 ; Get old OFFSET
        MOV OldOff, AX                  ; Save it
        MOV AX, ES:180H                 ; Get old SEGMENT
        MOV OldSeg, AX                  ; Save it

        MOV WORD PTR ES:180H, OFFSET CalcInt
                                        ; Set INT 60H OFFSET to CalcInt
        MOV ES:182H, CS                 ; Set INT 60H SEGMENT to current CS

        MOV AX, 2                       ; First number to add
        MOV BX, 3                       ; Second number to add

        INT 60H                         ; call CalcInt - DX = AX + BX

        MOV AX, OldOff                  ; Get old OFFSET
        MOV ES:180H, AX                 ; Restore it
        MOV AX, OldSeg                  ; Get old SEGMENT
        MOV ES:182H, AX                 ; Restore it


        MOV AX, 4C00H
        INT 21H                         ; Exit to DOS w/ error level 00
```

Figure 10-6 (*Continued*)

```
        END Begin
; This procedure computes DX = AX + BX
; This procedure is called as an interrupt
;
; Written by Tyson D. Sawyer

        DOSSEG
        .MODEL SMALL

        PUBLIC CalcInt

        .CODE
CalcInt:

        MOV DX, AX
        ADD DX, BX              ; DX = AX + BX
        IRET                    ; return from interrupt

        END
```

10.6 Files and Records

Files often are defined as a group of related information. The author has always maintained that they are related because they are in the same file! We will define a file as an object with a name upon which we can perform the following operations:

create
read
write
open
close
delete

Open informs the operating system that the file is about to become active; that is, we are going to read from or write to it. *Close* informs the operating system that the file is no longer going to be in active use.

We can implement each of these operations in assembly language using interrupts.

The information in a file can be a source program (a program before it has been assembled or compiled); an object program (a program after it has been assembled or compiled, but before it has been linked); an executable program (a program after it has been linked and is ready to execute); a list of data such as in a personnel file; or a list of commands to the operating system. In fact, just about any set of information can be contained in a file.

Files can be further subdivided into units called records. Like files, the size and content of records can be arbitrary. Some files consist of a sequence of records of the same size; other files consist of records of varying size. We can access the records in a file *sequentially,* that is, one at a time in the order in which they are stored, or *directly* if we know the location where the record is stored.

10.6.1 File Control Blocks

The files with which we will be concerned are stored on disk. Although the *content* of a file is arbitrary, DOS may need to know the following information in order to perform the operations listed above on the file:

The drive number
The file name
The extension
The current block
The record size
The file size
A date
The record number

This information is stored (some of it by the programmer) in a data structure called a *file control block* (FCB). The bytes in the FCB are shown in Figure 10-7.

Drive # indicates which drive is to be used:

0: default; the one indicated in the prompt: for example, A⟩ indicates that drive A is currently the default drive.
1: Drive A.
2: Drive B.
   .   .
   .   .
   .   .

The programmer sets this value.

File name indicates the part of the file name preceding the period, ".''; for example, *MyFile* in *MyFile.ASM*. This value is left-adjusted with blanks following for the remaining characters up to eight. The programmer defines the file name.

Figure 10-7 Bytes in the file control block

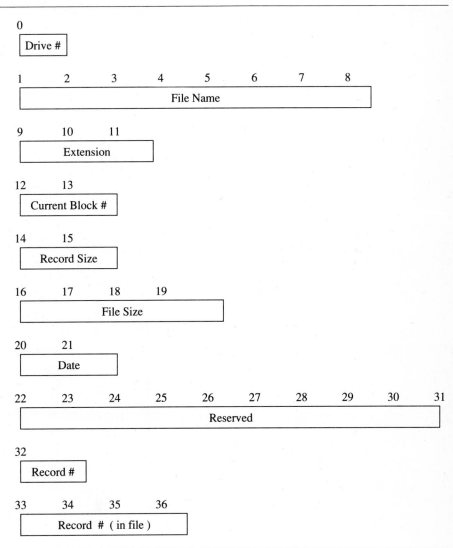

Extension indicates what kind of a file it is (although the programmer can create extensions consisting of any one, two, or three letters and digits). For example, *ASM* is the extension in the file name

    MyFile.ASM

When operating on files, the programmer must specify this field if the file contains an extension.

Current block # indicates the current block number counting from zero, relative to the beginning of the file where

```
block = 128 records
```

This number is used, together with the information in the next field, to read or write a record sequentially. The programmer must supply this information.

Record size is a "logical" size, i.e., it is the size (in bytes) that the programmer wants the records to be. This number is used for all read and write operations.

File size is the size of the file in bytes. The programmer may read this value, but not change it.

Date is the date the file was created or last updated. Like the file size, the programmer can read this field, but the operating system assigns it its value when the file is created or opened. (Of course, we saw in the previous section that we can use interrupts to change this value.) The date consists of three fields: day (bits 0-4), month (bits 5-8) and year (bits 9-15).

Record # indicates the record number, counting from zero, within the current block. Since blocks contain 128 records, this is an integer from 0 to 127. The programmer must set this field prior to performing a sequential read operation.

Record # within the file indicates the record number, counting from zero, from the beginning of the file. The programmer must set this field prior to performing a direct read operation.

10.6.2 Declaring File Control Blocks

File control blocks are easily declared using structures. Example 4 shows such a structure.

EXAMPLE 4

```
FCB      STRUC
;
Drive       DB    0
FileName    DB    "FileName"
Ext         DB    "Ext"
BlockNum    DW    0
RecSize     DW    128
FileSize    DD    0
Date        DW    0
Reserved    DT    0
RecNum1     DB    0      ; offset within block
RecNum2     DB    0      ; offset within file
;
FCB         ENDS
```

The file control block in Example 4 might be initialized as follows:

```
FILE    FCB    2,"MyFile","ASM",,80
```

This creates a structure (not a file) that refers to *File* (the structure name) with field *FileName* initialized to *MyFile,* field *Ext* initialized to *ASM,* and field *RecSize* initialized to 80. In the next section, we will learn how to create a file corresponding to this description.

10.6.3 File Operations

We can perform the operations listed at the beginning of Section 10.6 by using prewritten interrupt routines accessed by the

```
INT    21H
```

interrupt. As in Section 10.5, we first move into AH the number that corresponds to the operation we wish to perform. The numbers in hexadecimal that are used for the various operations are shown in Figure 10-8.

In addition, we can define a buffer area in which to read and from which to write by putting 1A into AH, putting the address of the buffer into DX, and then executing

```
INT 21H
```

EXAMPLE 5

```
          .
          .
Buffer  DB    128 Dup (?)
          .
          .
        LEA    DX,Buffer
        MOV    AH,1AH        ; define buffer area
        INT    21H
        LEA    DX,file       ; FCB name
        MOV    AH,16H        ; file create
        INT    21H
```

creates a file called *MyFile.ASM* if *File* is the FCB described in Example 4.

The file created in Example 5 will not show up in the file directory unless it is closed. Figure 10-9 shows a program that allots a buffer area, creates (and thus opens) a file, and then closes it. Exercises 6 through 8 explore adding more file operations to this example.

In Figure 10-9, we have added the buffer area to the FCB structure. This does not make it part of the file control block. When this program is executed, a new file named *MyFile.ASM* is added to the file directory on disk B. When a directory listing is requested, it will be listed as having 0 bytes length and the current date will be attached.

Figure 10-8 Hexadecimal equivalents of various operations

Operation	AH value	Description
Create	16	DS and DX must point to an unopened FCB. If a file of that name exists, it will be reused. If there is no space in the file directory for a new file, FF is returned in AL; otherwise, AL is set to 0, indicating space was found. The file is opened, and the file size field in the FCB is set to zero.
Open	F	DS and DX must point to the FCB. If a default drive is specified, the correct number is stored in the drive field. The current block number is set to 0. The record size is set to 128. The size of the file and the date are set. If no file with the name specified in the FCB exists, FF is stored in AL; otherwise, 0 is stored in AL.
Sequential Read	14	DS and DX must point to an opened FCB. The record indicated by the values in the fields Current Block Number and Record Number is read, and the Record Number field is then incremented. 1 is returned in AL if there is no data; 3 indicates that a partial.record is read; 2 indicates that the space in which the record is to be read is not large enough. If the record is successfully read, 0 is returned in AL.
Sequential Write	15	Analogous to Sequential Read except that 1 is returned in AL if the disk is full; 2 indicates too small an area from which to write; 0 indicates a successful write.
Direct Read	21	DS and DX must point to an opened FCB. Current Block and Record Number in file are set to point to the desired record. Values returned in AL are the same as for a Sequential Read.
Direct Write	22	Analogous to Direct Read. Values returned in AL are the same as for a Sequential Write.
Close	10	DS and DX point to an opened FCB. If file not found, FF returned in AL; otherwise, file directory is updated to reflect the current values in the FCB and 0 is returned to AL.
Delete	13	DS and DX must point to an unopened FCB. If no such file, FF returned in AL; otherwise, file deleted from directory, and 0 returned in AL.

10.6.4 Program Segment Prefix (PSP)

The linker adds 256 (100 hex) bytes to the front of all executable programs called a *program segment prefix* (PSP) control block. When .EXE files are executed, DS and ES are set to point to this value rather than to the data segment set up by the program. We reset DS by using our bookkeeping instructions described in Chapters 1 and 9. When the INT 21 or RET statement in our program is exe-

Figure 10-9 Adding a buffer area to the FCB structure

```
          ; Two necessary bookkeeping statements follow
          ;
              DOSSEG             ; Use Microsoft SEGment conventions
              .MODEL  SMALL      ; Use small memory model
          ;
          ; Stack Segment follows
          ;
              .STACK  100H
          ;
          FCB           STRUC
          ;
          Drive         DB  0
          Filename      DB  "filename"
          Ext           DB  "ext"
          BlockNum      DW  0
          RecSize       DW  128
          FileSize      DW  0
          Date          DW  0
          Reserved      DT  0
          RecNum1       DB  0    ; offset within block
          RecNum2       DB  0    ; offset within file
          ;
          Buffer        DB  128 DUP(?)  ; set aside buffer area

          FCB           ENDS
          ;
          ; Data segment follows
          ;
              .DATA
          ;
          File    FCB <2,"myfile","asm",,80>
          ;
          ; Code Segment follows
          ;
              .CODE
          ;
          ; Two more necessary bookkeeping statements follow
          ;
          Start: MOV AX,@Data     ; Define current
                 MOV DS,AX        ; Data Segment
          ;
          ; Main Program
          ;
                 MOV AX,0
                 LEA DX,File.Buffer
                 MOV AH,1AH       ; define buffer area
                 INT 21H
                 LEA DX,File      ; FCB name
                 MOV AH,16H       ; Create file
                 INT 21H
                 MOV AH,10H       ; Close file
                 INT 21H
                 NOP
          ;
                 MOV AH,4CH
                 INT 21H          ; Back to DOS
          ;
                 END Start        ; End of program.  Start is transfer address
```

cuted, the original value of DS is popped into CS. Since this is the value of the beginning of the PSP, we might wonder how control actually does get back to the calling program (DOS or the debugger, most likely). The answer is that the first element of the PSP is

```
INT     20H
```

Thus, when we execute INT 21H or RET, the DS value together with an IP value of 0 — which our first three bookkeeping instructions pushed onto the stack — are popped into CS and IP, causing the INT 20 instruction to be executed, which terminates the program.

Both the MASM and DOS manuals show the fields in the PSP. There is another executable file type whose extension is .COM rather than .EXE. When we use a .COM file, we make sure that our first executable instruction is at 100H, and DOS will set CS to point to this area when our program is executed. This saves us the need of the bookkeeping instructions that we have been using. Usually, this is accomplished by placing

```
ORG     100    ; .COM file
```

just before the ASSUME statement, and using:

```
INT     20H
```

in place of RET.

The DOS command EXE2BIN (see DOS Manual) will convert the resulting .EXE program (after assembly and linking) to a .COM file. Programs that execute an INT 27H (terminate and stay resident) often are written as .COM files since it is difficult in .EXE files to set CS to point to the PSP.

For more information about .EXE files versus .COM files, see the DOS Manual.

10.7 Summary

This chapter has been an introduction to systems programming. Terms such as ports and interrupts were discussed conceptually, with applications of their use to the 86-family. It is the intent of this chapter to prepare the reader to be able to extend this knowledge. Further information on ports and interrupts can be found in the Technical Reference Manual, an imposing document to the novice. Experimenting with the interrupts and ports while consulting the Technical Reference Manual is an excellent way to increase expertise in these areas. The exercises contain problems that will help the reader to study these system issues.

The ports and predefined interrupts discussed in this chapter are system dependent; specific locations and numbers may vary with different system configurations.

Although we generally create, read, and write files using the DOS commands and our editor, we can also create files directly by using the

```
INT     21H
```

instruction with the appropriate operation specified in AH. This allows us to access files sequentially and directly. There are many other operations associated with the INT 21H instruction, and we refer the reader to the DOS Manual for them as well as for a list of the other available interrupts and their functions.

Exercises

1. Consult the Technical Reference Manual System Unit section, and list the ports for each of the devices described in Figure 10-2, their functions, and their hexadecimal addresses. For example, a little digging will reveal that 3F4H is the main status register for the floppy disk controller.
2. Use the port addresses from Exercise 1 to write a program that will fill the screen with all 0's.
3. Use IN and OUT and the ports associated with the keyboard and display screen to write an assembly language program to input characters from the keyboard and echo them on the screen. Your program should LOOP back for each successive character until it finds a carriage return.
4. Consult the BIOS listing in the Technical Reference Manual to find the (relative) address of the various BIOS interrupts. For example, in the author's current listing, the interrupt routine for Interrupt 0 is at (relative) address E6DD (line 1485 of the listing).
5. It is common to use the system time clock in high-level languages to generate random numbers. Use the type 1AH interrupt and the value for seconds to generate a random number between 1 and 10 in assembly language. Store the random number generated at address *Random*.
6. Section 10.4 shows a macro to set the cursor position. Rewrite this as a procedure and call it from your favorite high-level language.
7. Do the problem described in Exercise 3, but using interrupts.
8. Write a procedure that will return True if a key is pressed.
9. Write a macro called *Scroll* that will scroll the screen a specified *Number* of lines.
10. Write a macro called *Display* that will display a single character at a current cursor position.
11. Write a procedure called *Cursor* that will change the cursor from a blinking line to a blinking box.
12. Write a procedure to draw a box on the video display screen.
13. Figure 10-9 shows a program that creates a file called *MyFile.ASM*. If you have only one disk drive, change the program to create the file on drive A. In any case, change the program to create a file called *MyFile.DAT*, execute the program, and then examine your file directory to see if it is there.
14. Edit the program of Exercise 13 to create a file containing names, one name per record. You should change the file type, too.
15. Add to the program and file of Exercises 13 and 14
    a. statements that will copy (sequentially) the records in your file to *YourFile.DAT*.
    b. statements that will change (directly) the third record of your original file to contain the name

        Jill Ann Lemone

Assembly

11.0 Introduction

In Chapter 1 we described an assembly language as a set of mnemonic symbols for the 1's and 0's of machine language and an assembler as a translator from assembly language to machine language. By now, the reader no doubt realizes that there is a lot more to assembly language than this definition indicates. Similarly, describing an assembler as a translator hardly indicates the vast number of actions involved.

In this chapter we will take a closer look at the MASM assembler—initially by learning some additional directives (pseudo-ops). The first group of these, described in Section 11.1, allows the programmer to control the assembly process; Section 11.2 describes some additional directives used in conjunction with macros; Section 11.3 introduces some program organization directives (also called listing directives).

In Sections 11.4 and 11.5, we take a closer look at the assembly process in general.

The chapter concludes with a description of a project for writing an assembler suitable for a classroom project.

11.1 Conditional Assembly

Assembly language is often used in applications where the amount of space allocated for the executable code is limited; in fact, most microcomputer applications involve space restrictions. In addition, we may wish to assemble different code based on various options. Conditional assembly directives provide a method for controlling the code that gets assembled. An instruction may be assembled or not assembled based upon the outcome of a condition. The form for a conditional assembly sequence is:

```
IfStatement    Expression
               .
               .
[ELSE]         .                        ,
               .
               .
ENDIF          .
```

where the dots indicate the instructions to be assembled as a result of the *IfStatement's* evaluation upon the *Expression*, and the brackets indicate that ELSE is optional. ELSE is *not* surrounded by brackets in an assembly language program.

The *IfStatement* may be one of the following:

1. IF
   evaluates to true if *Expression* is a nonzero arithmetic expression.
2. IFE   (if equal)
   evaluates to true if *Expression* is a zero valued arithmetic expression.
3. IFDEF   (if defined)
   evaluates to true if *Expression* is a symbol and it has either been defined or declared to be external.
4. IFNDEF   (if not defined)
   evaluates to true if *Expression* is a symbol and it has not been defined or declared to be external.

5. IFB   (if blank)
   evaluates to true if *Expression* is an argument and it is blank. The argument must be enclosed in angle brackets, < >.
6. IFNB   (if not blank)
   evaluates to true if *Expression* is an argument and it is not blank. The argument must be enclosed in angle brackets, < >.
7. IFIDN   (if identical)
   evaluates to true if *Expression* consists of two string arguments and they are identical. The two arguments must be enclosed in angle brackets, < >.
8. IFDIF   (if different)
   evaluates to true if *Expression* consists of two string arguments and they are not identical. The two arguments must be enclosed in angle brackets, < >.

EXAMPLE 1

```
X = . . .
    . . .
  IFE   X
  MOV   AX,0
  PUSH  AX
ENDIF
```

assembles the instructions that push a 0 onto the stack only if the symbol X is equal to 0 during assembly.

We will see two more forms of *IfStatement* in Section 11.4 when we discuss the two-pass assembly process.

11.1.1 %OUT

It is often convenient to know how our program is assembling (especially when it does not work correctly yet!). The assembler directive

```
%OUT     Message
```

will print out *Message* on the screen during assembly if it occurs in a sequence of code that is being assembled. This *Message* may occur twice. In Section 11.4, we will see why.

EXAMPLE 2

```
X = ...
    .
    .
    .
  IFE  X
```

```
%OUT    assembling a PUSH 0 onto stack
 MOV     AX,0
 PUSH    AX
ENDIF
```

prints out the message "assembling a PUSH 0 onto stack" every time those instructions are assembled, that is, whenever X is 0. (Again, the message may occur on the screen twice.)

11.2 Macro Directives

In Chapter 7 we introduced macros and a small number of directives and operators for their use. In this section, we describe facilities for writing more sophisticated macros and show an example using them. Strictly speaking, the next two directives may be used outside macros, but in reality rarely are.

11.2.1 REPT

Often we may wish to assemble a sequence of the same instructions. The form for such repetition is

```
REPT Expression
   .
   .
   .
ENDM
```

where *Expression* evaluates to the number of times the instructions represented by the dots are to be assembled.

EXAMPLE 3

```
MakeWord MACRO     N
            REPT   N
              DW
            ENDM
          ENDM
```

When this is invoked with

```
MakeWord 3
```

it will expand to

```
MakeWord 3
+           DW
+           DW
+           DW
```

═══════

11.2.2 IRP

It is possible to repeat the expansion of a sequence of instructions in an indefinite manner. At the same time, each expansion can include a different argument. The form for this is:

```
IRP        SymbolName <ArgumentList>
.
.
.
ENDM
```

where the angle brackets, $<\quad>$, are not metasymbols; the angle brackets are necessary. The instructions represented by the three dots are assembled as many times as there are arguments. Each repetition assigns to *SymbolName* the next name in the argument list. The following example illustrates IRP as well as some of the previous directives. It is a macro to generate instructions that will push up to 10 values onto the stack.

EXAMPLE 4

```
PUSH$  MACRO   N,A1,A2,A3,A4,A5,A6,A7,A8,A9,A10
       Count = N
       IFE Count            ; If Count = 0
           MOV   AX,0       ;   Then assemble instruction
           PUSH  AX         ;      to push 0 onto stack
       ENDIF
       IRP     A, <A1,A2,A3,A4,A5,A6,A7,A8,A9,A10>
           IFE    Count     ; While Count < > 0 Do
             EXITM
           ENDIF
           IFB    <A>       ;    If Count < > 0 and A is blank
             MOV  AX,0       ;       Then assemble instruction
             PUSH AX         ;          to push 0 onto stack
           ENDIF
           IFNB   <A>       ;       Else If A is nonblank
             PUSH  A         ;         Then assemble instruction
           ENDIF             ;            to push A onto stack
       Count = Count - 1     ;    Decrement Count
       ENDM                  ; EndWhile
       ENDM
```

The macro in Example 4 is called *Push$*. It is similar to the 86-family PUSH instruction, except that it will assemble instructions to push up to 10 values on the stack. This is very useful in procedures where we wish to save the registers we are going to reuse inside the procedure. The programmer can write

```
Push$        5,AX,BX,CX,DX,DI
```

instead of

```
PUSH         AX
PUSH         BX
PUSH         CX
PUSH         DX
PUSH         DI
```

When invoked with a 0 argument, this macro pushes a 0 onto the stack.

11.2.3 EXITM

Example 4 uses the EXITM macro directive. When EXITM is encountered during assembly, the macro being assembled is exited without further expansion.

Figure 11-1 shows an assembly language program using the macro of Example 4. Figure 11-2 is the assembled version showing the macro expansions.

11.2.4 IRPC

IRPC is similar to IRP, except the second operand is interpreted as a character string, and the instructions between IRPC and ENDM are repeated once for every character in the string. The format is

```
IRPC         SymbolName,String
    .
    .
    .
ENDM
```

As with IRP, *SymbolName* is successively substituted with each character of the string.

Figure 11-1 Assembly language program using Example 4 macro

```
; This macro pushes up to 10 arguments onto the stack,
; pushing a zero if none

        PUSH$   MACRO   N,A1,A2,A3,A4,A5,A6,A7,A8,A9,A10
        Count = N
        IFE Count           ; If Count = 0
            MOV    AX,0      ; Then assemble instruction
            PUSH   AX        ;      to push 0 onto stack
        ENDIF
        IRP     A, <A1,A2,A3,A4,A5,A6,A7,A8,A9,A10>
            IFE    Count     ; While Count < > 0 Do
              EXITM
            ENDIF
            IFB    <A>       ;   If Count < > 0 and A is blank
              MOV  AX,0      ;       Then assemble instruction
              PUSH AX        ;           to push 0 onto stack
            ENDIF
            IFNB   <A>       ;       Else If A is nonblank
              PUSH   A       ;           Then assemble instruction
            ENDIF            ;               to push A onto stack
        Count = Count - 1    ;   Decrement Count
        ENDM                 ; EndWhile
        ENDM


        DOSSEG
        .MODEL Small

        .STACK    100H       ; Stack segment

        .DATA                ; Data segment

        .CODE                ; Code segment

Start:  MOV AX,@Data         ; Define current
        MOV DS,AX            ; data segment

        PUSH$    1,BX         ; PUSH$ BX
        PUSH$    2,BX,CX      ; PUSH$ BX, then CX

        MOV      AH,4CH       ; Back to DOS
        INT      21H
        END      Start        ; End of Program. Start = Transfer address
```

Figure 11-2 Macro expansions

```
; This macro pushes up to 10 arguments onto the stack,
; pushing a 0 if none



        PUSH$   MACRO   N,A1,A2,A3,A4,A5,A6,A7,A8,A9,A10
        Count = N
          IFE Count         ; If Count = 0
            MOV   AX,0       ;   Then assemble instruction
            PUSH  AX         ;        to push 0 onto stack
          ENDIF
          IRP    A, <A1,A2,A3,A4,A5,A6,A7,A8,A9,A10>
            IFE    Count     ; While Count < > 0 Do
              EXITM
            ENDIF
            IFB    <A>       ;   If Count < > 0 and A is blank
              MOV  AX,0      ;      Then assemble instruction
                 PUSH AX     ;             to push 0 onto stack
            ENDIF
            IFNB   <A>       ;      Else If A is nonblank
               PUSH  A       ;         Then assemble instruction
            ENDIF            ;             to push A onto stack
      Count = Count - 1  ;     Decrement Count
          ENDM             ; EndWhile
        ENDM

        DOSSEG
        .MODEL Small

        .STACK    100H        ; Stack segment

        .DATA                 ; Data segment

        .CODE                 ; Code segment
0000  B8 ---- R   Start:  MOV AX,@Data       ; Define current
0003  8E D8              MOV DS,AX           ; data segment

                         PUSH$   1,BX        ; PUSH$ BX
0005  53            2    PUSH  BX      ;        Then assemble instruction
                         PUSH$   2,BX,CX     ; PUSH$ BX, then CX
0006  53            2     PUSH  BX     ;         Then assemble instruction
0007  51            2    PUSH  CX      ;         Then assemble instruction

0008  B4 4C             MOV     AH,4CH       ; Back to DOS
000A  CD 21             INT     21H
                        END     Start       ; End of Program.
                                            ; Start = Transfer address
```

11.3 Program Organization Directives

Designing a good assembly language program is usually more difficult than designing a good high-level language program. We have mentioned how important good comments are. It is not unusual to see assembly language programs with comments on each line.

Program organization directives, also called listing directives, continue this process of creating readable, well-documented programs.

In Chapter 7, we saw three directives for controlling the listing of macro expansions: .LALL, .SALL, and .XALL.

11.3.1 .LIST and .XLIST

When a list file (the .LST option described in Chapters 1, 5, and 9) is requested during assembly, .LIST and .XLIST can be used to list or not list certain segments of code. .LIST is the default and causes all executable machine code to be printed in the .LST file. (Don't confuse the .LIST assembler directive with the .LST file extension.) .XLIST suppresses the listing of both the source code and the object code in the .LST file until a .LIST (if any) is encountered.

11.3.2 PAGE

When a PAGE directive is encountered during assembly, the code following is printed on the next page of the assembler listing. PAGE is generally used at the beginning of macros, procedures, and segment declarations to make the .LST file more readable.

PAGE can also be used with one or two operands. If there are two operands, they should be separated by commas. The first operand must be an integer from 10 to 255, representing the number of lines to be printed on one page of the listing. Without the PAGE directive, the default is 66. The second operand indicates a change from the default width of 80 and may be an integer from 60 to 132. The higher numbers generally require that the MODE (see the MODE command in the DOS Manual) be changed before printing the .LST file. To change the width but not the length, use the default number (66) as a first operand or just precede the width with a comma. Thus

```
PAGE 66,80
```

and

```
PAGE ,80
```

both cause the assembler to create a new page in the listing file as well as to set the page length to 66 and the page width to 80. The directive PAGE + increments the section page numbering.

11.3.3 TITLE

The directive

```
TITLE      Name Comment
```

directs the assembler to give a *Name* to the code currently being assembled. Both *Name* and *Comment* (which combined must be fewer than 60 characters) are printed at the top of each page. Strictly speaking, the first six characters following TITLE after the separating blanks are used for *Name*. The rest are considered part of the *Comment*.

EXAMPLE 5

```
TITLE      Analyze  Compares two sorting procedures
```

will generate the title

```
Analyze Compares two sorting procedures
```

at the top of each page. The title of the module is *Analyz* since only the first six characters are part of the title; the comment is also printed, however, so that

```
Analyze  Compares two sorting procedures
```

appears on the top of each page of the assembler listing.
There can be only one TITLE directive in a program.

11.3.4 SUBTTL

A typical assembly language program consists of a number of smaller routines. The directive

```
SUBTTL     Name
```

directs the assembler to include *Name*, again a sequence of 60 or fewer characters, underneath the TITLE text. There may be more than one SUBTTL in a program.

EXAMPLE 6

```
TITLE      Analyze  Compares two sorting procedures
SUBTTL     BubbleSort      First sort routine
              .
              .
              .
SUBTTL     SelectionSort  Second sort routine
```

will print the same title as in Example 5, but different subtitles at different parts of the listing. The new subtitle, when a change is made, appears at the top of the next new page in the listing. SUBTTL itself does not cause a new page in the listing.

11.4 Two-Pass Assembly

An assembler is a systems program that accepts a symbolic assembly language as input and translates it into *object code*. It may optionally produce a listing (the .LST file for the MASM assembler) that contains machine code in readable form and error diagnostics. The object code is stored in a file with an .OBJ extension.

The object code consists of machine code as well as various information for the linker, all in a format known to the linker. [See the discussion of the program segment prefix (PSP) in Chapter 10.] Discussion of object file formats is beyond the scope of this book.

When we examine the assembler process, we can easily see that the essential function of an assembler is the *conversion of symbols*. This conversion is often broken into two phases called *passes*. Pass I's primary task is to recognize and define symbols, and Pass II translates these symbols to machine code.

It is difficult to generate machine code in one pass, as the following shows:

```
JG Pos
      .
      .
Pos:     .
```

When the JG instruction is being translated, the location of *Pos* is not known. This is called the *forward reference* problem. There are one-pass assemblers that recognize and translate in the same phase. This is usually accomplished by "backpatching." That is, the machine code for *Pos* is left blank, and when *Pos*'s location becomes known, this blank location is filled in. Needless to say, this involves some very complex bookkeeping. MASM and most modern assemblers are two-pass assemblers. Some assemblers may operate in either one-pass or two-pass mode. Blanks are filled in in the second pass.

The discussion in the remainder of this section applies to assemblers in general.

11.4.1 Assembler Symbols

Assembler symbols can be divided into two categories:

1. Predefined
2. User-defined

Predefined Symbols. Predefined symbols include instruction mnemonics, e.g., MOV; assembler directives, e.g., DW; and special characters, e.g., $. They are stored together with their associated machine code, if any, and other information, such as the number of operands for instructions, in a permanent *symbol table* called a machine code table. Instead of one such symbol table, there may be more than one. Thus there may be separate tables for instruction mnemonics and for assembler directives. Ultimately, each symbolic operation code must be replaced by its machine code and space reserved for all instructions and data.

User-Defined Symbols. User-defined symbols include labels, assignment statements, macro definitions, external symbols, and literals. The assembler creates and maintains a symbol table for these symbols during the assembly process. Ultimately, these symbolic addresses must be replaced by numeric addresses and constants translated into machine representation.

The *location counter* is maintained by the assembler during assembly. It is initialized to zero for each pass and contains the location (relative to zero) of the current byte of code.

11.4.2 Basic Assembler Algorithm

The following algorithm applies to both Pass I and Pass II:

```
                    Initialize Location Counter
                    Perform Other Bookkeeping Tasks
                    LOOP
                        Scan a line
                        CASE (Statement Type) IS

        Machine Instruction:   ...

        Assembler Directive:   ...

        Assignment Statement: ...


                            .
                            .
                            .
```

```
                    END CASE
                    Adjust Location Counter
             UNTIL .end or end of input
```

where

```
                        CASE (Statement Type) IS
      Machine Instruction:   ...

      Assembler Directive:   ...
          .
          .
          .
```

is equivalent pseudocode to

```
        IF (Statement Type) = Machine Instruction
           THEN ...
        IF (Statement Type) = Assembler Directive
           THEN ...
             .
             .
             .
```

The functions performed by the three dots (. . .) vary according to the statement type and according to which pass of the assembler is taking place.

Each line of the algorithm represents a function or a number of functions to be performed. For example, "Scan a line" involves picking off and categorizing the four possible fields: label, operation, operand, and comment. Labels must be inserted into the user-defined symbol table, or an error message produced if the label is already there.

Pass I.   During Pass I, user-defined symbols are evaluated and inserted into the user-defined symbol table. The location counter (LC) is updated after each line to define what the relative offset is for each line. Blocks of storage are indicated by assembler directives such as DW. The LC is initialized to zero, and LC offsets are generated consecutively. LC always contains the offset of the next byte to be assigned. As Pass I continues, LC is incremented by an appropriate amount, depending on the statement currently being processed. For example, when a DW directive is encountered, LC is incremented by 2, unless there is a DUP factor, in which case LC is incremented by the specified number of bytes.

When a symbolic name is encountered, it is entered into the symbol table. If the symbol is a label, its value is the current LC value. If the symbol appears in an assignment statement with either EQU or =, the value associated with the symbol is the value of the expression appearing to the right of EQU or =. If the assembler is unable to evaluate this expression, an error message is generated. If the symbol has previously been defined with an EQU, then again an error message is generated.

Literals and other constants are converted to their binary values. This involves conversions from any of the allowable number systems, such as hexadecimal. The length in bytes of each constant is used by the LC to update its value.

The assembler must be able to distinguish between executable instructions and assembler directives. Since instructions vary in the number of operands, this information must be kept in the machine code table in order to update the LC correctly. Thus, for each symbolic instruction, Pass I uses the size information, and Pass II uses both the size information and the machine code to which the instruction is to be translated from the permanent symbol table. Figure 11-3 shows the assembler algorithm with some of the Pass I details.

Figure 11-3 Pass I algorithm

—Basic Assembler Algorithm (Pass I)—

LC := 0
Perform Other Bookkeeping Tasks
LOOP

Scan a line, locating label, operation and operands and identifying Statement Type.
CASE (Statement Type) IS

Machine Instruction: Compute number of bytes needed.
Assembler Directive: Compute number of bytes needed.
Assignment Statement: Evaluate the expression and enter the symbol and its value into the symbol table (unless the symbol is $).

END CASE
If there is a label, set its value equal to the value of LC and enter it into the symbol table.
Adjust Location Counter.
UNTIL .end or end of input

Pass II. In Pass II, the actual machine code is generated. The permanent symbol table or machine code table is consulted to translate executable instructions. The program thus assembled is output to both the object module and to the list file (if requested). The object module contains binary machine code in the format required by the linker. The listing file contains the machine code, but in readable character form; each line of such machine code is attached to its source line.

Figure 11-4 shows the basic assembly algorithm, but with Pass II information inserted.

Figure 11-4, like Figure 11-3, does not contain any references to error conditions. For example, if an expression such as an addressing mode is evaluated

Figure 11-4 Pass II algorithm

--Basic Assembler Algorithm (Pass II)--

LC := 0
Perform Other Bookkeeping Tasks
LOOP
      Scan a line, placing source line into
      listing file, and determining the statement
      parts.
      CASE (Statement Type) IS

Machine Instruction: Fetch Opcode, evaluate any expressions and operands values not evaluated in Pass I and generate machine code.

Assembler Directive: Associated with each directive is the action that the assembler should take. For example, a PAGE directive affects only the listing, while a DB directive generates machine code.

Assignment Statement: Either fetch symbol's value from symbol table or evaluate any expressions to associate with the symbol (or both).

    .
    .
    .

      END CASE
      Adjust Location Counter.
UNTIL .end or end of input

Figure 11-5 List file from Figure 5-2

```
;   This program calculates Result := A + B when A = 2, B = 3.
;
; Two necessary bookkeeping statements follow
;
                      DOSSEG              ; Use Microsoft SEGment conventions
                      .MODEL   Small      ; Use small memory model
;; Stack Segment follows
;
                      .STACK   100H
;
; Data Segment follows
;
                      .DATA
0000   0002           A        DW   2
0002   0003           B        DW   3
0004   0000           Result   DW   ?
;
; Code Segment follows
;
                      .CODE
;
; Two more necessary bookkeeping statements follow
;
0000   B8 ---- R      Start:  MOV AX,@Data      ; Define current
0003   8E D8          MOV DS,AX           ; Data Segment
;
; Main Program
;
0005   A1 0000 R      MOV AX,A            ; Get A
0008   03 06 0002 R   ADD AX,B            ; Compute A + B
000C   A3 0004 R      MOV Result,AX       ; Result := A + B
;
000F   B4 4C          MOV AH,4CH
0011   CD 21          INT 21H             ; Back to DOS
;
                      END Start           ; End of program.
                                          ; Start is transfer address
```

during Pass II and it produces a result that does not fit into the space allotted to it, then an error message must be produced. Undefined symbols may occur in either pass, but by Pass II, any forward references should have been resolved. Undefined forward references produce error messages. Similarly, during Pass I, multiply defined symbols can be noted.

Figure 11-5 repeats the list file shown in Figure 5-2. The reader may wish to ''hand assemble'' the source program using the assembler algorithms for Pass I and Pass II.

MASM contains two more conditional assembly directives:

9. IF1   (if Pass I)
    evaluates to true if the assembler is in Pass I.
10. IF2   (if Pass II)
    evaluates to true if the assembler is in Pass II.

Some operations, such as INCLUDE, need be executed only in one pass.

EXAMPLE 7

```
IF1
        INCLUDE Macro.Lib
ENDIF
```

will assemble the instruction that includes the user's library of macros on Pass I (if that is what is contained in Macro.Lib).

11.5 Macro Processing

A macro is a user-defined assembly language instruction that is replaced during assembly with one or more other assembly language instructions or directives. *Macro processing* is the implementation of a translator that performs this substitution task, which is very similar to the substitution that occurs during text editing when one symbol or a sequence of symbols is replaced by another. Macro processing involves two tasks:

1. Macro definition
2. Macro expansion

11.5.1 Macro Definition

When a macro definition is encountered, all the statements between the statement containing MACRO and the final ENDM are entered (or perhaps pointers to such statements are entered) into a *macro definition table*. Since the formal parameters are to be substituted during expansion with actual arguments, it is useful to mark them throughout the code on entry into the table. This will save time since each time the macro is expanded these marked symbols can easily be found.

11.5.2 Macro Expansion

When an operation is encountered that is not an instruction or an assembler directive, the macro definition table is searched. If the macro is found there, then the actual arguments must be prepared to be substituted for the formal ones. Usually this is done as a positional match; that is, the first actual argument is matched with the first formal parameter, and so on.

When the matching process has been accomplished, each line of the macro is searched for specially marked characters; these markers are removed from a copy of this code, and the actual arguments are substituted. It is easy to see the parallel with text editing here. The expanded macro is then put in place of the macro call in the code.

Other issues must be dealt with, for example, a macro call that occurs in the body of a macro being expanded. Conditional assembly, local labels, and repeat blocks all complicate the macro processing operation.

11.6 An Assembler Project

Section 11.5 outlined the steps involved in the implementation of an assembler. In this section we carry this one step further by describing a project that will actually implement an assembler for a subset of the MASM assembly language. We describe this as a cross-assembler project since it can be carried out on any machine. This project is not intended to produce code that can then be transported back to an 86-family for execution! Although it can, itself, be written in assembler, we recommend a high-level language.

11.6.1 SUBMASM Assembler

Problem: To write a (cross-) assembler for a subset of the MASM assembly language. It is a cross-assembler because the resulting assembler may be executed on any machine for which its source code is implemented.

Discussion. Input for your program is a file containing MASM assembly language source statements; there are many example programs in this book with which to test your program.

Output from your program should consist of a listing similar to that found in the .LST file produced by the MASM assembler. This output listing contains the source program itself together with the assembled version, including the machine code (in hexadecimal) and appropriate error messages.

The assembler should correctly assemble programs that contain the following assembler directives and instructions:

Assembler directives

```
DB    DW    DD    END    EQU    =
.LIST       .XLIST
```

Instructions

```
ADD    AND    CBW    CLC    CLD    CLI    CMC    CMP    CWD
DEC    DIV    IDIV   IMUL   INC    JA     JAE    JB     JBE
JCXZ   JE     JG     JGE    JL     JLE    JMP    JNC    JNE
JNO    JNP    JNS    JO     JP     JS     LAHF   LDS    LEA
LES    LOOP   MOV    MUL    NEG    NOP    NOT    OR     POP
POPF   PUSH   PUSHF  RCL    RCR    ROL    ROR    SAHF   SAL
SAR    SHR    STC    STD    STI    SUB    TEST   XCHG   XOR
```

We will call this subset of the MASM assembly language SUBMASM.

Pass I. Pass I of the assembler should include evidence that

1. The opcode table (also called the machine code table) works correctly
2. The symbol table works correctly

You should also include

3. A preliminary output of the source listing
4. An explanation of your design and test runs

Pass II. Here, your program produces the actual listing file. You should include documentation for your design as well as example test runs showing how your assembler works on both correct and incorrect programs.

11.7 Summary

In this chapter we have described further details concerning the MASM assembler and assemblers in general. Conditional assembly directives and the repeat directives associated with macros are used by experienced and knowledgeable assembly language programmers. Program organizational directives should be used in all programs. They are as necessary for readability and modularity as are good comments.

Most assemblers are two-pass assemblers. The MASM assembler has two directives that refer to Pass I and Pass II: IF1 and IF2. Neither has arguments. IF1 is true if the assembler is currently in Pass I, and IF2 is true if the assembler is currently in Pass II. This is useful for controlling the %OUT directive; that is, there may be messages we would like to see only on one of the passes.

We concluded this chapter with a project for writing a small assembler. This is a favorite assignment in systems programming courses, and an extremely practical one. Although assembler functions were outlined and described, they give no indication of the myriad of details involved. Even a small assembler is a large program that needs appropriate data structures and lots of functions and procedures to make it a reasonable and readable piece of code. The exercises suggest various ways to expand on this project.

Exercises

1. Put documentation directives into the programs you have written.
2. Macro *Push$* in Example 4 does not save its own registers, even though its most likely use is to save registers! Fix this deficiency.
3. Rewrite macro *Push$* (see Exercise 2 first) so that the programmer need not specify the number of arguments. That is, the programmer should be able to invoke the macro with

   ```
   Push$        AX,BX,CX
   ```

   rather than

   ```
   Push$        Ǝ,AX,BX,CX
   ```

4. Define a macro called *BlkWInit* that is invoked with two parameters, *P1* and *P2,* that will assemble *P2* identical DW directives, each initializing a word of storage to the same value *P1*. If *P2* is left blank in the actual call to *BlkWInit,* then only 1 word of storage is to be initialized to *P1*. Assume *P1* and *P2* are values known at assembly time.
5. Write a macro called *IF* that simulates a high-level IF statement. For example,

   ```
   IF X,LT,Y,Label
   ```

   might cause control to pass to *Label* if $X < Y$. Make your macro as general as possible.
6. Extend Exercise 4 to simulate an If-Then-Else.
7. For each assembler directive in SUBMASM (defined in Section 11.6), consult the Macro Assembler Manual and try to specify as precisely as possible the actions taken by the assembler in processing it. Where applicable, distinguish between Pass I and Pass II actions.
8. Repeat Exercise 7 for the executable instructions of SUBMASM.
9. Identify and describe the functionality of the modules needed in the design of a two-pass assembler.
10. Rewrite the algorithms of Pass I and Pass II, inserting calls to the modules you identified in Exercises 7, 8, and 9.

11. Insert a general error handler module (if you have not already) into your design. Be specific about when it gets called. For example, if your module that is categorizing the four parts of an instruction finds an operation that is not an instruction, assembler directive, or macro call, then it should call the error handler.

12. Consult the Macro Assembler Manual and specify the actions that a macro assembler must take to deal with macros. Ignore conditional assembly and repeat blocks.

13. Extend your assembler design to process macros.

14. Consult a text that discusses linking and loading, for example. In particular, look at independent assembly and relocation issues. What must be changed in an assembler to allow it to refer to external symbols?

15. Continue Exercise 14 by expanding your assembler to produce relocatable object code.

16. Write a linker that will create a single load module from the relocatable object modules produced by the assembler of Exercise 15.

Floating-Point Instructions

12.0   Introduction

The 86-family instructions we have seen so far have been for integer or character manipulation. It is possible to write programs (in fact there are some on the market) that will manipulate floating-point numbers, using just 86-family (non-floating-point) instructions, but such software is quite slow. Students can also write their own if they wish. Fortunately, there is an additional piece of hardware that will perform floating-point operations more rapidly; this is the Intel 8087-family math coprocessor, sometimes called the 8087-family numeric data processor chip. With the 8086 or 8088 machine, the processor is an 8087. On an 80286 machine, it is an 80287; on an 80386 machine, it is an 80387. There is no 80487; the floating-point processor is part of the 80486.[1]

We will use the term *coprocessor* or *math coprocessor* to refer to the 8087-family, and *processor* or *CPU* to refer to the 86-family (8086, 8088, 80286, 80386, 80486).

Adding the math coprocessor to an 86-family computer is, in some sense, equivalent to combining two computers—one for the operations we have discussed in the previous 11 chapters and one for arithmetic operations involving real numbers—all under the same cover. The PC's are designed so that a coprocessor such as one of the 8087-family can simply be plugged into an empty socket on the system board. Although this is quite simple to do, you may wish to have it done at your local computer store since two system board switches must be reset.

Interfacing between these two "computers" is performed automatically. Since the instruction sets for the two processors are different, they can each recognize their own instructions. When an instruction occurs that involves the math coprocessor, processing "escapes" (see the ESCAPE instruction in Section 12.1.2) to the math coprocessor. Interestingly, the CPU can now continue with the next instructions, while the math coprocessor executes the instruction intended for it. This can be either an efficient or an erroneous action, depending on the circumstances. Additional instructions exist in both instruction sets to help the programmer synchronize these "parallel" processing activities. Often, the interfacing between the two processors is done by using memory as the intermediary.

12.1 Coprocessing

A true coprocessing system would, as the term implies, consist of two processors, each operating independently but in cooperation with the other, sharing memory and peripheral devices. True coprocessing systems are rare; instead, most coprocessing systems assign specific duties to each processor, and one of the processors is effectively "in charge." This master/slave situation exists to some extent when we add the math coprocessor to the 86-family. Although the coprocessor executes autonomously, the CPU is really in charge.

---

[1] But be careful; as of this writing there were versions of the 80486 that did not include a floating-point processor.

12.1.1 CPU/Coprocessor Interface

The instructions for the math coprocessor differ from those for the CPU. In particular, the assembler mnemonics are different—all math coprocessor instructions begin with an F (for floating-point). When one of these instructions occurs in a stream of instructions, the math coprocessor recognizes it and begins to decode it. At the same time, if there is a memory reference in the operand, the CPU calculates this address and makes it available to the coprocessor, which can now access the data. When the coprocessor knows what operation it is to perform and has the operand (if any) that represents a memory address or CPU register contents, it begins execution. The CPU, on the other hand, returns to the instruction stream and gets the next instruction. If it is also a coprocessor instruction, then it may have to wait; if it is not, then the CPU continues execution in parallel with the coprocessor, at times a dangerous situation since the coprocessor may store a result that the CPU reads and does not know was changed.

Thus, when the CPU and the coprocessor are operating in parallel, a number of problems can occur. The CPU may need a result that the coprocessor is computing; there is a WAIT instruction (Section 12.1.3) that the programmer can insert in the program that effectively causes the CPU to wait for the coprocessor's results.

Another situation that may occur during coprocessing is an attempt by both the CPU and the coprocessor to update the same memory location. Although this is resolved on a first-come basis, it may be difficult when the program is written to ascertain which processor will be first. The programmer can assert control by using the WAIT instruction or the LOCK instruction (Section 12.1.4).

12.1.2 Escape

The math coprocessor instructions are translated automatically by the assembler into an ESCAPE, whose mnemonic is ESC, together with the actual operation to be performed. Thus the programmer does not code an ESC when using math coprocessor instructions. We include it because it will be shown in the machine code listing when the floating-point instruction is assembled.

ESC fetches an operand and makes it available to an external processor. The syntax is

```
ESC    ExternalOpcode, Operand
```

and the semantics of this instruction cause *Operand*'s address (if a memory reference) to be accessed by the processor for which the external opcode is appropriate.

EXAMPLE 1

```
ESC  2FH, TestPlace
```

makes *TestPlace*'s address available to the 8087-family member, which performs the operation indicated by 2FH. We will see in Section 12.4 that this is the machine code for an instruction that stores an 8087-family register called the status register.

Machine Code. All math coprocessor instructions are encoded into 6 bits. These 6 bits are embedded (and separated) in 2 bytes that represent (a) an ESC, (b) the floating-point operation itself, and (c) some addressing mode information. We saw similar situations in Chapters 4 and 5 for instructions like ADD and SUB that had the same machine code in their first bytes for some operands. Instructions that access memory are 4–6 bytes in length. The machine code for ESC in the context of a floating-point instruction is

```
11011xxx  mmxxxrrr
```

where the x's represent the machine code for the coprocessor instruction, and mm and rrr are the addressing mode information (see Figure 5-3). Thus, in the assembled listing, "D" (1101) will occur as the first hexadecimal digit of one of the bytes of the translated code when a coprocessor instruction is translated.

EXAMPLE 2

The machine code for Example 1 is

```
DD 3E 0020 R
```

where 0020 R indicates that *TestPlace* is at 0020 (hex) in the program's data segment. The DD 3E in binary is

$$\underbrace{11011}101 \;\; 00111110$$
$$\text{ESC xxx mmxxxrrr}$$

so that the floating-point instruction (in binary) must be 11011101, which is the machine code for the instruction FSTSW (floating store the status word) when the operand (*TestPlace*) is a 16-bit integer.

In addition to ESC, there is another byte of machine code generated when a coprocessor instruction is assembled — the opcode for WAIT.

12.1.3 Wait

WAIT causes the CPU to wait until an external interrupt occurs. It has no operands, and its machine code is

    9B

WAIT, like ESC, is automatically generated by the assembler when a coprocessor instruction is translated. (There are a few coprocessor instructions that do not contain this wait byte.) During execution, if the coprocessor is busy, the CPU is put into a wait state until the coprocessor signals (via an interrupt) that it is available. There is, as we will see, a coprocessor instruction FWAIT that also causes the CPU to wait until the coprocessor is finished. Logically, it performs the same operation as WAIT and has the same machine code as WAIT.

12.1.4 Lock

LOCK is a prefix that precedes an instruction. No accesses can be made by the coprocessor for the duration of the instruction it precedes. It has no operands, and its machine code is

    F0

If we allow the CPU and the coprocessor to execute simultaneously and to access a common memory location, with at least one of them allowed to change the location, then we might want to use a LOCK instruction. In this text, however, we will force synchronization with the WAIT instruction.

12.2 Math Coprocessor Architecture

In Chapter 2, we saw that the term *architecture* refers to the structure of the processor—its registers and the operations that take place on them—as well as to other parts of the computer, such as memory. The math coprocessor shares memory with the CPU; thus we will be describing primarily the registers that are part of the math coprocessor, including their size and the notation needed to refer to them. In Section 12.3, we will discuss the floating-point data types and the ways in which they are stored in these registers.

12.2.1 Math Coprocessor Register Set

There are 10 registers in the math coprocessor register set. Eight of these are 80 bits long and organized into a stack, with the expression ST or ST(0) denoting the current stack top. ST(i) denotes the ith register from the top.

The remaining two registers are the control word register and the status word register, each of which is 16 bits in length. We will discuss these two registers first.

Status Word. The math coprocessor's status word is similar to the CPU's flags register. It reflects the overall state of the math coprocessor. Like the flags register, it contains information to determine whether to perform a conditional branch after a comparison. Unlike the flags register, it contains a pointer, a value from 0 to 7, to the math coprocessor's current stack top. In the CPU, an entire register is needed to address the top of the memory stack since it is an address in memory. Other bits in the status word indicate error situations such as overflow or a divide by zero. Figure 12-1 shows the names and meanings of the bits in the status word. These meanings vary among the 8087-family members.

The first 5 of these bits are also called exception bits since they are set when an exception, that is, an error, has occurred. Although the math coprocessor sets the condition codes (C0–C3), the status word must be stored in memory and examined by the CPU to perform a conditional branch instruction. We will see a program in Section 12.5 that does exactly this to find the maximum of a list of floating-point numbers.

The control word, described next, can affect whether these bits are actually set when these situations occur; that is, the programmer can control the setting of these bits.

Control Word. The control word is information that defines how the coprocessor is to operate during execution. The control word controls whether the bits in the status word are set or not. During instruction execution, the coprocessor consults the control word to determine what to do if an error has occurred (e.g., trying to pop from an empty stack element), to check for overflow or underflow, and to determine the degree of precision and rounding. When the appropriate bit in the control word is set (by the programmer), then these situations, called *exceptions,* are ignored; when the appropriate bits are clear, the exceptions are not ignored—when the exception occurs, the corresponding bits in the status word are set. This may cause a specific interrupt handler to be invoked. Figure 12-2 shows the names and meanings of the bits in the control word.

The first 6 bits in the control word are called exception masks since when they are set they effectively mask, that is, prevent, the corresponding bits in the status word from being set when the exception occurs. Bits 7 through 12 are called

Figure 12-1 Status word

15				7										0
B	C3	ST		C2	C1	C0	IR	SF	PE	UE	OE	ZE	DE	IE

IE (Bit 0) — Invalid operation except: Set if operation invalid on 8087; undefined on 80287 and 80387.

DE (Bit 1) — Denormalized operand exception: Set if operand not in normalized form (see Section 12.3).

ZE (Bit 2) — Zero divide exception: Set if an attempt to divide by 0 has occurred.

OE (Bit 3) — Overflow exception: Set if overflow has occurred.

UE (Bit 4) — Underflow exception: Set if underflow has occurred.

PE (Bit 5) — Precision exception: Set if the result of the operation is inexact.

SF (Bit 6) — Stack flag: Stack flag on 80387; undefined on 8087 and 80287.

IR or ES (Bit 7) — Interrupt request: Set if the Math Coprocessor interrupts the CPU on the 8087; Error Summary on 80287 and 80387.

C0 (Bit 8) — : Set by comparison instructions when the current stack top contains a value less than the operand.

C1 (Bit 9) — : Set by the Partial Remainder operation (see FPREM) and by the Examine Stack Top instruction when the current stack top is either negative or empty.

C2 (Bit 10) — : Set by comparison instructions when the current stack top contents are not interpretable.

ST (Bits 11–13) — Stack top pointer: Contains a value from 0–7 representing the stack register currently considered as the top.

C3 (Bit 14) — : Set by comparison instructions when the stack top contains a value equal to the operand.

B (Bit 15) — Busy flag: Set when the Math Coprocessor is busy, i.e., when it is executing an instruction. This value is made available to the 86-family CPU so that it knows whether the 8087-family processor is busy or not.

control bits since they control the way real numbers will be dealt with when approximations are necessary.

Floating-Point Stack. Most math coprocessor arithmetic operations that require operands operate on the floating-point stack. This stack consists of eight 80-bit registers. Do not confuse the 8087-family register stack with the 86-family memory stack. The 8087-family stack registers are accessed relatively, rather than absolutely, by referencing each from its offset from the current stack top. The ST bits in the status register, bits 11 through 13, contain the current stack

Figure 12-2 Control word

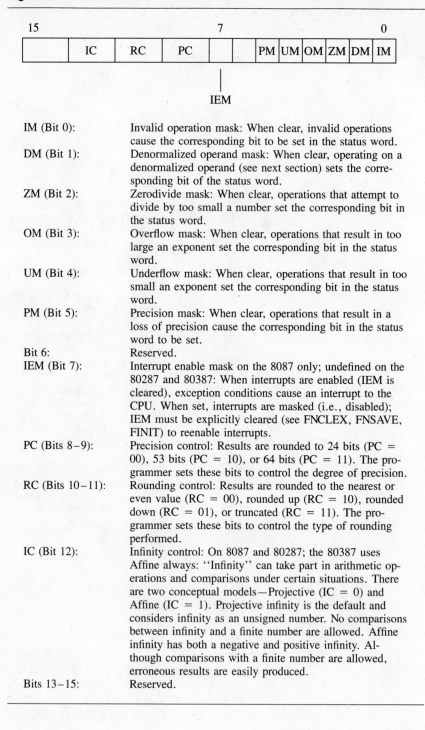

IM (Bit 0):	Invalid operation mask: When clear, invalid operations cause the corresponding bit to be set in the status word.
DM (Bit 1):	Denormalized operand mask: When clear, operating on a denormalized operand (see next section) sets the corresponding bit of the status word.
ZM (Bit 2):	Zerodivide mask: When clear, operations that attempt to divide by too small a number set the corresponding bit in the status word.
OM (Bit 3):	Overflow mask: When clear, operations that result in too large an exponent set the corresponding bit in the status word.
UM (Bit 4):	Underflow mask: When clear, operations that result in too small an exponent set the corresponding bit in the status word.
PM (Bit 5):	Precision mask: When clear, operations that result in a loss of precision cause the corresponding bit in the status word to be set.
Bit 6:	Reserved.
IEM (Bit 7):	Interrupt enable mask on the 8087 only; undefined on the 80287 and 80387: When interrupts are enabled (IEM is cleared), exception conditions cause an interrupt to the CPU. When set, interrupts are masked (i.e., disabled); IEM must be explicitly cleared (see FNCLEX, FNSAVE, FINIT) to reenable interrupts.
PC (Bits 8–9):	Precision control: Results are rounded to 24 bits (PC = 00), 53 bits (PC = 10), or 64 bits (PC = 11). The programmer sets these bits to control the degree of precision.
RC (Bits 10–11):	Rounding control: Results are rounded to the nearest or even value (RC = 00), rounded up (RC = 10), rounded down (RC = 01), or truncated (RC = 11). The programmer sets these bits to control the type of rounding performed.
IC (Bit 12):	Infinity control: On 8087 and 80287; the 80387 uses Affine always: "Infinity" can take part in arithmetic operations and comparisons under certain situations. There are two conceptual models—Projective (IC = 0) and Affine (IC = 1). Projective infinity is the default and considers infinity as an unsigned number. No comparisons between infinity and a finite number are allowed. Affine infinity has both a negative and positive infinity. Although comparisons with a finite number are allowed, erroneous results are easily produced.
Bits 13–15:	Reserved.

Figure 12-3 ST bits = 011

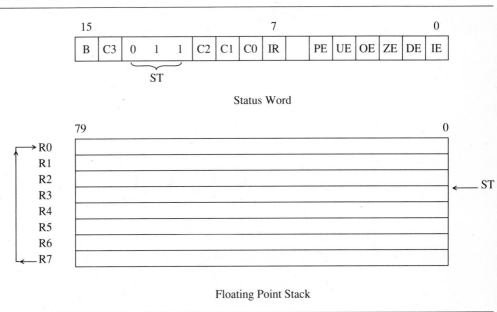

Status Word

Floating Point Stack

top. Figure 12-3 shows a situation where the ST bits in the status word contain 011 (binary). That is, ST contains 011, indicating that R3 is the current stack top.

The stack operations push and pop by decrementing and incrementing ST, respectively. Thus, when ST = 3 (011 binary), an operation that pushes a result onto the stack will change ST to 2 (010 binary), and an operation that pops a value from the stack will increase an ST value of 3 to 4 (100 binary).

The floating-point stack ''wraps around.'' Thus, popping the stack, which increments ST, will change an ST value of 111 (binary) to 000 (binary). Pushing a value onto the stack when ST = 000 changes ST to 111. Such wrap-arounds may represent errors if the programmer is not aware of their occurrence.

All registers in the floating-point stack are referenced relative to ST(0) (also denoted ST). Thus ST(1) denotes the register just ''below'' ST (in our picture).

12.2.2 Other Architecture Elements

The math coprocessor also contains a tag word that describes the contents of the floating-point registers and a set of exception pointers that contain the most recently executed instruction and operand. We refer the interested reader to the reference manuals.

12.3 Math Coprocessor Data Types

The math coprocessor operates on seven data types:

1. Word integer
2. Short integer
3. Long integer
4. Packed decimal
5. Short real
6. Long real
7. Temporary real

Short integers are the same size as doublewords, and long integers are the same size as quadwords. Their inclusion in the coprocessor allows such values to be stored in the coprocessor's registers, thus speeding up operations involving frequently referenced variables since they do not have to be transferred from memory. On the other hand, the math coprocessor converts each of these types to its internal temporary real format (described later), which adds to the time needed to process them.

12.3.1 Integer Types

Word integers are 16 bits in length, short integers are 32 bits, and long integers are 64 bits. These integer types have the same properties as integers in the CPU; in particular, negative integers are represented in two's complement.

Similarly, packed decimal integers in the coprocessor occupy 80 bits, but otherwise are the same as packed decimal types described in Chapter 3; that is, each byte represents 2 decimal digits. The leftmost bit is a sign bit, and the bits from 0 to 72 represent the packed decimal digits. Bits 73 through 78 are not used.

Integers and the operations on them are easily dealt with, whether they are in the CPU or the math coprocessor. Real, that is, floating-point, numbers are more complicated since frequently they represent an *approximation* of the actual value. For example, $1/3 = 0.333333$ . . . cannot be represented exactly in decimal. Even $1/10$, which can be represented finitely as 0.1 in decimal, cannot be represented exactly in binary since $1/10$ (decimal) is $0.000110011001100110011001100$. . .in binary. And, of course, there are numbers such as π that cannot be represented exactly in any number system. The best we can expect is an accurate approximation, and that real numbers that happen to be exact, for example, $1/4$ (decimal), which is 0.01 (binary), be represented correctly. The numbers that can be represented exactly vary with the size of the registers used to store them.

The math coprocessor converts all numbers (real or integer) to its internal 80-bit temporary real format, which allows a precision of 64 bits. This is actually the default value for the PC field of the control word. Short real and long real formats exist for convenience for interfacing with the CPU when short (or approximate) real numbers are to be loaded from or stored to memory.

12.3.2 Temporary Real Format

Temporary real format represents numbers in 80 bits; bits 63 through 0 represent the mantissa (positions following the decimal point); bits 64 through 78 represent the exponent; bit 79 encodes the sign.

```
79          63                                                        0
+-+--------+--------------------------------------------------------+
|S|Exponent|                      Mantissa                          |
+-+--------+--------------------------------------------------------+
```

The floating-point number is converted to *normalized* form before it is represented by a combination of these three fields. We will discuss each of these fields separately after an explanation of normalization.

Normalization. Normalization is similar to scientific notation, which would represent the number 345.67 as $3.4567 * 10^2$. Normalization uses a similar form, but (a) deals with the number in binary and (b) puts the leftmost 1 bit just to the left of the binary point. Thus 1011.111 (binary) is normalized to $1.011111 * 2^3$. Note that we are showing the base and exponent in decimal. A more consistent representation would be $1.011111 * (10)^{11}$, where all parts are shown in binary. At this point, the reader might wish to refer back to Chapter 3 to review how to convert from a decimal fraction to a binary fraction.

Mantissa. The bits from 63 through 0 represent the mantissa (also called the *significand*) of normalized binary fractions. The mantissa of $1.011111*2^3$ is

$$10111110 \leftarrow \text{all 0's} \rightarrow 0.$$

Exponent. Both positive and negative exponents must be represented. Although two's complement might seem to be the obvious way, it is not the representation that is actually used in most modern computers. Instead an integer representing a value about halfway through the range of exponents is selected and added to the exponent of the normalized number. This number is called a *bias,* and the resulting exponent is said to be *biased*.

For temporary real format, the bias is $2^{14} - 1$, which is 16383 (decimal) or 11111111111111 (binary). This bias is added to the exponent of a normalized binary number before it is stored in temporary real format. Thus the exponent of the normalized fraction $1.011111 * 2^3$ is $16383 + 3$ or 16386 (decimal), which is stored in binary as 100000000000010.

Sign.   The sign is stored in bit 79, 0 for a positive number and 1 for a negative number.

EXAMPLE 3

Show how the binary number 1011.111 (which is 11.875 decimal) is stored in temporary real format.

Step 1: Normalize: $1.011111 * 2^3$ or $1.011111 * (10)^{11}$.
Step 2. Identify the mantissa: 1011111.
Step 3: Bias the exponent: 11111111111111 + 11
                  = 100000000000010.
Step 4: Identify the sign: 0 (for positive).

Thus, 1011.111 (binary) is stored in temporary real format as:

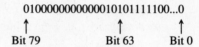

0100000000000010101111100...0
    ↑   ↑   ↑
  Bit 79   Bit 63   Bit 0

This is $4007BE00000000000000_{16}$. Note that the listing file shows the least significant bytes first.

EXAMPLE 4

Show -0.25 (decimal) as it would be stored using temporary real format.

Step 0: Convert to binary: -0.01.
          (See Chapter 3 for conversion method.)
Step 1: Normalize: $-1.0 * 2^{-2}$
Step 2: Identify the mantissa: 10000000. . .0
                  (64 bits in all).
Step 3: Identify the exponent: 11111111111111 − 2
                  = 11111111111101.
Step 4: Identify the sign: 1 (for negative).

Thus -0.25 (decimal) would be stored as

1011111111111101011000000...0
    ↑   ↑   ↑
  Bit 79   Bit 63   Bit 0

This is $BFFD8000000000000000_{16}$.

12.3.3 Short Real Format

A short integer represents a floating-point number in a format similar to temporary real format, but with fewer bits. A real number in short integer format has 32 bits, 1 for the sign, 8 for the biased exponent, and 23 for the mantissa.

The bias that is added to the exponent is $2^7 - 1 = 127$ (decimal) or 1111111 (binary).

There is one significant difference between temporary real format and short integer format. Since normalization requires a 1 to the left of the binary point, and space is limited, this bit is not actually stored. Thus a mantissa of 1011111 would be stored as 011111.

EXAMPLE 5

Show how 1011.111 (binary) would be represented using short integer format.

Step 1: Normalize: $1.011111 * 2^3$.
Step 2: Identify the mantissa: 1011111(but we will not store the leftmost 1).
Step 3: Identify the exponent: 1111111 − 11 = 10000010.
Step 4: Identify the sign: 0 (for positive).

Thus, 1011.111 (binary) is stored in short real format as

$$01000001001111100000000000000000$$

This is $413E0000_{16}$.

12.3.4 Long Real Format

Long real format is analogous to short real format, but allows for 64 bits, which are allotted as follows:

Bit 63:   Sign
Bits 52−62:   Exponent
Bits 51−0:   Mantissa

The exponent bias is $2^{10} - 1 = 1023$ (decimal) $= 1111111111$ (binary). Once again the 1 to the left of the binary point is not stored.

EXAMPLE 6

Show −0.25 (decimal) as it would be stored in long real format.

Step 0: Convert to binary: −0.25 (decimal) = −0.01 (binary).
Step 1: Normalize: $-0.01 = -1.0 * 2^{-2}$
Step 2: Identify the mantissa: 10 . . . 0 (52 bits total)
(remember: the 1 is
not stored).
Step 3: Calculate the exponent: 1111111111 − 10 = 1111111101.
Step 4: Identify the sign: 1 (for negative).

Thus, −0.25 (decimal) is stored as

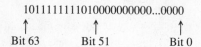

This is BF0000000000000$_{16}$.

12.3.5 Special Data Types

In Section 12.2, we saw that the math coprocessor can deal with infinity; in fact, it can deal with both positive and negative infinity. In addition, there are other bit patterns that the 8087-family interprets as special data types. In almost all cases, these types occur as intermediate values in a series of arithmetic operations. The entire sequence may result in a normal real number, but an intermediate result may be too large or small to exist in the standard real formats. Many of these types are created as a result of exception masking. For example, if exceptions are not masked, a "divide by zero" error would cause the 86-family to respond. With exceptions masked, the value infinity is created and used. There are special types other than those mentioned here. See the Intel Manual for more information.

Denormal Type.   Normalized real numbers have nonzero exponents. When a temporary value in the middle of a sequence of operations will result in a negative exponent, the 8087-family replaces the exponent by 0 and regards the binary point as having been shifted the appropriate number of places. Although the number is now denormalized, it can continue to be used in calculations.

Unnormal Type.   When a denormal is loaded from memory or used in an arithmetic operation, it must be converted to temporary real format. It is then called an unnormal. Normal real numbers in temporary real format have a 1 in bit 63 — the first bit of the mantissa. Unnormals have a 0 in bit 63.

NAN (Not a Number). When an operation is undefined, a result called a NAN can be produced. Trying to find the square root of a negative number can produce a NAN. The 8087-family allows arithmetic to continue using such (non-) numbers. NAN's are distinguished by the fact that they contain a string of 1's as the biased exponent.

Real Indefinite. When an invalid operation is performed, such as pushing a number onto the stack when it is full, a real indefinite type is created. It is distinguished by the negative sign bit, a biased exponent of all 1's, and two 1's followed by all 0's in the significand.

12.4 Math Coprocessor Instruction Set

The IEEE floating-point standard includes sizes and formats of data types, standard algorithms for operating on them, and recommendations for exception detection, exception handling, infinity arithmetic, and rounding controls. The math coprocessor conforms to this standard.

There are instructions for data transfer and conversion; arithmetic instructions, including operations for finding square roots, scaling, rounding, and computing absolute values; comparison instructions; transcendental operations, such as common trigonometric and exponential functions; and processor control instructions, such as enabling and disabling interrupts.

Mnemonically, all instructions begin with F. Some instructions have versions that end in P, meaning that the stack is to be popped after the instruction is performed. Some instructions have a variant that ends in R, which means to perform the operation with the operands reversed. In addition, some instructions have integer versions that begin with FI and perform the operation on an integer memory argument.

For example, the floating-point subtract operation has the following variants.

```
      FSUB      Operand1, Operand2
```

subtracts *Operand2* from *Operand1* and stores the difference in *Operand1* where one of the operands is ST. (ST denotes the *contents* of the register pointed to by ST.)

```
      FSUBP     Operand1, Operand2
```

performs the same actions, but then pops the stack.

The instruction

```
      FISUB     Operand
```

subtracts the integer argument *Operand* from ST.

```
      FSUBR     Operand1, Operand2
```

subtracts *Operand1* from *Operand2* and stores the difference in *Operand1*, where once again one of the arguments is ST. Note that this is a reverse operation from that performed by FSUB. If FSUB has only one operand (a memory reference), then ST is assumed and subtracted from it, and the difference stored in ST. Also, there is an FSUBRP, which subtracts, reverses, and pops, and an FISUBR, which subtracts an integer reversed similar to the FSUBR instruction.

We show each instruction group in a table that includes (a) the instruction name, (b) the instruction mnemonic, (c) the forms of its operands, (d) a brief description of its semantics, and (e) its machine code. The machine code consists of two groups of 3 bits embedded into the ESCAPE instruction and the addressing mode field, with a preceding WAIT byte. The terms *Source* and *Destination* refer to memory operands and generate different machine code depending on whether they are

SR—short real   (32 bits)
LR—long real   (64 bits)
TR—temporary real (80 bits)
SI—short integer   (32 bits)
LI—long integer   (64 bits)
WI—word integer   (16 bits)

In all cases, ST denotes the contents at the current top of the stack, and ST(i) denotes the contents of the stack, which are *i* entries "below" ST.

It is possible to leave out the operands for many of these instructions. Such instructions are said to have implicit arguments. For example, FSUB without operands performs the same function as

        FSUBP   ST(i),ST

not

        FSUB   ST(i),ST

We feel that it is too easy to make errors in these cases, and we have not shown the version of the instruction with implicit operands.

We may need to know how long it takes for an instruction to execute in order to synchronize the 8087-family with the 86-family. This is called the *cycle time*.

12.4.1 Data Transfer Instructions

The data transfer instructions load data from memory into the coprocessor stack, move data from one stack register to another, and store data from the coprocessor stack to memory. When data are moved into the coprocessor, they are automatically converted to temporary real format, no matter what their original type. Figure 12-4 shows the various flavors of data transfer instructions.

Figure 12-4 Data transfer instructions

Name	Operation	Operand(s)	Meaning	Machine code
Load Real	FLD	ST(i)	ST(i) is pushed onto the stack.	9B D9 C0 + i*
		SR	SR is pushed onto the stack.	9B D9 m0rm**
		LR	LR is pushed onto the stack.	9B DD m0rm
		TR	TR is pushed onto the stack.	9B DB m5rm
Store Real	FST	ST(i)	ST is stored in ST(i)	9B DD D0 + i
		SR	ST is stored in SR.	9B D9 m2rm
		LR	ST is stored in LR.	9B DD m2rm
Store Real & Pop	FSTP	ST(i)	ST is stored in ST(i) and stack popped.	9B DD D8 + i
		SR	ST is stored in SR and stack popped.	9B D9 m3rm
		LR	ST stored in LR and stack popped.	9B DD m3rm
		TR	ST stored in TR.	9B DB m7rm
Exchange Registers	FXCH	ST(i)	Swaps ST with ST(i)	9B D9 C8 + i
Integer Load	FILD	SI	Converts SI to TR, pushes it onto the stack.	9B DB m0rm
		WI	Same as for SI	9B DF m0rm
		LI	Same as for SI.	9B DF m5rm
Integer Store	FIST	SI	ST is rounded to the nearest integer and stored in source.	9B DB m2rm
		WI	Same as for SI.	9B DF m2rm
Integer Store & Pop	FISTP	SI	Same as FIST, but stack is popped.	9B DB m3rm
		WI	Same as for SI.	9B DF m3rm
		LI	Same as for SI.	9B DF m7rm
Packed Decimal (BCD) Load	FBLD	Source	Source is converted from BCD and pushed onto stack.	9B DF m4rm
Packed Decimal (BCD) Store & Pop	FBSTP	Destination	ST is converted to BCD and popped from the stack into source.	9B DF m6rm

*The notation C0 + i means that the machine code byte is C0 when the register is ST(0), C1 when the register is ST(1), and so on.
**The "mxrm" byte in the machine code denotes addressing mode information for the memory operand as well as the embedded 3 bits that complete the machine code for the instruction, where "mxrm" is short for

    mmxxxr/m

Thus

    m0rm

in the FLD SR instruction denotes

    mm000r/m

where 000 completes the machine code for FLD and mm...r/m is the addressing mode information for the short real operand. The entire machine code for this instruction, shown as:

    9B   D9   m0rm

could also be written:

    WAIT ESC,08H,SR

and the assembler would translate this to:

    WAIT   ESC.   08H.SR
    ‾‾‾‾   ‾‾‾‾   ‾‾‾‾‾‾
    1001 1011 11011 0001 mm000r/m

with mm. . .r/m the addressing mode information for the short real (SR).

12.4.2 Arithmetic Instructions

The coprocessor has instructions for adding, subtracting, multiplying, and dividing, as well as for other operations such as scaling and taking square roots. Figure 12-5 shows the details of these operations.

12.4.3 Comparison Instructions

The comparison instructions compare the stack top contents (ST) with other elements of the stack or a memory value. Bits C0–C3 of the status word may be set as a result of the comparison.

If ST is greater than the other operand, then C0, C2, and C3 are cleared.
If ST is less than the other operand, then C0 is set and C2 and C3 are cleared.
If ST equals the other operand, then C3 is set and C0 and C2 are cleared.
When the ST and the other operand cannot be compared, C0, C2, and C3 are set. This happens if the contents of either operand is a NAN or projective infinity and cannot be compared.

Other bits of the status word are also set as a result of the comparison instructions:

If ST is a positive unnormal, C0–C3 are cleared.
If ST is an unnormal, C1 is set.
If ST is a positive NAN, C0 is set.
If ST is a negative NAN, C0 and C1 are set.
If ST is a positive normal, C2 is set.
If ST is a negative normal, C1 and C2 are set.
If ST is positive infinity, C0 and C2 are set.
If ST is negative infinity, C0–C2 are set.
If ST is a positive denormal, C2 and C3 are set.
If ST is a negative denormal, C1 and C2 are set.
If ST is positive 0, C3 is set.
If ST is negative 0, C1 is set.
Any other combinations indicate that ST is empty.

Figure 12-6 shows the various compare instructions.

12.4.4 Transcendental Instructions

The math coprocessor has built-in instructions for computing trigonometric functions, logarithms, and exponentiation. They operate on ST or ST and ST(1). Figure 12-7 lists them.

Figure 12-5 Detailed arithmetic operations

Name	Operation	Operand(s)	Meaning	Machine code
Add Real	FADD	SR	Adds SR to ST.	9B D8 m0rm
		LR	Adds LR to ST.	9B DC m0rm
		ST,ST(i)	Adds ST(i) to ST.	9B D8 C0+i
		ST(i),ST	Adds ST to ST(i).	9B DC C0+i
Add Real & Pop	FADDP	ST(i),ST	Adds ST to ST(i) and pops the stack.	9B DE C0+i
Integer Add	FIADD	SI	Adds SI to ST.	9B DA m0rm
		LI	Adds LI to ST.	9B DE m0rm
Subtract Real	FSUB	SR	Subtracts SR from ST.	9B DB m4rm
		LR	Subtracts LR from ST.	9B DC m4rm
		ST,ST(i)	Subtracts ST(i) from ST.	9B D8 E0+i
		ST(i),ST	Subtracts ST from ST(i).	9B DC E8+i
Subtract Real & Pop	FSUBP	ST(i),ST	Subtracts ST from ST(i) and pops.	9B DE E8+i
Integer Subtract	FISUB	SI	Subtracts SI from ST.	9B DA m4rm
		LI	Subtracts LI from ST.	9B DE m4rm
Subtract Real Reversed	FSUBR	SR	Subtracts ST from SR and stores result in ST.	9B DA m5rm
		LR	Subtracts ST from LR and stores result in ST.	9B DE m5rm
Subtract Real Reversed & Pop	FSUBRP	ST(i),ST	Subtract ST(i) from ST, store in ST(i), and pop stack.	9B DE E0+i
Integer Subtract Reversed	FISUBR	SI	Subtract ST from SI and store in ST.	9B DA m5rm
		LI	Subtract ST from LI and store in ST.	9B DE m5rm
Multiply Real	FMUL	ST,ST(i)	Multiply ST by ST(i).	9B D8 C8+i
		ST(i),ST	Multiply ST(i) by ST.	9B DC C8+i
		SR	Multiply ST by SR.	9B D8 m1rm
		LR	Multiply ST by LR.	9B DC m1rm
Multiply Real & Pop	FMULP	ST(i),ST	Multiply ST(i) by ST and pop stack.	9B DE C8+i

Figure 12-5 (*continued*)

Name	Operation	Operand(s)	Meaning	Machine code
Integer Multiply	FIMUL	SI	Multiply ST by SI.	9B DA m1rm
		LI	Multiply ST by LI.	9B DE m1rm
Divide Real	FDIV	ST,ST(i)	Divide ST by ST(i).	9B D8 F0 + i
		ST(i),ST	Divide ST(i) by ST.	9B DC F8 + i
		SR	Divide ST by SR.	9B D8 m6rm
		LR	Divide ST by LR.	9B DC m6rm
Divide Real & Pop	FDIVP	ST(i),ST	Divide ST(i) by ST and pop stack.	9B DE F8 + i
Integer Divide	FIDIV	SI	Divide ST by SI.	9B DA m6rm
		LI	Divide ST by LI.	9B DE m6rm
Divide Real Reversed	FDIVR	ST,ST(i)	Divide ST(i) by ST and store in ST.	9B D8 F8 + i
		ST(i),ST	Divide ST by ST(i) and store in ST(i).	9B DC F0 + i
		SR	Divide SR by ST and store in ST.	9B D8 m7rm
		LR	Divide LR by ST and store in ST.	9B DC m7rm
Divide Real Reversed & Pop	FDIVRP	ST(i),ST	Divide ST by ST(i) and store in ST(i).	9B DE F0 + i
Integer Divide Reversed	FIDIVR	SI	Divide SI by ST and store in ST.	9B DA m7rm
		LI	Divide LI by ST and store in ST.	9B DE m7rm
Square Root	FSQRT	None	Replaces ST with its square root.	9B D9 FA
Scale	FSCALE	None	Replaces ST with ST * 2**ST(1).	9B D9 FD
Partial Remainder	FPREM	None	Replaces ST with ST mod ST(1).	9B D9 F8
Round to Integer	FRNDINT	None	Round ST to an integer.	9B D9 FC
Extract Exponent and Mantissa	FXTRACT	none	The exponent of ST replaces ST and its mantissa is pushed onto the stack.	9B D9 F4
Absolute Value	FABS	None	ST is replaced by |ST|.	9B D9 E1
Change Sign	FCHS	None	Replace ST with − ST.	9B D9 E0

Figure 12-6 Compare instructions

Name	Operation	Operand(s)	Meaning	Machine code
Compare Real	FCOM	ST(i)	ST is compared with ST(i).	9B D8 D0 + i
		SR	ST is compared with SR.	9B D8 m2rm
		LR	ST is compared with LR.	9B DC m2rm
Compare Real & Pop	FCOMP	ST(i)	Same as FCOM, except stack is popped.	9B D8 D8 + i
		SR source	Same as FCOM, except stack is popped.	9B D8 m3rm
		LR source	Same as FCOM, except stack is popped.	9B DC m3rm
Compare Real & Pop Twice	FCOMPP	ST(1)	ST is compared with ST(1) and stack is popped twice.	9B DE D9
Integer Compare	FICOM	SI	ST is compared with SI.	9B DA m2rm
		WI	Same as for SI.	9B DE m2rm
Integer Compare & Pop	FICOMP	SI	Same as FICOM, but pops the stack.	9B DA m3rm
		WI	Same as FICOM, but pops the stack.	9B DE m3rm
Test Stack Top Against +0.0	FTST	None	Compares ST with +0.	9B D9 E4
Examine ST	FXAM	None	Sets C0–C4 as described above.	9B D9 E5

Figure 12-7 Transcendental instructions

Name	Operation	Operand(s)	Meaning	Machine code
Partial Tangent	FPTAN	None	Calculates Tan(ST) and pushes it onto stack. ST must be between 0 and pi/4.	9B D9 F2
Partial Arctangent	FPATAN	None	Calculates Arctan of ST(1)/ST, where $0 < ST(1) < ST$, pops the stack, and pushes result onto stack.	9B D9 F3
2x − 1	F2XM1	None	2ST − 1 replaces ST where $0 < ST < 1/2$.	9B D9 F0
Y*$\log_2$X	FYL2X	None	ST(1)*$\log_2$ST replaces ST.	9B D9 F1
Y*$\log_2$(X + 1)	FYL2XP1	None	ST(1)*$\log_2$(1 + ST) replaces ST.	9B D9 F9

12.4.5 Constant Instructions

The math coprocessor contains instructions for pushing the values or approximate values of 0, 1, pi, $\log_2 10$, $\log_2 e$, $\log_{10} 2$, and $\log_e 2$ (ln 2) onto the stack. They are shown in Figure 12-8.

12.4.6 Processor Control Instructions

Processor control instructions manipulate the status word and the control word. The initialize-processor instruction FINIT sets the bits in the status word and in the control word to the following default values:

Control Word

IC:	0	(Projective infinity; default on 8087 and 80287)
RC:	00	(Round to nearest or even)
PC:	11	(64 bit mantissa)
IEM:	1	(Interrupts disabled on 8087; undefined on 80287 and 80387)
PM, UM, OM, ZM, DM, IM:	1	(Exceptions are masked)

Status Word

B:	0	(Not busy)
C0 – C3:	?	(Indeterminate on the 8087 and 80287; cleared on the 80387.)
ST:	000	(R0 is Stack Top)
IR:	0	(No interrupt)
PE, UE, OE, ZE, DE, IE:	0	(No exceptions)

Note that ST is set to R0 (000) so that the first FLD will change the stack top to R7 (111).

The processor control instructions are shown in Figure 12-9.

Figure 12-8 Constant instructions

Name	Operation	Operand(s)	Meaning	Machine code
Load Zero	FLDZ	None	Pushes 0.0 onto stack.	9B D9 EE
Load One	FLD1	None	Pushes 1.0 onto stack.	9B D9 E8
Load Pi	FLDPI	None	Pushes Pi onto stack.	9B D9 EB
Load $\log_2 10$	FLDL2T	None	Pushes $\log_2 10$ onto stack.	9B D9 E9
Load $\log_2 e$	FLDL2E	None	Pushes $\log_2 e$ onto stack.	9B D9 EA
Load $\log_{10} 2$	FLDLG2	None	Pushes $\log_{10} 2$ onto stack.	9B D9 EC
Load $\log_e 2$	FLDLN2	None	Pushes $\log_e 2$ onto stack	9B D9 ED

Figure 12-9 Processor control instructions

Name	Operation	Operand(s)	Meaning	Machine code
Initialize Processor	FINIT	None	Sets the control word and the status word to the initial values described earlier.	9B DB E3
Initialize Processor	FNINIT	None	Same as FINIT, except no WAIT first. (See machine code)	90 DB E3
Disable Interrupts	FDISI	None	Sets IEM on 8087 only.	9B DB E1
Disable Interrupts	FNDISI	None	Same as FDISI, except no WAIT.	90 DB E1
Enable Interrupts	FENI	None	Clears IEM on 8087 only.	9B DB E0
Enable Interrupts	FNENI	None	Same as FENI except no WAIT.	90 DB E0
Load Control Word	FLDCW	Mem16	Loads a 16-bit word into control word.	9B D9 m5rm
Store Control Word	FSTCW	Mem16	Stores control word into 16-bit memory word.	9B D9 m7rm
Store Control Word	FNSTCW	Mem16	Same as FSTCW, but no WAIT.	90 D9 m7rm
Store Status Word	FSTSW	Mem16 AX on80287 and 80387 only	Stores status word into 16-bit memory word.	9B DD m7rm
Store Status Word	FNSTSW	Mem16 AX on 80287 and 80387 only	Same as FSTSW, but into 16-bit memory word.	90 DD m7rm
Clear Exceptions	FCLEX	None	Clears exception flags: PE, UE, OE, ZE, DE, IE.	9B DB E2
Clear Exceptions	FNCLEX	None	Same as FCLEX, but no WAIT.	90 DB E2
Store Environment	FSTENV	14-byte mem (on 80287 and 80387, 28-byte mem on 80387)	Stores control word, status word, instruction pointer, tag word, and exception pointers into memory.	9B D9 m6rm
Store Environment	FNSTENV	14-byte mem (on 8087 and 80287)	Same as FSTENV, but no WAIT.	90 D9 m6rm
Load Environment	FLDENV	12-byte mem 28-byte mem on 80387	Loads control word, status word, etc., from a 12-byte memory location.	9B D9 m4rm
Save State	FSAVE	94-byte mem 108-bytes on 80387	Saves control word, status word, tag word, IP, OP, stack in memory. Initializes 8087. See Intel Manual.	9B DD m6rm
Save State	FNSAVE	94-byte mem (108 bytes mem on 80387)	Same as FSAVE, but no WAIT.	90 DD m6rm

Figure 12-9 (*continued*)

Name	Operation	Operand(s)	Meaning	Machine code
Restore State	FRSTOR	94-byte mem (108-bytes on 80387)	Restores control word, status word, tag word, IP, OP, stack in memory.	9B DD m4rm
Increment Stack Pointer	FINCSTP	None	Adds 1 to ST. If = 7 then changed to 0.	9B D9 F7
Decrement Stack Pointer	FDECSTP	None	Subtracts 1 from ST. If it = 0, then changed to 7.	9B D9 F6
Free Register	FFREE	ST(i)	ST(i) marked as empty.	9B DD C0 + i
No Operation	FNOP	None	Stores ST in ST. Used for time delays.	9B D9 D0
CPU Wait	FWAIT	None	Same as WAIT. CPU waits for coprocessor.	9B

12.5 Using the Math Coprocessor

Using the math coprocessor requires us to be aware of two parallel activities, that of the CPU (8086, 8088, 80286, 80386) and that of the math coprocessor (8087, 80287, 80387). Parallel processing is difficult for humans. We think better sequentially. (Try reading the first line from one book, the first line from another, then the second line from the first followed by the second line from the second, and so on.)

12.5.1 Basic Synchronization

Synchronization of the two processors is implemented with the FWAIT instruction. Simply insert it wherever the CPU should wait for a coprocessor result. Figure 12-10 shows our old friend *Calc,* the program that adds two numbers, this time real numbers, and stores them in memory. No synchronization need be done here.

Chapter 8 described assembly language procedures that are called from high-level language programs. Floating-point procedures are excellent examples of operations that are quite apt to be called from high-level language programs, especially if the high-level language translator does not take advantage of the 8087-family. (Many high-level language translators for 86-family machines were

Figure 12-10 *Calc* program using real numbers

```
; This program calculates RESULT := A + B when A = 2.0 , B = 3.0
;
; data segment follows
;
data    segment
;
a       dd      2.0
b       dd      3.0
result  dd      ?
;
data    ends
;
; code segment follows
;
code    segment
;
        assume cs:code,ds:data
;
main    proc    far
;
;       necessary bookkeeping statements follow
;
        push    ds      ; save caller's
        mov     ax,0    ; return
        push    ax      ; address
;
        mov     ax,data ; get current
        mov     ds,ax   ; data segment
;
; main procedure
;
        finit
        fld     a       ; get a
        fadd    b       ; add b
        fstp    result  ; put sum into location result
        ret
main    endp
code    ends
        end
```

written before the 8087-family was in common use.) Figure 12-11 shows procedure *Calc* in a form that can be called from a high-level language program.

We have added one synchronization instruction to Figure 12-11. FWAIT prevents the CPU from popping BP until we have finished using it to find the address at which to store our sum.

Figure 12-12 contains more examples of synchronization instructions. This is the same program as in Figure 6-1, but now the list contains floating-point

Figure 12-11 *Calc* called from a high-level language

```
;
; This procedure computes RESULT := A + B when called by
; CALL CALC(A,B,RESULT)
; It assumes ADDRESSES of arguments are passed rather than
; their values.
;
code      segment public
          assume  cs:code,ds:code
          public  calc
calc      proc    far
          finit
          push    si                      ; save SI
          push    bp                      ; save BP
          push    bx                      ; save BX
          mov     bp,sp                   ; point to args
          mov     bx,14[bp]               ; get A's address
          fld     dword ptr [bx]          ; get A
          mov     bx,12[bp]               ; get B's address
          fadd    dword ptr [bx]          ; add B
          mov     bx,10[bp]               ; get RESULT's address
          fst     dword ptr [bx]          ; store sum in RESULT
          fwait
          pop     bx                      ; restore BX
          pop     bp                      ; restore BP
          pop     si                      ; restore SI
          ret     6
calc      endp
code      ends
          end
```

numbers. Comments that pertain directly to the 8087-family operations are shown in parentheses.

12.5.2 Advanced Synchronization Techniques

Although synchronization can be accomplished safely by inserting FWAIT after every 8087-family instruction, this is often inefficient and unnecessary. A more intelligent insertion of FWAIT's will allow the CPU and the math coprocessor to proceed until the CPU must access a location into which the math processor stores a value. Even this use of FWAIT may be unnecessary if the CPU *access* is "far enough" from the math coprocessor *store*. It is possible to use cycle time information to calculate this, but the programmer should determine the exact cycle times for his or her machine.

Many compilers and interpreters do not take advantage of the math coprocessor when they compile or interpret. Even those that do often do not do so efficiently.

Figure 12-12 Additional synchronization instructions

```
;
; data segment follows
;
data    segment
list            dd      5.1,4.3,13.5,2.7,11.0,0.0
max             dd      ?
testplace       dw      ?
;
data    ends
;
; code segment follows
;
code    segment
;
        assume  cs:code,ds:data
;
main    proc    far
;
;       necessary bookkeeping statements follows
;
        push    ds      ; save caller's
        mov     ax,0    ; return
        push    ax      ; address
;
        mov     ax,data ; get current
        mov     ds,ax   ; data segment
;
;       main procedure
;
        finit
        fldz                            ; MAX :=0
        lea     bp,list
loop1:  nop
        mov     bx,ds:[bp]              ; places list[i] into bx
        fld     dword ptr [bx]          ; (push list[i] onto stack)
        ftst                            ; while list[i]<> 0.0
        fstsw   testplace               ; (store status word)
        fwait                           ; (wait for store)
        mov     ax,testplace            ; (AH now contains C0-C3)
        sahf                            ; (C0 and C3 now in CF and ZF)
        je      fini
        fcom    st(1)                   ; if list[i] > MAX
        fstsw   testplace               ; (store status word)
        fwait                           ; (wait for store)
        mov     ax,testplace            ; (AH now contains C0-C3)
        sahf                            ; (C0 and C3 now in CF and ZF)
        jb      next                    ;
        fst     st(1)                   ; then max := list[i]
next:   add     bp,4                    ; i := i + 1
        mov     bx,ds:[bp]              ;
        fcomp   st(1)                   ; (MAX now on top)
        jmp     loop1                   ; end while
fini:   fxch    st(1)                   ; (put MAX on top)
        fstp    max
        fwait
        ret
main    endp
;
code    ends
        end
```

12.5.3 MASM and the 8087-Family

Some early versions of MASM do not include the machine code for the 8087-family instructions. One way to deal with this is to use the machine code in the figures in this chapter to create macros that generate this machine code. For example,

```
MACRO       FInit

   DB       09BH       ;  WAIT
   DB       0DBH       ;  ESC,
   DB       0E3H       ;  INIT

ENDM        FInit
```

generates the machine code for FINIT. The INCLUDE directive can be used to include them during assembly.

12.6 Summary

This chapter describes the 8087-family math coprocessor. This involves learning not only a new architecture and new instructions, but also a new concept—that of synchronization. Coprocessing is a difficult process for people.

The 8087-family math coprocessor allows floating-point operations to be done in speeds that 86-family software simulators cannot even approach. In fact, the math coprocessor's speed is comparable to that of larger machines.

The 8087-family contains the single precision (32 bits) and double precision (64 bits) formats recommended by the IEEE. Internally, however, all data types are converted to the 80-bit temporary real format, allowing great accuracy in computations. In addition, intermediate values that are too large or small to be handled in the CPU are handled with ease by the 8087-family. There is even a representation for positive and negative infinity.

Math coprocessor instructions are easily distinguished from CPU instructions because they begin with F. The machine code for math coprocessor instructions begins with 9B D . . . representing an ESC WAIT. (A few instructions have variants that do not produce the WAIT.) This translation is automatic and allows the math coprocessor to "wake up" and access the address of the data (if any) before the CPU continues its processing.

The WAIT before an instruction is automatic. No WAIT is generated after a math coprocessor instruction (except by some macro libraries that include the WAIT in their macro expansions). This is the responsibility of the programmer, and there are many factors to consider. Maximum safety would require FWAIT following *every* math coprocessor instruction. Maximum speed would eliminate *all* such FWAIT's. A compromise usually is best, with FWAIT inserted just before any CPU instruction that accesses a memory location into which the math coprocessor has stored.

Exercises

1. Show (a) 1.0 and (b) −1.0 in
   i. short real format
   ii. long real format
   iii. temporary real format
2. Show machine code for the following math coprocessor instructions:
   a. `FADD AX`
   b. `FADD [SI]`
   c. `FADD ST(1)`
3. Show the effect on the math coprocessor of

   `FINIT`

   Describe how the initial settings of the status word and of the control word affect the operations of the math coprocessor.
4. Rewrite the program of Figure 6-2 to perform a sequential search for a real *Key* in a list of real numbers.
5. Rewrite the program of Figure 6-3 to sort a list of real numbers.
6. Rewrite the program of Figure 6-1 as a procedure callable from your favorite high-level language that will find the maximum of an array of real numbers.
7. Same as Exercise 6, but for Figure 6-2 (see Exercise 4).
8. Same as Exercise 6, but for Figure 6-3 (see Exercise 5).
9. Write a program to find the area bounded by the x-axis, the y-axis, the line $x = 2$, and the curve

   $$y = x^2$$

   (Hint: Use small trapezoidal "strips" and find their sum to approximate the area.)
10. Same as Exercise 9, but for the curve

    $$y = e^x$$
11. Write a procedure that will compute the area of a circle when called with the value of the radius.

There is one instruction, which we did not cover, that can be used to halt the 86-family processor. It is an appropriate one with which to end this book:

HLT

Answers to
Selected Exercises

Chapter 1

1. 0 and 1; bits.
2. The assembler translates the assembly language program into the corresponding machine language program.
3. Operation: the action to be performed; operand: object of the action.
4. Data segment.
5. Code segment.

Chapter 2

1. 1; $2^1 - 1 = 1$.
   8; $2^8 - 1 = 255$.
   16; $2^{16} - 1 = 65535$.
   32; $2^{32} - 1 = 4294967295$.
2. 20; (segment register) * 16 = address of beginning of segment.
3. AX, BX, CX, DX.
4. SS; SP, BP.
5. IP.
6. Flags register. See Section 2.3.5.
7. 000000011000000000001.
8. 1001000110011110 1000101011001010.
   10010001 10011110 10001010 11001010.
9. 0000000100001010.
10. SF, AF, CF.

===== **Chapter 3**

1. Storage sizes are multiples and fractions of 16; easy to convert from hexadecimal to binary; hexadecimal takes up less space than binary.
2. 6F3D; B4F5; CA; 19.
3. 1000110001001110; 11110101; 01010110; 00001111111111111111.
4. 00000000 and 10000000; 00000000 and 11111111; 00000000.
5. 1111111.
6. 11001011 in a byte; 1111111111001011 in a word; etc.
7. -2.
9. $-1.0 * 2^{-2} = .01_2 = .25_{10}$.
10. All zeros.
11. 61 73 63 69 69.
12. No.
13. K DB 12.
14. List DW 6 DUP (?).
15. ByteList = BYTE PTR List
    or
    ByteList LABEL BYTE (immediately preceding 14).
16. 2006.
17. 14.
18. A binary point.

===== **Chapter 4**

1. a. CX = 02?? (in hex).
   b. CX = 04?? (in hex).
   c. illegal.
   d. illegal.
   e. AX = 6869.
   f. AX = BF00.
   g. AX = 2.
2. a. MOV   AL,6
   b. MOV   BX,Datum
   c. XCHG   AX,BX
   d. MOV   AL, DataByte
      MOV   DL,NutherByte
      MOV   DataByte,BL
      MOV   NutherByte,AL
   e. LEA   BX,Table
      MOV   AL,4
      XLAT   Table

```
    f. BTable = BYTE PTR WTable
       MOV    AL,8
       LEA    BX,BTable
       XLAT   BTable
    g. MOV    DX, WORD PTR Dividend + 2
       MOV    AX, WORD PTR Dividend
       DIV    Divisor
       MOV    Quotient, AX
    h. MOV    AX,Dividend
       DIV    Divisor
       MOV    Quotient, AL
```

Chapter 5

1. An addressing mode is a way of calculating an effective address.
2. Single operand instructions contain addressing mode bytes if (a) the operand is not a register in direct mode, or (b) if the opcode does not specify the instruction uniquely. Two operand instructions usually have an addressing mode byte. Instructions with no operands rarely have addressing mode bytes.

   The parts of an addressing mode byte are (1) mode field, (2) r/m field, and (3) register field.
3. If two operands and they are both in direct mode, mode field is 11, register field contains code for destination (i.e., first) operand, r/m field contains code for source (i.e., second) operand. If two operands and one is not in direct mode, then register field contains code for direct mode operand, other fields code other operand.
4. Both unchanged.
5. AX = 2301;
   rest unchanged.
6. MOV [BX],DX.
8. a. MOV   DS,AX
   b. ADD   AX,[BX]
   c. ADD   [BX],AX
   d. ADD   AX,[DI]
9. a. 01 05
   b. 03.05
   c. 3B C2
   d. 39 06 0000
   e. 48
   f. FE CB
   g. FE OE 0001
   h. F6 36 0001

Chapter 7

1. Saves programmer time;
   more readable code.
2. MACRO; ENDM.
3. Macro name is substituted by the instructions defining it.
9a.

```
; This macro will convert a hexadecimal number to ASCII
; characters for  printing or displaying.  The hex number
; is in NUMH and the ASCII values will be returned in NUMA.
;
ITOA      MACRO     NUMH,NUMA,LENGTH
          LOCAL     NEXT
          PUSH      AX
          PUSH      SI
          PUSH      DI
          PUSH      CX
          MOV       SI,OFFSET NUMH
          MOV       DI,OFFSET NUMA
          MOV       CX,LENGTH
NEXT:     MOV       AL,[SI]
          PUSH      AX
          AND       AL,OFOH       ;extract first digit of pair
          ADD       AL,'0'        ;convert back to ASCII
          MOV       [DI],AL       ;save digit
          INC       DI
          POP       AX
          AND       AL,OFH        ;second digit
          ADD       AL, '0'       ;convert back to ASCII
          MOV       [DI],AL       ;save digit
          INC       DI
          INC       SI
          LOOP      NEXT
          POP       CX
          POP       DI
          POP       SI
          POP       AX
          ENDM
```

9b.

```
; This macro will accept a string of digits in ASCII and
; convert them to a  hexadecimal number.  The number will
; be in memory location NUMA and the hex value will be
; returned in NUMH.
;
```

```
ATOI      MACRO     NUMA,NUMH,LENGTH
          LOCAL     NEXT
          PUSH      AX
          PUSH      BX
          PUSH      CX
          MOV       CX,LENGTH
          MOV       BX,OFFSET NUMA
NEXT:     MOV       AL,[BX]
          SUB       AL,'0'          ;convert number by subtracting ASCII 0
          SAL       NUMH,4          ;multiply by 16
          ADC       NUMH,AL
          LOOP      NEXT
          POP       CX
          POP       BX
          POP       AX
          ENDM
```

10.

```
          ;       Delay for 1 millisecond on author's computer
          ;
          DLY1MS MACRO
                  LOCAL   DLY
          PUSH    CX              ;Save CX reg
          MOV     CX,238          ;Loop count

  DLY:    NOP
          LOOP    DLY

          POP     CX              ;Retrieve CX
          ENDM
```

11.

```
;This macro will generate a delay of one or more seconds
;
LONGDELAY MACRO     SECOND
          LOCAL     OVER,AGAIN
          PUSH      AX              ;save registers
          PUSH      CX
          PUSH      DX
          MOV       AX,SECOND       ;get length of delay
          MOV       CX,4
          MUL       CX              ;count for CX register
          MOV       CX,AX
OVER:     PUSH      CX              ;save count
          MOV       CX,OFFFFH       ;maximum count
AGAIN:    LOOP      AGAIN
```

```
        POP      CX              ;restore count
        LOOP     OVER
        POP      DX
        POP      CX
        POP      AX
        ENDM
```

Chapter 8

1. Last-in-first-out (LIFO) list.
2. Because the stack grows to lower addresses.
3. Yes.
4. On the stack; on the stack (after CS).
5. Push IP (after perhaps CS) on stack; change IP (and perhaps CS) to procedure location.

Chapter 10

6.

```
;*****************************************************************
; PROCEDURE GotoXY (x,y : INTEGER );
;
;    This procedure sets the cursor position to the indicated
;    coordinates.
;
;
;       Uses the DOS video interrupt.
;
;*****************************************************************

GotoXY  PROC     FAR

        PUSH     BP              ;Save old frame pointer
        MOV      BP,SP           ;Set up new frame pointer

        MOV      DL,8[BP]        ;Get column (x) coordinate
        MOV      DH,6[BP]        ;Get row (y) coordinate
        MOV      BH,0            ;Video page 0

        MOV      AH,2            ;Set cursor position
        INT      10H             ;Video interrupt

        POP      BP              ;Restore old frame pointer
        RET      4               ;Back to PASCAL

GotoXY  ENDP
```

7.

```
; This macro will read from the keyboard until a carriage return
; is entered and places the bytes read in at the location
; specified.
;
READLINE    MACRO      INBUFFER
            LOCAL      READN
            PUSH       AX          ;save AX register
            XOR        SI,SI
READN:      MOV        AH,0        ;select BIOS function for keyboard read
            INT        16H         ;call BIOS routine
            MOV        [INBUFFER][SI],AL ;save character just read
            INC        SI          ;one more character
            CMP        AL,0DH      ;check for carriage return
            JNZ        READN
            MOV        CX,SI
            POP        AX
            ENDM
```

8.

```
;****************************************************************
;
; FUNCTION KeyPress : BOOLEAN;
;
;        Return True if a key was pressed.
;
;****************************************************************
KeyPress         PROC    FAR

        MOV     AH,0BH          ;Read status
        INT     21H             ;DOS Keyboard interrupt
        AND     AX,True         ;Mask for TRUE bit, TRUE EQU 1
        RET

KeyPress         ENDP
```

9. (Note: The solution shown here uses some constructs introduced in Chapter 11.)

```
; SCROLL A SPECIFIED WINDOW A SPECIFIED AMOUNT
; this macro will invoke the proper BIOS interrupt
; to scroll the screen
;
Scroll     MACRO      TOPROW,TOPCOL,BOTROW,BOTCOL,ATTRIBUTE,NUMBER
           PUSH       DX
           PUSH       CX
           PUSH       BX
```

```
            PUSH      AX
            IFNB      <TOPROW>
            MOV       CH,TOPROW           ;row to start scrolling
            ELSE
            MOV       CH,1                ;default is top row
            ENDIF
            IFNB      <TOPCOL>
            MOV       CL,TOPCOL           ;column to start scrolling
            ELSE
            MOV       CL,1                ;default is first column
            ENDIF
            IFNB      <BOTROW>
            MOV       DH,BOTROW           ;row to end scroll region
            ELSE
            MOV       DH,24               ;default is last row
            ENDIF
            IFNB      <BOTCOL>
            MOV       DL,BOTCOL           ;column to end scroll region
            ELSE
            MOV       DL,80               ;default is last row
            ENDIF
            IFNB      <ATTRIBUTE>
            MOV       BH,ATTRIBUTE        ;set attribute for blanked lines
            ELSE
            MOV       BH,7                ;default is normal attribute
            ENDIF
            IFNB      <NUMBER>
            MOV       AL,NUMBER           ;number of lines to scroll
            ELSE
            MOV       AL,1                ;default is one line
            ENDIF
            MOV       AH,6                ;indicate scroll
            INT       10H
            POP       AX
            POP       BX
            POP       CX
            POP       DX
            ENDM
```

10.

```
; This macro will display a single character at a current
; cursor location
;
Display     MACRO     CHARACTER,ATTRIBUTE
            PUSH      AX
            PUSH      BX
```

```
          PUSH      CX
          PUSH      DX
          MOV       AX,CHARACTER         ;character to write
          MOV       AH,9                 ;BIOS function = write character
          MOV       BX,ATTRIBUTE         ;attribute of character
          MOV       BH,0                 ;display page
          MOV       CX,1                 ;write single character
          INT       10H
          POP       DX
          POP       CX
          POP       BX
          POP       AX
          ENDM
```

11.

```
;***************************************************************
;
; PROCEDURE cursor ( top, bot : INTEGER );
;
; This procedure will change the cursor.  A value such as 48,48
; will make the cursor go away (become invisible). A value of 0,9
; will make a large blinking cursor.
;
;***************************************************************
Cursor    PROC      FAR
          PUSH      BP                   ;Save old frame pointer
          MOV       BP,SP                ;Set up new frame pointer

          MOV       CH,8[BP]             ;Starting line
          MOV       CL,6[BP]             ;Ending line

          MOV       AH,1                 ;Set cursor type
          INT       10H                  ;Video Interrupt

          POP       BP                   ;Restore old frame pointer
          RET       4                    ;Back to calling program, 2 parms
Cursor    ENDP
```

12.

```
;***************************************************************
;
; TYPE boxes = (single, double, thick, points, solid, s1, s2, s3)
; PROCEDURE box ( kind : boxes; ulx,uly, xs,ys : INTEGER )
; PROCEDURE nbox ( kind : boxes; ulx,uly, xs,ys : INTEGER )
;
```

```
;       Draws a graphic box on the text screen where:
;          kind  is what type of box.
;          ulx,ul  are the inside coordinates of the upper left.
;          xs,ys are the inside dimensions of the box.
;          nbox is the same as box except that the box is cleared.
;
;******************************************************************


nbox     PROC     FAR

         PUSH     BP                ;Save old frame pointer
         MOV      BP,SP             ;Set up new frame pointer

         XOR      AL,AL             ;Clear entire window
         MOV      CL,12[BP]         ;CX := row,col upper left
         MOV      CH,10[BP]

         MOV      DX,CX             ;DX := row,col lower right
         ADD      DL,8[BP]
         ADD      DH,6[BP]
         MOV      BH,1              ;White on black
         MOV      AH,6              ;Scroll window
         INT      10H               ;Video Interrupt

         JMP      bxx
nbox     ENDP

box      PROC     FAR

         PUSH     BP                ;Save old frame pointer
         MOV      BP,SP             ;Set up new frame pointer

bxx:     MOV      AX,14[BP]         ;Get box type
         MOV      BX,8              ;Calc box table base index
         MUL      BX
         ADD      AX,OFFSET boxtable ;Add addr. of table
         MOV      SI,AX             ;SI indexes box type in table


         MOV      DL,12[BP]         ;Draw upper left corner:
         DEC      DL
         MOV      DH,10[BP]
         DEC      DH
         CALL     gotod
         MOV      AL,CS: [SI]
```

```
          CALL     wchar

          MOV      AL,CS: 1[SI]      ;Draw top line
          CALL     hlin

          MOV      AL,CS: 2[SI]      ;Draw upper right corner
          CALL     wchar

;Draw vertical lines:
          MOV      CX,6[BP]          ;Y size in count
          MOV      DH,10[BP]         ;Start Y row

vlin:     MOV      DL,12[BP]         ;Calc left X col
          DEC      DL
          CALL     gotod
          MOV      AL,CS: 3[SI]      ;Left char
          CALL     wchar
          MOV      DL,12[BP]         ;Calc right col
          ADD      DL,8[BP]
          CALL     gotod
          MOV      AL,CS: 7[SI]      ;Right char
          CALL     wchar

          INC      DH                ;Next line
          LOOP     vlin              ;Continue loop
          MOV      DL,12[BP]         ;Lower left corner
          DEC      DL
          CALL     gotod
          MOV      AL,CS: 4[SI]
          CALL     wchar

          MOV      AL,CS: 6[SI]
          CALL     hlin              ;Bottom line

          MOV      AL,CS: 5[SI]      ;Bottom right corner
          CALL     wchar

          MOV      DL,12[BP]         ;Position @ inside upper left corner
          MOV      DH,10[BP]
          CALL     gotod

          POP      BP
          RET      10                ;Return 5 args from PASCAL

;
```

```
;         Define box character codes in the order:
;          up left, top, up right, left, down left, lower right, bot,
;          right


;
boxtable:

; Single Line box:
          DB          0DAH;0C4H,0BFH,0B3H,0C0H,0D9H,0C4H,0B3H

; Double Line box:
          DB          0C9H,0CDH,0BBH,0BAH,0C8H,0BCH,0BAH

; Solid Line box:
          DB          220,220,220,221,223,223,223,222

; Pointed box:
          DB          32,30,32,17,32,32,31,16

; Solid border box:
          DB          0DBH,0DBH,0DBH,0DBH,0DBH,0DBH,0DBH,0DBH

; Shade 1
          DB          0B0H,0B0H,0B0H,0B0H,0B0H,0B0H,0B0H,0B0H

; Shade 2
          DB          0B1H,0B1H,0B1H,0B1H,0B1H,0B1H,0B1H,0B1H

; Shade 3
          DB          0B2H,0B2H,0B2H,0B2H,0B2H,0B2H,0B2H,0B2H

box       ENDP

hlin      PROC        NEAR
          MOV         CX,8[BP]          ;Get X size in CX
hlop:     CALL        wchar             ;Write to screen
          LOOP        hlop              ;Loop until done
          RET
hlin      ENDP

gotod     PROC        NEAR
          PUSH        AX
          PUSH        BX
          MOV         BX,0              ;Video page 0
          MOV         AH,2              ;Set cursor position
          INT         10H               ;Video Interrupt
```

```
          POP      BX
          POP      AX
          RET
gotod     ENDP

;char in AL
wchar     PROC     NEAR
          PUSH     AX
          PUSH     DX
          MOV      BH,0              ;Page num
          MOV      AH,14             ;Write char (glass teletype)
          INT      10H               ;Video Interrupt
          POP      DX
          POP      AX
          RET
wchar     ENDP
```

Chapter 12

1. a.(i) 001111111000000000000000000000000
    b.(i) 101111111000000000000000000000000

9.

```
.data
;
; constants
;
xfirst   dd     0.0       ;(a) start on x axis
xlast    dd     2.0       ;(b) end on x axis
numseg   dd     10        ;(n) Number of intervals to use
numsgl   =      word ptr numseg
two      dd     2         ;the constant 2
;
;variables
;
xcurr    dd     ?         ;current position on x axis
interv   dd     ?         ;interval between trapezoids
sum      dd     ?         ;sum: x1 + 2x2 + 2x3 ... + xn
area     d      ?         ;area computed
;
;
;
.code
;
start:   mov    ax,@data
         mov    ds, ax
```

```
        ;
        ;
                finit
                fldz            ;initialize variables
                fst     xcurr
                fst     interv
                fst     sum
                fst     area
        ;
        ; sum := f(xfirst)
        ;
                fld     xfirst
                fst     xcurr
                call    func
                fadd    sum
                fst     sum
        ;
        ; interv := (xlast - xfirst)/numseg
        ;
                fld     xlast
                fsub    xfirst
                fidiv   numseg
                fst     interv
        ;
        ; loop for all but first and last interval
        ;

                mov     ax,numsg1-2
        ;
        ; add interval to current position
        ;
looop:          fld     xcurr
                fadd    interv
                fst     xcurr
        ;
        ; sum := sum + 2*f(xcurr)
        ;
                call    func
                fadd    st,st(0)
                fadd    sum
                fst     sum
        ;
        ; loop until done
        ;
                dec     ax
                jg      looop
        ;
        ; add last interval to sum. sum := sum + f(xlast)
```

```
;
        fld     xlast
        fst     xcurr
        call    func
        fadd    sum
        fst     sum
;
; area := sum*h/2
;
        fmul    interv
        fidiv   two
        fst     area
        mov     AH, 4C00H
        int     21H
;
; function we are finding area under
;
func    proc    near
        fld     xcurr
        fmul    xcurr
        ret
func    endp
;
        end start
```

B

86-Family Alphabetically Ordered Instruction Set

37	AAA	.286
D5 0A	AAD	.286
D4 0A	AAM	.286
14 12	ADC AL,Imm8	.286
15 3456	ADC AX,Imm16	.286
66| 15 78901234	ADC EAX,Imm32	.386
12 FF	ADC Reg8,Reg8	.286
10 3E 0000r	ADC Mem8,Reg8	.286
80 D7 12	ADC Reg8,Imm8	.286
80 16 0000r 12	ADC Mem8,Imm8	.286
12 3E 0000r	ADC Reg8,Mem8	.286
13 DB	ADC Reg16,Reg16	.286
11 1E 0001r	ADC Mem16,Reg16	.286
81 D3 3456	ADC Reg16,Imm16	.286
81 16 0001r 3456	ADC Mem16,Imm16	.286
13 1E 0001r	ADC Reg16,Mem16	.286
83 D3 12	ADC Reg16,Imm8	.286
83 16 0001r 12	ADC Mem16,Imm8	.286
66| 13 DB	ADC Reg32,Reg32	.386
66| 11 1E 0003r	ADC Mem32,Reg32	.386
66| 81 D3 78901234	ADC Reg32,Imm32	.386
66| 81 16 0003r +	ADC Mem32,Imm32	.386
66| 13 1E 0003r	ADC Reg32,Mem32	.386
66| 83 D3 12	ADC Reg32,Imm8	.386
66| 83 16 0003r 12	ADC Mem32,Imm8	.386
04 12	ADD AL,Imm8	.286
05 3456	ADD AX,Imm16	.286
66| 05 78901234	ADD EAX,Imm32	.386
02 FF	ADD Reg8,Reg8	.286
00 3E 0000r	ADD Mem8,Reg8	.286
80 C7 12	ADD Reg8,Imm8	.286
80 06 0000r 12	ADD Mem8,Imm8	.286
02 3E 0000r	ADD Reg8,Mem8	.286
03 DB	ADD Reg16,Reg16	.286
01 1E 0001r	ADD Mem16,Reg16	.286
81 C3 3456	ADD Reg16,Imm16	.286
81 06 0001r 3456	ADD Mem16,Imm16	.286
03 1E 0001r	ADD Reg16,Mem16	.286
66| 03 DB	ADD Reg32,Reg32	.386
66| 01 1E 0003r	ADD Mem32,Reg32	.386
66| 81 C3 78901234	ADD Reg32,Imm32	.386
66| 81 06 0003r +	ADD Mem32,Imm32	.386
66| 03 1E 0003r	ADD Reg32,Mem32	.386
66| 83 C3 12	ADD Reg32,Imm8	.386
66| 83 06 0003r 12	ADD Mem32,Imm8	.386
24 12	AND AL,Imm8	.286
25 3456	AND AX,Imm16	.286
66| 25 78901234	AND EAX,Imm32	.386
22 FF	AND Reg8,Reg8	.286
20 3E 0000r	AND Mem8,Reg8	.286
80 E7 12	AND Reg8,Imm8	.286
80 26 0000r 12	AND Mem8,Imm8	.286
22 3E 0000r	AND Reg8,Mem8	.286
23 DB	AND Reg16,Reg16	.286

21 1E 0001r	AND Mem16,Reg16	.286
81 E3 3456	AND Reg16,Imm16	.286
81 26 0001r 3456	AND Mem16,Imm16	.286
23 1E 0001r	AND Reg16,Mem16	.286
83 E3 12	AND Reg16,Imm8	.286
83 26 0001r 12	AND Mem16,Imm8	.286
66| 23 DB	AND Reg32,Reg32	.386
66| 21 1E 0003r	AND Mem32,Reg32	.386
66| 81 E3 78901234	AND Reg32,Imm32	.386
66| 81 26 0003r +	AND Mem32,Imm32	.386
66| 23 1E 0003r	AND Reg32,Mem32	.286
66| 83 E3 12	AND Reg32,Imm8	.286
66| 83 26 0003r 12	AND Mem32,Imm8	.286
63 DB	ARPL Reg16,Reg16	.386P
63 1E 0001r	ARPL Mem16,Reg16	.386P
62 1E 0003r	BOUND Reg16,Mem32	.386
66| 62 1E 000Dr	BOUND Reg32,Mem64	.386
0F BC DB	BSF Reg16,Reg16	.386
0F BC 1E 0001r	BSF Reg16,Mem16	.386
66| 0F BC DB	BSF Reg32,Reg32	.386
66| 0F BC 1E 0003r	BSF Reg32,Mem32	.386
0F BD DB	BSR Reg16,Reg16	.386
0F BD 1E 0001r	BSR Reg16,Mem16	.386
66| 0F BD DB	BSR Reg32,Reg32	.386
66| 0F BD 1E 0003r	BSR Reg32,Mem32	.386
66| 0F CB	BSWAP Reg32	.486
0F A3 DB	BT Reg16,Reg16	.386
0F A3 1E 0001r	BT Mem16,Reg16	.386
66| 0F A3 DB	BT Reg32,Reg32	.386
66| 0F A3 1E 0003r	BT Mem32,Reg32	.386
0F BA E3 12	BT Reg16,Imm8	.386
0F BA 26 0001r 12	BT Mem16,Imm8	.386
66| 0F BA E3 12	BT Reg32,Imm8	.386
66| 0F BA 26 0003r 12 +	BT Mem32,Imm8	.386
0F BB DB	BTC Reg16,Reg16	.386
0F BB 1E 0001r	BTC Mem16,Reg16	.386
66| 0F BB DB	BTC Reg32,Reg32	.386
66| 0F BB 1E 0003r	BTC Mem32,Reg32	.386
0F BA FB 12	BTC Reg16,Imm8	.386
0F BA 3E 0001r 12	BTC Mem16,Imm8	.386
66| 0F BA FB 12	BTC Reg32,Imm8	.386
66| 0F BA 3E 0003r 12 +	BTC Mem32,Imm8	.386
0F B3 DB	BTR Reg16,Reg16	.386
0F B3 1E 0001r	BTR Mem16,Reg16	.386
66| 0F B3 DB	BTR Reg32,Reg32	.386
66| 0F B3 1E 0003r	BTR Mem32,Reg32	.386
0F BA F3 12	BTR Reg16,Imm8	.386
0F BA 36 0001r 12	BTR Mem16,Imm8	.386
66| 0F BA F3 12	BTR Reg32,Imm8	.386
66| 0F BA 36 0003r 12 +	BTR Mem32,Imm8	.386
0F AB DB	BTS Reg16,Reg16	.386
0F AB 1E 0001r	BTS Mem16,Reg16	.386
66| 0F AB DB	BTS Reg32,Reg32	.386
66| 0F AB 1E 0003r	BTS Mem32,Reg32	.386
0F BA EB 12	BTS Reg16,Imm8	.386
0F BA 2E 0001r 12	BTS Mem16,Imm8	.386
66| 0F BA EB 12	BTS Reg32,Imm8	.386
66| 0F BA 2E 0003r +	BTS Mem32,Imm8	.386
E8 FFFD	CALL near ptr Rel_call	.286
9A 00000448sr	CALL far ptr Rel16	.286
FF 16 0001r	CALL Mem16	.286
FF D3	CALL Reg16	.286
E8 0000040D	CALL Rel_32	.386
FF D3	CALL Reg32	.386
67| FF 16 0003r	CALL Mem32	.386
66| 9A 00000003sr	CALL far ptr Mem32	.386

98	CBW	.286
66| 99	CDQ	.386
66| 98	CWDE	.386
F8	CLC	.386
FC	CLD	.386
FA	CLI	.386
0F 06	CLTS	.286P
F5	CMC	.286
3C 12	CMP AL,Imm8	.286
3D 3456	CMP AX,Imm16	.286
66| 3D 78901234	CMP EAX,Imm32	.386
3A FF	CMP Reg8,Reg8	.286
38 3E 0000r	CMP Mem8,Reg8	.286
80 FF 12	CMP Reg8,Imm8	.286
80 3E 0000r 12	CMP Mem8,Imm8	.286
3A 3E 0000r	CMP Reg8,Mem8	.286
3B DB	CMP Reg16,Reg16	.286
39 1E 0001r	CMP Mem16,Reg16	.286
81 FB 3456	CMP Reg16,Imm16	.286
81 3E 0001r 3456	CMP Mem16,Imm16	.286
3B 1E 0001r	CMP Reg16,Mem16	.286
83 FB 12	CMP Reg16,Imm8	.286
83 3E 0001r 12	CMP Mem16,Imm8	.286
66| 3B DB	CMP Reg32,Reg32	.386
66| 39 1E 0003r	CMP Mem32,Reg32	.386
66| 81 FB 78901234	CMP Reg32,Imm32	.386
66| 81 3E 0003r +	CMP Mem32,Imm32	.386
66| 3B 1E 0003r	CMP Reg32,Mem32	.386
66| 83 FB 12	CMP Reg32,Imm8	.386
66| 83 3E 0003r 12	CMP Mem32,Imm8	.386
A6	CMPSB	.286
A7	CMPSW	.286
66| A7	CMPSD	.386
0F A6 FF	CMPXCHG Reg8,Reg8	.486
0F A6 3E 0000r	CMPXCHG Mem8,Reg8	.486
0F A7 DB	CMPXCHG Reg16,Reg16	.486
0F A7 1E 0001r	CMPXCHG Mem16,Reg16	.486
66| 0F A7 DB	CMPXCHG Reg32,Reg32	.486
66| 0F A7 1E 0003r	CMPXCHG Mem32,Reg32	.486
99	CWD	.286
66| 99	CDQ	.386
27	DAA	.286
2F	DAS	.286
FE CF	DEC Reg8	.286
FE 0E 0000r	DEC Mem8	.286
FF 0E 0001r	DEC Mem16	.286
48	DEC AX	.286
49	DEC CX	.286
4A	DEC DX	.286
4B	DEC BX	.286
4C	DEC SP	.286
4D	DEC BP	.286
4E	DEC SI	.286
4F	DEC DI	.286
66| FF 0E 0003r	DEC Mem32	.386
66| 48	DEC EAX	.386
66| 49	DEC ECX	.386
66| 4A	DEC EDX	.386
66| 4B	DEC EBX	.386
66| 4C	DEC ESP	.386
66| 4D	DEC EBP	.386
66| 4E	DEC ESI	.386
66| 4F	DEC EDI	.386
F6 F7	DIV Reg8	.286
F6 36 0000r	DIV Mem8	.286
F7 F3	DIV Reg16	.286

F7 36 0001r	DIV Mem16	.286
66| F7 F3	DIV Reg32	.386
66| F7 36 0003r	DIV Mem32	.386
C8 3456 00	ENTER Imm16,0	.286
C8 3456 01	ENTER Imm16,1	.286
C8 3456 12	ENTER Imm16,Imm8	.286
DA D3	ESC Imm8,Reg16	.287
F4	HLT	.286
F6 FF	IDIV Reg8	.286
F6 3E 0000r	IDIV Mem8	.286
F7 FB	IDIV Reg16	.286
F7 3E 0001r	IDIV Mem16	.286
66| F7 FB	IDIV Reg32	.386
66| F7 3E 0003r	IDIV Mem32	.386
F6 EF	IMUL Reg8	.386
F6 2E 0000r	IMUL Mem8	.386
F7 EB	IMUL Reg16	.386
F7 2E 0001r	IMUL Mem16	.386
66| F7 EB	IMUL Reg32	.386
66| F7 2E 0003r	IMUL Mem32	.386
0F AF DB	IMUL Reg16,Reg16	.386
0F AF 1E 0001r	IMUL Reg16,Mem16	.386
66| 0F AF DB	IMUL Reg32,Reg32	.386
66| 0F AF 1E 0003r	IMUL Reg32,Mem32	.386
6B DB 12	IMUL Reg16,Reg16,Imm8	.386
6B 1E 0001r 12	IMUL Reg16,Mem16,Imm8	.386
66| 6B DB 12	IMUL Reg32,Reg32,Imm8	.386
66| 6B 1E 0003r 12	IMUL Reg32,Mem32,Imm8	.386
6B DB 12	IMUL Reg16,Imm8	.386
66| 6B DB 12	IMUL Reg32,Imm8	.386
69 DB 3456	IMUL Reg16,Reg16,Imm16	.386
69 1E 0001r 3456	IMUL Reg16,Mem16,Imm16	.386
66| 69 DB 78901234	IMUL Reg32,Reg32,Imm32	.386
66| 69 1E 0003r +	IMUL Reg32,Mem32,Imm32	.386
69 DB 3456	IMUL Reg16,Imm16	.386
66| 69 DB 78901234	IMUL Reg32,Imm32	.386
E4 12	IN AL,Imm8	.286
E5 12	IN AX,Imm8	.286
EC	IN AL,dx	.286
ED	IN AX,dx	.286
66| E5 12	IN EAX,Imm8	.386
66| ED	IN EAX,dx	.386
FE C7	INC Reg8	.286
FE 06 0000r	INC Mem8	.286
FF 06 0001r	INC Mem16	.286
40	INC AX	.286
41	INC CX	.286
42	INC DX	.286
43	INC BX	.286
44	INC SP	.286
45	INC BP	.286
46	INC SI	.286
47	INC DI	.286
66| FF 06 0003r	INC Mem32	.386
66| 40	INC EAX	.386
66| 41	INC ECX	.386
66| 42	INC EDX	.386
66| 43	INC EBX	.386
66| 44	INC ESP	.386
66| 45	INC EBP	.386
66| 46	INC ESI	.386
66| 47	INC EDI	.386
6C	INSB	.286
6D	INSW	.286
66| 6D	INSD	.386
CC	INT 3	.286

CD 12	INT Imm8	.286
CE	INTO	.286
0F 08	INVD	.486P
0F 01 3E 0003r	INVLPG Mem32	.486P
CF	IRET	.286
66| CF	IRETD	.386
77 FE	JA Rel8	.286
73 FC	JAE Rel8	.286
72 FA	JB Rel8	.286
76 F8	JBE Rel8	.286
72 F6	JC Rel8	.286
E3 F4	JCXZ Rel8	.286
67| E3 F1	JECXZ Rel8	.386
74 EF	JE Rel8	.286
7F ED	JG Rel8	.286
7D EB	JGE Rel8	.286
7C E9	JL Rel8	.286
EB E7	JMP short Rel8	.286
E9 0421	JMP near ptr Rel_8	.286
FF E3	JMP Reg16	.286
FF 26 0001r	JMP Word Ptr [Mem16]	.286
EA 00000448sr	JMP far ptr Rel16	.286
FF 2E 0001r	JMP DWord Ptr [Mem16]	.286
7E D3	JLE Rel8	.286
73 D1	JNC Rel8	.286
75 CF	JNE Rel8	.286
71 CD	JNO Rel8	.286
7B CB	JNP Rel8	.286
79 C9	JNS Rel8	.286
70 C7	JO Rel8	.286
7A C5	JP Rel8	.286
78 C3	JS Rel8	.286
0F 87 0444	JA Rel16	.386
0F 83 0440	JAE Rel16	.386
0F 82 043C	JB Rel16	.386
0F 86 0438	JBE Rel16	.386
0F 82 0434	JC Rel16	.386
0F 84 0430	JE Rel16	.386
0F 8F 042C	JG Rel16	.386
0F 8D 0428	JGE Rel16	.386
0F 8C 0424	JL Rel16	.386
0F 8E 0420	JLE Rel16	.386
0F 83 041C	JNC Rel16	.386
0F 85 0418	JNE Rel16	.386
0F 81 0414	JNO Rel16	.386
0F 8B 0410	JNP Rel16	.386
0F 89 040C	JNS Rel16	.386
0F 80 0408	JO Rel16	.386
0F 8A 0404	JP Rel16	.386
0F 88 0400	JS Rel16	.386
0F 82 00000470	JB Rel32	.386
0F 86 0000046A	JBE Rel32	.386
0F 82 00000464	JC Rel32	.386
0F 84 0000045E	JE Rel32	.386
0F 8F 00000458	JG Rel32	.386
0F 8D 00000452	JGE Rel32	.386
0F 8C 0000044C	JL Rel32	.386
0F 8E 00000446	JLE Rel32	.386
E9 00000441	JMP Rel32	.386
FF E3	JMP Reg32	.386
67| FF 26 0003r	JMP Mem32	.386
67| FF 2E 0007r	JMP Mem48	.386
67| FF 2E 0007r	JMP FWord ptr [Mem48]	.386
0F 83 0000042A	JNC Rel32	.386
0F 85 00000424	JNE Rel32	.386
0F 89 00000412	JNS Rel32	.386

0F 80 0000040C	JO Rel32	.386
0F 8A 00000406	JP Rel32	.386
0F 88 00000400	JS Rel32	.386
9F	LAHF	.286
0F 02 DB	LAR Reg16,Reg16	.386P
0F 02 1E 0001r	LAR Reg16,Mem16	.386P
66¦ 0F 02 DB	LAR Reg32,Reg32	.386P
66¦ 0F 02 1E 0003r	LAR Reg32,Mem32	.386P
C5 1E 0003r	LDS Reg16,Mem32	.286
66¦ C5 1E 0007r	LDS Reg32,Mem48	.386
BB 0001r	LEA Reg16,Mem16	.286
66¦ 8D 1E 0003r	LEA Reg32,Mem32	.386
C4 1E 0003r	LES Reg16,Mem32	.286
66¦ 0F B2 1E 0007r	LSS Reg32,Mem48	.386
0F B4 1E 0003r	LFS Reg16,Mem32	.386
66¦ 0F B4 1E 0007r	LFS Reg32,Mem48	.386
0F B5 1E 0003r	LGS Reg16,Mem32	.386
66¦ 0F B5 1E 0007r	LGS Reg32,Mem48	.386
C9	LEAVE	.386
0F 01 16 0007r	LGDT Mem48	.286P
0F 01 1E 0007r	LIDT Mem48	.286P
0F 00 D3	LLDT Reg16	.286P
0F 00 16 0001r	LLDT Mem16	.286P
0F 01 F3	LMSW Reg16	.286P
0F 01 36 0001r	LMSW Mem16	.286P
F0> 90	LOCK nop	.286
AC	LODSB	.286
AD	LODSW	.286
66¦ AD	LODSD	.386
E2 FE	LOOP Rel__8	.286
E1 FC	LOOPE Rel__8	.286
E0 FA	LOOPNE Rel__8	.286
0F 03 DB	LSL Reg16,Reg16	.286P
0F 03 1E 0001r	LSL Reg16,Mem16	.286P
66¦ 0F 03 DB	LSL Reg32,Reg32	.386P
66¦ 0F 03 1E 0003r	LSL Reg32,Mem32	.386P
0F B2 1E 0003r	LSS Reg16,Mem32	.386
66¦ 0F B2 1E 0007r	LSS Reg32,Mem48	.386
0F 00 DB	LTR Reg16	.286P
0F 00 1E 0001r	LTR Mem16	.286P
88 3E 0000r	MOV Mem8,Reg8	.286
89 1E 0001r	MOV Mem16,Reg16	.286
8A 3E 0000r	MOV Reg8,Mem8	.286
8A FF	MOV Reg8,Reg8	.286
8B 1E 0001r	MOV Reg16,Mem16	.286
8B DB	MOV Reg16,Reg16	.286
8C DB	MOV Reg16,SR	.286
8C 1E 0001r	MOV Mem16,SR	.286
8E DB	MOV SR,Reg16	.286
8E 1E 0001r	MOV SR,Mem16	.286
A0 0000r	MOV AL,Mem8	.286
A1 0001r	MOV AX,Mem16	.286
B0 12	MOV AL,Imm8	.286
B1 12	MOV CL,Imm8	.286
B2 12	MOV DL,Imm8	.286
B3 12	MOV BL,Imm8	.286
B4 12	MOV AH,Imm8	.286
B5 12	MOV CH,Imm8	.286
B6 12	MOV DH,Imm8	.286
B7 12	MOV BH,Imm8	.286
BA 3456	MOV DX,Imm16	.286
BB 3456	MOV BX,Imm16	.286
BC 3456	MOV SP,Imm16	.286
BD 3456	MOV BP,Imm16	.286
BE 3456	MOV SI,Imm16	.286
BF 3456	MOV DI,Imm16	.286

```
C6 06 0000r 12          MOV Mem8,Imm8            .286
C7 06 0001r 3456        MOV Mem16,Imm16          .286
0F 03 DB                LSL Reg16,Reg16          .286P
0F 03 1E 0001r          LSL Reg16,Mem16          .286P
66| 0F 03 DB            LSL Reg32,Reg32          .386P
66| 0F 03 1E 0003r      LSL Reg32,Mem32          .386P
0F B2 1E 0003r          LSS Reg16,Mem32          .386
66| 0F B2 1E 0007r      LSS Reg32,Mem48          .386
0F 00 DB                LTR Reg16                .286P
0F 00 1E 0001r          LTR Mem16                .286P
88 3E 0000r             MOV Mem8,Reg8            .286
89 1E 0001r             MOV Mem16,Reg16          .286
8A 3E 0000r             MOV Reg8,Mem8            .286
8A FF                   MOV Reg8,Reg8            .286
8B 1E 0001r             MOV Reg16,Mem16          .286
8B DB                   MOV Reg16,Reg16          .286
8C DB                   MOV Reg16,SR             .286
8C 1E 0001r             MOV Mem16,SR             .286
8E DB                   MOV SR,Reg16             .286
8E 1E 0001r             MOV SR,Mem16             .286
A0 0000r                MOV AL,Mem8              .286
A1 0001r                MOV AX,Mem16             .286
A2 0000r                MOV Mem8,AL              .286
A3 0001r                MOV Mem16,AX             .286
B0 12                   MOV AL,Imm8              .286
B1 12                   MOV CL,Imm8              .286
B2 12                   MOV DL,Imm8              .286
B3 12                   MOV BL,Imm8              .286
B4 12                   MOV AH,Imm8              .286
B5 12                   MOV CH,Imm8              .286
B6 12                   MOV DH,Imm8              .286
B7 12                   MOV BH,Imm8              .286
B8 3456                 MOV AX,Imm16             .286
B9 3456                 MOV CX,Imm16             .286
BA 3456                 MOV DX,Imm16             .286
BB 3456                 MOV BX,Imm16             .286
BC 3456                 MOV SP,Imm16             .286
BD 3456                 MOV BP,Imm16             .286
BE 3456                 MOV SI,Imm16             .286
BF 3456                 MOV DI,Imm16             .286
C6 06 0000r 12          MOV Mem8,Imm8            .286
C7 06 0001r 3456        MOV Mem16,Imm16          .286
66| 89 1E 0003r         MOV Mem32,Reg32          .386
66| 8B 1E 0003r         MOV Reg32,Mem32          .386
66| 8B DB               MOV Reg32,Reg32          .386
A0 0000r                MOV AL,Mem8              .386
66| A1 0003r            MOV EAX,Mem32            .386
66| A3 0003r            MOV Mem32,EAX            .386
66| B8 78901234         MOV EAX,Imm32            .386
66| B9 78901234         MOV ECX,Imm32            .386
66| BA 78901234         MOV EDX,Imm32            .386
66| BB 78901234         MOV EBX,Imm32            .386
66| BC 78901234         MOV ESP,Imm32            .386
66| BD 78901234         MOV EBP,Imm32            .386
66| BE 78901234         MOV ESI,Imm32            .386
66| BF 78901234         MOV EDI,Imm32            .386
66| C7 06 0003r     +   MOV Mem32,Imm32          .386
0F 22 C3                MOV cr0,Reg32            .386P
0F 20 C3                MOV Reg32,cr0_2          .386P
0F 22 DB                MOV cr2_3,Reg32          .386P
0F 21 C3                MOV Reg32,dr0_3          .386P
0F 21 F3                MOV Reg32,dr6_7          .386P
0F 23 C3                MOV dr0_3,Reg32          .386P
0F 23 F3                MOV dr6_7,Reg32          .386P
0F 24 E3                MOV Reg32,tr4_7          .386P
0F 26 E3                MOV tr4_7,Reg32          .386P
```

0F 24 DB	MOV Reg32,tr3	.386P
0F 26 DB	MOV tr3,Reg32	.386P
A4	MOVSB	.286
A5	MOVSW	.286
66| A5	MOVSD	.386
0F BE 1E 0000r	MOVSX Reg16,Mem8	.386
0F BE DF	MOVSX Reg16,Reg8	.386
66| 0F BE 1E 0000r	MOVSX Reg32,Mem8	.386
66| 0F BE DF	MOVSX Reg32,Reg8	.386
66| 0F BF 1E 0001r	MOVSX Reg32,Mem16	.386
66| 0F BF DB	MOVSX Reg32,Reg16	.386
0F B6 1E 0000r	MOVZX Reg16,Mem8	.386
0F B6 DF	MOVZX Reg16,Reg8	.386
66| 0F B6 1E 0000r	MOVZX Reg32,Mem8	.386
66| 0F B6 DF	MOVZX Reg32,Reg8	.386
66| 0F B7 1E 0001r	MOVZX Reg32,Mem16	.386
66| 0F B7 DB	MOVZX Reg32,Reg16	.386
F6 E7	MUL Reg8	.286
F6 26 0000r	MUL Mem8	.286
F7 E3	MUL Reg16	.286
F7 26 0001r	MUL Mem16	.286
66| F7 E3	MUL Reg32	.386
66| F7 26 0003r	MUL Mem32	.386
F6 DF	NEG Reg8	.286
F6 1E 0000r	NEG Mem8	.286
F7 DB	NEG Reg16	.286
F7 1E 0001r	NEG Mem16	.286
66| F7 DB	NEG Reg32	.386
66| F7 1E 0003r	NEG Mem32	.386
90	NOP	.286
F6 D7	NOT Reg8	.286
F6 16 0000r	NOT Mem8	.286
F7 D3	NOT Reg16	.286
F7 16 0001r	NOT Mem16	.286
66| F7 D3	NOT Reg32	.386
66| F7 16 0003r	NOT Mem32	.386
0C 12	OR AL,Imm8	.286
0D 3456	OR AX,Imm16	.286
66| 0D 78901234	OR EAX,Imm32	.386
0A FF	OR Reg8,Reg8	.286
08 3E 0000r	OR Mem8,Reg8	.286
80 CF 12	OR Reg8,Imm8	.286
80 0E 0000r 12	OR Mem8,Imm8	.286
0A 3E 0000r	OR Reg8,Mem8	.286
0B DB	OR Reg16,Reg16	.286
09 1E 0001r	OR Mem16,Reg16	.286
81 CB 3456	OR Reg16,Imm16	.286
81 0E 0001r 3456	OR Mem16,Imm16	.286
0B 1E 0001r	OR Reg16,Mem16	.286
66| 0B DB	OR Reg32,Reg32	.386
66| 09 1E 0003r	OR Mem32,Reg32	.386
66| 81 CB 78901234	OR Reg32,Imm32	.386
66| 81 0E 0003r +	OR Mem32,Imm32	.386
66| 0B 1E 0003r	OR Reg32,Mem32	.386
66| 83 CB 12	OR Reg32,Imm8	.386
66| 83 0E 0003r 12	OR Mem32,Imm8	.386
E6 12	OUT Imm8,AL	.286
E7 12	OUT Imm8,AX	.286
66| E7 12	OUT Imm8,EAX	.386
EE	OUT DX,AL	.286
EF	OUT DX,AX	.286
66| EF	OUT DX,EAX	.386
6E	OUTSB	.286
6F	OUTSW	.286
66| 6F	OUTSD	.286
8F 06 0001r	POP Mem16	.286

1F	POP DS	.286
07	POP ES	.286
17	POP SS	.286
58	POP AX	.286
59	POP CX	.286
5A	POP DX	.286
5B	POP BX	.286
5C	POP SP	.286
5D	POP BP	.286
5E	POP SI	.286
5F	POP DI	.286
66| 8F 06 0003r	POP Mem32	.386
0F A1	POP FS	.386
0F A9	POP GS	.386
66| 58	POP EAX	.386
66| 59	POP ECX	.386
66| 5A	POP EDX	.386
66| 5B	POP EBX	.386
66| 5C	POP ESP	.386
66| 5D	POP EBP	.386
66| 5E	POP ESI	.386
66| 5F	POP EDI	.386
61	POPA	.286
66| 61	POPAD	.386
9D	POPF	.286
66| 9D	POPFD	.386
FF 36 0001r	PUSH Mem16	.286
6A 12	PUSH Imm8	.286
68 3456	PUSH Imm16	.286
0E	PUSH CS	.286
1E	PUSH DS	.286
06	PUSH ES	.286
16	PUSH SS	.286
50	PUSH AX	.286
51	PUSH CX	.286
52	PUSH DX	.286
53	PUSH BX	.286
54	PUSH SP	.286
55	PUSH BP	.286
56	PUSH SI	.286
57	PUSH DI	.286
66| FF 36 0003r	PUSH Mem32	.386
66| 68 78901234	PUSH Imm32	.386
0F A0	PUSH FS	.386
0F A8	PUSH GS	.386
66| 50	PUSH EAX	.386
66| 53	PUSH EBX	.386
66| 54	PUSH ESP	.386
66| 55	PUSH EBP	.386
66| 56	PUSH ESI	.386
66| 57	PUSH EDI	.386
60	PUSHA	.286
66| 60	PUSHAD	.386
9C	PUSHF	.286
66| 9C	PUSHFD	.386
D0 D7	RCL Reg8,1	.286
D0 16 0000r	RCL Mem8,1	.286
D2 D7	RCL Reg8,cl	.286
D2 16 0000r	RCL Mem8,cl	.286
C0 D7 12	RCL Reg8,Imm8	.286
C0 16 0000r 12	RCL Mem8,Imm8	.286
D1 D3	RCL Reg16,1	.286
D1 16 0001r	RCL Mem16,1	.286
D3 D3	RCL Reg16,cl	.286
D3 16 0001r	RCL Mem16,cl	.286
C1 D3 12	RCL Reg16,Imm8	.286

C1 16 0001r 12		RCL Mem16,Imm8	.286
66| D1 D3		RCL Reg32,1	.386
66| D1 16 0003r		RCL Mem32,1	.386
66| D3 D3		RCL Reg32,cl	.386
66| D3 16 0003r		RCL Mem32,cl	.386
66| C1 D3 12		RCL Reg32,Imm8	.386
66| C1 16 0003r 12		RCL Mem32,Imm8	.386
D0 DF		RCR Reg8,1	.286
D0 1E 0000r		RCR Mem8,1	.286
D2 DF		RCR Reg8,cl	.286
D2 1E 0000r		RCR Mem8,cl	.286
C0 DF 12		RCR Reg8,Imm8	.286
C0 1E 0000r 12		RCR Mem8,Imm8	.286
D1 DB		RCR Reg16,1	.286
D1 1E 0001r		RCR Mem16,1	.286
D3 DB		RCR Reg16,cl	.286
D3 1E 0001r		RCR Mem16,cl	.286
C1 DB 12		RCR Reg16,Imm8	.286
1E 0001r 12		RCR Mem16,Imm8	.286
66| D1 DB		RCR Reg32,1	.386
66| D1 1E 0003r		RCR Mem32,1	.386
66| D3 DB		RCR Reg32,cl	.386
66| D3 1E 0003r		RCR Mem32,cl	.386
66| C1 DB 12		RCR Reg32,Imm8	.386
66| C1 1E 0003r 12		RCR Mem32,Imm8	.386
F3> A6		REP cmpsb	.286
F3> A6		REPZ cmpsb	.286
F2> A6		REPNZ cmpsb	.286
F3> A7		REP cmpsw	.286
F3> A7		REPZ cmpsw	.286
F2> A7		REPNZ cmpsw	.286
F3> 66| A7		REP cmpsd	.386
F3> 66| A7		REPZ cmpsd	.386
F2> 66| A7		REPNZ cmpsd	.386
F3> 6C		REP insb	.286
F3> 6C		REPZ insb	.286
F2> 6C		REPNZ insb	.286
F3> 6D		REP insw	.286
F3> 6D		REPZ insw	.286
F2> 6D		REPNZ insw	.286
F3> 66| 6D		REP insd	.386
F3> 66| 6D		REPZ insd	.386
F2> 66| 6D		REPNZ insd	.386
F3> AC		REP lodsb	.286
F3> AC		REPZ lodsb	.286
F2> AC		REPNZ lodsb	.286
F3> AD		REP lodsw	.286
F3> AD		REPZ lodsw	.286
F2> AD		REPNZ lodsw	.286
F3> 66| AD		REP lodsd	.386
F3> 66| AD		REPZ lodsd	.386
F2> 66| AD		REPNZ lodsd	.386
F3> A4		REP movsb	.286
F3> A4		REPZ movsb	.286
F2> A4		REPNZ movsb	.286
F3> A5		REP movsw	.286
F3> A5		REPZ movsw	.286
F2> A5		REPNZ movsw	.286
F3> 66| A5		REP movsd	.386
F3> 66| A5		REPZ movsd	.386
F2> 66| A5		REPNZ movsd	.386
F3> 6E		REP outsb	.286
F3> 6E		REPZ outsb	.286
F2> 6E		REPNZ outsb	.286
F3> 6F		REP outsw	.286
F3> 6F		REPZ outsw	.286

F2> 6F	REPNZ outsw	.286
F3> 6E	REP outsb	.386
F3> 6E	REPZ outsb	.386
F2> 6E	REPNZ outsb	.386
F3> AE	REP scasb	.286
F3> AE	REPZ scasb	.286
F2> AE	REPNZ scasb	.286
F3> AF	REP scasw	.286
F3> AF	REPZ scasw	.286
F2> AF	REPNZ scasw	.286
F3> 66| AF	REP scasd	.386
F3> 66| AF	REPZ scasd	.386
F2> 66| AF	REPNZ scasd	.386
F3> AA	REP stosb	.286
F3> AA	REPZ stosb	.286
F2> AA	REPNZ stosb	.286
F3> AB	REP stosw	.286
F3> AB	REPZ stosw	.286
F2> AB	REPNZ stosw	.286
F3> 66| AB	REP stosd	.386
F3> 66| AB	REPZ stosd	.386
F2> 66| AB	REPNZ stosd	.386
C3	RET	.286
CB	RETF	.286
C2 3456	RET Imm16	.286
CA 3456	RETF Imm16	.286
D0 C7	ROL Reg8,1	.286
D0 06 0000r	ROL Mem8,1	.286
D2 C7	ROL Reg8,cl	.286
D2 06 0000r	ROL Mem8,cl	.286
C0 C7 12	ROL Reg8,Imm8	.286
C0 06 0000r 12	ROL Mem8,Imm8	.286
D1 C3	ROL Reg16,1	.286
D1 06 0001r	ROL Mem16,1	.286
D3 C3	ROL Reg16,cl	.286
D3 06 0001r	ROL Mem16,cl	.286
C1 C3 12	ROL Reg16,Imm8	.286
C1 06 0001r 12	ROL Mem16,Imm8	.286
66| D1 C3	ROL Reg32,1	.386
66| D1 06 0003r	ROL Mem32,1	.386
66| D3 C3	ROL Reg32,cl	.386
66| D3 06 0003r	ROL Mem32,cl	.386
66| C1 C3 12	ROL Reg32,Imm8	.386
66| C1 06 0003r 12	ROL Mem32,Imm8	.386
D0 CF	ROR Reg8,1	.286
D0 0E 0000r	ROR Mem8,1	.286
D2 CF	ROR Reg8,cl	.286
D2 0E 0000r	ROR Mem8,cl	.286
C0 CF 12	ROR Reg8,Imm8	.286
C0 0E 0000r 12	ROR Mem8,Imm8	.286
D1 CB	ROR Reg16,1	.286
D1 0E 0001r	ROR Mem16,1	.286
D3 CB	ROR Reg16,cl	.286
D3 0E 0001r	ROR Mem16,cl	.286
C1 CB 12	ROR Reg16,Imm8	.286
C1 0E 0001r 12	ROR Mem16,Imm8	.286
66| D1 CB	ROR Reg32,1	.386
66| D1 0E 0003r	ROR Mem32,1	.386
66| C1 CB 12	ROR Reg32,Imm8	.386
66| C1 0E 0003r 12	ROR Mem32,Imm8	.386
9E	SAHF	.286
D0 E7	SAL Reg8,1	.286
D0 26 0000r	SAL Mem8,1	.286
D2 E7	SAL Reg8,cl	.286

D2 26 0000r	SAL Mem8,cl	.286
C0 E7 12	SAL Reg8,Imm8	.286
C0 26 0000r 12	SAL Mem8,Imm8	.286
D1 E3	SAL Reg16,1	.286
D1 26 0001r	SAL Mem16,1	.286
D3 E3	SAL Reg16,cl	.286
D3 26 0001r	SAL Mem16,cl	.286
C1 E3 12	SAL Reg16,Imm8	.286
C1 26 0001r 12	SAL Mem16,Imm8	.286
66| D1 E3	SAL Reg32,1	.386
66| D1 26 0003r	SAL Mem32,1	.386
66| D3 E3	SAL Reg32,cl	.386
66| D3 26 0003r	SAL Mem32,cl	.386
66| C1 E3 12	SAL Reg32,Imm8	.386
66| C1 26 0003r 12	SAL Mem32,Imm8	.386
D0 FF	SAR Reg8,1	.286
D0 3E 0000r	SAR Mem8,1	.286
D2 FF	SAR Reg8,cl	.286
D2 3E 0000r	SAR Mem8,cl	.286
C0 FF 12	SAR Reg8,Imm8	.286
C0 3E 0000r 12	SAR Mem8,Imm8	.286
D1 FB	SAR Reg16,1	.286
D1 3E 0001r	SAR Mem16,1	.286
D3 FB	SAR Reg16,cl	.286
D3 3E 0001r	SAR Mem16,cl	.286
C1 FB 12	SAR Reg16,Imm8	.286
C1 3E 0001r 12	SAR Mem16,Imm8	.286
66| D1 FB	SAR Reg32,1	.386
66| D1 3E 0003r	SAR Mem32,1	.386
66| D3 FB	SAR Reg32,cl	.386
66| D3 3E 0003r	SAR Mem32,cl	.386
66| C1 FB 12	SAR Reg32,Imm8	.386
66| C1 3E 0003r 12	SAR Mem32,Imm8	.386
1C 12	SBB AL,Imm8	.286
1D 3456	SBB AX,Imm16	.286
66| 1D 78901234	SBB EAX,Imm32	.386
80 DF 12	SBB Reg8,Imm8	.286
80 1E 0000r 12	SBB Mem8,Imm8	.286
81 DB 3456	SBB Reg16,Imm16	.286
81 1E 0001r 3456	SBB Mem16,Imm16	.286
66| 81 DB 78901234	SBB Reg32,Imm32	.386
66| 81 1E 0003r +	SBB Mem32,Imm32	.386
83 DB 12	SBB Reg16,Imm8	.286
83 1E 0001r 12	SBB Mem16,Imm8	.286
66| 83 DB 12	SBB Reg32,Imm8	.386
66| 83 1E 0003r 12	SBB Mem32,Imm8	.386
1A FF	SBB Reg8,Reg8	.286
18 3E 0000r	SBB Mem8,Reg8	.286
66| 1B DB	SBB Reg32,Reg32	.386
66| 19 1E 0003r	SBB Mem32,Reg32	.386
1A FF	SBB Reg8,Reg8	.286
1A 3E 0000r	SBB Reg8,Mem8	.286
1B DB	SBB Reg16,Reg16	.286
1B 1E 0001r	SBB Reg16,Mem16	.286
66| 1B DB	SBB Reg32,Reg32	.386
66| 1B 1E 0003r	SBB Reg32,Mem32	.386
AE	SCASB	.286
AF	SCASW	.286
66| AF	SCASD	.386
0F 97 06 0000r	SETA Mem8	.286
0F 97 C7	SETA Reg8	.286
0F 93 06 0000r	SETAE Mem8	.286
0F 93 C7	SETAE Reg8	.286
0F 92 06 0000r	SETB Mem8	.286
0F 92 C7	SETB Reg8	.286
0F 96 06 0000r	SETBE Mem8	.286

0F 96 C7	SETBE Reg8	.286
0F 92 06 0000r	SETC Mem8	.286
0F 92 C7	SETC Reg8	.286
0F 94 06 0000r	SETE Mem8	.286
0F 94 C7	SETE Reg8	.286
0F 9F 06 0000r	SETG Mem8	.286
0F 9F C7	SETG Reg8	.286
0F 9D 06 0000r	SETGE Mem8	.286
0F 9D C7	SETGE Reg8	.286
0F 9C 06 0000r	SETL Mem8	.286
0F 9C C7	SETL Reg8	.286
0F 9E 06 0000r	SETLE Mem8	.286
0F 9E C7	SETLE Reg8	.286
0F 93 06 0000r	SETNC Mem8	.286
0F 93 C7	SETNC Reg8	.286
0F 95 06 0000r	SETNE Mem8	.286
0F 95 C7	SETNE Reg8	.286
0F 91 06 0000r	SETNO Mem8	.286
0F 91 C7	SETNO Reg8	.286
0F 9B 06 0000r	SETNP Mem8	.286
0F 9B C7	SETNP Reg8	.286
0F 99 06 0000r	SETNS Mem8	.286
0F 99 C7	SETNS Reg8	.286
0F 90 06 0000r	SETO Mem8	.286
0F 90 C7	SETO Reg8	.286
0F 9A 06 0000r	SETP Mem8	.286
0F 9A C7	SETP Reg8	.286
0F 98 06 0000r	SETS Mem8	.286
0F 98 C7	SETS Reg8	.286
0F 01 06 0007r	SGDT Mem48	.386P
D0 E7	SHL Reg8,1	.286
D0 26 0000r	SHL Mem8,1	.286
D2 E7	SHL Reg8,cl	.286
D2 26 0000r	SHL Mem8,cl	.286
C0 E7 12	SHL Reg8,Imm8	.286
C0 26 0000r 12	SHL Mem8,Imm8	.286
D1 E3	SHL Reg16,1	.286
D1 26 0001r	SHL Mem16,1	.286
D3 E3	SHL Reg16,cl	.286
D3 26 0001r	SHL Mem16,cl	.286
C1 E3 12	SHL Reg16,Imm8	.286
C1 26 0001r 12	SHL Mem16,Imm8	.286
66| D1 E3	SHL Reg32,1	.386
66| D1 26 0003r	SHL Mem32,1	.386
66| D3 E3	SHL Reg32,cl	.386
66| D3 26 0003r	SHL Mem32,cl	.386
66| C1 E3 12	SHL Reg32,Imm8	.386
66| C1 26 0003r 12	SHL Mem32,Imm8	.386
D0 EF	SHR Reg8,1	.286
D0 2E 0000r	SHR Mem8,1	.286
D2 EF	SHR Reg8,cl	.286
D2 2E 0000r	SHR Mem8,cl	.286
C0 EF 12	SHR Reg8,Imm8	.286
C0 2E 0000r 12	SHR Mem8,Imm8	.286
D1 EB	SHR Reg16,1	.286
D1 2E 0001r	SHR Mem16,1	.286
D3 EB	SHR Reg16,cl	.286
D3 2E 0001r	SHR Mem16,cl	.286
C1 EB 12	SHR Reg16,Imm8	.286
C1 2E 0001r 12	SHR Mem16,Imm8	.286
66| D1 EB	SHR Reg32,1	.386
66| D1 2E 0003r	SHR Mem32,1	.386
66| D3 EB	SHR Reg32,cl	.386
66| D3 2E 0003r	SHR Mem32,cl	.386
66| C1 EB 12	SHR Reg32,Imm8	.386
66| C1 2E 0003r 12	SHR Mem32,Imm8	.386

0F 01 0E 0007r	SIDT Mem48	.386P
0F A4 DB 12	SHLD Reg16,Reg16,Imm8	.386
0F A4 1E 0001r 12	SHLD Mem16,Reg16,Imm8	.386
66| 0F A4 DB 12	SHLD Reg32,Reg32,Imm8	.386
66| 0F A4 1E 0003r +	SHLD Mem32,Reg32,Imm8	.386
0F AC DB 12	SHRD Reg16,Reg16,Imm8	.386
0F AC 1E 0001r 12	SHRD Mem16,Reg16,Imm8	.386
66| 0F AC DB 12	SHRD Reg32,Reg32,Imm8	.386
66| 0F AC 1E 0003r +	SHRD Mem32,Reg32,Imm8	.386
0F AD DB	SHRD Reg16,Reg16,CL	.386
0F AD 1E 0001r	SHRD Mem16,Reg16,CL	.386
0F 00 C3	SLDT Reg16	.286P
0F 00 06 0001r	SLDT Mem16	.286P
0F 01 E3	SMSW Reg16	.286P
0F 01 26 0001r	SMSW Mem16	.286P
F9	STC	.286
FD	STD	.286
FB	STI	.286
AA	STOSB	.286
AB	STOSW	.286
66| AB	STOSD	.386
0F 00 CB	STR Reg16	.286P
0F 00 0E 0001r	STR Mem16	.286P
2C 12	SUB AL,Imm8	.286
2D 3456	SUB AX,Imm16	.286
66| 2D 78901234	SUB EAX,Imm32	.386
2A FF	SUB Reg8,Reg8	.286
28 3E 0000r	SUB Mem8,Reg8	.286
80 EF 12	SUB Reg8,Imm8	.286
80 2E 0000r 12	SUB Mem8,Imm8	.286
2A 3E 0000r	SUB Reg8,Mem8	.286
2B DB	SUB Reg16,Reg16	.286
29 1E 0001r	SUB Mem16,Reg16	.286
81 EB 3456	SUB Reg16,Imm16	.286
81 2E 0001r 3456	SUB Mem16,Imm16	.286
2B 1E 0001r	SUB Reg16,Mem16	.286
83 EB 12	SUB Reg16,Imm8	.286
83 2E 0001r 12	SUB Mem16,Imm8	.286
66| 2B DB	SUB Reg32,Reg32	.386
66| 29 1E 0003r	SUB Mem32,Reg32	.386
66| 81 EB 78901234	SUB Reg32,Imm32	.386
66| 81 2E 0003r +	SUB Mem32,Imm32	.386
66| 2B 1E 0003r	SUB Reg32,Mem32	.386
66| 83 EB 12	SUB Reg32,Imm8	.386
66| 83 2E 0003r 12	SUB Mem32,Imm8	.386
A8 12	TEST AL,Imm8	.286
A9 3456	TEST AX,Imm16	.286
F6 C7 12	TEST Reg8,Imm8	.286
F6 06 0000r 12	TEST Mem8,Imm8	.286
F7 C3 3456	TEST Reg16,Imm16	.286
F7 06 0001r 3456	TEST Mem16,Imm16	.286
84 FF	TEST Reg8,Reg8	.286
84 3E 0000r	TEST Mem8,Reg8	.286
85 DB	TEST Reg16,Reg16	.286
85 1E 0001r	TEST Mem16,Reg16	.286
66| A9 78901234	TEST EAX,Imm32	.386
66| F7 C3 78901234	TEST Reg32,Imm32	.386
66| F7 06 0003r +	TEST Mem32,Imm32	.386
66| 85 DB	TEST Reg32,Reg32	.386
66| 85 1E 0003r	TEST Mem32,Reg32	.386
0F 00 E3	VERR Reg16	.286P
0F 00 26 0001r	VERR Mem16	.286P
0F 00 EB	VERW Reg16	.286P
0F 00 2E 0001r	VERW Mem16	.286P
9B	WAIT	.286
0F 09	WBINVD	.486P

```
0F C0 FF                XADD Reg8,Reg8          .486
0F C0 3E 0000r          XADD Mem8,Reg8          .486
0F C1 DB                XADD Reg16,Reg16        .486
0F C1 1E 0001r          XADD Mem16,Reg16        .486
66| 0F C1 DB            XADD Reg32,Reg32        .486
66| 0F C1 1E 0003r      XADD Mem32,Reg32        .486
93                      XCHG AX,Reg16           .286
93                      XCHG Reg16,AX           .286
86 FF                   XCHG Reg8,Reg8          .286
86 3E 0000r             XCHG Reg8,Mem8          .286
86 3E 0000r             XCHG Mem8,Reg8          .286
87 DB                   XCHG Reg16,Reg16        .286
87 1E 0001r             XCHG Reg16,Mem16        .286
87 1E 0001r             XCHG Mem16,Reg16        .286
90                      XCHG AX,AX              .286
91                      XCHG CX,AX              .286
92                      XCHG DX,AX              .286
93                      XCHG BX,AX              .286
94                      XCHG SP,AX              .286
95                      XCHG BP,AX              .286
96                      XCHG SI,AX              .286
97                      XCHG DI,AX              .286
66| 93                  XCHG EAX,Reg32          .386
66| 93                  XCHG Reg32,EAX          .386
66| 87 DB               XCHG Reg32,Reg32        .386
66| 87 1E 0003r         XCHG Reg32,Mem32        .386
66| 87 1E 0003r         XCHG Mem32,Reg32        .386
66| 90                  XCHG EAX,EAX            .386
66| 91                  XCHG ECX,EAX            .386
66| 92                  XCHG EDX,EAX            .386
66| 93                  XCHG EBX,EAX            .386
66| 94                  XCHG ESP,EAX            .386
66| 95                  XCHG EBP,EAX            .386
66| 96                  XCHG ESI,EAX            .386
66| 97                  XCHG EDI,EAX            .386
D7                      XLAT Table              .286
34 12                   XOR AL,Imm8             .286
35 3456                 XOR AX,Imm16            .286
66| 35 78901234         XOR EAX,Imm32           .386
80 F7 12                XOR Reg8,Imm8           .286
80 36 0000r 12          XOR Mem8,Imm8           .286
32 3E 0000r             XOR Reg8,Mem8           .286
33 DB                   XOR Reg16,Reg16         .286
31 1E 0001r             XOR Mem16,Reg16         .286
81 F3 3456              XOR Reg16,Imm16         .286
81 36 0001r 3456        XOR Mem16,Imm16         .286
33 1E 0001r             XOR Reg16,Mem16         .286
83 F3 12                XOR Reg16,Imm8          .286
83 36 0001r 12          XOR Mem16,Imm8          .286
66| 33 DB               XOR Reg32,Reg32         .386
66| 31 1E 0003r         XOR Mem32,Reg32         .386
66| 81 F3 78901234      XOR Reg32,Imm32         .386
66| 81 36 0003r    +    XOR Mem32,Imm32         .386
66| 33 1E 0003r         XOR Reg32,Mem32         .386
66| 83 F3 12            XOR Reg32,Imm8          .386
66| 83 36 0003r 12      XOR Mem32,Imm8          .386
```

86-Family Numerically
Ordered Instruction Set

```
00 3E. 0000r        ADD Mem8,Reg8          .286
01 1E 0001r         ADD Mem16,Reg16        .286
02 3E 0000r         ADD Reg8,Mem8          .286
02 FF               ADD Reg8,Reg8          .286
03 1E 0001r         ADD Reg16,Mem16        .286
03 DB               ADD Reg16,Reg16        .286
04 12               ADD AL,Imm8            .286
05 3456             ADD AX,Imm16           .286
06                  PUSH ES                .286
07                  POP ES                 .286
08 3E 0000r         OR Mem8,Reg8           .286
09 1E 0001r         OR Mem16,Reg16         .286
0A 3E 0000r         OR Reg8,Mem8           .286
0A FF               OR Reg8,Reg8           .286
0B 1E 0001r         OR Reg16,Mem16         .286
0B DB               OR Reg16,Reg16         .286
0C 12               OR AL,Imm8             .286
0D 3456             OR AX,Imm16            .286
0E                  PUSH CS                .286
0F 00 06 0001r      SLDT Mem16             .286P
0F 00 0E 0001r      STR Mem16              .286P
0F 00 16 0001r      LLDT Mem16             .286P
0F 00 1E 0001r      LTR Mem16              .286P
0F 00 1E 0001r      LTR Mem16              .286P
0F 00 26 0001r      VERR Mem16             .286P
0F 00 2E 0001r      VERW Mem16             .286P
0F 00 C3            SLDT Reg16             .286P
0F 00 CB            STR Reg16              .286P
0F 00 D3            LLDT Reg16             .286P
0F 00 DB            LTR Reg16              .286P
0F 00 DB            LTR Reg16              .286P
0F 00 E3            VERR Reg16             .286P
0F 00 EB            VERW Reg16             .286P
0F 01 06 0007r      SGDT Mem48             .386P
0F 01 0E 0007r      SIDT Mem48             .386P
0F 01 16 0007r      LGDT Mem48             .286P
0F 01 1E 0007r      LIDT Mem48             .286P
0F 01 26 0001r      SMSW Mem16             .286P
0F 01 36 0001r      LMSW Mem16             .286P
0F 01 3E 0003r      INVLPG Mem32           .486P
0F 01 E3            SMSW Reg16             .286P
0F 01 F3            LMSW Reg16             .286P
0F 02 1E 0001r      LAR Reg16,Mem16        .386P
0F 02 DB            LAR Reg16,Reg16        .386P
0F 03 1E 0001r      LSL Reg16,Mem16        .286P
0F 03 1E 0001r      LSL Reg16,Mem16        .286P
0F 03 DB            LSL Reg16,Reg16        .286P
0F 03 DB            LSL Reg16,Reg16        .286P
0F 06               CLTS                   .286P
0F 08               INVD                   .486P
0F 09               WBINVD                 .486P
0F 20 C3            MOV Reg32,cr0_2        .386P
```

```
0F 21 C3              MOV Reg32,dr0_3          .386P
0F 21 F3              MOV Reg32,dr6_7          .386P
0F 22 C3              MOV cr0,Reg32            .386P
0F 22 DB              MOV cr2_3,Reg32          .386P
0F 23 C3              MOV dr0_3,Reg32          .386P
0F 23 F3              MOV dr6_7,Reg32          .386P
0F 24 DB              MOV Reg32,tr3            .386P
0F 24 E3              MOV Reg32,tr4_7          .386P
0F 26 DB              MOV tr3,Reg32            .386P
0F 26 E3              MOV tr4_7,Reg32          .386P
0F 80 0000040C        JO Rel32                 .386
0F 80 0408            JO Rel16                 .386
0F 81 0414            JNO Rel16                .386
0F 82 00000464        JC Rel32                 .386
0F 82 00000470        JB Rel32                 .386
0F 82 0434            JC Rel16                 .386
0F 82 043C            JB Rel16                 .386
0F 83 0000042A        JNC Rel32                .386
0F 83 041C            JNC Rel16                .386
0F 83 0440            JAE Rel16                .386
0F 84 0000045E        JE Rel32                 .386
0F 84 0430            JE Rel16                 .386
0F 85 00000424        JNE Rel32                .386
0F 85 0418            JNE Rel16                .386
0F 86 0000046A        JBE Rel32                .386
0F 86 0438            JBE Rel16                .386
0F 87 0444            JA Rel16                 .386
0F 88 00000400        JS Rel32                 .386
0F 88 0400            JS Rel16                 .386
0F 89 00000412        JNS Rel32                .386
0F 89 040C            JNS Rel16                .386
0F 8A 00000406        JP Rel32                 .386
0F 8A 0404            JP Rel16                 .386
0F 8B 0410            JNP Rel16                .386
0F 8C 0000044C        JL Rel32                 .386
0F 8C 0424            JL Rel16                 .386
0F 8D 00000452        JGE Rel32                .386
0F 8D 0428            JGE Rel16                .386
0F 8E 00000446        JLE Rel32                .386
0F 8E 0420            JLE Rel16                .386
0F 8F 00000458        JG Rel32                 .386
0F 8F 042C            JG Rel16                 .386
0F 90 06 0000r        SETO Mem8                .286
0F 90 C7              SETO Reg8                .286
0F 91 06 0000r        SETNO Mem8               .286
0F 91 C7              SETNO Reg8               .286
0F 92 06 0000r        SETB Mem8                .286
0F 92 06 0000r        SETC Mem8                .286
0F 92 C7              SETB Reg8                .286
0F 92 C7              SETC Reg8                .286
0F 93 06 0000r        SETAE Mem8               .286
0F 93 06 0000r        SETNC Mem8               .286
0F 93 C7              SETAE Reg8               .286
0F 93 C7              SETNC Reg8               .286
0F 94 06 0000r        SETE Mem8                .286
0F 94 C7              SETE Reg8                .286
0F 95 06 0000r        SETNE Mem8               .286
0F 95 C7              SETNE Reg8               .286
0F 96 06 0000r        SETBE Mem8               .286
0F 96 C7              SETBE Reg8               .286
0F 97 06 0000r        SETA Mem8                .286
0F 97 C7              SETA Reg8                .286
0F 98 06 0000r        SETS Mem8                .286
0F 98 C7              SETS Reg8                .286
0F 99 06 0000r        SETNS Mem8               .286
0F 99 C7              SETNS Reg8               .286
```

0F 9A 06 0000r	SETP Mem8	.286
0F 9A C7	SETP Reg8	.286
0F 9B 06 0000r	SETNP Mem8	.286
0F 9B C7	SETNP Reg8	.286
0F 9C 06 0000r	SETL Mem8	.286
0F 9C C7	SETL Reg8	.286
0F 9D 06 0000r	SETGE Mem8	.286
0F 9D C7	SETGE Reg8	.286
0F 9E 06 0000r	SETLE Mem8	.286
0F 9E C7	SETLE Reg8	.286
0F 9F 06 0000r	SETG Mem8	.286
0F 9F C7	SETG Reg8	.286
0F A0	PUSH FS	.386
0F A1	POP FS	.386
0F A3 1E 0001r	BT Mem16,Reg16	.386
0F A3 DB	BT Reg16,Reg16	.386
0F A4 1E 0001r 12	SHLD Mem16,Reg16,Imm8	.386
0F A4 DB 12	SHLD Reg16,Reg16,Imm8	.386
0F A6 3E 0000r	CMPXCHG Mem8,Reg8	.486
0F A6 FF	CMPXCHG Reg8,Reg8	.486
0F A7 1E 0001r	CMPXCHG Mem16,Reg16	.486
0F A7 DB	CMPXCHG Reg16,Reg16	.486
0F A8	PUSH GS	.386
0F A9	POP GS	.386
0F AB 1E 0001r	BTS Mem16,Reg16	.386
0F AB DB	BTS Reg16,Reg16	.386
0F AC 1E 0001r 12	SHRD Mem16,Reg16,Imm8	.386
0F AC DB 12	SHRD Reg16,Reg16,Imm8	.386
0F AD 1E 0001r	SHRD Mem16,Reg16,CL	.386
0F AD DB	SHRD Reg16,Reg16,CL	.386
0F AF 1E 0001r	IMUL Reg16,Mem16	.386
0F AF DB	IMUL Reg16,Reg16	.386
0F B2 1E 0003r	LSS Reg16,Mem32	.386
0F B2 1E 0003r	LSS Reg16,Mem32	.386
0F B3 1E 0001r	BTR Mem16,Reg16	.386
0F B3 DB	BTR Reg16,Reg16	.386
0F B4 1E 0003r	LFS Reg16,Mem32	.386
0F B5 1E 0003r	LGS Reg16,Mem32	.386
0F B6 1E 0000r	MOVZX Reg16,Mem8	.386
0F B6 DF	MOVZX Reg16,Reg8	.386
0F BA 26 0001r 12	BT Mem16,Imm8	.386
0F BA 2E 0001r 12	BTS Mem16,Imm8	.386
0F BA 36 0001r 12	BTR Mem16,Imm8	.386
0F BA 3E 0001r 12	BTC Mem16,Imm8	.386
0F BA E3 12	BT Reg16,Imm8	.386
0F BA EB 12	BTS Reg16,Imm8	.386
0F BA F3 12	BTR Reg16,Imm8	.386
0F BA FB 12	BTC Reg16,Imm8	.386
0F BB 1E 0001r	BTC Mem16,Reg16	.386
0F BB DB	BTC Reg16,Reg16	.386
0F BC 1E 0001r	BSF Reg16,Mem16	.386
0F BC DB	BSF Reg16,Reg16	.386
0F BD 1E 0001r	BSR Reg16,Mem16	.386
0F BD DB	BSR Reg16,Reg16	.386
0F BE 1E 0000r	MOVSX Reg16,Mem8	.386
0F BE DF	MOVSX Reg16,Reg8	.386
0F C0 3E 0000r	XADD Mem8,Reg8	.486
0F C0 FF	XADD Reg8,Reg8	.486
0F C1 1E 0001r	XADD Mem16,Reg16	.486
0F C1 DB	XADD Reg16,Reg16	.486
10 3E 0000r	ADC Mem8,Reg8	.286
11 1E 0001r	ADC Mem16,Reg16	.286
12 3E 0000r	ADC Reg8,Mem8	.286
12 FF	ADC Reg8,Reg8	.286
13 1E 0001r	ADC Reg16,Mem16	.286
13 DB	ADC Reg16,Reg16	.286

```
14 12             ADC AL,Imm8          .286
15 3456           ADC AX,Imm16         .286
16                PUSH SS              .286
17                POP SS               .286
18 3E 0000r       SBB Mem8,Reg8        .286
1A 3E 0000r       SBB Reg8,Mem8        .286
1A FF             SBB Reg8,Reg8        .286
1A FF             SBB Reg8,Reg8        .286
1B 1E 0001r       SBB Reg16,Mem16      .286
1B DB             SBB Reg16,Reg16      .286
1C 12             SBB AL,Imm8          .286
1D 3456           SBB AX,Imm16         .286
1E                PUSH DS              .286
1E 0001r 12       RCR Mem16,Imm8       .286
1F                POP DS               .286
20 3E 0000r       AND Mem8,Reg8        .286
21 1E 0001r       AND Mem16,Reg16      .286
22 3E 0000r       AND Reg8,Mem8        .286
22 FF             AND Reg8,Reg8        .286
23 1E 0001r       AND Reg16,Mem16      .286
23 DB             AND Reg16,Reg16      .286
24 12             AND AL,Imm8          .286
25 3456           AND AX,Imm16         .286
27                DAA                  .286
28 3E 0000r       SUB Mem8,Reg8        .286
29 1E 0001r       SUB Mem16,Reg16      .286
2A 3E 0000r       SUB Reg8,Mem8        .286
2A FF             SUB Reg8,Reg8        .286
2B 1E 0001r       SUB Reg16,Mem16      .286
2B DB             SUB Reg16,Reg16      .286
2C 12             SUB AL,Imm8          .286
2D 3456           SUB AX,Imm16         .286
2F                DAS                  .286
31 1E 0001r       XOR Mem16,Reg16      .286
32 3E 0000r       XOR Reg8,Mem8        .286
33 1E 0001r       XOR Reg16,Mem16      .286
33 DB             XOR Reg16,Reg16      .286
34 12             XOR AL,Imm8          .286
35 3456           XOR AX,Imm16         .286
37                AAA                  .286
38 3E 0000r       CMP Mem8,Reg8        .286
39 1E 0001r       CMP Mem16,Reg16      .286
3A 3E 0000r       CMP Reg8,Mem8        .286
3A FF             CMP Reg8,Reg8        .286
3B 1E 0001r       CMP Reg16,Mem16      .286
3B DB             CMP Reg16,Reg16      .286
3C 12             CMP AL,Imm8          .286
3D 3456           CMP AX,Imm16         .286
40                INC AX               .286
41                INC CX               .286
42                INC DX               .286
43                INC BX               .286
44                INC SP               .286
45                INC BP               .286
46                INC SI               .286
47                INC DI               .286
48                DEC AX               .286
49                DEC CX               .286
4A                DEC DX               .286
4B                DEC BX               .286
4C                DEC SP               .286
4D                DEC BP               .286
4E                DEC SI               .286
4F                DEC DI               .286
50                PUSH AX              .286
51                PUSH CX              .286
```

```
52                           PUSH DX                        .286
53                           PUSH BX                        .286
54                           PUSH SP                        .286
55                           PUSH BP                        .286
56                           PUSH SI                        .286
57                           PUSH DI                        .286
58                           POP AX                         .286
59                           POP CX                         .286
5A                           POP DX                         .286
5B                           POP BX                         .286
5C                           POP SP                         .286
5D                           POP BP                         .286
5E                           POP SI                         .286
5F                           POP DI                         .286
60                           PUSHA                          .286
61                           POPA                           .286
62 1E 0003r                  BOUND Reg16,Mem32              .386
63 1E 0001r                  ARPL Mem16,Reg16               .386P
63 DB                        ARPL Reg16,Reg16               .386P
66| 01 1E 0003r              ADD Mem32,Reg32                .386
66| 03 1E 0003r              ADD Reg32,Mem32                .386
66| 03 DB                    ADD Reg32,Reg32                .386
66| 05 78901234             ADD EAX,Imm32                  .386
66| 09 1E 0003r              OR Mem32,Reg32                 .386
66| 0B 1E 0003r              OR Reg32,Mem32                 .386
66| 0B DB                    OR Reg32,Reg32                 .386
66| 0D 78901234             OR EAX,Imm32                   .386
66| 0F 02 1E 0003r           LAR Reg32,Mem32                .386P
66| 0F 02 DB                 LAR Reg32,Reg32                .386P
66| 0F 03 1E 0003r           LSL Reg32,Mem32                .386P
66| 0F 03 1E 0003r           LSL Reg32,Mem32                .386P
66| 0F 03 DB                 LSL Reg32,Reg32                .386P
66| 0F 03 DB                 LSL Reg32,Reg32                .386P
66| 0F A3 1E 0003r           BT Mem32,Reg32                 .386
66| 0F A3 DB                 BT Reg32,Reg32                 .386
66| 0F A4 1E 0003r    +      SHLD Mem32,Reg32,Imm8          .386
66| 0F A4 DB 12              SHLD Reg32,Reg32,Imm8          .386
66| 0F A7 1E 0003r           CMPXCHG Mem32,Reg32            .486
66| 0F A7 DB                 CMPXCHG Reg32,Reg32            .486
66| 0F AB 1E 0003r           BTS Mem32,Reg32                .386
66| 0F AB DB                 BTS Reg32,Reg32                .386
66| 0F AC 1E 0003r    +      SHRD Mem32,Reg32,Imm8          .386
66| 0F AC DB 12              SHRD Reg32,Reg32,Imm8          .386
66| 0F AF 1E 0003r           IMUL Reg32,Mem32               .386
66| 0F AF DB                 IMUL Reg32,Reg32               .386
66| 0F B2 1E 0007r           LSS Reg32,Mem48                .386
66| 0F B2 1E 0007r           LSS Reg32,Mem48                .386
66| 0F B2 1E 0007r           LSS Reg32,Mem48                .386
66| 0F B3 1E 0003r           BTR Mem32,Reg32                .386
66| 0F B3 DB                 BTR Reg32,Reg32                .386
66| 0F B4 1E 0007r           LFS Reg32,Mem48                .386
66| 0F B5 1E 0007r           LGS Reg32,Mem48                .386
66| 0F B6 1E 0000r           MOVZX Reg32,Mem8               .386
66| 0F B6 DF                 MOVZX Reg32,Reg8               .386
66| 0F B7 1E 0001r           MOVZX Reg32,Mem16              .386
66| 0F B7 DB                 MOVZX Reg32,Reg16              .386
66| 0F BA 26 0003r    +      BT Mem32,Imm8                  .386
66| 0F BA 2E 0003r    +      BTS Mem32,Imm8                 .386
66| 0F BA 36 0003r    +      BTR Mem32,Imm8                 .386
66| 0F BA 3E 0003r    +      BTC Mem32,Imm8                 .386
66| 0F BA E3 12              BT Reg32,Imm8                  .386
66| 0F BA EB 12              BTS Reg32,Imm8                 .386
66| 0F BA F3 12              BTR Reg32,Imm8                 .386
66| 0F BA FB 12              BTC Reg32,Imm8                 .386
66| 0F BB 1E 0003r           BTC Mem32,Reg32                .386
66| 0F BB DB                 BTC Reg32,Reg32                .386
```

```
66| 0F BC 1E 0003r        BSF Reg32,Mem32          .386
66| 0F BC DB              BSF Reg32,Reg32          .386
66| 0F BD 1E 0003r        BSR Reg32,Mem32          .386
66| 0F BD DB              BSR Reg32,Reg32          .386
66| 0F BE 1E 0000r        MOVSX Reg32,Mem8         .386
66| 0F BE DF              MOVSX Reg32,Reg8         .386
66| 0F BF 1E 0001r        MOVSX Reg32,Mem16        .386
66| 0F BF DB              MOVSX Reg32,Reg16        .386
66| 0F C1 1E 0003r        XADD Mem32,Reg32         .486
66| 0F C1 DB              XADD Reg32,Reg32         .486
66| 0F CB                 BSWAP Reg32              .486
66| 11 1E 0003r           ADC Mem32,Reg32          .386
66| 13 1E 0003r           ADC Reg32,Mem32          .386
66| 13 DB                 ADC Reg32,Reg32          .386
66| 15 78901234           ADC EAX,Imm32            .386
66| 19 1E 0003r           SBB Mem32,Reg32          .386
66| 1B 1E 0003r           SBB Reg32,Mem32          .386
66| 1B DB                 SBB Reg32,Reg32          .386
66| 1B DB                 SBB Reg32,Reg32          .386
66| 1D 78901234           SBB EAX,Imm32            .386
66| 21 1E 0003r           AND Mem32,Reg32          .386
66| 23 1E 0003r           AND Reg32,Mem32          .286
66| 23 DB                 AND Reg32,Reg32          .386
66| 25 78901234           AND EAX,Imm32            .386
66| 29 1E 0003r           SUB Mem32,Reg32          .386
66| 2B 1E 0003r           SUB Reg32,Mem32          .386
66| 2B DB                 SUB Reg32,Reg32          .386
66| 2D 78901234           SUB EAX,Imm32            .386
66| 31 1E 0003r           XOR Mem32,Reg32          .386
66| 33 1E 0003r           XOR Reg32,Mem32          .386
66| 33 DB                 XOR Reg32,Reg32          .386
66| 35 78901234           XOR EAX,Imm32            .386
66| 39 1E 0003r           CMP Mem32,Reg32          .386
66| 3B 1E 0003r           CMP Reg32,Mem32          .386
66| 3B DB                 CMP Reg32,Reg32          .386
66| 3D 78901234           CMP EAX,Imm32            .386
66| 40                    INC EAX                  .386
66| 41                    INC ECX                  .386
66| 42                    INC EDX                  .386
66| 43                    INC EBX                  .386
66| 44                    INC ESP                  .386
66| 45                    INC EBP                  .386
66| 46                    INC ESI                  .386
66| 47                    INC EDI                  .386
66| 48                    DEC EAX                  .386
66| 49                    DEC ECX                  .386
66| 4A                    DEC EDX                  .386
66| 4B                    DEC EBX                  .386
66| 4C                    DEC ESP                  .386
66| 4D                    DEC EBP                  .386
66| 4E                    DEC ESI                  .386
66| 4F                    DEC EDI                  .386
66| 50                    PUSH EAX                 .386
66| 53                    PUSH EBX                 .386
66| 54                    PUSH ESP                 .386
66| 55                    PUSH EBP                 .386
66| 56                    PUSH ESI                 .386
66| 57                    PUSH EDI                 .386
66| 58                    POP EAX                  .386
66| 59                    POP ECX                  .386
66| 5A                    POP EDX                  .386
66| 5B                    POP EBX                  .386
66| 5C                    POP ESP                  .386
66| 5D                    POP EBP                  .386
66| 5E                    POP ESI                  .386
66| 5F                    POP EDI                  .386
```

66|	60		PUSHAD	.386
66|	61		POPAD	.386
66|	62 1E 000Dr		BOUND Reg32,Mem64	.386
66|	68 78901234		PUSH Imm32	.386
66|	69 1E 0003r	+	IMUL Reg32,Mem32,Imm32	.386
66|	69 DB 78901234		IMUL Reg32,Imm32	.386
66|	69 DB 78901234		IMUL Reg32,Reg32,Imm32	.386
66|	6B 1E 0003r 12		IMUL Reg32,Mem32,Imm8	.386
66|	6B DB 12		IMUL Reg32,Imm8	.386
66|	6B DB 12		IMUL Reg32,Reg32,Imm8	.386
66|	6D		INSD	.386
66|	6F		OUTSD	.286
66|	81 06 0003r	+	ADD Mem32,Imm32	.386
66|	81 0E 0003r	+	OR Mem32,Imm32	.386
66|	81 16 0003r	+	ADC Mem32,Imm32	.386
66|	81 1E 0003r	+	SBB Mem32,Imm32	.386
66|	81 26 0003r	+	AND Mem32,Imm32	.386
66|	81 2E 0003r	+	SUB Mem32,Imm32	.386
66|	81 36 0003r	+	XOR Mem32,Imm32	.386
66|	81 3E 0003r	+	CMP Mem32,Imm32	.386
66|	81 C3 78901234		ADD Reg32,Imm32	.386
66|	81 CB 78901234		OR Reg32,Imm32	.386
66|	81 D3 78901234		ADC Reg32,Imm32	.386
66|	81 DB 78901234		SBB Reg32,Imm32	.386
66|	81 E3 78901234		AND Reg32,Imm32	.386
66|	81 EB 78901234		SUB Reg32,Imm32	.386
66|	81 F3 78901234		XOR Reg32,Imm32	.386
66|	81 FB 78901234		CMP Reg32,Imm32	.386
66|	83 06 0003r 12		ADD Mem32,Imm8	.386
66|	83 0E 0003r 12		OR Mem32,Imm8	.386
66|	83 16 0003r 12		ADC Mem32,Imm8	.386
66|	83 1E 0003r 12		SBB Mem32,Imm8	.386
66|	83 26 0003r 12		AND Mem32,Imm8	.286
66|	83 2E 0003r 12		SUB Mem32,Imm8	.386
66|	83 36 0003r 12		XOR Mem32,Imm8	.386
66|	83 3E 0003r 12		CMP Mem32,Imm8	.386
66|	83 C3 12		ADD Reg32,Imm8	.386
66|	83 CB 12		OR Reg32,Imm8	.386
66|	83 D3 12		ADC Reg32,Imm8	.386
66|	83 DB 12		SBB Reg32,Imm8	.386
66|	83 E3 12		AND Reg32,Imm8	.286
66|	83 EB 12		SUB Reg32,Imm8	.386
66|	83 F3 12		XOR Reg32,Imm8	.386
66|	83 FB 12		CMP Reg32,Imm8	.386
66|	85 1E 0003r		TEST Mem32,Reg32	.386
66|	85 DB		TEST Reg32,Reg32	.386
66|	87 1E 0003r		XCHG Mem32,Reg32	.386
66|	87 1E 0003r		XCHG Reg32,Mem32	.386
66|	87 DB		XCHG Reg32,Reg32	.386
66|	89 1E 0003r		MOV Mem32,Reg32	.386
66|	8B 1E 0003r		MOV Reg32,Mem32	.386
66|	8B DB		MOV Reg32,Reg32	.386
66|	8D 1E 0003r		LEA Reg32,Mem32	.386
66|	8F 06 0003r		POP Mem32	.386
66|	90		XCHG EAX,EAX	.386
66|	91		XCHG ECX,EAX	.386
66|	92		XCHG EDX,EAX	.386
66|	93		XCHG EAX,Reg32	.386
66|	93		XCHG EBX,EAX	.386
66|	93		XCHG Reg32,EAX	.386
66|	94		XCHG ESP,EAX	.386
66|	95		XCHG EBP,EAX	.386
66|	96		XCHG ESI,EAX	.386
66|	97		XCHG EDI,EAX	.386
66|	98		CWDE	.386
66|	99		CDQ	.386

```
66| 99                        CDQ                      .386
66| 9A 00000003sr             CALL far ptr Mem32       .386
66| 9C                        PUSHFD                   .386
66| 9D                        POPFD                    .386
66| A1 0003r                  MOV EAX,Mem32            .386
66| A3 0003r                  MOV Mem32,EAX            .386
66| A5                        MOVSD                    .386
66| A7                        CMPSD                    .386
66| A9 78901234              TEST EAX,Imm32           .386
66| AB                        STOSD                    .386
66| AD                        LODSD                    .386
66| AF                        SCASD                    .386
66| B8 78901234              MOV EAX,Imm32            .386
66| B9 78901234              MOV ECX,Imm32            .386
66| BA 78901234              MOV EDX,Imm32            .386
66| BB 78901234              MOV EBX,Imm32            .386
66| BC 78901234              MOV ESP,Imm32            .386
66| BD 78901234              MOV EBP,Imm32            .386
66| BE 78901234              MOV ESI,Imm32            .386
66| BF 78901234              MOV EDI,Imm32            .386
66| C1 06 0003r 12            ROL Mem32,Imm8           .386
66| C1 0E 0003r 12            ROR Mem32,Imm8           .386
66| C1 16 0003r 12            RCL Mem32,Imm8           .386
66| C1 1E 0003r 12            RCR Mem32,Imm8           .386
66| C1 26 0003r 12            SAL Mem32,Imm8           .386
66| C1 26 0003r 12            SHL Mem32,Imm8           .386
66| C1 2E 0003r 12            SHR Mem32,Imm8           .386
66| C1 3E 0003r 12            SAR Mem32,Imm8           .386
66| C1 C3 12                  ROL Reg32,Imm8           .386
66| C1 CB 12                  ROR Reg32,Imm8           .386
66| C1 D3 12                  RCL Reg32,Imm8           .386
66| C1 DB 12                  RCR Reg32,Imm8           .386
66| C1 E3 12                  SAL Reg32,Imm8           .386
66| C1 E3 12                  SHL Reg32,Imm8           .386
66| C1 EB 12                  SHR Reg32,Imm8           .386
66| C1 FB 12                  SAR Reg32,Imm8           .386
66| C5 1E 0007r               LDS Reg32,Mem48          .386
66| C7 06 0003r        +      MOV Mem32,Imm32          .386
66| CF                        IRETD                    .386
66| D1 06 0003r               ROL Mem32,1              .386
66| D1 0E 0003r               ROR Mem32,1              .386
66| D1 16 0003r               RCL Mem32,1              .386
66| D1 1E 0003r               RCR Mem32,1              .386
66| D1 26 0003r               SAL Mem32,1              .386
66| D1 26 0003r               SHL Mem32,1              .386
66| D1 2E 0003r               SHR Mem32,1              .386
66| D1 3E 0003r               SAR Mem32,1              .386
66| D1 C3                     ROL Reg32,1              .386
66| D1 CB                     ROR Reg32,1              .386
66| D1 D3                     RCL Reg32,1              .386
66| D1 DB                     RCR Reg32,1              .386
66| D1 E3                     SAL Reg32,1              .386
66| D1 E3                     SHL Reg32,1              .386
66| D1 EB                     SHR Reg32,1              .386
66| D1 FB                     SAR Reg32,1              .386
66| D3 06 0003r               ROL Mem32,cl             .386
66| D3 16 0003r               RCL Mem32,cl             .386
66| D3 1E 0003r               RCR Mem32,cl             .386
66| D3 26 0003r               SAL Mem32,cl             .386
66| D3 26 0003r               SHL Mem32,cl             .386
66| D3 2E 0003r               SHR Mem32,cl             .386
66| D3 3E 0003r               SAR Mem32,cl             .386
66| D3 C3                     ROL Reg32,cl             .386
66| D3 D3                     RCL Reg32,cl             .386
66| D3 DB                     RCR Reg32,cl             .386
66| D3 E3                     SAL Reg32,cl             .386
```

```
66| D3 E3                            SHL Reg32,cl                        .386
66| D3 EB                            SHR Reg32,cl                        .386
66| D3 FB                            SAR Reg32,cl                        .386
66| E5 12                            IN EAX,Imm8                         .386
66| E7 12                            OUT Imm8,EAX                        .386
66| ED                               IN EAX,dx                           .386
66| EF                               OUT DX,EAX                          .386
66| F7 06 0003r       +              TEST Mem32,Imm32                    .386
66| F7 16 0003r                      NOT Mem32                           .386
66| F7 1E 0003r                      NEG Mem32                           .386
66| F7 26 0003r                      MUL Mem32                           .386
66| F7 2E 0003r                      IMUL Mem32                          .386
66| F7 36 0003r                      DIV Mem32                           .386
66| F7 3E 0003r                      IDIV Mem32                          .386
66| F7 C3 78901234                   TEST Reg32,Imm32                    .386
66| F7 D3                            NOT Reg32                           .386
66| F7 DB                            NEG Reg32                           .386
66| F7 E3                            MUL Reg32                           .386
66| F7 EB                            IMUL Reg32                          .386
66| F7 F3                            DIV Reg32                           .386
66| F7 FB                            IDIV Reg32                          .386
66| FF 06 0003r                      INC Mem32                           .386
66| FF 0E 0003r                      DEC Mem32                           .386
66| FF 36 0003r                      PUSH Mem32                          .386
67| E3 F1                            JECXZ Rel8                          .386
67| FF 16 0003r                      CALL Mem32                          .386
67| FF 26 0003r                      JMP Mem32                           .386
67| FF 2E 0007r                      JMP FWord ptr [Mem48]               .386
67| FF 2E 0007r                      JMP Mem48                           .386
68 3456                              PUSH Imm16                          .286
69 1E 0001r 3456                     IMUL Reg16,Mem16,Imm16              .386
69 DB 3456                           IMUL Reg16,Imm16                    .386
69 DB 3456                           IMUL Reg16,Reg16,Imm16             .386
6A 12                                PUSH Imm8                           .286
6B 1E 0001r 12                       IMUL Reg16,Mem16,Imm8               .386
6B DB 12                             IMUL Reg16,Imm8                     .386
6B DB 12                             IMUL Reg16,Reg16,Imm8              .386
6C                                   INSB                                .286
6D                                   INSW                                .286
6E                                   OUTSB                               .286
6F                                   OUTSW                               .286
70 C7                                JO Rel8                             .286
71 CD                                JNO Rel8                            .286
72 F6                                JC Rel8                             .286
72 FA                                JB Rel8                             .286
73 D1                                JNC Rel8                            .286
73 FC                                JAE Rel8                            .286
74 EF                                JE Rel8                             .286
75 CF                                JNE Rel8                            .286
76 F8                                JBE Rel8                            .286
77 FE                                JA Rel8                             .286
78 C3                                JS Rel8                             .286
79 C9                                JNS Rel8                            .286
7A C5                                JP Rel8                             .286
7B CB                                JNP Rel8                            .286
7C E9                                JL Rel8                             .286
7D EB                                JGE Rel8                            .286
7E D3                                JLE Rel8                            .286
7F ED                                JG Rel8                             .286
80 06 0000r 12                       ADD Mem8,Imm8                       .286
80 0E 0000r 12                       OR Mem8,Imm8                        .286
80 16 0000r 12                       ADC Mem8,Imm8                       .286
80 1E 0000r 12                       SBB Mem8,Imm8                       .286
80 26 0000r 12                       AND Mem8,Imm8                       .286
80 2E 0000r 12                       SUB Mem8,Imm8                       .286
80 36 0000r 12                       XOR Mem8,Imm8                       .286
```

```
80 3E 0000r 12       CMP Mem8,Imm8          .286
80 C7 12             ADD Reg8,Imm8          .286
80 CF 12             OR Reg8,Imm8           .286
80 D7 12             ADC Reg8,Imm8          .286
80 DF 12             SBB Reg8,Imm8          .286
80 E7 12             AND Reg8,Imm8          .286
80 EF 12             SUB Reg8,Imm8          .286
80 F7 12             XOR Reg8,Imm8          .286
80 FF 12             CMP Reg8,Imm8          .286
81 06 0001r 3456     ADD Mem16,Imm16        .286
81 0E 0001r 3456     OR Mem16,Imm16         .286
81 16 0001r 3456     ADC Mem16,Imm16        .286
81 1E 0001r 3456     SBB Mem16,Imm16        .286
81 26 0001r 3456     AND Mem16,Imm16        .286
81 2E 0001r 3456     SUB Mem16,Imm16        .286
81 36 0001r 3456     XOR Mem16,Imm16        .286
81 3E 0001r 3456     CMP Mem16,Imm16        .286
81 C3 3456           ADD Reg16,Imm16        .286
81 CB 3456           OR Reg16,Imm16         .286
81 D3 3456           ADC Reg16,Imm16        .286
81 DB 3456           SBB Reg16,Imm16        .286
81 E3 3456           AND Reg16,Imm16        .286
81 EB 3456           SUB Reg16,Imm16        .286
81 F3 3456           XOR Reg16,Imm16        .286
81 FB 3456           CMP Reg16,Imm16        .286
83 16 0001r 12       ADC Mem16,Imm8         .286
83 1E 0001r 12       SBB Mem16,Imm8         .286
83 26 0001r 12       AND Mem16,Imm8         .286
83 2E 0001r 12       SUB Mem16,Imm8         .286
83 36 0001r 12       XOR Mem16,Imm8         .286
83 3E 0001r 12       CMP Mem16,Imm8         .286
83 D3 12             ADC Reg16,Imm8         .286
83 DB 12             SBB Reg16,Imm8         .286
83 E3 12             AND Reg16,Imm8         .286
83 EB 12             SUB Reg16,Imm8         .286
83 F3 12             XOR Reg16,Imm8         .286
83 FB 12             CMP Reg16,Imm8         .286
84 3E 0000r          TEST Mem8,Reg8         .286
84 FF                TEST Reg8,Reg8         .286
85 1E 0001r          TEST Mem16,Reg16       .286
85 DB                TEST Reg16,Reg16       .286
86 3E 0000r          XCHG Mem8,Reg8         .286
86 3E 0000r          XCHG Reg8,Mem8         .286
86 FF                XCHG Reg8,Reg8         .286
87 1E 0001r          XCHG Mem16,Reg16       .286
87 1E 0001r          XCHG Reg16,Mem16       .286
87 DB                XCHG Reg16,Reg16       .286
88 3E 0000r          MOV Mem8,Reg8          .286
88 3E 0000r          MOV Mem8,Reg8          .286
89 1E 0001r          MOV Mem16,Reg16        .286
89 1E 0001r          MOV Mem16,Reg16        .286
8A 3E 0000r          MOV Reg8,Mem8          .286
8A 3E 0000r          MOV Reg8,Mem8          .286
8A FF                MOV Reg8,Reg8          .286
8A FF                MOV Reg8,Reg8          .286
8B 1E 0001r          MOV Reg16,Mem16        .286
8B 1E 0001r          MOV Reg16,Mem16        .286
8B DB                MOV Reg16,Reg16        .286
8B DB                MOV Reg16,Reg16        .286
8C 1E 0001r          MOV Mem16,SR           .286
8C 1E 0001r          MOV Mem16,SR           .286
8C DB                MOV Reg16,SR           .286
8C DB                MOV Reg16,SR           .286
8E 1E 0001r          MOV SR,Mem16           .286
8E 1E 0001r          MOV SR,Mem16           .286
8E DB                MOV SR,Reg16           .286
```

```
8E DB                    MOV SR,Reg16                        .286
8F 06 0001r              POP Mem16                           .286
90                       NOP                                 .286
90                       XCHG AX,AX                          .286
91                       XCHG CX,AX                          .286
92                       XCHG DX,AX                          .286
93                       XCHG AX,Reg16                       .286
93                       XCHG BX,AX                          .286
93                       XCHG Reg16,AX                       .286
94                       XCHG SP,AX                          .286
95                       XCHG BP,AX                          .286
96                       XCHG SI,AX                          .286
97                       XCHG DI,AX                          .286
98                       CBW                                 .286
99                       CWD                                 .286
9A 00000448sr            CALL far ptr Rel16                  .286
9B                       WAIT                                .286
9C                       PUSHF                               .286
9D                       POPF                                .286
9E                       SAHF                                .286
9F                       LAHF                                .286
A0 0000r                 MOV AL,Mem8                         .286
A0 0000r                 MOV AL,Mem8                         .286
A0 0000r                 MOV AL,Mem8                         .386
A1 0001r                 MOV AX,Mem16                        .286
A1 0001r                 MOV AX,Mem16                        .286
A2 0000r                 MOV Mem8,AL                         .286
A3 0001r                 MOV Mem16,AX                        .286
A4                       MOVSB                               .286
A5                       MOVSW                               .286
A6                       CMPSB                               .286
A7                       CMPSW                               .286
A8 12                    TEST AL,Imm8                        .286
A9 3456                  TEST AX,Imm16                       .286
AA                       STOSB                               .286
AB                       STOSW                               .286
AC                       LODSB                               .286
AD                       LODSW                               .286
AE                       SCASB                               .286
AF                       SCASW                               .286
B0 12                    MOV AL,Imm8                         .286
B0 12                    MOV AL,Imm8                         .286
B1 12                    MOV CL,Imm8                         .286
B1 12                    MOV CL,Imm8                         .286
B2 12                    MOV DL,Imm8                         .286
B2 12                    MOV DL,Imm8                         .286
B3 12                    MOV BL,Imm8                         .286
B3 12                    MOV BL,Imm8                         .286
B4 12                    MOV AH,Imm8                         .286
B4 12                    MOV AH,Imm8                         .286
B5 12                    MOV CH,Imm8                         .286
B5 12                    MOV CH,Imm8                         .286
B6 12                    MOV DH,Imm8                         .286
B6 12                    MOV DH,Imm8                         .286
B7 12                    MOV BH,Imm8                         .286
B7 12                    MOV BH,Imm8                         .286
B8 3456                  MOV AX,Imm16                        .286
B9 3456                  MOV CX,Imm16                        .286
BA 3456                  MOV DX,Imm16                        .286
BA 3456                  MOV DX,Imm16                        .286
BB 0001r                 LEA Reg16,Mem16                     .286
BB 3456                  MOV BX,Imm16                        .286
BB 3456                  MOV BX,Imm16                        .286
BC 3456                  MOV SP,Imm16                        .286
BC 3456                  MOV SP,Imm16                        .286
BD 3456                  MOV BP,Imm16                        .286
```

```
BD 3456                 MOV BP,Imm16               .286
BE 3456                 MOV SI,Imm16               .286
BE 3456                 MOV SI,Imm16               .286
BF 3456                 MOV DI,Imm16               .286
BF 3456                 MOV DI,Imm16               .286
C0 06 0000r 12          ROL Mem8,Imm8              .286
C0 0E 0000r 12          ROR Mem8,Imm8              .286
C0 16 0000r 12          RCL Mem8,Imm8              .286
C0 1E 0000r 12          RCR Mem8,Imm8              .286
C0 26 0000r 12          SAL Mem8,Imm8              .286
C0 26 0000r 12          SHL Mem8,Imm8              .286
C0 2E 0000r 12          SHR Mem8,Imm8              .286
C0 3E 0000r 12          SAR Mem8,Imm8              .286
C0 C7 12                ROL Reg8,Imm8              .286
C0 CF 12                ROR Reg8,Imm8              .286
C0 D7 12                RCL Reg8,Imm8              .286
C0 DF 12                RCR Reg8,Imm8              .286
C0 E7 12                SAL Reg8,Imm8              .286
C0 E7 12                SHL Reg8,Imm8              .286
C0 EF 12                SHR Reg8,Imm8              .286
C0 FF 12                SAR Reg8,Imm8              .286
C1 06 0001r 12          ROL Mem16,Imm8             .286
C1 0E 0001r 12          ROR Mem16,Imm8             .286
C1 16 0001r 12          RCL Mem16,Imm8             .286
C1 26 0001r 12          SAL Mem16,Imm8             .286
C1 26 0001r 12          SHL Mem16,Imm8             .286
C1 2E 0001r 12          SHR Mem16,Imm8             .286
C1 3E 0001r 12          SAR Mem16,Imm8             .286
C1 C3 12                ROL Reg16,Imm8             .286
C1 CB 12                ROR Reg16,Imm8             .286
C1 D3 12                RCL Reg16,Imm8             .286
C1 DB 12                RCR Reg16,Imm8             .286
C1 E3 12                SAL Reg16,Imm8             .286
C1 E3 12                SHL Reg16,Imm8             .286
C1 EB 12                SHR Reg16,Imm8             .286
C1 FB 12                SAR Reg16,Imm8             .286
C2 3456                 RET Imm16                  .286
C3                      RET                        .286
C4 1E 0003r             LES Reg16,Mem32            .286
C5 1E 0003r             LDS Reg16,Mem32            .286
C6 06 0000r 12          MOV Mem8,Imm8              .286
C6 06 0000r 12          MOV Mem8,Imm8              .286
C7 06 0001r 3456        MOV Mem16,Imm16            .286
C7 06 0001r 3456        MOV Mem16,Imm16            .286
C8 3456 00              ENTER Imm16,0              .286
C8 3456 01              ENTER Imm16,1              .286
C8 3456 12              ENTER Imm16,Imm8           .286
C9                      LEAVE                      .386
CA 3456                 RETF Imm16                 .286
CB                      RETF                       .286
CC                      INT 3                      .286
CD 12                   INT Imm8                   .286
CE                      INTO                       .286
CF                      IRET                       .286
D0 06 0000r             ROL Mem8,1                 .286
D0 0E 0000r             ROR Mem8,1                 .286
D0 16 0000r             RCL Mem8,1                 .286
D0 1E 0000r             RCR Mem8,1                 .286
D0 26 0000r             SAL Mem8,1                 .286
D0 26 0000r             SHL Mem8,1                 .286
D0 2E 0000r             SHR Mem8,1                 .286
D0 3E 0000r             SAR Mem8,1                 .286
D0 C7                   ROL Reg8,1                 .286
D0 CF                   ROR Reg8,1                 .286
D0 D7                   RCL Reg8,1                 .286
D0 DF                   RCR Reg8,1                 .286
```

```
D0 E7                    SAL Reg8,1                              .286
D0 E7                    SHL Reg8,1                              .286
D0 EF                    SHR Reg8,1                              .286
D0 FF                    SAR Reg8,1                              .286
D1 06 0001r              ROL Mem16,1                             .286
D1 0E 0001r              ROR Mem16,1                             .286
D1 16 0001r              RCL Mem16,1                             .286
D1 1E 0001r              RCR Mem16,1                             .286
D1 26 0001r              SAL Mem16,1                             .286
D1 26 0001r              SHL Mem16,1                             .286
D1 2E 0001r              SHR Mem16,1                             .286
D1 3E 0001r              SAR Mem16,1                             .286
D1 C3                    ROL Reg16,1                             .286
D1 CB                    ROR Reg16,1                             .286
D1 D3                    RCL Reg16,1                             .286
D1 DB                    RCR Reg16,1                             .286
D1 E3                    SAL Reg16,1                             .286
D1 E3                    SHL Reg16,1                             .286
D1 EB                    SHR Reg16,1                             .286
D1 FB                    SAR Reg16,1                             .286
D2 06 0000r              ROL Mem8,cl                             .286
D2 0E 0000r              ROR Mem8,cl                             .286
D2 16 0000r              RCL Mem8,cl                             .286
D2 1E 0000r              RCR Mem8,cl                             .286
D2 26 0000r              SAL Mem8,cl                             .286
D2 26 0000r              SHL Mem8,cl                             .286
D2 2E 0000r              SHR Mem8,cl                             .286
D2 3E 0000r              SAR Mem8,cl                             .286
D2 C7                    ROL Reg8,cl                             .286
D2 CF                    ROR Reg8,cl                             .286
D2 D7                    RCL Reg8,cl                             .286
D2 DF                    RCR Reg8,cl                             .286
D2 E7                    SAL Reg8,cl                             .286
D2 E7                    SHL Reg8,cl                             .286
D2 EF                    SHR Reg8,cl                             .286
D2 FF                    SAR Reg8,cl                             .286
D3 06 0001r              ROL Mem16,cl                            .286
D3 0E 0001r              ROR Mem16,cl                            .286
D3 16 0001r              RCL Mem16,cl                            .286
D3 1E 0001r              RCR Mem16,cl                            .286
D3 26 0001r              SAL Mem16,cl                            .286
D3 26 0001r              SHL Mem16,cl                            .286
D3 2E 0001r              SHR Mem16,cl                            .286
D3 3E 0001r              SAR Mem16,cl                            .286
D3 C3                    ROL Reg16,cl                            .286
D3 CB                    ROR Reg16,cl                            .286
D3 D3                    RCL Reg16,cl                            .286
D3 DB                    RCR Reg16,cl                            .286
D3 E3                    SAL Reg16,cl                            .286
D3 E3                    SHL Reg16,cl                            .286
D3 EB                    SHR Reg16,cl                            .286
D3 FB                    SAR Reg16,cl                            .286
D4 0A                    AAM                                     .286
D5 0A                    AAD                                     .286
D7                       XLAT Table                              .286
DA D3                    ESC Imm8,Reg16                          .287
E0 FA                    LOOPNE Rel__8                           .286
E1 FC                    LOOPE Rel__8                            .286
E2 FE                    LOOP Rel__8                             .286
E3 F4                    JCXZ Rel8                               .286
E4 12                    IN AL,Imm8                              .286
E5 12                    IN AX,Imm8                              .286
E6 12                    OUT Imm8,AL                             .286
E7 12                    OUT Imm8,AX                             .286
E8 0000040D              CALL Rel_32                             .386
E8 FFFD                  CALL near ptr Rel_call                  .286
```

```
E9 00000441          JMP  Rel32                      .386
E9 0421              JMP  near ptr Rel_8             .286
EA 00000448sr        JMP  far ptr Rel16             .286
EB E7                JMP  short Rel8                 .286
EC                   IN   AL,dx                      .286
ED                   IN   AX,dx                      .286
EE                   OUT  DX,AL                      .286
EF                   OUT  DX,AX                      .286
F0> 90               LOCK nop                        .286
F2> 66| 6D           REPNZ  insd                     .386
F2> 66| A5           REPNZ  movsd                    .386
F2> 66| A7           REPNZ  cmpsd                    .386
F2> 66| AB           REPNZ  stosd                    .386
F2> 66| AD           REPNZ  lodsd                    .386
F2> 66| AF           REPNZ  scasd                    .386
F2> 6C               REPNZ  insb                     .286
F2> 6D               REPNZ  insw                     .286
F2> 6E               REPNZ  outsb                    .286
F2> 6E               REPNZ  outsb                    .386
F2> 6F               REPNZ  outsw                    .286
F2> A4               REPNZ  movsb                    .286
F2> A5               REPNZ  movsw                    .286
F2> A6               REPNZ  cmpsb                    .286
F2> A7               REPNZ  cmpsw                    .286
F2> AA               REPNZ  stosb                    .286
F2> AB               REPNZ  stosw                    .286
F2> AC               REPNZ  lodsb                    .286
F2> AD               REPNZ  lodsw                    .286
F2> AE               REPNZ  scasb                    .286
F2> AF               REPNZ  scasw                    .286
F3> 66| 6D           REP   insd                      .386
F3> 66| 6D           REPZ  insd                      .386
F3> 66| A5           REP   movsd                     .386
F3> 66| A5           REPZ  movsd                     .386
F3> 66| A7           REP   cmpsd                     .386
F3> 66| A7           REPZ  cmpsd                     .386
F3> 66| AB           REP   stosd                     .386
F3> 66| AB           REPZ  stosd                     .386
F3> 66| AD           REP   lodsd                     .386
F3> 66| AD           REPZ  lodsd                     .386
F3> 66| AF           REP   scasd                     .386
F3> 66| AF           REPZ  scasd                     .386
F3> 6C               REP   insb                      .286
F3> 6C               REPZ  insb                      .286
F3> 6D               REP   insw                      .286
F3> 6D               REPZ  insw                      .286
F3> 6E               REP   outsb                     .286
F3> 6E               REP   outsb                     .386
F3> 6E               REPZ  outsb                     .286
F3> 6E               REPZ  outsb                     .386
F3> 6F               REP   outsw                     .286
F3> 6F               REPZ  outsw                     .286
F3> A4               REP   movsb                     .286
F3> A4               REPZ  movsb                     .286
F3> A5               REP   movsw                     .286
F3> A5               REPZ  movsw                     .286
F3> A6               REP   cmpsb                     .286
F3> A6               REPZ  cmpsb                     .286
F3> A7               REP   cmpsw                     .286
F3> A7               REPZ  cmpsw                     .286
F3> AA               REP   stosb                     .286
F3> AA               REPZ  stosb                     .286
F3> AB               REP   stosw                     .286
F3> AB               REPZ  stosw                     .286
F3> AC               REP   lodsb                     .286
F3> AC               REPZ  lodsb                     .286
```

F3> AD	REP lodsw	.286
F3> AD	REPZ lodsw	.286
F3> AE	REP scasb	.286
F3> AE	REPZ scasb	.286
F3> AF	REP scasw	.286
F3> AF	REPZ scasw	.286
F4	HLT	.286
F5	CMC	.286
F6 06 0000r 12	TEST Mem8,Imm8	.286
F6 16 0000r	NOT Mem8	.286
F6 1E 0000r	NEG Mem8	.286
F6 26 0000r	MUL Mem8	.286
F6 2E 0000r	IMUL Mem8	.386
F6 36 0000r	DIV Mem8	.286
F6 3E 0000r	IDIV Mem8	.286
F6 C7 12	TEST Reg8,Imm8	.286
F6 D7	NOT Reg8	.286
F6 DF	NEG Reg8	.286
F6 E7	MUL Reg8	.286
F6 EF	IMUL Reg8	.386
F6 F7	DIV Reg8	.286
F6 FF	IDIV Reg8	.286
F7 06 0001r 3456	TEST Mem16,Imm16	.286
F7 16 0001r	NOT Mem16	.286
F7 1E 0001r	NEG Mem16	.286
F7 26 0001r	MUL Mem16	.286
F7 2E 0001r	IMUL Mem16	.386
F7 36 0001r	DIV Mem16	.286
F7 3E 0001r	IDIV Mem16	.286
F7 C3 3456	TEST Reg16,Imm16	.286
F7 D3	NOT Reg16	.286
F7 DB	NEG Reg16	.286
F7 E3	MUL Reg16	.286
F7 EB	IMUL Reg16	.386
F7 F3	DIV Reg16	.286
F7 FB	IDIV Reg16	.286
F8	CLC	.386
F9	STC	.286
FA	CLI	.386
FB	STI	.286
FC	CLD	.386
FD	STD	.286
FE 06 0000r	INC Mem8	.286
FE 0E 0000r	DEC Mem8	.286
FE C7	INC Reg8	.286
FE CF	DEC Reg8	.286
FF 06 0001r	INC Mem16	.286
FF 0E 0001r	DEC Mem16	.286
FF 16 0001r	CALL Mem16	.286
FF 26 0001r	JMP Word Ptr [Mem16]	.286
FF 2E 0001r	JMP DWord Ptr [Mem16]	.286
FF 36 0001r	PUSH Mem16	.286
FF D3	CALL Reg16	.286
FF D3	CALL Reg32	.386
FF E3	JMP Reg16	.286
FF E3	JMP Reg32	.386

Quick C Environment*

This appendix describes how to create, assemble, and execute a program just as in Chapter 1 but using the Quick C environment instead of the MASM environment. Since both are written by Microsoft, there are many similarities, and the assembly language programs themselves are virtually indistinguishable. Only the editor and the commands for assembling, linking, and running are different. The output on the screen also differs. There are five steps:

Step 0:	Boot:	Load the operating system.
Step 1:	Edit:	Create or correct the program.
Step 2:	Assemble:	Translate the program to machine language. If there are errors, return to Step 1.
Step 3:	Link:	Have memory locations assigned (automatically) to the assembled program.
Step 4:	Execute:	Use Quick C's Debug function to execute the program and to view results. If there are errors, return to Step 1.

These steps will be described in detail. They presume a built-in hard disk drive and one floppy drive.

 ## D.1 The Operating System and Quick C Editor

Step 0. Load the operating system.
This happens automatically by turning on the computer with no disk in drive A. You may need to answer some questions before seeing the DOS prompt *C>*.

*Quick C © is a product of Microsoft Corporation

The *C>* means that the operating system is awaiting a command. The next step may be to change to the directory that contains Quick C. The command to change directories is:

```
C> CD DirectoryName
```

Try

```
C> CD QC\BIN
```

(It may be the case that when you turned on the computer this directory appeared automatically.) To use Quick C, a mouse is usually used, although pressing the arrow keys will also suffice to move around the screen.

Step 1. Create a program using the editor.
This is done by choosing the *File* menu with the mouse or by using the *Alt* and arrow keys. Select *Open*. The cursor shows *. ASM*. Name this first program *Sum.ASM*. Choose *Yes* to create the new file containing the program. Type in the program of Figure 1-1 using arrow and delete and insert keys when a mistake is made.

D.2 The Assembler

The assembler translates the program to machine language.

Step 2. Assemble the program.
To assemble the program, choose *Compile File* from the *Make* menu. If there are any errors, the assembler will list them. If there are errors, compare the program closely with Figure 1-1 and return to the Editor to make changes.

D.3 The Linker

The linker automatically determines the addresses where the program is to be stored. Linking can also be used to link more than one assembled or compiled program into a single executable program. Once a program has been *linked,* it is ready to be executed.

Step 3. Link the assembled program. Choose *Build* from the *Make* menu.
(The assemble and link steps can be combined by selecting *Build All* from the *Make* menu. Also, *Run* will assemble, link, *and* execute the program.)

D.4 The Debugger

There is little need for traditional print statements for assembly language programs, although they are described in Appendix E. The debugger is used to view the execution of a program. Thus, the program can be executed instruction by instruction, viewing the changes in registers and in memory along the way. Alternatively, we can instruct the debugger to execute the entire program and *then* examine registers and memory.

Step 4. Execute the program with the debugger.
Select *Registers* and *Watch Window* from the Debug menu. (If your system includes *Windows,* select *Windows* from the *View* menu.)

To execute the program one instruction at a time, use the *Trace* command. Each time an instruction is executed, the debugger will update the contents of the registers on the screen and highlight the next instruction to be executed. The F8 key will highlight register AX. When the *INT 21H* instruction is reached, AX and *Result* both contain a 5. The program can be restarted by holding down the shift key and pressing F5. To leave Quick C, select the *Exit* command from the *File* menu.

E

Input/Output Operations

This appendix describes operations that can be inserted into assembly language programs to perform simple input and output. These routines allow input and output of strings and integers. We describe them and then show them for Figure 1-1 from Chapter 1. The reader should be familiar with the steps in Chapter 1 or Appendix D for editing, assembling, and linking an assembly language program.

To use the macros described here, the following command should be added to the program *before* any of these routines are used. (The file *IOOps.MLB* should also have been copied to your directory.)

To print a string of characters to the screen, use *PrintString$*.

EXAMPLE 1   To Print a String

```
      .DATA
  A   DB    "The value is"
      DB    "$"
      ...
      .CODE
      ...
      PrintString$    A
      ...
```

When *PrintString$* is executed, the string *The value is* will appear on the screen. *PrintString$* is useful for typing out prompts and values on the screen. Note that the string to be printed is terminated with *$*.

To print a word integer on the screen (in decimal), use *PrintWord$*.

EXAMPLE 2 To Print a Word Integer

```
        .DATA
A       DW      2
        ...
        .CODE
        ...
        PrintWord$    A
        ...
```

When *PrintWord$* is executed, the value of its operand (here *A*) will appear on the screen.

To input a word integer from the keyboard (again, in decimal), use *ReadWord*.

EXAMPLE 3 To Read a Word Integer

```
        .DATA
A       DW      ?
Prompt  DB      "ENTER A VALUE FOR A"
        ...
        DB      $
        .CODE
        ...
        PrintString$    Prompt
        ReadWord$    A
        ...
```

In Example 3, *PrintString$* is used to output a prompt telling the user to enter a value for *A*.

Example 4 shows these I/O macros being used in the *Sum.ASM* program from Chapter 1.

EXAMPLE 4

```
; This program calculates Result := A + B when A = 2, B = 3
;
; Two necessary bookkeeping statements follow

        DOSSEG                      ;Use Microsoft SEGment conventions
        .MODEL  small               ;Use small memory model
        INCLUDE IOOps.mlb

;
; Stack Segment follows
;

        .STACK  100H
```

```
;
; Data Segment follows
;

        .DATA

A                DW      ?
B                DW      ?
Result           DW      ?
StartBuff        DB      07H
                 DB      ?
Buffer           DB      7          DUP(?)
Prompt           DB      "Enter value for A and B on separate lines"
                 DB      "$"
;
; Code segment follows
;

                .CODE

;
; Two more necessary bookkeeping statements follow

Start:
        MOV     AX,     @DATA     ;Define current
        MOV     DS,     AX        ;Data Segment

;
; Main Program
;

        PrintString$    Prompt
        ReadWord$       A
        ReadWord$       B

        MOV     AX,     A         ;Get A
        ADD     AX,     B         ;Compute A + B
        MOV     Result, AX        ;Result := A + B

        PrintWord$      Result

        MOV     AH,     4CH
        INT     21H               ;Back to DOS

        END     Start             ;End of Program. Start is transfer address
```

Figure E-1 shows the code for these macros, which must be in the user's directory (in file *IOOps.MLB*) before the macros may be used.

Figure E-1 Code for input/output macros

```
         COMMENT          #       MACRO    HEADER
         MACRO    NAME            PrintString$   FILE:  IOOps.mlb
         PURPOSE                  Prints a $ terminated string on the screen
         CALLED  AS       #       PrintString$   Buffer


PrintString$    MACRO    string

         PUSH     DX                      ;Push the registers to be used
         PUSH     AX

         MOV      AH,     02H              ;Print a newline
         MOV      DL,     0DH
         INT      21H
         MOV      DL,     0AH
         INT      21H

         MOV      DX,     OFFSET   string  ;Move the string address into DX
         MOV      AH,     09H              ;Set up finction 09H
         INT      21H                      ;dos interrupt to print this string

         MOV      AH,     02H              ;Print a newline
         MOV      DL,     0DH
         INT      21H
         MOV      DL,     0AH
         INT      21H

         POP      AX                       ;Pop the registers
         POP      DX

     ENDM

     ;-------------------------------------------------------------------------

         COMMENT          #       MACRO    HEADER
         MACRO    NAME            PrintWord$     FILE:  IOOps.mlb
         PURPOSE                  Prints a word in decimal on the screen
                                  First converts the word into the ASCII string and
                                  then prints it
         CALLED  AS       #       PrintWord$     word


PrintWord$      MACRO    word
         LOCAL    Notneg                  ;Local labels
         LOCAL    Convert
         LOCAL    Countdigits
         LOCAL    Convertloop

         PUSH     DX                      ;Push the registers to be used
         PUSH     AX
         PUSH     CX
         PUSH     BX
         PUSH     DI

         MOV      AX,     Word            ;Move the word to be printed in AX
         LEA      BX,     Buffer          ;Use the Buffer to hold the string
         AND      AX,     AX              ;See if negative
         JGE      Notneg
         NEG      AX                      ;if negative
         MOV      BYTE PTR [BX],  '-'     ;store a - sign in the string begining
         INC      BX                      ;increment the string pointer
Notneg:

         PUSH     AX                      ;Have to use AX, so push it
         MOV      DI,     10              ;Move 10 in DI, to be used for division
         XOR      CX,     CX              ;Clear CX to hold the number of digits
```

```
Countdigits:

        XOR     DX,     DX              ;Clear DX for division
        INC     CX                      ;Increment CX
        DIV     DI                      ;divide by 10
        AND     AX,     AX              ;if more digits
        JNE     Countdigits             ;then loop back
        POP     AX                      ;else restore AX

Convert:
        ADD     BX,     CX              ;Point to the end of string
        MOV     BYTE PTR [BX],  '$'     ;Put a sentinel to mark end
        DEC     BX                      ;Point to one less than the end

Convertloop:

        XOR     DX,     DX              ;Clear DX for division
        DIV     DI                      ;Divide the number by 10
        ADD     DX,     '0'             ;convert the digit value to ASCII
        MOV     [BX],   DL              ;Move the character into the string
        DEC     BX                      ;Decrement the string pointer
        LOOP    Convertloop             ;Loop back as long as more digits

        PrintString$    Buffer          ;Print this string using the old macro

        POP     DI                      ;Pop the registers used
        POP     BX
        POP     CX
        POP     AX
        POP     DX

    ENDM


;--------------------------------------------------------------------

COMMENT         #       MACRO   HEADER
MACRO   NAME            ReadWord$       FILE:   IOOps.mlb
PURPOSE                 Reads the input (as string), converts it into
                        one word binary and stores it in the arg :word
CALLED  AS      #       ReadWord$       word


ReadWord$       MACRO   word
        LOCAL   Notneg                  ;Local labels
        LOCAL   Convert
        LOCAL   Convertloop
        LOCAL   Firstdigit
        LOCAL   Endconvert

        PUSH    DX                      ;Push the registers to be used
        PUSH    AX
        PUSH    CX
        PUSH    BX
        PUSH    DI
        PUSH    SI

        XOR     AX,     AX              ;Clear SI
        MOV     SI,     AX

                                        ;Get the string input

        MOV     DX,     OFFSET  StartBuff
        MOV     AH,     0AH
        INT     21H
```

Figure E-1 (*Continued*)

```
                MOV     BX,     DX          ;Move the string pointer in BX

                INC     BX
                MOV     AX,     [BX]
                MOV     CX,     AX          ;Move the number of characters in CX
                INC     BX

                CMP     BYTE PTR [BX], '-'
                JNE     Firstdigit
                MOV     SI,     -1          ;if negative, store a -1 in SI
                INC     BX

Firstdigit:

                XOR     AX,     AX          ;Clear AX
                MOV     DI,     10          ;Move 10 in DI for multiplication

Convertloop:

                CMP     BYTE PTR [BX],  '0'     ;Check if a digit
                JL      Endconvert              ;if not, end conversion
                CMP     BYTE PTR [BX],  '9'
                JG      Endconvert
                MUL     DI                      ;else multiply by 10
                SUB     DX,     DX              ;clear DX
                MOV     DL,     BYTE PTR [BX]   ;Move the character in DL
                SUB     DL,     '0'             ;convert ASCII code to the value
                ADD     AX,     DX              ;Add this to the previous value
                INC     BX                      ;Move pointer ahead
                LOOP    Convertloop             ;Go back as long as more charcters

Endconvert:

                AND     SI,     SI          ;if negative
                JE      Notneg
                NEG     AX                  ;negate the value in AX

Notneg:

                MOV     word,   AX          ;store the final value in word

                MOV     AH,     02H         ;print a newline after reading
                MOV     DL,     0DH
                INT     21H
                MOV     DL,     0AH
                INT     21H

                POP     SI                  ;restore the registers
                POP     DI
                POP     BX
                POP     CX
                POP     AX
                POP     DX

        ENDM

        ;---------------------------------------------------------------------
```

F

Machine Organization: Introduction to Fundamentals

F.0 Introduction

Chapter 2 describes the function of computer components such as registers, memory, and the arithmetic and logic unit (ALU). This appendix describes in general terms how several of these components might be implemented and how they operate. Our introduction here is solely intended to show how the computer components described in Chapter 2 are implemented logically and is not meant to substitute for a more extensive study of these components. Further discussion of the topics here can be found in basic computer organization texts. Hardware implementation of these devices is also beyond the scope of this discussion. We presume devices exist (they do) that perform the operations we describe.

The most elementary component is a *binary signal*, one whose values can be represented by the binary digits 0 or 1. A low and high voltage or any other easily sensed distinct representation can be used. We use the terms *set, on,* or *high* to denote a signal represented by the binary digit 1 and the terms *clear, off,* or *low* to denote signals represented by the binary digit 0. (Note: In some logic systems, the low signals are denoted by 1.)

Our next most elementary element is called, formally, a *logic gate* or sometimes just a *gate*. A gate is a device that transforms binary signals to other binary signals according to the rules of Boolean algebra. We can combine gates to form circuits called *combinational logic circuits*. When we add a time dependency to these circuits, we call the circuit a *sequential circuit*.

Binary signals, gates, and their connections into circuits are the building blocks of today's computers. How these devices are organized is called *computer organization*.

F.1 Combinational Logic Circuits

Underlying memory, registers, I/O devices, and processors such as the ALU are the components that implement them. These components are (a) *gates,* (b) *circuits* (which are collections of gates), and (c) *chips* (which are collections of circuits). We combine logic gates to create some basic circuits such as the ALU's *adder,* which adds *n*-bit integers.

F.1.1 Logic Gates

A gate implements one of the Boolean operations such as AND, OR, XOR, or NOT. It thus has inputs that can be 0 or 1, and a single output whose value is also 0 or 1. The corresponding gates are called AND gates, OR gates, XOR gates, and NOT gates. AND, OR, and XOR gates may have two or more inputs. NOT gates have a single input. There are standard symbols for these gates:

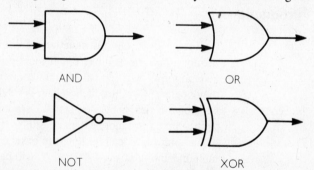

The output of the NOT gate is 1 if and only if its input is *not* 1. NOT gates are also called *inverters*. The output of the OR gate is 1 if and only if one or more of the inputs are 1. The output of the AND gate is 1 if and only if all inputs are 1. The output of the XOR gate is 1 if and only if an odd number of its inputs are 1. Sometimes the following notation is used for NOT gates:

The Boolean operation *NOT-AND* AND's all inputs and then complements (NOT's) them. It is implemented using a NAND gate:

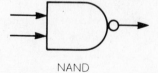

NAND

The little circle, $\bigcirc$, denotes the NOT part of the operation. Similarly, there is a gate that represents the combination *NOT-OR*, which means to OR all inputs and then complement (NOT) the result. It is called a NOR gate:

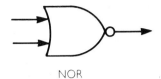

NOR

Example 1 shows the output for the various gates when all the inputs are 1. The NAND or NOR gates are "universal" in the sense that either is sufficient to implement any logic function. This is significant when one is actually building such circuits.

F.1.2 Computer Applications

In this section, we will show how the gates described in Section F.1.1 might be combined to implement some of the computer parts described in the first two chapters.

Adders. One of the functions of the ALU described earlier is to perform addition. Addition can be performed with combinations of the previously de-scribed gates. Now that we have described gates, we can show how they can be combined to perform typical operations.

EXAMPLE 1   Various gate outputs when the inputs are all 1

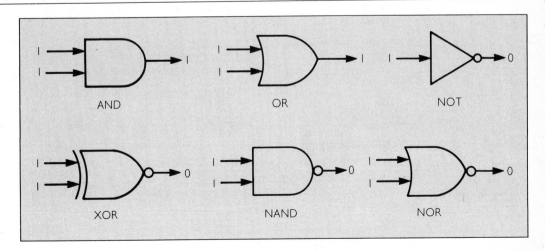

Example 2 uses an XOR gate in combination with an AND gate to add 2 bits. It implements the following operation. The values of a_i and b_i can be 0 or 1:

$$\begin{array}{r} a_i \\ + b_i \\ \hline ? \end{array}$$

There are actually two outputs here — the sum output that is set (that is, equals 1) if one and only one of the inputs is set and the carry bit that is set if both of the inputs are set. (The reader might wish to combine various gates to try to implement this before looking at the circuit in Example 2.) This circuit is called a *half-adder* because it performs half of the add function.

The reader should check that the half-adder operates as shown in the following truth table:

a_i	b_i	Sum	Carry
0	0	0	0
0	1	1	0
1	0	1	0
1	1	0	1

A more useful problem is to add *n*-bit binary numbers in parallel:

$$\begin{array}{l} a_{n-1} \cdots a_{i+1} a_i a_{i-1} \cdots a_0 \\ + b_{n-1} \cdots b_{i+1} b_i b_{i-1} \cdots b_0 \\ \hline ? \quad\;\; \cdots ? \quad ?\,? \quad\; \cdots ? \end{array}$$

Note that to compute the result at bit position i, we have to consider the carry from the next lower position as well as the values of a_i and b_i. The sum bit is set if only one of these is set or if all three of them are set. The carry bit is set if any two of these are set or if all three are set.

EXAMPLE 2   Half-adder

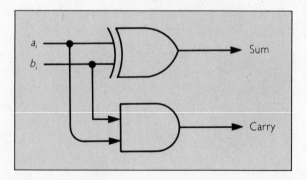

We can perform this sum $a_i + b_i$ by combining two half-adders and an OR gate. The circuit is called a *full-adder* (Example 3).

To perform the entire n-bit addition, we use n full-adders, inputting each carry bit to the next adder. The initial carry bit $Carry_0$ is set to 0 (Example 4).

Encoders and Decoders. Another class of circuits composed of logic gates includes those known as *encoders* and *decoders*. Decoders can be used to interpret the contents of memory addresses; encoders can be used to interpret data on I/O devices.

EXAMPLE 3 Full-adder

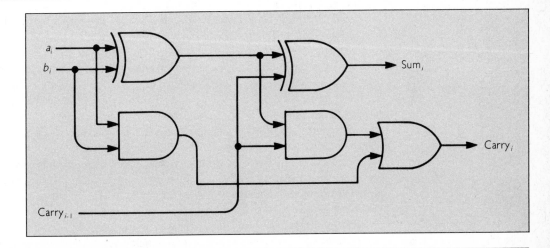

EXAMPLE 4 Implementing n-bit addition

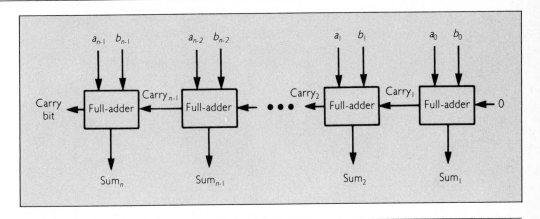

As we have seen, n bits can represent 2^n things. We can use decoders to decide which of the 2^n possible numbers is being represented with these n bits. Thus a decoder has n input lines and 2^n possible outputs numbered $0, 1, \ldots, 2^n - 1$. Output line i is 1 if the binary representation of i is on the n input lines; the other output lines are 0.

An *enable* line is often present. When this enable line is 0, all output lines are set to 0. (When an enable line is present, we often call the n input lines *select* lines.) We show this for a 2×4 decoder (2 input lines, 4 output lines) and an input representing the number 1. Note that the 0 input line contains 1, while the 1 input line contains 0. Thus, the input represents the binary number 1 and output line 1 contains 1, while output lines 0, 2, and 3 contain 0. This simple decoder can recognize only the integers 0 through 3 (see Figure F-1).

How do we use gates to implement such a device? The reader may wish to try it before looking at the Figure F-1 (as with adders, there is more than one way to implement this). Figure F-2 represents a 2×4 decoder with an enable line.

An encoder operates in opposite fashion from a decoder. An encoder has up to 2^n input lines and n output lines. We can thus use encoder output to represent the binary code for the 2^n possible inputs. For example, if input line 5 is 1, we might wish to output . . . 101; that is, we want to output the binary code for 5.

A problem arises if two of the input lines are *on* for an encoder when we only want to be able to interpret one *on* line. This is solved by looking at the lowest numbered line containing 1 (alternatively, the highest numbered line can be given top priority). An extra enable line is often used with encoders. If the enable line is 0 or if no input line contains 1, then an output of 00 . . . 00 is produced. If the enable line is 1, then the lowest (or highest) numbered line containing 1 is encoded into its binary equivalent.

Figure F-3 shows an encoder with two output lines. The input represents the integer 3; thus, input lines 0, 1, and 2 are off, and line 3 is on. The output is $a_0 = 1$ and $a_1 = 1$ (representing the binary code for 3). Note that line 0 goes

Figure F-1 2×4 decoder

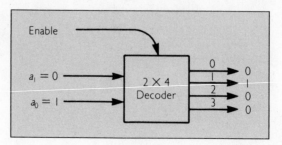

nowhere; we explain this later. For this reason, we call the encoder a 3×2 priority encoder rather than a 4×2. In fact, line 0 usually is not even shown.

When the enable line for a 3×2 priority encoder is off or all input lines are off, both outputs are 0. Thus, to avoid ambiguity, we do not encode 0.

When the enable line for a 3×2 priority encoder is on:

1. Output line a_0 is 1 and a_1 is 0, representing 1 if input line 1 is on (regardless of what is on the other lines).
2. Output line a_1 is 1 and output line a_0 is 0, representing 2 if input line 2 is on and input line 1 is 0 (higher lines may be either on or off) since the lowest numbered bit that is 1 is the one output.
3. Output lines a_0 and a_1 are 1, representing 3 if input line 3 is on and input lines 1 and 2 are off. This is the example shown in the Figure F-3.

Because of the priority hardware, this circuit is more complicated than the 2×4 decoder shown in Figure F-2, but once again we invite the reader to give it a try.

Figure F-2 2×4 decoder with enable

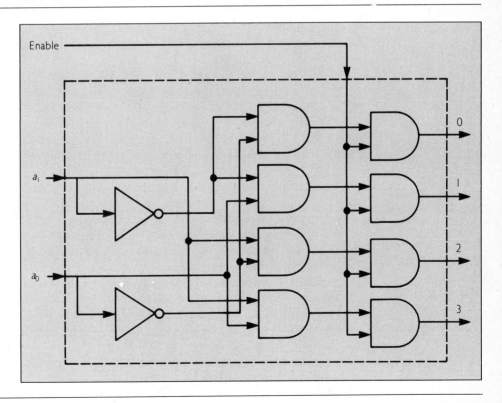

Figure F-3 3×2 priority encoder

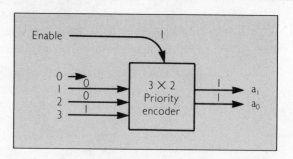

The circuitry for the 3×2 encoder is shown in Figure F-4. In this logic, a box encloses the part that implements the priority described previously. The outputs of this box are x, $x'y$ (denoting the complement of x AND'd with y) and $x'y'z$ (denoting the complements of x, the complement of y, and z all AND'd together).

Demultiplexer.   We can look at a decoder with an enable line in a different light if we interpret the enable line as a data line consisting of a stream of 0's and 1's. When the enable line contains 0, we would like all outputs to be 0, and when the enable line contains 1, we would like only one of the output lines to be 1 and the rest to be 0. The select lines will control which of these outputs is to be 1 according to the desired application. Such a decoder is called a *demultiplexer*, also called a *DEMUX* for short, and a 2×4 decoder would be called a 1×4 DEMUX, where the 1 represents the enable line and the 4 again represents the four possible outputs, as shown in Figure F-5.

Multiplexer.   Just as there is a circuit that effectively goes from one to many (the demultiplexer), so is there a circuit that goes from many to one. Not too surprisingly, this is called a *multiplexer,* often called a *MUX*. Since there is only one output line, the n select lines now function to direct the 2^n input lines to one output line. In addition, we can still have an enable line. When the enable line is 0, the output is 0 regardless of what is input; if the enable line is 1, then the n select lines are interpreted as a binary number, say i, and an output of 1 means that input line i is on; an output of 0 from the same multiplexer means that input line i is off (or the enable line is off). This may seem like a complicated device for what it does, but as we shall see, multiplexers are common useful circuits in computer systems.

A 4×1 multiplexer with an enable line would be denoted by a diagram such as the one shown in Figure F-6. In this figure, if input line 1 is on and the select lines represent the integer 1, then the output here is 1. If the select lines represent

Figure F-4 3×2 priority encoder

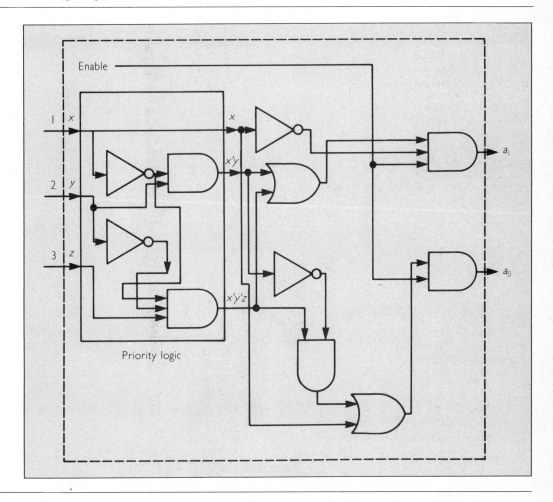

any other integer, an input of 1 has an output of 0. If the enable line is off or if input line 1 is off with the select lines representing 1, then again the output would be 0.

This 4×1 MUX with an enable line might be implemented as shown in Figure F-7 (try it first!). MUXs and DEMUXs often turn up in device controllers since they function to route devices. Example 5 shows a schematic of several terminals connected to a MUX with a single line to the CPU.

In this example, the MUX is used to select the desired terminal, with the assumption that each terminal has been assigned a distinct select code. To transmit more than 1 bit of data, we repeat the basic design for as many bits as desired.

Figure F-5 1×4 demultiplexer

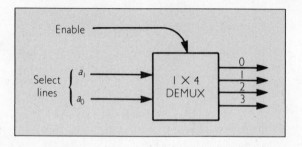

Figure F-6 4×1 multiplexer

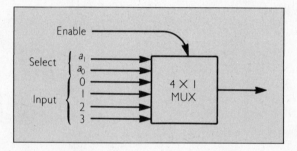

EXAMPLE 5 Device controller

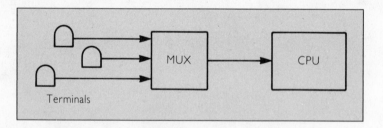

Modularity. Hardware designers, like software designers, modularize their designs. In fact, hardware is considerably more standardized than software, making it easier to use standard chips. Once we have a useful circuit such as a full-adder or a particular demultiplexer, we can stop worrying about what is inside and represent it by a box that we know has certain characteristics. Thus, circuit design works with standard components much as a program designer works with

Figure F-7 4 × 1 multiplexer

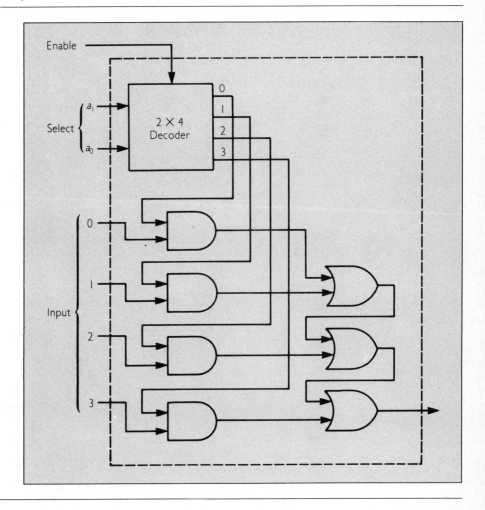

a library of modules. For example, we can build a 4 × 16 decoder from two
3 × 8 decoders using a single enable line (see Exercise 8 at the end of this
appendix).

Read-Only Memory.   One of the major applications of decoders is the design
of read-only memory (ROM). Suppose, for simplicity, that we have 4-bit
words, and altogether our ROM contains eight of these 4-bit words. This might
be called a 32-bit ROM since there are 32 bits in total in the memory. From
Chapter 2, we know that we can represent any one of the eight addresses using
3 bits (see Figure F-8).

Figure F-8 32-bit ROM

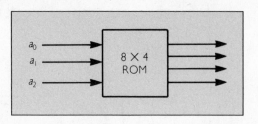

EXAMPLE 6   32-bit ROM

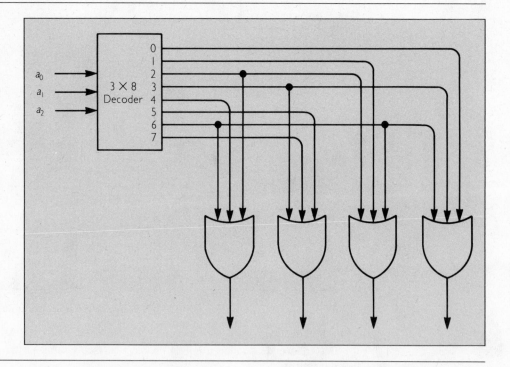

We input one of these addresses on the three select lines to a decoder with an enable line. For this reason, select lines are often called *address* lines. To select the contents of the address selected, we need only OR the eight decoder outputs using four OR gates.

Example 6 shows the logical construction of this 32-bit ROM.

In this example we have not described the contents of each of the addresses. These contents are (permanently) stored in the ROM by cutting the lines to the OR gates so that the desired value is returned for each address (0 for a cut line, 1 for an uncut line). This is called *programming* the ROM. We will not discuss this here, but the interested reader could "cut" some of the lines in this example and see what values are actually returned for each of the eight addresses.

F.2   Sequential Circuits

The previous circuits were all strictly combinational; that is, they had no time dependence. We simply apply a set of inputs and get a fixed result regardless of hat happened previously in the circuit. Devices such as registers require components that will maintain their current value until an external stimulus causes it to change.

In this section, we introduce memory elements and describe systems whose outputs vary with time. The values of the memory elements at any time are called the *state* of the system. A new state of such a system depends on both the previous state and the combinational circuit.

The basic component of computer storage devices is a *flip-flop,* a device capable of maintaining a binary 0 or 1 state indefinitely (as long as power is on) until directed by one of its input signals to change its state. Circuits containing flip-flops are called *sequential circuits.*

F.2.1 Flip-Flops

Flip-flops come in several flavors. In Section F.1, we saw that many useful circuits contain an extra input called an enable input. Similarly, flip-flops generally contain an extra line, called a *clock pulse.* This input changes from high to low (binary 1 to binary 0) and from low to high at a regular rate, although nonregular clock signals can be used as well.

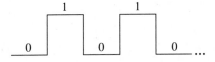

This regular change in the clock pulse causes all flip-flops in a system to change at defined intervals and in unison (synchronously). The study of asynchronous sequential circuits is beyond the scope of this discussion.

The flip-flops we will look at first are designed to change their state when the clock changes from 0 to 1. Later we will see flip-flops designed to change their state when the clock changes from 1 to 0.

The most basic flip-flop is called the *set-reset* flip-flop or, more commonly, an *RS flip-flop*.

RS Flip-Flop.   In an RS flip-flop there are two inputs, called R and S. We denote (clocked) RS flip-flops pictorially as shown in Figure F-9. The inputs are R, S, and the clock pulse, CP; the outputs are Q and Q', where Q' means NOT Q. Q' is sometimes denoted $\overline{Q}$. Thus, although we have not yet described the function of the RS flip-flop, we already know that it has two inputs (besides the clock pulse) and two outputs that are complements. Q is called the state of the flip-flop.

Since the flip-flop changes with time, we must somehow incorporate this fact into our truth tables. There are various ways of representing this; the one we show is called a *characteristic table*. The characteristic table for a clocked RS flip-flop is

R	S	$Q(t^+)$	$Q'(t^+)$
0	0	$Q(t^-)$	$Q'(t^-)$
0	1	1	0
1	0	0	1
1	1	Not allowed	

In the characteristic table, $Q(t^+)$ indicates the output Q just after the clock pulse has changed to 1; $Q(t^-)$ is the output Q just prior to the change.

We now know a little more about an RS flip-flop. The characteristic table is shown just after the clock pulse has become 1; this time is denoted t^+. Similarly, the time just prior to the clock pulse becoming 1 is denoted t^-. We can assume that the change occurred at time t.

Figure F-9 Clocked RS flip-flop

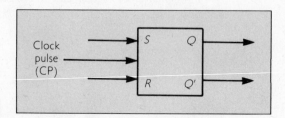

The characteristic table tells us the following. When the clock pulse changes from 0 to 1

1. and both inputs are 0, the outputs Q and Q' are whatever they were before the clock changed; that is, the state does not change
2. and R is 0 and S is 1, output Q becomes 1 and Q' becomes 0; that is, the flip-flop is set
3. and R is 1 and S is 0, output Q becomes 0 and Q' becomes 1; that is, the flip-flop is reset

Figure F-10 shows an RS flip-flop implemented using NOR gates; the R, S, and clock pulses are AND'd. In the figure, let us suppose that R and S are both 0 when the clock pulse changes to 1. Then the output from each AND gate is necessarily 0 and the output of the NOR gate leading to Q will be the complement of Q' (its other input). But the complement of Q' is Q. Thus, the output Q is whatever Q was before the clock change. Similarly, the output leading to Q' will be whatever the Q' output was just prior to the clock pulse becoming 1.

Also in the figure, if $R = 0$ and $S = 1$ when the clock changes to 1, then the output of R's AND gate is 0 and the output of S's AND gate is 1. The inputs to the NOR gate leading to Q are thus 0 and Q'. The inputs to the NOR gate leading to Q' are 1 and Q. No matter what Q is, the output leading to Q' will thus be 0 since the output of a NOR gate will be 0 if any input is 1. The output to Q is

```
NOT( □ OR Q')
```

Since Q' is 0, this output Q is 1. We leave it to the reader to check the other combinations and to discover why $S = R = 1$ is disallowed.

Figure F-10 Clocked RS flip-flop

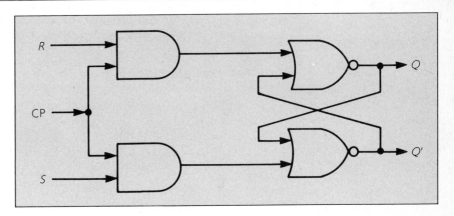

D Flip-Flop. A variant of the RS flip-flop is called the *data* or *D* flip-flop. It has the property that the Q output assumes the value on the input line when the clock pulse goes high. Figure F-11 shows a D flip-flop.

We can implement this using NAND gates, as shown in Figure F-12. The clocked D flip-flop is sometimes called a *latch* since it latches onto (holds) the input. There are also no unallowed input combinations as in the RS flip-flop. The characteristic table for a D flip-flop is:

D	$Q(t^+)$	$Q'(t^+)$
0	0	1
1	1	0

The reader should check that the figure corresponds to this table.

JK Flip-Flop. Another flip-flop that can be implemented from an RS flip-flop is the *JK* flip-flop shown in Figure F-13. It differs from the RS flip-flop in its output when both the J and K inputs are 1; the outputs in this state are complementary to what they were before the clock pulse was applied. Thus, it has no unallowed states. The characteristic table is

J	K	$Q(t^+)$	$Q'(t^+)$
0	0	$Q(t^-)$	$Q'(t^-)$
0	1	0	1
1	0	1	0
1	1	$Q'(t^-)$	$Q(t^-)$

We can implement the JK flip-flop from an RS flip-flop by ANDing the Q output with the K input and the Q' output with the J input, as shown in Figure F-14. The

Figure F-11 Clocked D flip-flop

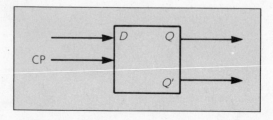

Figure F-12 Clocked D flip-flop

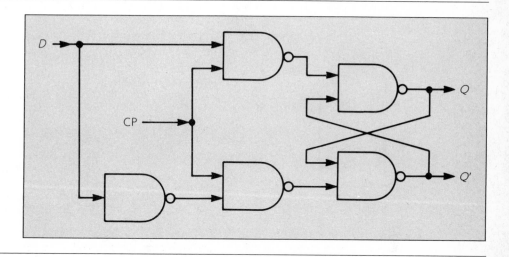

Figure F-13 Clocked JK flip-flop

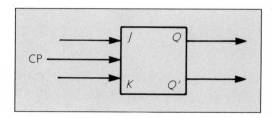

reader should check that the JF flip-flop produces the values shown in its characteristic table.

T Flip-Flop. The *toggle* or *T* flip-flop has the useful property that it changes state every time the input becomes 1 and only then, as shown in Figure F-15. Its characteristic table is thus

T	$Q(t^+)$	$Q'(t^+)$
0	$Q(t^-)$	$Q'(t^-)$
1	$Q'(t^-)$	$Q(t^-)$

Figure F-14 JK flip-flop

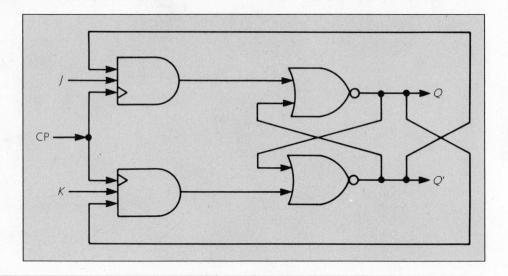

Figure F-15 Clocked T flip-flop

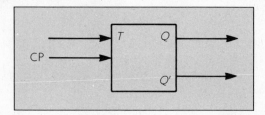

We can build a T flip-flop by tying the two inputs of the JL flip-flop together, as shown in Figure F-16.

Now that we have a variety of flip-flops to work with, we can see how some common computer components are implemented.

F.2.2 Computer Applications

Counters.   Counting is an operation performed frequently in a computer. If the clock inputs are evenly spaced, then a counter can be used as a timer. For simplicity, we will show a 3-bit binary counter. It thus counts from 000 to 111.

Figure F-16 Clocked T flip-flop

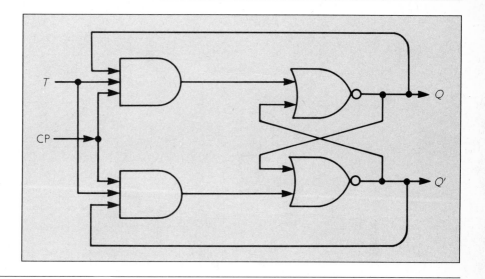

If we denote the 3 bits in the binary number as

$$A_2 A_1 A_0$$

then $A_0 = A_1 = A_2 = 0$ initially. At the first clock pulse, A_0 should become 1. At the second clock pulse, A_1 becomes 1, and A_0 becomes 0. At the third clock pulse, A_1 remains 1, A_0 becomes 1, and so on.

The algorithm here (for any size counter) is:

1. A_0 always changes (is toggled)
2. A_i changes if the value of $A_{i-1} A_{i-2} \ldots A_0$ is currently 11 . . . 1

(The reader should check this out for the 3-bit counter.)

We can thus build a 3-bit binary counter from T flip-flops and a single AND gate (Example 7).

Note that in this example, the Q' output is unused and the clock pulse is called a count pulse. The reader should check that this circuit "counts" 000, 001, 010, 011, . . . , 111, 000, . . .

Registers.   Registers are used to store temporary results during evaluation of arithmetic expressions. An n-bit register can be constructed by combining n flip-flops. We want our register to function as a latch with a bit assuming the state of the input when the clock pulse is on. Thus, we can create an n-bit register as a series of n D flip-flops. The clock pulse is often called a *Load* since this permits the data (D) to be loaded. Similarly a *Read* line allows us to read the contents of

EXAMPLE 7   3-bit binary counter

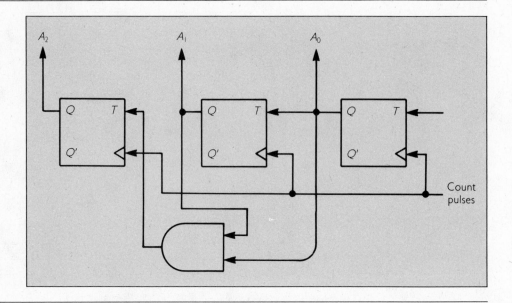

the register when it is AND'd with the Q outputs. We show this for a 3-bit register (Example 8).

Notice that in this example all bits in the register are written or read at once. This is called *parallel* writing (reading).

Shift Registers.   Shifting is an operation often performed on computers. For example, multiplication and division involve shifting. In addition, many computers, including the 86-family, have instructions for shifting. An internal register whose function is to shift bits is called, not too surprisingly, a *shift register*.

Example 9 shows a 3-bit register being loaded by shifting bits to the left. In this example, the circles on the clock pulse indicate that the register shifts its contents as the clock pulse goes from 1 to 0 rather than as it goes from 0 to 1. This is called *negative edge triggering* rather than the *positive edge triggered* flip-flops we have been seeing. Such flip-flops are designed as before, but with the clock pulse complemented.

To create an actual register that can be loaded and shifted, we can combine Examples 8 and 9 and add three 4×1 multiplexers. The four inputs to the multiplexer are as follows:

0: No change
1: Shift to right
2: Shift to left
3: Load

EXAMPLE 8 3-bit register

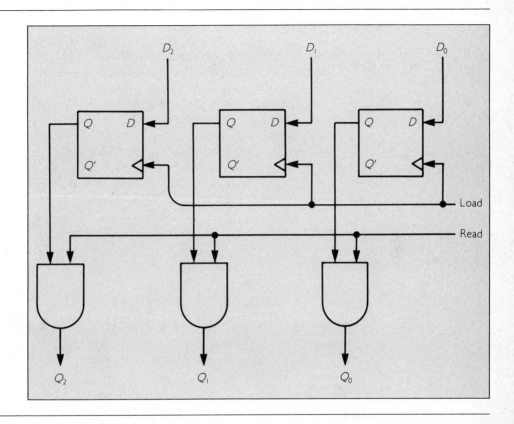

EXAMPLE 9 Loading by shifting

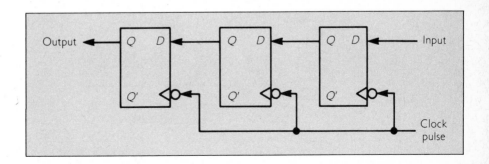

In Example 10, there is an extra input line, which we have labeled *clear*. This clear signal clears the register to 0. The parallel inputs are $D_2D_1D_0$; the "outputs" (data that are read) are $Q_2Q_1Q_0$.

Memory.   Memory has the same components as registers except the only operations we perform are to read and write. This read/write memory is often called random access memory (RAM).

Two internal registers are used in accessing memory: the memory address register (MAR) and the memory buffer register (MBR), which is also sometimes called a memory data register (MDR). The MAR is loaded with the address of the word that we want to store (write) or fetch (read). The MBR is loaded with the contents of the location into which we want to store or from which we fetch. An extra input called the read/write line is also used. A 1 on this line will cause a write, a 0 will cause a read (see Figure F-17).

EXAMPLE 10   3-bit shift register with parallel load

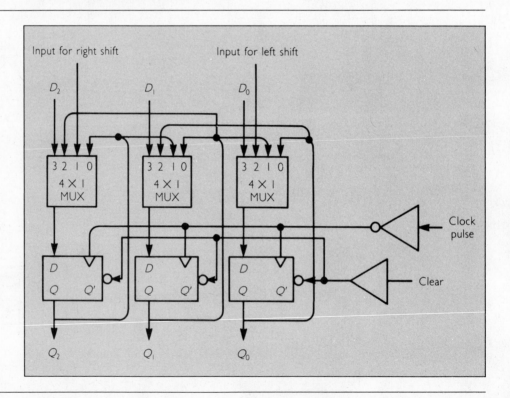

Figure F-17 Read/write memory

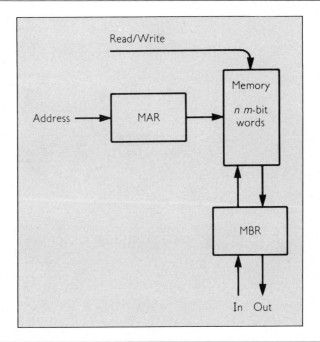

A memory read consists of three steps:

1. Put address (to read from) in the MAR
2. Set read/write line to 0
3. Fetch contents from MBR

Similarly, we can describe a memory write in three steps:

1. Put the data (to be written) in the MBR
2. Put address in MAR
3. Set read/write line to 1

Since an n-bit MAR contains one of 2^n addresses, it can be decoded with an $n \times 2^n$ decoder.

Example 11 shows a 4-word memory where each word is 3 bits. The decoder is 2×4, and each memory cell is essentially a D flip-flop with extra gates. There may also be an enable line (not shown), called the memory enable, that initiates a memory operation.

When the RAM in the example is in write mode, the 2-bit address A_1A_0 is decoded by the decoder, and the input data are written in parallel into the four memory registers at the designated address. In read mode, the 2-bit address B_1B_0

EXAMPLE 11 RAM—random access memory

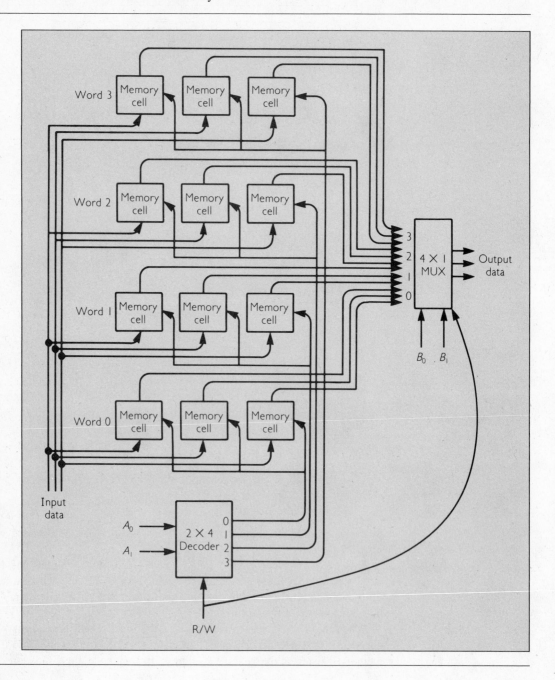

causes the contents at that address to be selected by the MUX as output data. The single 4 × 1 MUX shown is actually three 4 × 1 MUXs. The 3-bit output corresponds to the bits in the MBR, and the 2-bit addresses correspond to the bits in the MAR.

Core Memory.   There is another, older implementation of RAM called *core memory*. Each memory cell consists of a doughnut-shaped magnetic device that when magnetized in one direction represents 1 and when magnetized in another direction represents 0. To sense the direction of magnetism (read), we must change (and then change back) the magnetism. The circuit for such a memory contains different inputs from those shown for the flip-flop implementation.

We have seen two kinds of memory—ROM and RAM (actually, read/write memory). There are some variants of these two, including:

1. *programmable read-only memory*—(PROM) The user permanently programs this memory that then functions as ROM.
2. *erasable programmable read-only memory*—(EPROM) Using special equipment, the user can reprogram this ROM.

Still other variants exist, such as EEPROMs (electrically erasable PROMs).

Content-Addressable Memory.   Content-addressable memory, or associative memory as it is also called, differs from the other memories described in that a word is selected on the basis of its content rather than its location. With associative memory, the desired value is placed in the MBR, and the address (if any) of the word containing that value is returned in the MAR. All words in the memory are ''searched'' at the same time (in parallel). Such memory must incorporate additional logic to handle cases in which the desired contents are not in memory or in which two words have the same value.

Since content-addressable memory is more elaborate and expensive, its use is limited to a few special applications. One of these is the paging management in virtual memory systems.

F.3 Bus Structure

Information is passed between the various devices in a computer system along connections called *buses*. Buses can connect registers to one another and to main memory.

There are many varieties and classifications of buses, and we will describe a few of them. Some computer systems have many types of buses, some only a very few, perhaps one. A system with very few buses will use these buses for many transfers, and since more than one transfer may be initiated at a time, a *bus controller* is needed to coordinate transfers. Usually *priorities* are assigned to the various devices attached to the bus, and the one with the highest priority gets to use the bus first. A system with many buses can often perform more than one transfer at a time. This can again require coordination (perhaps by the programmer!) since an instruction to change an item should not be executed before the item is fetched. Other coordination problems can also arise.

F.3.1 Serial versus Parallel Buses

Parallel buses allow all bits to be transferred simultaneously, much as we loaded the bits in the 3-bit register in Example 8 in parallel (simultaneously). To transfer between two n-bit registers requires a bus with n or more lines, the extra lines being used for coordination and error checking. Parallel buses are fast but expensive. Internal buses such as between two registers are often parallel buses.

Serial buses transfer bits one at a time over a single line, much as we did in loading the register of Example 9. Serial buses are slower but cheaper. Buses to external I/O devices such as printers are often serial buses.

F.3.2 Unidirectional Buses versus Bidirectional Buses

As the names imply, *unidirectional* buses allow information to flow in only one direction, while *bidirectional* buses allow transfer in either direction. Enabling of *selection* lines similar to those we have seen previously controls the direction of the flow of information.

F.3.3 Synchronous versus Asynchronous Buses

A *synchronous* bus is one whose signals are sent with each clock pulse. The devices to which it connects must also operate at the same speed. *Asynchronous* buses communicate with devices that respond at their own rate. Coordination is performed by interrupts or by *handshaking* (signals sent between the devices that are using or want to use the bus).

F.3.4 Special-Use Buses

Common Bus.   A single bus structure is often used in smaller computer systems. All components use the same set of wires. This is an inexpensive, but less efficient, bus structure. The common bus is often called a *system* bus (see Figure F-18).

Figure F-18 Single bus system

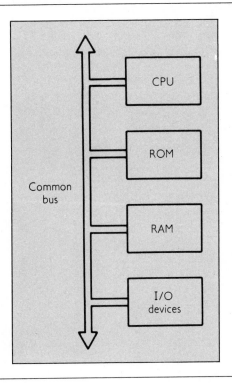

Data and Address Buses. Sometimes buses are designated for special purposes. For example, a system might have a *data* bus and an *address* bus. As the names imply, one bus is used to transfer data, the other to transfer addresses. Parallel data buses are generally the computer word size in width; if they are less than word size, two or more transfers are necessary to move a word of data (see Figure F-19). Note that in the figure the address bus is unidirectional, while the data bus is bidirectional.

Each device in the system (or, more accurately, the registers that interface with them) is given an address. Memory addresses sometimes must be distinguished from other device "addresses." Usually a device in such a system recognizes its own address when it is loaded onto the address bus and either loads or fetches the appropriate information onto or from the data bus.

Address and data buses can be used between memory and external devices, or between memory and the CPU (or both). However, many computers use the same bus for both data and addresses.

Figure F-19 Two-bus system

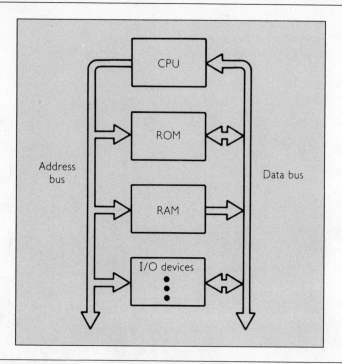

Parallel processing is often performed with data and address buses—selecting a word in memory over the address line can be overlapped with transferring the word over the data line.

Control Bus. Some systems have three types of buses: an address bus, a data bus, and a *control* bus for transferring control information, perhaps specifying whether an address is for a register or memory (if they have not been assigned distinct addresses). See Figure F-20 for an illustration.

I/O Buses and Memory Buses. Some systems have separate buses for I/O to and from memory and for memory to and from the CPU. These are called, respectively, *I/O* buses and *memory* buses as shown in Figure F-21. A microcomputer system might consist of four types of buses: an address bus, a control bus, a data bus, and an I/O bus.

Figure F-20 Address, data, and control buses

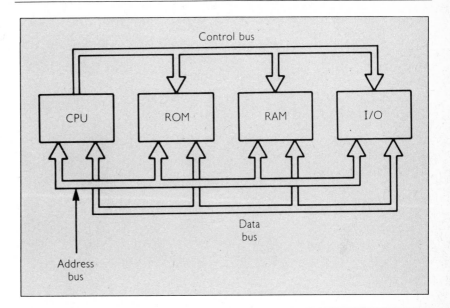

F.3.5 Implementation of Buses

The gates described in this appendix have been binary; that is, there are two output states corresponding to 0 and 1. Buses are implemented with three-state gates, with the third state called a high *impedance* state. This extra state disconnects the gate from the circuit, effectively disabling the output. We will not discuss three-state gates here.

F.3.6 Standard Buses

Some buses are used by many computer systems. When standard buses are used, it is easy to expand the system by ''plugging'' in new devices that interface with standard buses. We mention a few of them.

(EIA) RS-232C—This is a well-known, much used, inexpensive unidirectional serial bus, used to connect to external I/O devices such as terminals.

UNIBUS—This is a 120-bit-wide parallel bidirectional bus.

Figure F–21 Memory and I/O buses

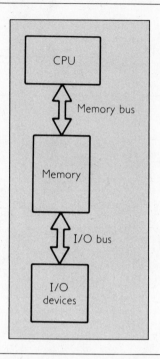

IEEE-488 — A standard parallel bus, 24 bits wide, the IEEE-488 transfers one byte at a time. It is often used with data acquisition devices and for interfacing with instrumentation.

S-100 — This is a standard 100-bit-width parallel bidirectional bus. The IEEE has proposed standard uses for many of the lines (e.g., 16 lines for data, 24 lines for addresses, 11 lines for control signals). The S-100 is often used as the single common bus in microcomputers.

F.4 Microcode

When an operation such as MUL in the 86-family is initiated, it causes various suboperations such as repeated (loops!) *shifts* and *adds,* much as we multiply by hand. These suboperations may not appear as part of the computer's instruction set. Many, though not all, computers have an internal instruction set into which assembly instructions are translated. Like circuits, it is hardware's analogue to the structured modular design so encouraged in software. These suboperations are called *microcode* or *microinstructions*. The trade-offs between assembler and microcode are similar to the trade-offs between high-level languages and assembler. Often it is possible to perform actions more efficiently by writing directly in microcode rather than in the translated microcode, much as better code can be written in assembly language than that generated by a compiler. A much more detailed knowledge of the CPU is required, however. Finally, it is easier to effect simple architecture changes in a microcoded system.

Computers that incorporate the microcode concept may have a special *micromemory* (often called the *control store*), where such *microprograms* can be stored, and a *microprogram counter* to keep track of their execution.

A clock pulse initiates a microcycle that may be divided into subcycles, each of which performs some basic action on devices (generally registers) not programmable at the assembly language level. For example, at the assembly language level, we expect a memory *read* to take place by referring to the memory location, often by a mnemonic name. If our assembly language instruction is to copy a memory location to a register, the following actions might take place at the microcode level. Each step represents a microcode instruction:

1. Load memory address onto address bus
2. Store address in MAR
3. Initiate memory access (this may take a while)
4. Load data into MBR
5. Transfer data over data bus
6. Load into appropriate register (see Example 8)

During Step 3, the microprogram might perform some other activity (e.g., checking for interrupts or fetching the next assembly language instruction) or, less efficiently, just wait, effectively repeating Step 3.

Microprograms often do not have a program counter but contain the address of the next microinstruction within the current one!

The various fields of the microinstruction reference the specific buses and internal registers, such as MAR. The syntax of most microprogramming languages is difficult (at best) to read.

F.5 RISC Machines

Computers such as the 86-family are complex instruction set computers (CISC). Reduced Instruction Set Computers (RISC) are designed for simplicity. The return to smaller instruction sets and simpler addressing modes is not a return to the past, however. Random access memory is faster and cheaper. Registers and buses remain larger (generally 32 bits). Hardware design and implementation as well as compiler techniques are much better understood.

F.5.1 RISC Machine Features

There is some controversy concerning what is or is not a RISC processor. The debate centers upon whether to classify a machine as RISC, as opposed to CISC, by architectural differences such as an abundance of registers or by performance measures such as performance of benchmark programs. In this section, we mention a number of architectural features commonly associated with RISC machines.

Small, Simpler Instruction Set and Few Addressing Modes. *Small, simple,* and *few* are relative terms. Instruction set sizes are typically less than 150. Four or fewer addressing modes are common, although some processors have more.

Instruction set formats tend to be fixed in size, in contrast to variable length instruction formats or CISC machines. The number of these fixed-length formats is small, often on the order of two or three. This results in a faster (hard-wired) decoding.

Single-cycle operations allow the instructions to execute rapidly. *Load-Store* design dictates that only Load and Store instructions access memory. Ideally, these are the only instructions which take more than one machine cycle to execute.

Elimination of complex instructions eliminates the need for microcode.

Many Registers. Operations execute faster when the data is in a register. Thirty-two or more registers are common for RISC machines. Some have more. Hardware maintained sets of registers, called *register windows,* are organized in a circular queue, with a new set added to the tail of the queue and an older set removed from the head of the queue.

Levels of Memory. In addition to secondary memory, and a large number of registers, RISC processors include cache memory. Sometimes there is a separate cache memory for operations and operands. There may be separate buses to each cache.

Special-Purpose Architectures. RISC machines are often designed for a particular application or language or operating system. There are RISC machines for signal processing, symbolic processing, AI, image processing, scientific calculations, graphics processing, multiprocessing, and parallel processing. In addition, there are several general-purpose RISC machines on the market.

F.5.2 Super-Scalar Processors

Processors capable of executing *more* than one instruction per cycle are termed *super-scalar processors*. Architecturally, they combine RISC features with parallel processing. To maintain an instruction rate of two instructions per cycle requires sophisticated branch prediction.

Much is known about achieving concurrency for scientific calculations, but for wider applications, non-vectorizable instruction concurrency is needed.

Algorithms for finding non-numerical instructions which can be executed in parallel in a general application or business application environment are needed.

F.6 Parallel Processing Machines

Parallel processing which overlaps fetch and execute instructions at both the hardware level and the compiler level is not new. Instruction pipelining is actually an example of parallel processing.

F.6.1 Parallel Machine Features

RISC architectures are often parallel processing environments. Other parallel processing environments include multiple CPU's (multiprocessing) and multiple ALU's (array processors and supercomputers) and systems with enough back-up components to execute even if there is a hardware error (fault-tolerant computers).

Multiple processors which have their own memory and I/O ports (loosely coupled systems) have different compiler issues from those which have multiple CPU's, but share memory and I/O ports (tightly coupled systems).

F.7 Fault-Tolerant Machines

Previous sections of this appendix have described special architecture for increasing performance. There is also a growing need for systems that ''produce correct results or actions even in the presence of faults or other anomalous or unexpected conditions.'' Fault-tolerant systems increase dependability through redundancy. Applications such as robotics, navigational systems and others require reliable systems. The purpose of a fault-tolerant system is to be able to execute an algorithm in the presence of hardware or software errors. Fault tolerance may be implemented in hardware with back-up devices or in software.

F.7.1 Fault-Tolerant Hardware Features

Fault-tolerant machines have a back-up for every critical part of the machine. This includes the CPU, I/O ports, buses, and the ALU.

F.8 Summary

Chapter 2 describes the logical architecture of the 86-family. In this appendix, we have suggested how the arithmetic logic unit (ALU), memory, and bus structure might be implemented and organized. To do this, we introduced some simple logic circuits, both combinational and sequential, and their building blocks—gates and flip-flops.

Our introduction here is basic and elementary. Even so, the reader may be overwhelmed with the logical complexity of some of the computer's components. For mere mortals, computers are complicated machines.

Our goal is not only to give some ideas about the underlying structure of computer organization but also to whet the reader's appetite to learn more. The further study of logic circuits includes many design techniques for logic circuits. In addition, there are many other topics that we could not explore here. We strongly recommend that serious students of computer science and computer engineering continue to examine how the components in a computer system are implemented.

Exercises

1. Show the outputs for the various gates when
   a. all inputs are 0.
   b. exactly one input is 1.
   (Use two inputs for those gates that allow more than two inputs.)
2. Implement a NOT gate from a circuit consisting entirely of NOR gates. How many are needed? Similarly, implement OR and AND gates entirely from NOR gates.
3. Repeat Exercise 2 using NAND gates.
4. A half-adder can be implemented in many ways. Show one not covered in this chapter.
5. Show a truth table for a full-adder.
6. A half-subtractor is a circuit that computes a difference by subtracting two bits. Like the adder, it has an extra output, in this case specifying whether a 1 has been borrowed. Implement a half-subtractor.
7. Repeat Exercise 5 but for a full-subtractor.
8. Using a single enable line, build a 4×16 decoder from two 3×8 decoders. (Hint: Invert the enable line to the 3×8 decoder representing the first eight outputs and use the same three inputs to the second 3×8 decoder as to the first 3×8 decoder.) Assume the existence of the 3×8 decoders.
9. Show a diagram analogous to that in Example 7 for transmitting output bits from the CPU to several terminals.
10. Synthesize an 8×1 MUX out of 4×1 MUXs using the enable line of the 4×1 MUXs and any other gates you think necessary. Develop a general modular technique for building larger MUXs out of smaller ones.

11. A ROM consisting of 512 8-bit words would be called a ?-bit ROM.
12. Design a 3×8 ROM that outputs, for input combination $a_2a_1a_0$ having decimal value j ($0 \leqslant j \leqslant 7$), the binary equivalent of j^2 (written left to right). For example, if 101 is input (as the ''address''), the 6-bit pattern ''read'' should be 011001.
13. Show how the 3×8 decoder shown in the 32-bit ROM in Example 6 might be implemented.
14. Implement an RS flip-flop using NAND gates.
15. Implement a D flip-flop as a variant of a JK flip-flop.
16. Implement a T flip-flop by feeding the outputs of an RS flip-flop back to the S and R inputs and letting T be C.
17. Implement a 4-bit binary counter.
18. Show how to combine n 8-bit parallel load registers into a single $n \times 8$ register.
19. Design a 4-bit register with the following controls: load, left shift, complement, set, and clear.
20. Reverse the direction of the counting sequence in Example 7.
    a. Devise an algorithm for a down-counter (called a *decrementor*).
    b. Create a design for a decrementor using your procedure.
21. An n-bit *ring counter* is a device whose output contains $n - 1$ zero bits. Thus, only a single bit is 1 at any time. This 1 rotates either right or left through the register. Design an 8-bit ring counter using a 3-bit up-counter and a 3×8 decoder. How can you control the direction of this counter?
22. Assume the availability of a RAM with a capacity of only 3 words and 2 bits per word. How many of these memories would have to be combined to equal the information storage capacity of the RAM in Example 11?
23. Show a computer system with two types of buses: I/O buses and a memory bus. The memory bus is bidirectional; the I/O buses are unidirectional.
24. Draw a two-bus system consisting of an m-bit data bus and an n-bit address bus. Include memory, the MBR, the MAR, and two registers in your drawing. Show how parallelism (doing two operations at once) might be achieved.
25. How might decoders and multiplexers be used in a bus structure?

Index